I0894287

A Remarkable Story to Tell

A Remarkable Story to Tell

TCU 1973-2023

EDITED BY
Sarah Horning, Abigail Jennings, Leo Munson, Mark Wassenich,
Peggy Watson, Dan Williams

ASSOCIATE EDITORS
Chloe Creed, Emma Graham, Kareyn Hellmann,
Wafa Shaikh, Amy Yin

This project has been blessed with the help of 112 students who served as assistant editors.

TCU Press

Fort Worth, Texas

Copyright © 2023 by TCU Press

Library of Congress Cataloging-in-Publication Data

Names: Horning, Sarah-Marie, editor. | Jennings, Abigail, editor. | Munson, Leo W., editor. | Wassenich, Mark, editor. | Watson, Peggy W., 1948- editor. | Williams, Daniel E., 1951- editor.
Title: A remarkable story to tell : TCU 1973-2023 / editors, Sarah Horning, Abigail Jennings, Leo Munson, Mark Wassenich, Peggy Watson, Dan Williams; associate editors, Nicole Choi, Chloe Creed, Emma Graham, Kareyn Hellmann, Wafa Shaikh, Amy Yin.
Description: Fort Worth : TCU Press, [2023] | "This project has been blessed with the help of 122 students who served as assistant editors." | Summary: "As part of its sesquicentennial celebration, this history of Texas Christian University examines the growth of the school over the past fifty years. Following on the heels of Images and Stories of TCU's First 100 Years, this volume examines the remarkable advances made by the university since 1973 in terms of its campus, its sports programs, its student enrollment, its endowment, and its academic profile and offerings—growth that most recently includes a new medical school. An institution long associated with the Disciples of Christ denomination and the Brite Divinity School, TCU from the outset has emphasized a values-centered education. It is committed to diversity, equity, and inclusion, and to preparing students to be ethical leaders in the global community."– Provided by publisher.
Identifiers: LCCN 2023011525 | ISBN 9780875658513 (hardback)
Subjects: LCSH: Texas Christian University—History. | Private universities and colleges—Texas—Fort Worth—History.
Classification: LCC LD5311.T382 R46 2023 | DDC 378.764/5315–dc23/eng/20230411
LC record available at https://lccn.loc.gov/2023011525

TCU Press

TCU Box 298300
Fort Worth, Texas 76129
www.tcupress.com

Design by Bill Brammer

Contents

Preface

In these competitive and challenging times, we must be very good at what we do. Day after day, week after week, year after year, we must become better. We must know—and clearly communicate—who we are and what we want to be. Simply put, TCU has a remarkable story to tell.

Chancellor Victor Boschini, 2006 Convocation Speech

The pages that follow recount TCU's remarkable story during the past fifty years, a half-century journey that started when the university was a small regional school with high aspirations but burdened with money, enrollment, and morale issues. Due to the leadership of Chancellors Tucker, Ferrari, and Boschini, and the efforts of hundreds of trustees, faculty, staff, alumni, and community members, TCU rapidly progressed to become a highly respected, financially stable, and uniquely successful independent university of recognized distinction and merit. In higher education, this is truly a remarkable story.

This book, however, is not a conventional retelling of TCU's growth and achievements. The remarkable story of recent decades resulted from the work and dedication of scores of people, and in this book "TCU's story" is narrated by literally hundreds of people. In the truest sense, this book is a multi-voiced work incorporating the perspectives and observations of TCU community members from the 1970s to the present. For the most part, these voices were recorded by the TCU Oral History Project in one hundred and forty interviews over the span of a dozen years. In 2011, while talking over coffee in the bookstore, Leo Munson, then Associate Provost, mentioned that TCU's recent recognitions and achievements resulted from commitments made decades earlier. Since Emeritus Chancellor Bill Tucker and most of his administrative team were still around, he wondered if it would be possible to record their stories.

Thus the TCU Oral History Project was conceived. Since that time a sizeable list of administrators, trustees, faculty, staff, and alumni were interviewed, and most of these interviews were conducted by several dozen TCU Honors students. Thanks to the support of Peggy Watson, Founding Dean of the John V. Roach Honors College, a series of Honors colloquia were created to support the project. Ultimately, the Honors students who participated in the project, the many people they interviewed, and numerous others who contributed their time researching, writing, and editing are all—one way or another—the authors of this book. A core Disciples belief is that everyone has a place at the table, and this book was created in the belief that every voice should be heard.

Assembling a book around hundreds of voices and nearly fifteen hundred transcript pages—totaling more than nine hundred thousand words—required careful organization. At the outset, questions about order and arrangement had to be considered, but there was one unifying theme that the editorial team—Sarah Horning, Abigail Jennings, Leo Munson, Mark Wassenich, Peggy Watson, and Dan Williams—quickly agreed would provide the necessary connections. In TCU's earliest days, after the devastations of the Civil War, brothers Addison and Randolph Clark had committed to helping students develop as responsible citizens by founding AddRan Male and Female College. They wanted to teach, but they also wanted to give students "a purpose in life and the foundation on which to build character" (Randolph Clark, *Reminiscences: Biographical and Historical* 49). This high-minded goal has remained a central part of TCU's mission for one hundred and fifty years. Fifty years ago Chancellor Moudy declared that TCU was a "values-affirming institution"; today TCU's website proclaims that it is a "values-centered university." This book is organized around TCU's efforts to educate responsible citizens and its commitment to uphold the values it espouses.

"Values" is a loose term, and at different times TCU has held different kinds of values. Consequently, this book begins with a chapter written by Vice Chancellor for Student Affairs Emeritus Don Mills, whose TCU history literally connects the past fifty years and who has astutely commented on the university's changes and connections. This is followed by a chapter on TCU's values that traces TCU's ethical standards and institutional commitments from Thorp Spring to the present. While there is no constant, unequivocal set of values, there is a remarkably consistent history of the university's willingness not only to declare its values but also to reexamine them in the context of its ever-evolving history. It is this commitment to responsible citizenship and ethical leadership that connects TCU's past and present.

The examination of TCU's values is followed by a three-part narrative that outlines TCU's history during the administrations of Chancellors Tucker, Ferrari, and Boschini, and documents how TCU's leadership teams jointly managed the university's progress. This section describes most of the events, actions, and situations that define the university's history since the 1970s, providing a framework for examining TCU's remarkable growth and progress and sketching the many ways the university has connected the curricular and cocurricular areas of student life to promote citizenship and leadership.

Following the narrative is a series of twenty-two smaller, thematic chapters, Voices and Images. Using innovative layouts that merge word and image, these chapters offer concise and visual insight into relevant areas that complement the preceding historical narrative. While the narrative continually quotes from many of the participants who took part in shaping TCU's history, these final chapters are primarily made of multiple voices. While human memory is not particularly a precision instrument, the use of multiple perspectives on comparable situations offers a chorus, mostly harmonious but sometimes dissonant, that adds dimension and depth to the historical narrative.

After examining its recent past, this book concludes with Chancellor Boschini's message on the future of TCU. Over the past two decades, Chancellor Boschini has directed TCU's growth and progress, and in his conclusion he comments on how the university's core commitments will direct its future growth. Just as Chancellor Moudy looked into TCU's future fifty years ago, Chancellor Boschini offers his understanding of the university's mission, vision, and values. Following this glimpse into the future is a statistical survey, visually displayed, of TCU's growth.

Throughout this manuscript journey, the editorial team was graced with the help of many others along the way and was deeply humbled by this help. Students Chloe Creed and Kareyn Hellmann contributed much during the project's early stages, and students Emma Graham, Wafa Shaikh, and Amy Yin joined later but were equally helpful. All of these students did such excellent work that they also became trusted core colleagues. Ma'lisa Yost attended dozens of meetings to offer her insights. With patience and support, Kathy Walton, Marco Roc, and James Lehr at TCU Press provided considerable assistance to turn a motley manuscript into a book. Mary Saffell and her colleagues in the Mary Couts Burnett Library's Special Collections were always responsive and supportive with numerous requests, and the editors are grateful for all of the help they received from Dean Tracy Hull. Special thanks also to Jean Pickett and Janine Cox in the Chancellor's Office. Throughout the project their help was invaluable, and they graciously responded to an endless stream of emails. Equally valuable has been the help of colleagues such as Cathan Coghlan and Maggie Williams in TCU's Institutional Research. TCU's remarkable story would not be complete without their statistical analysis of TCU's growth. Many friends along the way read various draft pieces and provided helpful comments, particularly Rich Enos, Newell Williams, Frederick Gooding, Bobby Hawley, Kay Higgins, and Michael Lee Stallard. Despite her workload and responsibilities, Cynthia Shearer was an especially astute reader. Considering all of the interviewers and interviewees, and the dozens who helped along the way, this book is the product of a community.

This account focuses on the past fifty years, but it owes much to the two exceptional TCU histories that preceded it, Colby Hall's *History of Texas Christian University: A College on the Cattle Frontier*, published by TCU Press in 1947 and 2014, and Jerome Moore's centennial celebration, *Texas Christian University: One Hundred Years of History*, published by TCU Press in 1974. Another TCU Press book, Joan Hewatt Swaim's *Walking TCU: A Historical Perspective*, first published in 1992, has been equally valuable and is currently being republished in a new and revised edition by Joan Swaim and Phil Hartman. Many other books were also quite helpful, including Randolph Clark's *Reminiscences: Biographical and Historical* (1919), but special note should be made of *Thank God We Made It: A Family Affair and Education* (1969). Written by Joseph Lynn Clark, Randolph Clark's son, the book is an account of the Clark family and offers great insight into TCU's early years in Thorp Spring and Waco; it should be especially recognized for preserving the remarkable stories of Charley and Kate Thorp. Finally, the three primary sources repeatedly relied on for research and inspiration were the TCU yearbooks, *TCU Magazine*, and the TCU *Skiff*. All of the writers and editors of these publications deserve much thanks for timely help.

Recognizing such help for such an ambitious project is humbling. Recognizing the gift of trust and responsibility given the editors is equally humbling. With gratitude and dedication, they accepted the task with the confidence that the university will continue to thrive by sustaining its foundational values of inclusiveness, tolerance, and service. The Clark Brothers established the AddRan Male and Female College amid post-Civil War instability in the belief that education fostered a stable, rational society, and from the beginning they sought to nurture students to become responsible citizens in service to others and their communities. Throughout its history TCU has always affirmed this higher purpose. What connects TCU past, present, and future is the conviction that education is a process, not a product, that it is a life-long undertaking "in pursuit of the greater good" (TCU website).

The remarkable story that follows is not simply a listing of growth and achievement; rather, it is an attempt to capture the spirit and ethos that stimulated TCU's progress. Knowing that their task was difficult, if not impossible, the editors recognize that their historical survey is only a step in a movement of ages. This story will be retold in fifty years, in one hundred years, and whenever the university pauses to consider its past and recommit to its future. The editors are grateful for having had the opportunity to contribute to TCU's remarkable story.

This book celebrates that story not only by connecting its present with its past but also by anticipating its future. This history reflects the generous spirit of all those who contributed to it and the hope that their work will not only endure but will help advance greater levels of achievement as TCU's future unfolds. Greater good will come.

To study history means submitting yourself to chaos, but nevertheless retaining your faith in order and meaning.

Herman Hesse

A Remarkable Story Assistant Editors

Rema Abdeljalil
Sarah Adams
Rachel Adcock
Carmen Allums
Sarah Amend

Taylor Balch
Katie Baxter
Josh Blankenship
Alec Bloom
Adam Blue
Ashley Bomm
Sara Bond
Patrick Borer
Abby Boyd
Kathryn Briggs
Megan Brown
Sam Bruton
Madison Burnett

Preston Chilton
Jason Cline
Nicole Choi
Jessica Cook
Mary Cordell
Jeremy Culhane
Sarah Cullen

Michael Dabbs
Ashlynn Deaton
Emily Denney
Kristi Dena
Mary Doyle

Pearce Edwards
Olivia Ernst

Aubrey Fearer
Leah Fiorini
Demi Fritz

Anna Gass
David Gearhart
Sarah Gordon
Justine Grace
Ellyn Grantham
Michael Gutierrez

Lyndsi Hardin
Hope Hardy
Ashley Hart
Joe Hartshorn
Luke Harville
Nathan Hearnsberger
Kaitlin Helm
Eivy Herrera
Courtney Hicks
Nick Hill
Raymond Hill, III
Rachel Hilton
Luke Hockett
Carolyn Howell
Kimberly Hughes
Aubree Hutchison

Gabrielle Jackson
Kyle Jaggers
Cameron Jordan
Nick Julian

Kourtney Kinsel
Anna Knuth
Emily Knuth
Audrey Koetting
Alex Kostel
Addy Kryger

Shannon Listorti

Bianca Mariottini
Kortnie Maxoutopoulis
Catherine McSweeney
Holman Moores, III
Meg Moran
Mackie Moreno
William Morris
Katie Myers

Senna Nilsson

Alexis Olivas
Liz O'Malley

Jigna Patel

Ashley Rea
Emily Ricks
Tia Robb
Kristen Robinson
Stephanie Rocco
Sean Roddich
Jordan Rubio
Caroline Ryan

Anna Schraer
Sarah Scott
Ariana Sheridan
Christie Shields
Caleb St. Laurent
Alex Smith
Bailey Snyder
Hannah Stevens
Madison Stottle
Kaitlin Stutts
Jeremy Sweeney

Ben Taylor
Abby Till
Kristin Trumble
Erica Turner

Daniel Vial
Natalie Vilcek

Katie Walker
Ben Warren
Cora Watanabe
Marie Watson
Ashley Winther
Ben Wright

Julia Zellers

I.

Dreams and Aspirations: How Then Became Now

Don Mills

Vice-Chancellor for Student Affairs Emeritus

Why do some places foster an emotional response among those who experience them? If there were an easy answer to that question, then a formula could be developed and every place would have it. But the truth of the matter is that each person has a response that may share characteristics with those of others, yet ultimately is unique. This book is part of the story of a place that has generated mostly positive reaction from those affiliated with it for the past half century. Over that time there has been drama, joy, contention, celebration, challenge, frustrations, and achievements. It is the story of Texas Christian University (TCU). It is a story of opportunity presented and seized.

LEFT
Don Mills. Courtesy of Texas Christian University. Photograph by Glen E. Ellman.

Would 150-year-old TCU be recognized by students who attended the 100-year-old TCU? The financial condition of the institution was not always stellar; the football team was not always winning; the residence halls were not always co-educational or beautiful; academic facilities were not always state of the art; Frog Camp was not always a tradition for new students; and the center of the campus was not always a commons area for use by the residents. But these things are true now. Parking, needless to say, always was, and is, a problem. Through all of the changes, the primary constant over the last fifty years is TCU's commitment to community, connection, and relationships.

When I arrived at TCU in the late 1960s, I knew nothing of its founding, its early days, or its significance in the higher education community in Texas. What I quickly learned is that TCU had strong roots in West Texas. TCU had a national reputation in the world of collegiate sports but was not as widely known for its academic offerings or for its faculty committed to students and excellence. Indeed, it would be fair to say that TCU was a good regional university. Over the last five decades its academic profile has changed significantly, as TCU is now considered to be a top-one-hundred national university. This is testament to hard work from faculty and staff in addition to institutional vision from trustees and administrative leadership. But it wasn't a straight-line path to excellence. The discerning reader will recognize the challenges confronting TCU along the way, and especially its willingness to confront those challenges and accept the risks that come with reaching for greater prominence. Understanding the choices faced and decisions made illuminates the past five decades of the TCU story.

I have had the good fortune to be affiliated with TCU for over fifty years first as a student at Brite Divinity School, then as an administrator for over forty years, and finally a decade as a professor of Higher Education. My plan was to get a degree from Brite and then return to the familiarity of the east coast. I had barely been to Texas before, and never to Fort Worth. Serendipitously, the first person I met in Fort Worth and at TCU was future Chancellor William Tucker, who was Associate Dean at Brite at the time. I had driven from the east coast to TCU to begin my graduate studies at Brite. I arrived in the middle of August during the noon hour, so when I walked into Brite it was empty, as everyone appeared to have left for lunch. So I passed the time reading bulletin board material. Quietly I was joined in the corridor by a person who looked at me with a serious face and a piercing stare which quickly, to my relief, turned into a welcoming smile. In those days we were asked to send a picture after we were admitted, and apparently Dr. Tucker had taken the time to recognize and know the name of each new student. "You must be Don Mills," the man said. "I'm Bill Tucker." And so began my affiliation to, and affection for, TCU.

The student experience has been at the heart of TCU for many decades. When provided the opportunity to discuss their TCU experience, common statements of students from the seventies and eighties were "great experience, treated students as individuals," and praise for the camaraderie in the dorms. Those same statements are reflected by graduates of the last ten or fifteen years as well. There are also constants in the composition of the student body over the decades, but the present student body might be somewhat unrecognizable to an observer from 1973. Some characteristics of students are similar. Women still represent the majority of students. Greek life remains an important part of school social life for the majority of attendees. Friendliness is a noticeable feature of the campus. However, when the TCU centennial celebration ended in 1973, it would be fair to say the student body was neither ethnically nor geographically diverse.

As TCU heads into the sesquicentennial celebration, not only is ethnic diversity much more evident, it is a stated focus of the university. Only about half of TCU students are from the southwest, and almost one hundred countries are represented in the student body. The number of students has almost doubled. Students still greet each other while walking across campus but just as frequently may be engaged with their phone rather than with other students.

The growth of the student body has created some challenges. TCU is not immune from other difficult issues facing the country generally and higher education specifically. Mental health is a significant problem. Implementing legislative mandates is challenging. Cost affects every aspect of the student experience, from who attends and who is able to take advantage of international programs to the size of debt upon graduation. The student body has become more diverse, but not every student has felt the campus is as welcoming or supportive as it could be. The story of how the university has navigated the challenges of a growing, diversifying, and technologically dependent student body without changing the essential nature of a TCU education is a theme that runs throughout this book.

When I arrived at TCU in the late 1960s, I knew nothing of its founding, its early days, or its significance in the higher education community in Texas.

One very significant change since 1973 is the open expression of school spirit. It is hard to walk the campus in 2023 without seeing virtually everyone wearing TCU-branded clothing. This was not the case four decades ago. In the early 1990s, the main dining room in the old Brown-Lupton Student Center was undergoing a facelift. The design committee, including students, rejected the idea of purple and white being the primary colors of the renovated dining facility. When the new Brown-Lupton University Union was built in 2008, purple and white dominated not just the food service areas, but many of the offices and public areas. Students insisted on it. Hand signs at sporting events were common at many Southwest Conference schools in the seventies. Not at TCU. But by the eighties the Horned Frog hand sign was ubiquitous. "Go Frogs" has become a common parting phrase.

The increase in school spirit is also a reflection of the sense of community that is part of TCU's culture. Over the years I have asked students if there is a TCU community and, if so, where to find it. The most common answer I would get was around sports. The second most common response was residence halls and a third was student organizations, including fraternities and sororities. Students also remember the professors who challenged and inspired them—those that sparked a lifelong, intellectual journey.

Over the first one hundred years of TCU providing an education to students, it could arguably be said that teaching was the primary academic mission of faculty. The relationship established between students and faculty was a hallmark of the TCU academic experience. However, the most prestigious national institutions have faculty that engage in research as well as teaching. In some instances, research has a higher priority than anything that happens in the classroom. TCU has tried to navigate the teacher/researcher conundrum by establishing a teacher-scholar model. It is one of many academic decisions that have been instrumental in shaping the academic experience for students. How this and other significant academically focused decisions spurred increased prominence is presented in some detail in this history. These decisions defined the school's academic and intellectual environment as they advanced TCU's national reputation.

A cursory observation of the past fifty years might lead to a conclusion that student body growth, increased school spirit, national prominence, campus redevelopment, and financial stability are the result of athletic success. Of course, success on the field of play has had a highly significant influence on the gains TCU has experienced, but it would be a mistake to overstate its impact. The balance of factors and decisions is one of the intriguing storylines in the history.

A visitor to the TCU Centennial Celebration in 1973 might describe the campus as pleasant but unremarkable. Buildings shared the same TCU "buff" brick (supplied since 1910 by Acme Brick Company); trees seemed small; parking was located near residence halls (although never enough); utility lines stretched between buildings, limiting any clear vista across the campus, and landscaping was modest. The campus was roughly organized into three primary sectors—athletic facilities, residential and student life facilities, and academic facilities. University Drive and Stadium Drive served as challenges to pedestrian traffic and in some measure divided units of the campus. Some units were housed in World War II-era barracks. Still others were housed in trailers similar to construction trailers.

But a new recreation center (the Rickel Building) had recently opened; a new science facility (the Sid Richardson Building)

The relationship established between students and faculty was a hallmark of the TCU academic experience.

was dedicated only two years previously, and fraternity and sorority housing was less than a decade old. Brachman Hall, established on the Oxbridge model of faculty being affiliated with the residence hall, had housed its first students just three years previously. To that 1973 visitor the physical campus was a balance of old and new, with clear boundaries between the adjacent residential communities and the campus. If the Centennial year visitor were to return to TCU during its Sesquicentennial year, they would find an almost unbelievable transformation. In fact it is not uncommon to hear older alums returning to TCU say, "I don't recognize the place" or "I can hardly find my way around the campus." I like to say the trees grew up.

The 2023 campus has more space for human connections both on the Campus Commons and in campus buildings. Buildings function both as places where certain activities occur, but also as opportunities for serendipitous interactions and the unstructured exchange of ideas and experiences. Thus relationships are built between students and students, students and faculty, and faculty with faculty. Building these connections and relationships has been a core value for 150 years, and now the physical plant supports that value.

I believe it is accurate to say the physical campus has grown to realize the vision and aspirations of the university family. The four chancellors, the boards of trustees, faculty, students, administration, and countless other leaders articulated a vision of TCU as a university of national import. There are a number of elements necessary for that to happen, but one of those is a physical plant that supports the vision and values. TCU is frequently described as beautiful. The goal at TCU was never to create beauty for beauty's sake but to create an environment where it would be possible to create an incontrovertibly excellent student experience, where faculty had the teaching and research space to reach their potential as teacher-scholars, and where athletic teams had the facilities to allow them to be successful on the field of play.

But do not be misled. The development of the campus was not a straight-line progression. There were disagreements and compromises. Sometimes the decision process became quite contentious. Questions of how to design aspirations into a structure, questions of priorities, and questions of resource allocations are described throughout the book. Ultimately, though, campus design decisions resulted in a campus that works, meets the needs of users, and reflects the values of the campus. How and why decisions affecting the physical campus are made is part of what makes this story so fascinating.

To suggest that neighbors were always happy with TCU, however, would be a gross overstatement. With student growth came the need for student off-campus housing. As students moved into nearby rental houses, and later new private mini-dorms, some neighbors voiced concern about noise and parking issues in their neighborhood.

The area around TCU has seen dramatic changes in the past five decades. Berry Street was full of student hangouts and retail stores in the early seventies. Then it was designated as a major interior artery by the city, widened, and became pedestrian unfriendly and basically avoided by students. (The phrase "scary Berry" was part of the student lexicon.) By the mid-nineties, TCU, the city, and area businesses had teamed to form the Berry Street Initiative to make the Berry area friendlier to pedestrians and more encouraging to entrepreneurs so as to establish new businesses appealing to both residents and students. TCU was a lead player in the transformation of the area of Berry Street around the campus into a more vibrant area. The neighbors of the university were generally appreciative.

To suggest that neighbors were always happy with TCU, however, would be a gross overstatement. With student growth came the need for student off-campus housing. As students moved into nearby rental houses, and later new private mini-dorms, some neighbors voiced concern about noise and parking issues in their neighborhood. Expanded athletic facilities led some to have concern about property values. More than one neighborhood meeting was a contentious gathering. But over time, as residents of Fort Worth recognized the quality of TCU incursions into the neighborhood along Berry Street, in the Worth Hills area, and directly east of the campus, most came to see TCU as both a good neighbor and an integral part of the city. The story of how TCU responded to neighborhood issues is reflective of the commitment to be a university not just in Fort Worth, but also a part of Fort Worth.

How to read this book

If you are an alum or a member of the TCU community, I suggest you read this book with your experiences at TCU always in the forefront of your thoughts. The history of an institution is a memoir of sorts. There exist certain elements of history that are factually correct. Leaders are named. Scores are posted. Buildings are constructed. Financial reports are published. Trustees pursue policies. These are history. But for students, faculty, and staff, these facts are filtered through the lens of lived experience. The role of the Chancellor is a significant one, but for students the Chancellor may have little direct impact on daily life. More students graduated from TCU in the past fifty years than in the entire history of the previous one hundred. Every student has their own story, their own history of the institution. In that interpretive sense, this history is a memoir. I encourage alumni who read this volume to filter it through their own personal memories and experiences.

The story of TCU, however, also has value for a reader interested in the history of higher education in the US. There are many descriptions in this book that provide lessons on ways to move an institution forward. Texas Christian University has evolved from a good regional institution to a university rated among the top one hundred in the nation. A close reading provides clues on how an institution moves from the present to a more dynamic future. What decisions needed to be made? How were priorities established? What resources

... it would be fair to say that TCU was a good regional university. Over the last five decades its academic profile has changed significantly, as TCU is now considered to be a top-one hundred national university.

are needed and where do resources come from? What leadership decisions proved to be essential in moving the institution forward? Understanding these and many other questions and answers provides hints for other institutions that may wish to make similar institutional gains.

If I were to summarize the history of the most recent half century at TCU in a word, I think I would choose opportunity. Under the direction of four chancellors, the leadership of TCU has focused on finding those critical moments to enhance the university's financial position, elevate the institutional profile, expand academic capacity, improve the student experience, raise the student profile, diversify the campus community, strengthen the faculty, and augment the physical plant. These moments became the opportunities for institutional growth and development. Opportunity is not limited to the organization. The opportunities for students to engage on campus and throughout the world have multiplied dramatically. Expansion of faculty research, travel, and professional reach have improved TCU's academic reputation while highlighting the strength of the faculty.

In 1973 TCU was a small regional institution; any national identity was primarily the result of football. TCU used the tagline "TCU has the feel of a residential college with the opportunities of a major university" or variations of that theme. TCU's historical values of respect and dignity for all persons, of the search for truth and wisdom, of strength through differences have all been tested in the rush of changing environments and aspirations. While TCU can point with justifiable pride at many accomplishments, this history reflects that the university was not immune to challenges and setbacks, too. If nothing else, the last fifty years at TCU reflects Heraclitus's observation "the only constant is change." Change brings challenge, but we are also reminded of Ben Franklin's reflection that "When you are finished changing, you are finished." TCU is not finished.

II.

A Values-Centered University: 1873, 1973, 2023

TCU has always been a values-affirming institution.

Chancellor James M. Moudy

While TCU was celebrating its history during the 1973 centennial observances, Chancellor James Moudy was worried about its future. In "A Look to the Future," his closing essay in Jerome Moore's centennial history, *Texas Christian University: A Hundred Years of History*, he voiced his unease that if TCU yielded to "external pressures for the neutralization of values," its future would be in jeopardy. Disturbed by the civil, social, financial, and political turbulence of the 1960s and 1970s, Chancellor Moudy perceived a decline not simply of ethical standards and but also of discernment, the capacity and will to make value judgments.
To endure as a unique, viable, and relevant independent university, he believed that TCU needed to remain a "values-affirming institution."

Yet Chancellor Moudy was fully cognizant that values are variable and that value judgments are products of circumstance. Aware that the university had changed considerably since the AddRan Male and Female College held its first classes on September 1, 1873, he believed that, rather than a specific set of values, it was the university's enduring commitment to actively uphold and publicly declare its values that informed its institutional character. Despite the troubled times, he believed that the university's future would be determined by its willingness to sustain its high standards and high-minded expectations as it continually examined how best to fulfill its mission in an ever-evolving world. If TCU continued to affirm its values, Chancellor Moudy concluded: "...it will probably survive many centuries, and the world will be better for its having survived" (262).

Fifty years later TCU remains a "value-affirming institution." The university's website unmistakably proclaims this commitment. Its familiar mission statement, "To educate individuals to think and act as ethical leaders and responsible citizens in the global community," is decidedly values-laden, and its "Vision" announces its aspiration "to be a world-class, values-centered university." To elucidate its commitments, the website explicitly articulates its values:

> At TCU, we value:
> Academic and personal achievement
> Intellectual inquiry and the creation of knowledge
> Artistic and creative expression
> A heritage of service in pursuit of the greater good
> Personal freedom and integrity
> The dignity and respect for the individual
> Active appreciation for the array of human experience and the potential of every human being

By publicly affirming these values, TCU embraces its heritage and instructs its future.

Yet values change over time. As cultural contexts evolve, so, too, do standards and expectations. What is accepted as fundamental at one time inevitably shifts as situations change and new perceptions develop. Chancellor Moudy understood this contingency of values when he acknowledged that TCU in 1973 was not as austere as it once had been: "TCU has always been a value-affirming institution. The values it affirmed in the early days were much more precise, even dogmatic, perhaps; but TCU does not cease to affirm both general ethical values and more specifically Christian values" (261). In his essay "Toward Wonder: Education and Recognition," he similarly acknowledged that values are contingent on context: "...for what we call 'education' is not an exact science and probably cannot become so: principles that seem certain at one time are at other times uncertain" (*A Hope of Wisdom,* 50-51). When discussing TCU as a "value-affirming institution," Chancellor Moudy was not simply voicing his hope that TCU would always be willing to express its values. Rather, he hoped

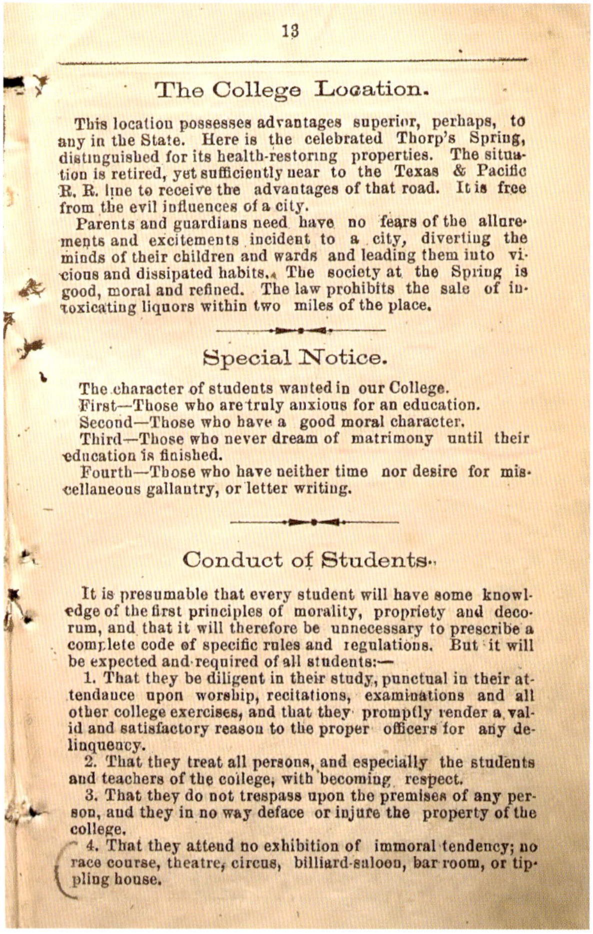

13

The College Location.

This location possesses advantages superior, perhaps, to any in the State. Here is the celebrated Thorp's Spring, distinguished for its health-restoring properties. The situation is retired, yet sufficiently near to the Texas & Pacific R. R. line to receive the advantages of that road. It is free from the evil influences of a city.

Parents and guardians need have no fears of the allurements and excitements incident to a city, diverting the minds of their children and wards and leading them into vicious and dissipated habits. The society at the Spring is good, moral and refined. The law prohibits the sale of intoxicating liquors within two miles of the place.

Special Notice.

The character of students wanted in our College.
First—Those who are truly anxious for an education.
Second—Those who have a good moral character.
Third—Those who never dream of matrimony until their education is finished.
Fourth—Those who have neither time nor desire for miscellaneous gallantry, or letter writing.

Conduct of Students.

It is presumable that every student will have some knowledge of the first principles of morality, propriety and decorum, and that it will therefore be unnecessary to prescribe a complete code of specific rules and regulations. But it will be expected and required of all students:—

1. That they be diligent in their study, punctual in their attendance upon worship, recitations, examinations and all other college exercises, and that they promptly render a valid and satisfactory reason to the proper officers for any delinquency.
2. That they treat all persons, and especially the students and teachers of the college, with becoming respect.
3. That they do not trespass upon the premises of any person, and they in no way deface or injure the property of the college.
4. That they attend no exhibition of immoral tendency; no race course, theatre, circus, billiard-saloon, bar room, or tippling house.

ABOVE
Page from 1875-1876 AddRan Male and Female College Catalogue. Courtesy of Mary Couts Burnett Library.

ABOVE
Chancellor James Moudy welcomes guests to the Centennial Convocation, 1973. Courtesy of Mary Couts Burnett Library.

It is surprising how many items which were once matters of the most serious concern are now regarded as within the student's prerogative to decide.

Colby Hall, History of Texas Christian University: A College of the Cattle Frontier, 149

That they [students] attend no exhibition of immoral tendency; no race course, theatre, circus, billiard-saloon, bar room, or tippling house.

1876 AddRan Catalogue

No extravagance or superfluous ornamentation will be allowed in this College. Heretofore we have endeavored to regulate the character and style of dress by giving directions in general terms; but as there is such a variety of ability, taste, and judgment among those who attend school, we have found that something more than general directions are necessary; and are, therefore, compelled to adopt a uniform for students.

1883 AddRan Catalogue

...we regard the love of dress and devotion to fashion as one of the greatest temptations to the young to be vain and frivolous...

1890 AddRan Catalogue

that TCU would remain willing to periodically reassess its values. Being committed to high values necessarily requires a readiness to appraise the needs of context and circumstance, and at times acknowledge the inconsistencies between principles and practice.

TCU values are reflected in its catalogues, especially in its statements on student conduct, and from Thorp Spring to the present, TCU catalogues document a whimsical evolution of student policies and rules. Stocked with language evoking a *College of the Cattle Frontier*, TCU's first conduct code appeared in catalogues for over two decades, and its regulations clearly demonstrate a distant set of student behavior requirements:

Conduct of Students

It is presumable that every student will have some knowledge of the first principles of morality, propriety, and decorum, and that it will therefore be unnecessary to prescribe a complete code of rules and regulations. But it will be expected and required of all students:

1. That they be diligent in their study, punctual in their attendance on worship, recitation, examinations and all other college exercises, and that they promptly render a valid and satisfactory reason to the proper officers for any delinquency.

2. That they treat all persons, and especially students and teachers of the college, with becoming respect.

3. That they do not trespass upon the premises of any person, and they in no way deface or injure the property of the college.

4. That they attend no exhibition of immoral tendency; no race course, theatre, circus, billiard-saloon, bar room, or tippling house.

5. That they neither introduce upon the premises of the college, nor use there or elsewhere, any kind of intoxicating beverage; and that they abstain from the use of tobacco in the buildings of the college.

6. That they neither keep in their possession nor use any firearms, a dirk, a bowie-knife, nor any kind of deadly weapon.

7. That they abstain from profanity, the desecration of the Lord's day, all kinds of gaming for a reward or prize of any kind, and from card playing even for amusement; and also whatever else is inconsistent with good order, good taste, and good morals.

8. That they attend public worship every Lord's day.

9. That they do not leave the college until regularly dismissed at the close of the session, without special permission of the Faculty.

10. That they do not change their place of boarding without the permission of the Faculty.

11. That they shun and discountenance all disorderly combinations and associations of students or citizens; and that they co-operate with the Faculty in every honorable way to promote the interests and reputation of the college. (AddRan Catalogue, 1876)

In his account of TCU's early decades, *A Histoy of Texas Christian University: A College of the Cattle Frontier* (1947), TCU's first historian, Colby Hall, noted that early catalogues repeatedly attempted to regulate how students dressed and concluded that "extravagance of any kind was discouraged" (59). An 1875 catalogue, for example, stated: "Parents are advised to prepare their children for this school with plain, neat but comfortable clothing. It is thought best that no encouragement should be given to gaudy or extravagant dress." Evidently students then, as today, were more concerned with being fashionable than being comfortable. A few years later, an 1883 catalogue declared more forcefully that "no extravagance or superfluous ornamentation will be allowed in this College" and then instituted a mandatory dress code. Still unable to stifle "extravagance," TCU's 1890 catalogue

The pernicious effects of tobacco smoking, especially cigarette smoking, upon the young, impel us to this decision.

1888 AddRan Catalogue

As the judgment of girls can not be relied upon in making judicious purchases, all their shopping will be done by supervision of the Matron, and parents will please give instructions as to limit in expense money. They will also please address us freely with regard to peculiarties of body and of mind that need special attention.

In conclusion we will say that we regard love of dress and devotion to fashion one of the greatest temptations of the young to be vain and frivolous, absorbing mind and time that should be devoted to the earnest work of life. Viewing this question from every stand point, physically, financially, morally, we think a reformation is needed.

1890 AddRan Catalogue

emphatically declared: "In conclusion, we will say that we regard the love of dress and devotion to fashion as one of the greatest temptations to the young to be vain and frivolous, absorbing mind and time that should be devoted to the earnest work of life." But the "devotion to fashion" was impossible to suppress. After recording a series of catalogue adjustments to dress restrictions, Hall described how female students staged their final revolt:

> The girls increasingly rebelled against wearing a uniform. Gradually the requirement was relaxed. Any white blouse and any blue skirt would do! Finally, all regulation was removed except one: they had to wear a regulation hat. These were ordered, delivered, and each girl must purchase one and wear one. There was nothing the girls could do about it—except lose them. And lose hats they did. How could a girl wear a hat if the hat was lost? That ended the whole uniform affair forever. (149)

Tobacco was also a sensitive issue. Its use was widespread among men at this time, but Addison and Randolph Clark abstained from both tobacco and alcohol. Their abstemious standards, however, were not popular and hard to enforce. An 1888 catalogue required students to pledge "a hearty endorsement" of the "Conduct of Students" and specifically asserted that resistance to the tobacco ban would result in immediate expulsion: "The use of tobacco is forbidden in this college. Let all concerned take notice of this, and if they cannot or will not stop the use of tobacco, they are requested *not to come here to school*. The pernicious effects of tobacco, especially cigarette smoking, upon the young, impel us to this decision . . . . We may lose some students on account of the restriction, but we shall retain a good conscience"(Hall 57-58).

In addition to dress and tobacco, Hall disclosed that regulating the conduct between genders was also a matter of most serious concern. Although progressive for its time as a coeducational institution, the AddRan Male and Female College had strict policies to compel proper decorum between female and male students. Men and women were forbidden from walking alone together across campus, and communication between them was even quite limited. Writing letters to each other, for example, was forbidden. At one point, after being seen walking with her brother, a young woman was "called before the faculty" and reprimanded to "avoid the appearance of evil." Similarly, "one of the finest young men of the senior class" was nearly expelled days before graduation after being seen walking "with a young lady," despite that they were engaged and "were to be married in two weeks" (Hall 60, 61). In commenting on the changes in school regulations, Hall also acknowledged the flux of values: "It is surprising how many items which were once matters of the most serious concern are now regarded as within the student's prerogative to decide" (Hall 149).

In his review of early student behavior policies, TCU's second historian, Jerome Moore, documented a progression of stern warnings and ultimately an unusual expulsion. An 1892 catalogue took the peculiarly public step of identifying and dismissing fourteen recalcitrant students: "These are not desirable pupils. We do not wish them back at this school;

The kind of students wanted in this college: Those who have neither the time nor the desire for miscellaneous gallantry or letter writing. . . . Those who never dream of matrimony until their education is finished.

1876 AddRan Catalogue

"Century" Program Approved (See Page 2)

The Skiff

TEXAS CHRISTIAN UNIVERSITY ★ ★ ★ ★ FORT WORTH, TEXAS

Virtue Triumphs In Morality Play (See Page 3)

VOL. 67, No. 52 TUESDAY, MAY 13, 1969 8 PAGES

Nation's Protest Finds Campus

By JAMES GORDON

The nationwide wave of student unrest aroused a few glimmers at TCU last weekend—glimmers that did not immediately die out.

A demonstration held to protest the expulsion of a student from Clark Dormitory resulted in the formation of a "Student Rights Organization" which prepared to launch a campaign for administration approval of a list of "student rights" proposals.

The protest began when administration officials ordered a sophomore from Spotswood, N.J. to vacate his room in Clark Dormitory.

He was ordered to leave after it was discovered that he owed the school $186 from the fall semester and had been living on campus while not a registered student.

He had signed up for classes at the beginning of the spring semester but was denied permission to complete registration when it was discovered that he owed money.

Attending Classes

The student had been attending several classes since then, however, and did so until April 29, when administration officials discovered that he was in class attendance but not on the business office rolls.

* * *

Friends of the student began circulating a petition protesting the expulsion, and gathered over 500 names.

Administration officials learned of the petition before it was presented, and met with over 60 of the organizers behind Pete Wright dormitory.

The organizers were protesting the fact that the student, who said he finally was prepared to pay the money he owed, was being ejected from campus despite attending classes.

Not Registered

Administration officials, including Dean of Men Col. John W. Murray and Assistant Dean of Men Kenneth Gordon, placated the students by suggesting he might be readmitted to school through late registration, subject to the decision of Dean Jerome Moore of Add-Ran College.

Dean Moore refused to admit the student, however, saying that late registration was impossible after the first week or so after the end of regular registration.

Dr. Moore said he was "startled" to learn that a student had been allowed to attend classes for which he was not officially registered for such a long period.

"I knew nothing about him until I found out that he had been attending this long," he said. "I immediately sent out a note to his professors to remove him from their rolls."

Administration officials apparently did not become aware that the student was on campus illegally until he became involved in a disciplinary action two weeks ago.

Five Meetings

But business office officials and Dean Murray said they had had "at least five appointments" with the student about the unpaid bill since the start of spring semester. The student had promised several times to pay the bill, they said, but had not come up with the money.

"Legally they're right; morally they're wrong," said one organizer of the petition. "Why did they let him stay on campus all semester and then kick him out with just three weeks left to go?"

Friday evening the petition organizers held a rally attended by about 60 persons at the partially constructed quadrangle fountain.

They discarded the issue of the student's expulsion when they apparently became dissatisfied with his explanation of the affair.

DEANS, PETITIONERS AND ONLOOKERS MEET
Friday meeting took place behind Clark Dorm

Fire Guts ROTC Buildings

ABOVE
Courtesy of the *Skiff*. May 13, 1969.

Other things have changed with the buildings. In recent years black students have been admitted to the University and accepted on campus.

Also, the student body has come to life several times over burning issues. When the library closed its doors on Sundays in 1963, activists picketed to open them. Students were riled again in 1969 when construction began on the Frog Fountain, but this time the fountain won. They offered meek protests against the war in Vietnam from time to time, but got down to serious demonstrations this year when visitation rights were denied.

The years have brought changes now and then in all parts of the University. Students have changed in interests and appearance, the original buildings are no longer recognizable and even the faculty and administration have changed.

It comes down to 1973, and Dr. James Moudy, a man who has led the University through several years of something less than economic security, is named TCU's "Man of the Century." M. E. Sadler, who served the University for 25 prosperous years, is now only the name of a building.

It may not all be right, but it is TCU.

OPPOSITE PAGE, ABOVE LEFT: Skirts were long and hair was short on campus in the 40's. OPPOSITE PAGE, ABOVE RIGHT: The TCU Theater drew a crowd way back when. OPPOSITE PAGE, MIDDLE: Freshmen donned beanies for Howdy Week in the 30's. OPPOSITE PAGE, BELOW: Students protest the violence at Kent State. THIS PAGE: Students of 1972-73 give TCU a new look.

ABOVE
Page from 1973 TCU yearbook. Courtesy of Mary Couts Burnett Library.

neither can we commend them to others." Four years later, an 1896 catalogue offered an uncompromising warning to parents:

> Parents who know that their sons have bad habits, and find it difficult, if not impossible, to keep them out of mischievous and sinful ways at home, should send such sons to a reformatory and not to this University. . . . One thing is promised: vicious and incurable pupils will not be retained in this school to the detriment and demoralization of other pupils.

Rules and regulations reflect what an institution values. TCU today still supervises student conduct, but its expectations are far different from the stringent restrictions of the school's earliest decades. What constituted "good order, good taste, and good morals" at one time has been adjusted as cohorts of students matriculated and as codes and circumstances evolved. Values change with the times.

Writing at the same time as Chancellor Moudy, the student editors of the 1973 yearbook were equally concerned with changes in standards and expectations. Equally disturbed by the social turbulence of 1960s and 1970s, they believed they lived in an unprecedented time when traditional values were being challenged, if not shattered. Looking back over the university's first century, they too acknowledged that over time TCU's values had varied nearly as often as fashions. To point out some of these alterations, they catalogued how student issues had evolved since the early days in Thorp Spring. After noting that TCU's former "Code of Conduct" had eventually disappeared from catalogues, they chronicled several other regulations that came and went. With wry amusement, the editors stated around the turn of century "the administration had decided to let the ladies stay out until 8 at night, but still required them to wear uniforms. The concerned officials protected their young by building a fence around the campus site" (24).

Similarly, they remarked that as late as 1916 "coeds were still forbidden to go to the library at night, and the boys and girls had to eat in separate cafeterias" (26).

Writing at a time of widespread student activism, particularly protests opposing the Vietnam War, they ironically described how "the quiet country campus was shaken" in the fall of 1919—not with the devastations of WWI, but by football. To force the administration to revoke the suspensions of five football players who had been disciplined for hazing, numerous young men threatened to leave school and, to demonstrate their resolve, they stacked their packed trunks seven feet high and thirty feet long in front of Clark Hall. When an administrator obligingly offered to have the trunks transferred to the railway station free of charge, the students quietly moved them back into the dorms, and the protest ended (26-27).

TCU celebrated its first one hundred years during difficult times. Across the country students protested the war, and deep surges of unrest erupted during the Civil Rights Movement, particularly after Selma's Bloody Sunday in 1965 and the assassination of Martin Luther King Jr. in 1968, as well as by the women's rights movement, the gay and lesbian movement, the protests of various ethnic identities and communities across the United Sates, and the youth movement's general resistance to the status quo. In May 1970 the country was shocked when four unarmed students were killed and nine others wounded at Kent State University, and again eleven days later when two more students were killed and twelve others wounded at Jackson State University.

Despite such turbulence, the student editors believed that most TCU students were generally less interested in the national news than they were with campus issues. After declaring that "in recent years Black students have been admitted to the University and accepted on campus," a momentous change deserving greater recognition, they satirically listed several student protests on campus:

> The student body has come to life several times over burning issues. When the library closed its doors on Sundays in 1963, activists picketed to open them again. Students were riled again in 1969 when construction began on Frog Fountain . . . they offered meek protests against the war in Vietnam from time to time, but got down to serious demonstrations this year when visitation rights were denied. (30)

To remind readers of their serious context, the student editors dedicated their yearbook to those fighting in Vietnam.

Despite the relative quiet on campus, the student editors recognized—though still with satiric amusement—that TCU had undergone significant transitions: "The years have brought changes now and then in all parts of the University. Students have changed in interests and appearance, the original buildings are no longer recognizable, and even the faculty and administration have changed" (30). To illustrate these changes, they contrasted photos from previous times with current scenes and included an interesting triptych of three photos: a Black female student speaking, two long-haired, tie-dyed students in conversation, and another female student wearing shorts and a top that—in previous decades—would have caused an indignant stir. To emphasize that they lived in an unprecedented time of changing values, they added the caption: "Skirts were long and hair was short on campus in the 40s . . . Students of 1972-73 give TCU a new look" (31).

In reviewing TCU's first century, Hall, Moore, and the 1973 yearbook editors all found elements of quaint humor in the school's early attempts to supervise student behavior, but beneath their amusement there is a serious question. If so many values have changed, what has remained consistent?

Chancellor Moudy believed that TCU always maintained certain core commitments, particularly its deep and abiding concern for student welfare. In tracing TCU's history, Hall described how this concern extended well beyond the classroom. While relating how the AddRan Male and Female College pro-

Questions of value are vital.

Chancellor Emeritus Bill Tucker

Valuing people is a signature character strength of TCU's culture.

Michael Lee Stallard, *Connection Culture,* 2020

Vicious and incurable pupils will not be retained in this school to the detriment and demoralization of other pupils.

1896 AddRan Christian College Catalogue

NO CASTE: The quality of the student body is unsurpassed. No secret societies, no hazing, no plutocracy is allowed. Character and conduct, not clothes and money, determine one's standing.

1896 AddRan Christian College Catalogue

Core Values reaffirm the essential character of TCU. Strategic planning at TCU must be consistent with the following core values: (1) valuing the individual and public good, (2) valuing the liberal arts and sciences, (3) valuing the teacher-scholar model, (4) valuing academic quality as a cornerstone.

Kaludis Synthesis Report, 2005

The purpose was to make a strong academy in which boys and girls would be taught how to study, would be given a purpose in life, and a foundation on which to build character.

Randolph Clark, *Reminiscences*, 49

moted itself, he noted that the school boosted its enrollments by publicizing its commitment to "the high standards of character building and lofty ideals of life and service" (Hall 55). The aim was not simply to educate students but as well to help them build lives of integrity, service, and commitment. An 1875 catalogue, for example, announced the school's resolve to build character as well as minds when it declared that its "large faculty" [all nine of them] would "spare no pains for the moral and mental improvement of those committed to their charge." While listing AddRan's "Advantages," an 1885 catalogue described the college as being "away from the alluring vices of a city" and declared: "It is unsurpassed in moral bearing and social worth."

When describing their high purpose in his 1919 memoir, *Reminiscences*, Randolph Clark was unequivocal about TCU's commitment to character building: "The purpose was to make a strong academy in which boys and girls would be taught how to study, would be given a purpose in life, and a foundation on which to build character" (49). Influenced by the Disciples' encouragement to live an ethical life in service to others, TCU developed as a university dedicated to helping students build conscientious, rational lives. To rebuild their society after the desolations of the Civil War, AddRan faculty were not only accountable for curriculum and classrooms but also for helping students develop as responsible citizens. That commitment has endured and is clearly evident in TCU's mission statement. While its expectations of student behavior have altered, TCU's commitment to building character has not.

While contemplating TCU's future, Chancellor Moudy believed that its history, reputation, and momentum would shape its future, that its high expectations and its devotion to students would ensure its destiny. When reflecting on TCU's achievements, he declared: "What has been achieved at TCU . . . is an amazing and marvelous thing" (259). Yet worried by the tumult of the times, he concluded his look into TCU's future with caution as well as confidence: "If TCU, which in its best forms is highly conscious of the past and intensely thoughtful of the future, can more often live up to its best forms, and if its faculty can imbue each generation of students with the same high outlook, the future of TCU is good" (263). By encouraging TCU to "live up to its best forms," to practice what it preaches, Chancellor Moudy believed that "the noble work started by Addison and Randolph Clark" would continue (263).

Fifty years later, TCU sustains its "high outlook" and remains committed to achieving "its best forms." Just as 1973 yearbook editors perceived their time, today nearly everyone recognizes that we are living in unprecedented times. One way or another, everyone has been touched by the COVID-19 pandemic. Along with the pandemic, there has been political divisiveness, financial instability, social unrest, racial bigotry, environmental cataclysm, and a pervasive collective anxiety. For the first time in over a century TCU has faced serious issues that have challenged its security and tested its values. Working to achieve "its best forms" during the pandemic has been an unsteady process requiring continual adjustment and accommodation. What is most notable, however, is not the day-by-day results, but the conviction to preserve what is best about TCU—its commitment to affirm its values and its focus on students.

While TCU remains a "values-centered university," its values are not widely known. Few on campus can recite the seven values listed on TCU's website. Moreover, this list is a recent inclusion, having been formally adopted by the Board of Trustees in 2019. After a two-year process to review and possibly make changes to the mission statement, and after receiving recommendations from the Student Government Association, the Faculty Senate, the Staff Assembly, and a special task force chaired by Dr. Kristie Bunton, Dean of the Bob Schieffer College of Communication,

ABOVE
Amiso George, Associate Professor of Strategic Communication, right, assists a student while they wear masks for protection during the coronavirus pandemic, 2020. Courtesy of TCU Marketing and Communication. Photograph by Carolyn Cruz.

Chancellor Boschini and the trustees decided not to change the mission statement but to amend the list of values, placing greater emphasis on the "creation of knowledge" and on the potential of every individual. Yet this recent list itself might be further amended. Currently, Vice Chancellor for Student Affairs Kathy Cavins-Tull is leading an initiative to explore, refine, and reaffirm what TCU values. As Chancellor Moudy indicated fifty years ago, TCU—as a values-affirming institution—is obliged to periodically and publicly confirm the values it upholds.

Until further changes are made, the best elucidation of TCU's high outlook and best forms is found in the Faculty and Staff Handbook's "Our Heritage, Philosophy and Goals." Although often passed over as Handbook users search for policy statements, this remarkable declaration of the university's philosophical convictions remains not only the fullest affirmation of TCU's principles, but it also constitutes the university's most consistent and enduring vision of itself. What few recognize is that "Our Heritage, Philosophy and Goals" was written forty years ago by Chancellor Bill Tucker.

Rightfully recognized for starting TCU on its upward trajectory from a small regional school beset with financial worries to a highly respected, well-endowed national and global university, Chancellor Tucker secured TCU's future at a time it was less than certain. His contributions are many and extensive. Yet one of his least-known contributions—submitting a brief four-page document of TCU's philosophy, objectives, and goals to the Board of Trustees in March 1983—is perhaps one of his most significant. His statement of TCU's core values remains as relevant and purposeful today as it was when he first drafted it.

Along with announcing its curriculum and expectations for student conduct, TCU catalogues have continually published brief statements of its vision and intentions. Its earliest catalogues announced its qualifications as a "A Christian College" far removed from Hell's Half Acre's "dram shops and their attendant soul-destroying vices" and praised its pastoral location as being "unsurpassed by that of any college in the State." Starting in 1965, TCU catalogues included explicit statements of its "Philosophy and Objectives," which were revised in 1973 by the TCU Priorities Committee in time for centennial celebrations. Not long after assuming TCU's highest administrative office, Chancellor Tucker redrafted the university's values in a statement that remained in catalogues up until Chancellor Ferrari formulated TCU's well-known mission statement in 1998. Although omitted from catalogues, Chancellor Tucker's statement was transferred to the TCU *Faculty and Staff Handbook*, where it remains today—nearly word for word—as "Our Heritage, Philosophy, and Goals."

Chancellor Tucker believed that TCU was best defined by the commitments it maintained: "A community dedicated to learning, the University affirms its commitments to rationality, objectivity, diversity, freedom of inquiry, and civility." Viewing the considerable growth since TCU's start as "a small school on the cattle frontier," he stated that the university's past and present were connected by the dedication of its campus members: "As agents of change in our time as our predecessors were in theirs, we—faculty, staff, students, and trustees—are united in striving for the constant improvement of the University on the basis of its philosophy and objectives" ("Philosophy, Objectives, Goals of Texas Christian University," 1983).

Chancellor Tucker, however, broke with the past in one statement that signally deviated from earlier catalogue copy. Previous catalogues had proclaimed TCU's primary purpose was "to seek, advance, conserve, and transmit truth" (1978 TCU Catalogue). In his revision, Chancellor Tucker offered a different perception of TCU's fundamental purpose: "TCU is committed as well to the preservation, appraisal, and transmission of knowledge and wisdom and to the discovery of new ideas and knowledge by which the understanding of truth may be extended or corrected." Rather than a monolith, Chancellor Tucker described truth as being open to multiple understandings contingent on time and place and, by recasting TCU's purpose on the transmission of knowledge and the discovery of new ideas, he concluded that the university's responsibility was to foster "rational decision-making, creative thinking and expression, and responsible living."

Identifying TCU with the Disciples heritage of seeking unity through service, tolerance, and compassion, Chancellor Tucker's philosophy statement asserted that seeking knowledge and questioning values are inseparable and, therefore, that TCU was obligated to protect and encourage free inquiry: "though knowledge may be treated as ethically neutral, we believe that questions of value are vital and that the exploration of the moral and religious dimensions of human existence is basic to the love of wisdom." To address the gaps between

Leadership and values are really important to us. It's not any one value, but we want our students to embrace understanding and be able to recognize when they are in ethical situations that arise in business or society. We want them to have practice while they are students and think about ethical issues. It's a lot easier to practice when you are a student than when you are in a workplace.

Homer Erekson, Emeritus Dean and Professor of Entrepreneurship, at TCU 2008-2023

Our objective is to provide undergraduate and graduate instruction informed by research, to offer such undergraduate and graduate studies as will enable students to enter fruitful careers, to promote the mental, spiritual, and physical well-being of our students, to encourage continuous self-education, and to maintain a vital and inviting setting for learning and living . . . while the atmosphere of a residential college is preserved.

Chancellor Emeritus Bill Tucker, *"Philosophy, Objectives, Goals of Texas Christian University"*

principles and practice, he emphasized the need for diversity: "We are convinced that there must be a general compatibility among the values and daily practices of the University . . . We hope to perpetuate diversity in our programs and people, for we believe that no single vision will suffice."

Like those before him, Chancellor Tucker believed that TCU was distinguished by its commitments to people: "At the center of the educational endeavor are people. Affirming the incalculable worth of each individual, TCU seeks to be a caring community, encouraging close working relationships among all members of the University and challenging students, faculty, and staff alike to high achievement."

Chancellor Tucker's statement of TCU as a caring community articulates its highest ideals, and his statement remains the fullest expression of TCU's values. Though specific values have shifted over time, the university's commitment to maintaining its philosophical values has not. Continually improving as a caring community where every individual is esteemed remains central to TCU's educational endeavor. The university's recent commitment to improving diversity, equity, and inclusion and to achieving reconciliation on campus exemplifies its desire to be a caring campus where connections are promoted and differences embraced, where the incalculable worth of every individual is esteemed. Though the process is uneven and progress unsteady, TCU's commitment to being a caring community that esteems its members and affirms its values remains resolute. When remarking on recent Lead On goals, Chancellor Boschini reiterated the university's commitment to diversity when he stated that TCU was "a place where differences can become strengths, where personal attention brings success, and where great things happen when we learn from one another."

Viewing the considerable growth since TCU's start as "a small school on the cattle frontier," he stated that the university's past and present were connected by the dedication of its campus members: "As agents of change in our time as our predecessors were in theirs, we–faculty, staff, students, and trustees–are united in striving for the constant improvement of the University on the basis of its philosophy and objectives" (Chancellor Tucker, "Philosophy, Objectives, Goals of Texas

TCU is a place where differences can become strengths.

Chancellor Victor Boschini

Christian University," March 1983).

Chancellor Tucker, however, broke with the past in one statement that signally deviated from earlier catalogue copy. Previous catalogues had proclaimed TCU's primary purpose was "to seek, advance, conserve, and transmit truth" (1978 Catalogue). In his revision, Chancellor Tucker offered a different perception of TCU's fundamental purpose: "TCU is committed as well to the preservation, appraisal, and transmission of knowledge and wisdom and to the discovery of new ideas and knowledge by which the understanding of truth may be extended or corrected." Rather than a monolith, Chancellor Tucker described truth as being open to multiple understandings contingent on time and place and, by recasting TCU's purpose on the transmission of knowledge and the discovery new ideas, he concluded that the university's responsibility was to foster "rational decision-making, creative thinking and expression, and responsible living."

Identifying TCU with the Disciples heritage of seeking unity through service, tolerance, and compassion, Chancellor Tucker's philosophy statement asserted that seeking knowledge and questioning values are inseparable and, therefore, that TCU was obligated to protect and encourage free inquiry: "though knowledge may be treated as ethically neutral, we believe that questions of value are vital and that the exploration of the moral and religious dimensions of human existence is basic to the love of wisdom." To address the gaps between principles and practice, he emphasized the need for diversity: "We are convinced that there must be a general compatibility among the values and daily practices of the University . . . We hope to perpetuate diversity in our programs and people, for we believe that no single vision will suffice."

Like those before him, Chancellor Tucker believed that TCU was distinguished by its commitments to people: "At the center of the educational endeavor are people. Affirming the incalculable worth of each individual, TCU seeks to be a caring community, encouraging close working relationships among all members of the University and challenging students, faculty, and staff alike to high achievement." Chancellor Tucker's statement of TCU as a caring community articulates its highest ideals.

Chancellor Tucker's statement remains the fullest expression of TCU's values. Though specific values have shifted over time, the university's commitment to maintaining its philosophical values has not. Continually improving as a caring community where every individual is esteemed remains central to TCU's educational endeavor. The university's recent commitment to improving diversity, equity, and inclusion and to achieving reconciliation on campus exemplifies its desire to be a caring campus where connections are promoted and differences embraced, where the incalculable worth of every individual is esteemed. Though the process is uneven and progress unsteady, TCU's commitment to being a caring community that esteems its members and affirms its values remains resolute. When remarking on recent Lead On goals, Chancellor Boschini reiterated the university's commitment to diversity when he stated that TCU was "a place where differences can become strengths, where personal attention brings success, and where great things happen when we learn from one another."

Voices on Values

Previous students will come back and say, "I can't believe how campus has changed." Universities should change, but they should also stay the same. TCU has changed dramatically since I was here as an undergraduate, but I bet it's also stayed the same, and that's exactly the way we want it to be—the interest in students, its core mission and values. That's what TCU is about. This grand old institution will continue to stay true to its core mission, and yet it's always going to change and adapt.

Larry Adams, Interview, April 2012

There's no better place to talk about values than a college campus where you really have open, authentic conversations . . . TCU's legacy, the Disciples of Christ denomination, is about those conversations. I hope we embrace those conversations, that we talk about values.

Homer Erekson, Interview, November 2014

The students have just written a creed, and it's what students want to own: "learning with passion, serving with respect, and leading with integrity." It's not in place of the mission statement, but it's what the students want to be known for. I think the founders would be real proud of what the students are saying. We've got this great big circle.

Susan Adams, Interview, April 2012

I think the chancellors have kept us true to our values, which goes back a long way to our founding brothers. In strategic planning, they have tried to project what the community needs, and I think the key word is teamwork. Nobody can do something by themselves . . . they have to expect teamwork, quality, and no excuses. I think that's true in the academic classroom. We have some of the best faculty in the country here.

Susan Adams, Interview, April 2012

Compared to when I first started teaching, the values are about the same. The reason I say this is because there are church-related schools where the churches call the shots. That's not the way the Disciples are set up. Disciples are for freedom of inquiry and freedom of religion. I always say the Disciples are a perfect match for education because what you want are students and faculty to think for themselves. You want them to study what others have thought and what others have lived for, what their values and commitments were, but ultimately you want people to make up their own minds. What you don't want is somebody telling you what's good for your life, and telling you what you ought to believe. That just doesn't work. Intelligent people need to make their own decisions. The Disciples have always stood for that.

Jim Atwood, Interview, November 2016

We stand for dignity. We stand for respect. We stand for the idea that people count and that they have intrinsic value. We stand for the idea that people should not be clones of one another. Those are the values we have.

Jim Atwood, Interview, November 2016

In the old days, all Chancellors were Disciples of Christ members . . . But that went away with Dr. Ferrari and Dr. Boschini. Both are people who support Disciples values, which are freedom of inquiry, respect for people, living a clean life, and walking the walk.

Jim Atwood, Interview, November 2016

There are all kinds of values that cannot be reduced to economic value. There's aesthetic value, and there's moral value. But we live in a culture that is so driven by the notion of value being equal to money that it's hard for us to understand distinctions. I worry sometimes that, as my granddaughter grows up, she'll grow up in a world in which economic values have simply overwhelmed those other values.

David Grant, Interview, November 2012

I think the biggest difference between my first day at TCU and now, and it's really not even a difference, but what makes it special, is that the University is bigger. It's more complicated, and there are more students, more activities, more national attention. I could go on and on about things that make TCU a different experience from what it was ten years ago. Yet at its core, the values of the University have remained just as strong—the appreciation for the culture, the friendliness of the culture—those continue to remain intact. I think that, with all the change, the one thing that hasn't changed is probably the most important thing. The University's heart seems to be just as strong as it was when I got here.

Brian Gutierrez, Interview, February 2015

The person that I worked for, a woman named Elizabeth Proffer, who later became Dean of Students at TCU, was actively engaged in the Christian church. We talked a lot about my career in the sense that this work—Student Affairs work—was a ministry, particularly in a school like TCU that was church related and values oriented. I began to see what I did then as a ministry and actually considered it a ministry throughout my career.

Don Mills, Interview, April 2012

I think that undergraduate research is one of our core values.

Manfred Reinecke, Interview, November 2011

I'm a Disciples of Christ minister, and when I hear Victor say, "TCU's a wonderful place because of the Disciples of Christ influence," I'm pleased to hear that. . . . I do think TCU is a special place in many respects, and I see alignment with that Disciples DNA. . . . The Disciples of Christ continues to be a community that supports TCU and the pursuit of academic excellence and academic freedom, that supports seeking an awake conscience, that addresses a changing world and the issues of our day in a way that makes for wholeness and flourishing in the whole universe. Those are values of the Disciples of Christ, those are values of Texas Christian University.

Newell Williams, Interview, March 2014

The Disciples that established TCU wanted a first-rate university. Well, that's what we keep striving to be, that's what TCU is.

Newell Williams, Interview, March 2014

III.

Vision and Leadership: A Narrative

Part 1
Vision: The Tucker Years

TCU has a remarkable story to tell. During the past half century, TCU experienced exceptional growth in every way possible, and it was the shared vision, optimism, and effort of TCU's administrators, trustees, faculty, staff, students, and alumni that enabled the university's advancement. When TCU celebrated its 1973 centennial, however, there was little indication that the university would ever be much more than it then was, a small regional school with high aspirations but burdened with little money, low morale, and modest enrollments.

LEFT
Chancellor Bill Tucker, 1970s.
Courtesy of Mary Couts Burnett Library.
Photograph by Regal Arts Studio.

When Dr. William (Bill) E. Tucker returned to campus in August of 1979 to become the school's eighth chancellor, TCU faced serious challenges. Like many of the nation's private colleges and universities, it had been adversely affected by the decade's economic problems of high inflation, high unemployment, and relentless recession. Along with financial distress, the 1960s and 1970s were decades of social turbulence and discord. In successive waves of activism, thousands of disgruntled people, a majority of whom were college students, had filled the streets and had showed up at rallies not only to protest the Vietnam War but also to oppose the discriminatory practices and policies that sustained the political, racial, and sexual injustices experienced by numerous marginalized communities. Women, Blacks, Hispanics, Native Americans, Gays, and Lesbians all had marched for equal rights. Across the country higher education was deeply impacted, particularly after the convulsive shocks of Martin Luther King's assassination in 1968 and the shootings that took place on the campuses of Kent State and Jackson State in 1970.

Inevitably, TCU had been directly affected by the nation's financial and social upheavals. The oil embargoes of 1973 and 1977 more than tripled the price of gas, which in turn caused some of the highest inflation rates in the nation's history. When Chancellor Tucker was officially inaugurated on April 16, 1980, TCU had been operating at a deficit of around two million dollars each year for two years. Faced with increased competition from the state schools, the university had also experienced a decline in enrollment, and due to rising prices and stagnant salaries, morale was low among faculty and staff. In reflecting back on his early years as TCU's chief executive, Chancellor Tucker commented: "When I became Chancellor in 1979, higher education in America was at a time of low tide . . . [and] it was especially low tide at TCU. . . . Those were difficult times" (Interview, November 2011).

Coming to TCU from Bethany College, a small Disciples of Christ school near Pittsburgh, Chancellor Tucker had hoped to "listen for a while" before taking action, but the issues of budget deficits and low morale required immediate attention. Quickly addressing the problems, he made several key decisions that later had profound impacts. The first decision was to ensure that TCU would never again operate with budget deficits. While describing his initial steps to balance the TCU budget, he commented:

> At the very outset I decided that TCU had to operate on a balanced budget, and early on I used for the first time a statement that the faculty of TCU must have grown weary of hearing me say, "A university that is not fiscally sound cannot remain academically strong for long." That became a statement I tried to honor from day one to the day I stepped aside." (Interview, November 2011)

To support this commitment, Chancellor Tucker made two pivotal decisions that soon reshaped TCU's finances. The first, and perhaps the most far-sighted and impactful, was to transfer ninety-five percent of the income from the Barnett Daniel Trust into a quasi-endowment. Having gained insight into the oil and gas industry from his wife Jean's family and working summers in the field, he was quite aware that wells eventually stopped producing, which in turn stopped the income stream, and that steps had to be taken to manage that inevitability. This decision was of immense significance. When Chancellor Tucker started, the TCU endowment totaled a modest $53,000,000; when he retired nineteen years later in 1998, the endowment had reached over $650,000,000. All of TCU's subsequent achievements and milestones were made possible by Chancellor Tucker's firm determination to grow the university's endowment.

The decision, however, to grow the endowment and stop spending oil and gas income, while prescient, was not popular on campus. Previously, much of that revenue had been allocated to TCU's operating budget, and the loss of these funds caused considerable concern among faculty and staff. Having some of the lowest faculty and staff salaries in the nation, and seeing their buying power steadily decline as inflation rapidly rose, some faculty and staff complained that Chancellor Tucker was more concerned with the future than he was with the present, and this concern increased when he announced that, in order for TCU to operate in the black for the fiscal

I like the idea of TCU becoming a major university with the atmosphere of a residence college, and that became the priority. That is the spirit of this place.

Chancellor Emeritus Bill Tucker

Those who stand still fall behind.

Chancellor Emeritus Bill Tucker

When I became Chancellor, the morale at TCU was just at the bottom. We were losing enrollment, and we were operating at a deficit.

Chancellor Emeritus Bill Tucker
Interview, March 2012

I knew the endowment needed to grow, and grow substantially, if TCU were ever to fulfill its mission to become what it is today.

Chancellor Emeritus Bill Tucker
Interview, November 2012

There were those who said, and they were probably half right, maybe three-quarters right, "he's crimping the present to prepare for the future."

Chancellor Emeritus Bill Tucker
Interview, November 2011

There were a bunch of decisions that were made fairly early, and I cannot say 100 percent of the faculty said, "Bill Tucker is doing the right thing." I'm sure there were those who said, "What is going on?"

Chancellor Emeritus Bill Tucker
Interview, March 2012

It [the campus] wasn't barren, but we needed to make an effort to make the grounds more attractive."

Chancellor Emeritus Bill Tucker
TCU Magazine, Summer 2007

The grass was brown, the ground was brown, the trees were brown, the buildings were brown.

Kay Higgins, Interview,
October 2013

From Chancellor Bill Tucker's Inauguration Speech

ABOVE
Chancellor Bill Tucker. Courtesy of Mary Couts Burnett Library.

Remembering the past and anticipating the future, we must take care lest we be mesmerized by the one and frozen by the other. Our time, no matter how difficult and demanding and complex, is now.

In view of climbing prices and sagging morale, growing numbers of alarmists have adopted Chicken Little as the patron saint of American higher education in the 1980s.

The stakes are high precisely because the vitality of universities and colleges is essential to the life and welfare of this nation and to women and men across the face of the earth.

In a time of bubbling emotion and epidemic-like yearning for instant everything, do we not need leaders who are thinkers with a sense of history and a grasp of the human situation in all its grandeur and misery?

For too long we have watched in sophisticated silence as the seeds of anti-intellectualism spread, sprout, and flower. For too long we have enjoyed the fruits without attending to the roots of our civilization.

The decade of the 1980s is no time for us to huddle together in our robes and feel our way from fear and trembling to atrophy. It is a time to live out our stated mission, to confirm or if necessary to revise our goals and objectives, to celebrate our strengths, to acknowledge our weaknesses, and to seize every opportunity to close the gap between what is and what can be and ought to be.

Let us celebrate our diversity of programs.

Let us reaffirm in word and deed the wholeness of Texas Christian University and cultivate a sense of oneness in the midst of our diversity.

Let us reaffirm the bold decision in the 1960s to encourage and support excellent teaching and significant research on the ground that each enhances the other.

Let us deepen and broaden the unusual concern for individual students that really helps to make TCU distinctive among universities.

Let us answer commitment with commitment.

ABOVE
Dan Rogers Hall on TCU campus, ca. 1960s. Courtesy of Mary Couts Burnett Library.

LEFT
Texas oil derrick.

ABOVE
Bayard Friedman. Courtesy of Mary Couts Burnett Library.

But the most important thing we did, Bayard Friedman, Bill Tucker, and I, [is that we] decided . . . to save a large part of the oil and gas minerals revenue that was coming into the university. A big part of the endowment was oil and gas minerals, and at the time, there was pressure for faculty salaries and keeping tuition increases minimal, but we needed to recognize the fact that the oil and gas revenues were going to deplete over time, and so we wanted to set aside a substantial amount of it so we could build up the portfolio of investments . . . in the endowment. We set up a ten-year plan to do that, and I think we accomplished it in less than ten years. We set aside enough money into the endowment that would produce income that would totally replace the oil and gas income. Today's endowment . . . is attributable to that decision.

Denny Alexander, Interview, March 2013

year 1980, there would not be money available mid-year for salary bonuses, a considerable disappointment to many struggling with inflation as their financial positions continued to deteriorate.

In his first address to the Board of Trustees in November, Chancellor Tucker insisted that TCU "must operate in the black in fiscal year 1980" ("Report to the Board," Trustee Minutes, November 1979). Despite his determination to balance TCU's budget, he was by no means insensitive to low morale and low salaries. After erasing the university's deficits, increasing faculty and staff salaries became one of his highest priorities. In the same report to the trustees, he stressed this concern:

> Please do not take my comments to mean that I am of a mind to dismiss with a passing reference the widespread campus concern about remuneration. Quite the contrary, the need for substantial improvement is clear and pressing, so much so that I think merit increases in salary for faculty and staff should be assigned the highest priority in budget planning for the next fiscal year. (Report to the Board, November 1979)

True to his word, Chancellor Tucker proposed "compensation adjustments" of $1.2 million in his 1980 March report to the Trustees, hoping that the 1981 budget would "clearly if not dramatically" reflect his priority to help faculty and staff (Report to the Board, March 1980). A year later, however, he acknowledged that, with inflation continuing to rise erratically and the price of oil and gas fluctuating wildly, his efforts had only succeeded in keeping salaries "from not falling further behind." To help faculty and staff from further financial distress, he again proposed to the trustees that more help was needed: "It is simply not right that TCU, compared to other Category 1 universities in Texas, is near the top in teaching and research and dead last in salaries." The trustees responded by approving an overall merit increase of 13 percent in 1981 followed by a 14 percent increase in the next budget cycle (Report to the Board, March 1981).

Chancellor Tucker quickly made another significant decision when he resolved to improve TCU's physical appearance. Making TCU more physically attractive was, he believed, necessary to attract more students, and the campus in the 1970s was not particularly appealing. According to Lynn Guy, who worked in the Chancellor's Office, TCU "had practically gone back to prairie . . . it was stark, dry, and pretty woebegone." Long-time Student Affairs administrator Dr. Kay Higgins was decidedly unimpressed by what she saw when she arrived on campus: "I arrived the first week of August, walked onto campus, and thought pretty much, this was the ugliest place I had ever been in my whole entire life. The grass was brown, the ground was brown, the trees were brown, the buildings were brown. It was all pretty much brown or light brown" (Interview, October 2013).

Chancellor Tucker resolved that campus beautification was a priority. Since TCU's budget was—as it remains—dependent on tuition dollars, the university could not afford to remain visually unappealing if it wanted higher enrollments. When prospective students and their parents visit a university, first impressions matter greatly. If a campus looked neglected, they might suspect that its academics were also neglected. The chancellor, trustees, and many on campus realized that having an attractive campus was a crucial part of the recruitment process.

In commenting on his decision to improve campus appearance, Chancellor Tucker stated: "The other thing that was an absolute priority to me was making the campus more inviting and attractive; that meant flowers and shrubbery . . . If we were going . . . to have more success in admissions, we needed to have an attractive campus." Yet at a time when salaries were low and inflation high, he realized that "not everyone [would] agree when they saw flowers sprouting up here and there" (Interview, November 2011). Realizing that many would complain if tuition dollars were being spent on "flowers and shrubbery," Chancellor Tucker successfully identified a donor who was willing to create an endowment dedicated to improving TCU's campus landscape. That donor was Mary Evans Beasley. She and her husband Theodore (as well his former wife Beulah) were among TCU's most generous benefactors. In recalling the gift, Chancellor Tucker stated: "The Beasleys and I had been talking, as we regularly did, and I suggested a gift for campus beautification. For Mary, it became the perfect match of donor and project." In 1987 the Mary Evans Beasley

ABOVE
Summertime flowers bloom under shady oak trees on TCU Campus, 2006. Courtesy of Texas Christian University.

Endowment Fund for Campus Beautification was established, and for nearly a decade Mary Evans Beasley kept contributing to the fund to keep the campus visually appealing. In expressing his thanks for her donation, Chancellor Tucker said that she was someone "interested in all things beautiful," adding that "she was a person of wonderful taste and delighted in beauty where she found it. Her gift will last for decades to come. It is difficult to place a value on just how beautiful a campus we have. That was her gift." Today TCU has around 11,000 square feet of annual flower beds and another 15,350 of perennial flower beds (*TCU Magazine*, Summer 2007).

During his time in Sadler, Chancellor Tucker continually helped TCU to progress, and he never hesitated responding to challenges and obstacles, including several serious and urgent situations. But Chancellor Tucker always expressed discomfort at taking credit for what was accomplished during his administration, and he was quick to acknowledge the crucial contributions of those he worked closely with: "I really back away from saying Bill Tucker did this or Bill Tucker did that . . . I was part of a team . . . and there were many people who played a prominent, and sometimes a decisive, role in moving TCU from point A to point B" (Interview, March 2012). When asked about what TCU achieved during his nineteen years in office, he modestly responded: "One of my accomplishments was that I was able to attract and retain a remarkable executive team" (Interview, November 2011). Of those who played decisive roles in his administration, he named Bill Koehler, who became Provost and Vice Chancellor for Academic Affairs, and Leigh Secrest, who became TCU's chief financial officer as Vice Chancellor for Finance. Chancellor Tucker additionally mentioned the significant contributions of Don Mills, who served as Vice Chancellor of Student Affairs; Paul Hartman, who served as Vice Chancellor for University Relations and Development; and Bronson Davis, who served as Vice Chancellor of University Advancement. He particularly expressed gratitude to Bayard Friedman and John Roach, both of whom served as the Board of Trustees Chair during his years as TCU's chief administrator. In different ways and in different roles, each one of these individuals was instrumental in TCU's upward trajectory.

In the spring of 1984 Bill Koehler made one of the most significant contributions of the Tucker years when he proposed closing TCU enrollments. Up to this time, enrollments

I was able to attract and retain a remarkable executive team.

Chancellor Emeritus
Bill Tucker

Chancellor Tucker used to call Athletics . . . the window through which people viewed the university . . . if you have a great athletic program, people are going . . . to get a glimpse of what the university is all about.

Roby Key, Interview,
November 2014

I am firmly committed to the conviction that intercollegiate athletics must be seen and kept in proper perspective. But it also must be recognized that spectator sports are windows through which the public views the University. Like it or not, our basketball team's victory over Arkansas in the Southwest Conference tournament attracted more favorable publicity for TCU than we might receive if two of our professors should be selected as Nobel Prize winners in the same year.

Chancellor Emeritus
Bill Tucker, Report to the Board,
March 1983

They wanted football . . . that was a challenge.

Chancellor Emeritus Bill Tucker,
Interview, November 2011

RIGHT
Leigh Secrest. Courtesy of Mary Couts Burnett Library. Photograph by Linda Kaye.

LEFT
Bill Koehler. Published in TCU 1984 yearbook. Courtesy of Mary Couts Burnett Library.

Chancellor's Statement

During a team meeting on Thursday night (Sept. 19), Coach Wacker reviewed TCU's commitment to integrity in light of rumors or allegations of violations of NCAA rules at other universities in the Southwest conference. Following the meeting, a player—recruited prior to the arrival of Coach Wacker—revealed to an assistant coach that he had been illegally recruited and had continued to receive payments. . . . Five others—all recruited prior to Coach Wacker's arrival—also admitted to improprieties.

The decision we made and the promptness of our actions were intended to underscore the uncompromising commitment of Texas Christian University to integrity in intercollegiate athletics.

***Skiff*, September 24, 1985**

The chancellor said he was "shocked" and "saddened" when he first heard the news, and added, "the first things that popped into my mind was to do the right thing."

***Skiff*, September 24, 1985**

were open, allowing students to apply throughout the academic year without any deadlines, which led many people on the outside to assume that the university was easy to get into. Prospective first-year students often considered TCU a safe application. This open-door policy was thought to offer the best way to maximize enrollments and consequently tuition dollars. As Chancellor Tucker recalls, Provost Koehler took the opposite approach:

> We had been struggling with admissions, a real struggle, with some declining enrollments . . . and I remember Bill Koehler coming into my office and saying, "Chancellor, let's close freshman admissions." That was something unheard of . . . and all that did was make entrance into TCU more dear. (Interview, November 18, 2011)

Changing this admission policy indeed heightened TCU's value in the admissions marketplace. Contrary to the conventional wisdom of the time, the number of applications actually increased, and over the years has continued to increase. Recently the number TCU applications topped the twenty thousand mark for roughly two thousand places.

In moving TCU forward, Chancellor Tucker and his team also made a strong commitment to improve athletics, especially football. Achieving success in other sports mattered little to alumni eager for gridiron victories. In recalling the commitment he and his team made to football, Chancellor Tucker commented:

> I would get all these letters saying, "I will give you money, [but] your football team is an embarrassment." . . . and I'd write back and say look at what our record was in tennis this year, look at what our record was in women's golf. . . . but they didn't care a bit about what was happening in tennis and women's golf. They wanted football . . . that was a challenge. (Interview, November 2011)

Yet after making a commitment to improve football and hiring Jim Wacker as the new football coach, Chancellor Tucker and his team encountered one of their most serious challenges:

> One of the big challenges for me and our team was the emphasis we placed on having a viable athletics program, but we got clobbered, but not just in terms of wins and losses. When I became Chancellor, I was told that we had to do better than we'd been doing in football. . . . our goal was to make the football team more viable. I used to say in speeches, "we want a football team of the same quality as the university." Well, it didn't work out (Interview, November 2011).

The clobbering that Chancellor Tucker referred to did not take place on the field in Amon Carter Stadium, but in serious recruitment violations: "We found out we had been violating rules, and we received the second worst penalty ever imposed, and it happened on my watch in the mid-80s [1984]. That's when we were found guilty of major infractions, serious recruitment irregularities." (Interview, November 2011).

After learning of the violations, Coach Jim Wacker directly reported them to Athletic Director Frank Windegger, who quickly relayed the news to Chancellor Tucker and Provost Koehler. As soon as he heard of the infractions, Chancellor Tucker stopped what he was doing and, to verify the reports, went that same evening to see one of the people suspected of paying several football players. When he learned the reports were true—that some players were receiving payments for playing—he called a news conference to announce the violations and to promise full compliance with the NCAA. Coach Wacker, Athletic Director Windegger, Provost Koehler, and Chancellor Tucker's immediate response was "to do the right thing." TCU's celerity of response, self-reporting, and willingness to correct and comply were intended to lessen the inevitable NCAA penalties that were expected, but they were as well a clear public demonstration of TCU's institu-

ABOVE
Jim Wacker. Courtesy of TCU Athletics.

ABOVE
Frank Windegger. Courtesy of Texas Christian University.

LEFT
Ross Bailey. Courtesy of Ross Bailey.

It was rumored that a number of schools in the Southwest Conference were paying football players, and some of our alums, well-intentioned, said we can't be competitive unless we also recruit some players. So, for a couple of years, a few players, I don't know, maybe a half a dozen, were being paid. And nobody knew that except the handful of alums that were actually doing the paying. . . . I remember one of my daughters was in school, [and] she calls us in the middle of the night and starts talking about the rumors and what's going on on campus. It turned out to be true. It really set the football program back.

John V. Roach, Interview, March 2012

We had a situation when our football team got sanctioned for breaking the rules because of alumni trying to recruit and retain players. The way TCU handled that said a lot about the institution. No one was angry at the individual students who were involved. The day the news broke we put police in the resident halls where those particular young men lived to keep the press away. We warned the press that this is a private institution and they were not going to get access to our residence halls.

The students had enough on their minds. They were our students, and we were going to take care of them. I was not pleased with their behavior, but I was not going to let them be harassed by local or national media. The way the institution responded to that is an extraordinarily good story about living out our values.

If you care about people, even if they do something wrong, you will continue to care about them and make sure they don't come to harm.

Peggy Barr, Interview, December 2013

ABOVE
Anti-Apartheid protest organized by Students for a Democratic South Africa, 1986. Published in the TCU yearbook. Courtesy of TCU Marketing and Communication. Photograph by David Martin.

tional commitment to its ethical values. Yet such openness and compliance did not mitigate the punitive measures that were soon handed down. TCU received "onerous sanctions that crippled TCU football" (Interview, November 2011). For years the loss of scholarships and probation plagued the program, resulting in a succession of losing seasons, and undoubtedly contributed to the university not being invited to join the new Big XII conference ten years later. Both TCU and SMU, the two schools with the worst NCAA sanctions, were left out of the Big XII.

Just as he made a commitment to raise the endowment and salaries, Chancellor Tucker ultimately helped athletics achieve greater success, and that success helped TCU gain national recognition. In describing the relationship between athletics and academics, former Associate Athletic Director of Operations Ross Bailey credited Chancellor Tucker with raising expectations: "I think you have seen the university change the way it views athletics. I think Dr. Tucker said athletics was the window through which the university was viewed. Whether that's right or wrong, that's the part that [shows up in] headlines. We have to be willing to live up to those expectations in the community, and in the athletic world, which means competing at a higher level" (Interview, December 2012). Success in athletics contributes significantly to success in academics. Ross Bailey further commented that winning seasons, especially in football, elevated "the desirability of the university . . . which lets us bring more students in, which helps bring in

There's one other thing that I remember Bill Tucker for in particular and that was during the 1980s. He was really caught in . . . the apartheid in South Africa. There was a great movement among people in lots of places but very much so in the Christian church, the Disciples of Christ, to divest investments from companies and businesses in South Africa. Brite Divinity School divested its endowment and the church divested and there was a lot of pressure on Bill to do that. The board members just would not hear of it. Bill took the side of the board, which he had to do, frankly.

Paul Hartman, Interview, November 2011

If you are part of a university with everyone in lockstep, that's got to be a sorry university. If everyone is thinking the same way, that's not what a university is. That would be scary.

Chancellor Emeritus Bill Tucker, Interview, March 2012

more financial resources to the university, and maybe makes the alumni a little bit more willing to give back because they have a new sense of pride in the university" (Interview, December 2012).

An equally great challenge during the 1980s was divesture: whether TCU should divest its investments in corporations doing business with South Africa. This was particularly difficult for Chancellor Tucker, who was caught between conflicting commitments and loyalties. At the heart of the divesture conflict was a global movement to ostracize and penalize the South African government for apartheid. A particularly oppressive political system of policies and laws intended to buttress the power of South Africa's small white minority at the expense of the country's vast Black majority, apartheid had become a global cause during the 1970s as the winds of change blew across the world. Frequent reportage of Black militant resistance being violently and viciously confronted by South African police and military had led to global outrage, and many governments and the United Nations called on the South African government to end its racial oppression. Among the many steps taken globally was a movement to boycott South Africa, and throughout the 1980s numerous universities and corporations were pressured to discontinue their investments with the country. During the late 1980s the divestment movement had achieved critical mass, with over two hundred global corporations and over 150 universities having divested.

Chancellor Tucker was caught in the middle. As the Disciples of Christ historian and its moderator from 1983 to 1985, he was a prominent figure in the church, and when the denomination joined the apartheid boycott the Disciples leadership pressured Chancellor Tucker to have TCU, the largest of the schools associated with the Disciples, publicly divest its South African investments. In recalling the divesture issues, he stated:

> When the apartheid struggle came along, the denomination of which I was a part, and its past moderator, wanted colleges and universities related to the Disciples to divest of stocks and companies that had any interest in South Africa, and that became a major thing. I thought it was a simplistic approach, and I thought there were better ways of addressing apartheid, and we did. We started trying to get scholarships for students in South Africa . . . [but] there was a lot of animosity. I took the position as Chancellor of TCU . . . that the church denomination through its offices could not tell TCU what to do with its endowment. The trustees had fiduciary responsibility that I did not think they could relinquish. That's what put me in hot water with the Church, and we wound up having people protesting on the steps of Robert Carr Chapel. That went on for a long time. It was troubling to me. (Interview, November 2011)

TCU

TEXAS CHRISTIAN UNIVERSITY
Fort Worth, Texas 76129
817-921-7469

Department of Sociology
Undergraduate Social Work Program

DATE: February 7, 1991

TO: Faculty Senate

FROM: Linda Moore (for the SOWO 4843 class)

RESOLUTION

Whereas Martin Luther King, Jr. stood for social justice, equality, and world peace, and

Whereas Texas Christian University strives to promote the development of mature individuals who respect others, who understand the past, who cherish a free and just society, and who are prepared to act as responsible citizens, and

Whereas the United States government recognizes Martin Luther King, Jr.'s birthday as a national holiday, and

Whereas Chancellor Tucker has presented to the University a goal of multicultural awareness,

Therefore, be it resolved that Texas Christian University recognize Martin Luther King, Jr.'s birthday as a university holiday.

ABOVE
TCU Faculty Senate minutes, February 7, 1991.

ABOVE
Linda Moore. Courtesy of TCU Race and Reconciliation Initiative.

One of the big things that occurred during my tenure there [in the Chancellor's Office] was the controversy over apartheid . . . There was a faction of people who really wanted the university to divest itself from any corporations that were invested in . . . South Africa.

It was very controversial not only for Brite Divinity School, Texas Christian University, but for the Disciples of Christ Church as a whole. Chancellor Tucker was a prominent figure in the Disciples . . . but he took the stand not to divest . . . That was not popular. There were shanties built on campus, and there were sit-ins in hallways. He received a lot of opposition about that, and I think it took a great deal of strength and character and courage to stand his ground.

Lynn Guy, Interview, November 2013

From the early nineteenth century, the Disciples represented unity. We were there to bring people together. Christian unity was our polar star. And now TCU—as a university affiliated with the Disciples, is also concerned with unity across faiths. What is essential to this university is inclusiveness—inclusiveness in every meaning of that term.

Chancellor Emeritus Bill Tucker, TCU At a Glance, February 2000

I think Chancellor Tucker did a fantastic job in taking the first steps to making the university more a presence not only in the state but nationally.

Denny Alexander, Interview, March 2013

Despite the stream of protests and publicity, which at one point included a hunger strike, sit-ins, and protest shanties on campus, Chancellor Tucker and the Trustees withstood the pressure and preserved the university's autonomy through this difficult period.

Not long after the apartheid contention, there was another campus-wide dispute over whether TCU should officially celebrate Martin Luther King Jr. Day. Efforts to honor Martin Luther King Jr. with a national holiday started shortly after his assassination in 1968, but it was not until 1983 that President Ronald Reagan signed a bill making the third Monday of January a national holiday to celebrate King's birthday, and MLK Day was observed for the first time on January 20, 1986. States and municipalities were slow to recognize MLK Day, but by 1991 both Fort Worth and Dallas recognized the day as an official holiday, as did most schools in the metroplex. TCU was an exception. In January 1991, Professor Linda Moore and one of her social work classes began asking why TCU was not officially celebrating the day. By the end of the semester—after successive waves of discussion and demonstration that included local and national media coverage—Chancellor Tucker announced that TCU would recognize Martin Luther King Jr.'s birthday as an official TCU holiday.

There was a lot of opposition at the outset, including Chancellor Tucker, who along with many believed that there were better ways of commemorating Dr. King, but there was such "an outpouring of support" for the holiday's official recognition that he, his administrative team, and the trustees were persuaded to relent. In describing the movement to recognize MLK Day on campus as one of her most significant experiences during her distinguished career as a professor of social work, Linda Moore stated: "One of my proudest achievements is one [when] my class in 1991 decided that we should celebrate Martin Luther King Jr.'s birthday as a holiday," adding that "It was the most exciting collaborative experience that I have ever seen on this campus (Interview, November 2012).

In recalling how it started, Moore explained: "I had a class of students that were engaged in community practice, and I said we have to come up with a project. What do y'all want to do?" In response, her students, an "all-white class," asked why TCU did not celebrate

There were also times in the early 1980s when apartheid was an issue, and people wanted TCU to divest of any investments in South Africa until apartheid [was eliminated]. . . we had a lot of students saying, "We need to divest," and there was a whole shanty of building projects that went on. This was funny. They are building shanties, like in front of the library, and as soon they were built the campus police would tear it down. While they were tearing it down they put up a new one across the street. But it brought a lot of attention to the issue on campus.

Linda Moore, Interview, November 2012

The buildings have life to me. They walk and talk with me.

Chancellor Emeritus Bill Tucker, Interview, November 2011

I made my way to Brite [from Barton College] but became very much involved in the life of the university. I would have never come to Brite had it not been affiliated with a university.

Chancellor Emeritus Bill Tucker, Interview, March 2012

Martin Luther King Jr. Day. When she told them they had to ask the TCU administration why it did not, they collectively responded: "We want it to be an official holiday because it should be." When she told them that "policy change takes a long time" and that "you won't get it this semester," the class nevertheless took on the challenge: "Never tell students they can't do something. They went out [and] interviewed everybody on campus. What they found was that most of leadership said, we don't need a holiday; we will just celebrate his activities" (Interview, November 2012).

Undiscouraged by a lack of initial support, Linda Moore and her class submitted a resolution to the TCU Faculty Senate in February 1991, which was discussed and defeated in the March Faculty Senate meeting. Opposing viewpoints cited the cost of making MLK Day an official holiday and questioned whether "broadening the event over a longer period of time was better than simply closing class for one day," while those in favor stated that "not observing Martin Luther King Jr.'s birthday would send a message to the community that TCU does not endorse the policies of equality and social justice proposed by Martin Luther King Jr." (Faculty Senate Minutes, March 1991). Although Professor Moore and her class took part in the discussion, a majority of those present sided with the argument that there were better ways of honoring Dr. King than cancelling class.

Momentum for recognizing MLK Day continued to grow on campus, particularly among students. In recalling campus support, Professor Moore commented:

> The Black Student Caucus got involved. Then a professor at the School of Business offered his consulting skills for free . . . it was fabulous. The Bright Divinity School and the House of Student Representatives all said, we need to have this, and passed resolutions. . . . The entire football team cancelled spring practice the day before the spring game and came to the [April] senate meeting . . . with Channel 4, Channel 8, and Channel 11 in tow. (Interview, November 2012)

To support the movement, Professor Moore's students also circulated a petition calling for recognizing MLK Day as an official university holiday and gathered signatures of over 1300 students and 180 faculty members.

During the Faculty Senate's April meeting, Professor Moore resubmitted the resolution to recognize MLK Day, and—despite the strong student support—the resolution was again not approved. But the Faculty Senate April 1991 minutes recorded the words of several students who spoke on behalf of the resolution:

> Teto Garcia, a TCU student, expressed to the Senate that he was concerned about the negative impact of not recognizing Martin Luther King Jr.'s birthday on athletic recruitment. Garcia further urged the Senate to recognize the support from the students present regarding the proposal. Sadd Jackson, a freshman business major and football player, stated that the causes supported by Martin Luther King Jr., such as justice and Christian ideals, should be honored and supported by TCU. Laura Whitworth, a senior social work major, stated that a holiday is the best and only way of supporting Martin Luther King Jr.'s birthday. (Faculty Senate Minutes, April 1991)

The April minutes close with an announcement from Chancellor Tucker: "A letter from Chancellor Tucker was read to the faculty regarding the establishment of an ad hoc committee to study the merits and ways of recognizing Martin Luther King Jr.'s birthday" (Faculty Senate Minutes, April 1991). The committee quickly held three listening sessions to gather opinions and perspectives, and Chancellor Tucker did not wait long to announce his decision. In concluding her recollection, Professor Moore stated: "At the spring leadership meeting [and] award ceremony in May, Chancellor Tucker . . . said, 'I once met a leader I think is very important, Martin Luther King Jr., and as of August 1991 we will celebrate it [his birthday] as an official holiday'" (Interview, November 2012).

Ironically, one of Chancellor Tucker's most impactful achievements resulted from an unsuccessful attempt to manage a constant enrollment issue, the gender imbalance of having more female than male students on campus. TCU needed to grow academically, and Chancellor Tucker and his executive team discussed and researched what kinds of programs would best complement TCU's curriculum and profile while attracting more male applicants. Ultimately the decision was made to develop an engineering program:

> We needed to have more programs at that time that would be attractive to men because the percentage of women on campus was growing . . . We also needed something that was complementary to some of the programs we had

> The creation of an engineering program at TCU was a dream that the then Dean of the College of Sciences, Michael McCracken, and I both shared. We tried on several occasions to start an engineering program and were not successful, and finally it seemed like the right time and the right thing to do, and we were able to start an engineering program . . . there was concern among some trustees that an engineering school may bring some risk that we will not be successful because there were so many well-established engineering schools in the state. But I think that they obviously came to understand that it would truly be beneficial to the university, which I think it has been.
>
> **Bill Koehler, Interview, November 2011**

> in science and technology, and the decision was made to move into engineering, [although] it was an expensive program. I've always felt good about that decision because engineering is a splendid program at TCU. (Interview, March 2012)

Chancellor Tucker had ample reason to feel good about bring engineering to campus. Although it did not change TCU's gender imbalance, engineering was a successful program from the start. He commented that "It received full accreditation in the first year it was possible to get full accreditation" (Interview, March 2012).

During his years at TCU's helm, Chancellor Tucker helped to build many university programs and areas, but he remained cautious about constructing new buildings. When he arrived on campus, the Moudy Building was being built, and while its construction was funded, its maintenance was not, and Chancellor Tucker and his executive team were concerned that there were insufficient funds to cover what was needed both to maintain the building and upgrade its academic programs:

> I did not want to build a building if there was not money to heat, cool, and clean it . . . We began seriously to look at what it cost to heat, cool, and clean the non-revenue buildings, and we determined what it cost and added it to the project budget, so we would not become what I call "building poor." That is to say, you build a building and then you are obligated . . . to keep it up. I thought it made sense to have a designated endowment attached, so it could be heated, cooled, and kept up without infringing on money that could be spent for other academic purposes. It was a different way of doing things, and the Moudy Building is a classic example. (Interview, March 2012)

With new buildings, Chancellor Tucker wanted to make sure that all costs were anticipated, including those well beyond the actual construction, particularly maintenance, upkeep, and service. During his time in Sadler, several more new buildings and additions were completed on campus. At the same time the Moudy Building was being built in 1982, a new addition was added to Mary Couts Burnett Library, nearly doubling its size. A new student residence, Moncrief Hall, opened in 1988, and a new Neeley School building, Tandy Hall, was connected to the Dan D. Rogers Hall in 1989. In the 1990s several more construction projects were completed on campus. The Walsh Complex, a $2,500,000 weight training and rehabilitation center, opened in 1994, and in 1997, the Dee J. Kelly Alumni and Visitors Center was completed. One of the most unique and ambitious projects on campus, The Walsh Center for the Performing Arts, was finished a year later in 1998 and included two unique theaters, the Pepsico Recital Hall and the Marlene and Spencer Hays Theater.

ABOVE
Chancellor Emeritus Bill Tucker, 1990s.
Courtesy of Mary Couts Burnett Library.

To fully fund these projects, Chancellor Tucker utilized what he referred to as a "rifle shoot" in fundraising. Although he played a significant role in TCU's Next Frontier campaign, he preferred to focus on projects one at a time. The Walsh Center's Hays Theater is a good example of Chancellor Tucker's preferring a rifle over a shotgun. Sometime in 1994 he approached Marlene and Spencer Hays with a proposal to fund a new theater and, wanting to help support both Chancellor Tucker and TCU, they quickly agreed. In describing his efforts at fundraising, he stated:

> My approach to fundraising didn't go by the handbook. . . . The Next Frontier Campaign was halfway through my term as chancellor, but I preferred to rifle shoot rather than shotgun shoot; that is, I wanted to take project A, B, C in succession. I didn't care about all of the bells and whistles in terms of fundraising . . . my colleagues in advancement wanted to do campaigns . . . but I preferred to rifle shoot. Instead of a broad-based campaign, I preferred to take one project, complete it, and move on . . . I think the most important work I did was before the Next Frontier Campaign . . . but I was part of a team, and I mean that sincerely. I had some wonderful colleagues and developed some wonderful friends in this city and beyond. Let's just say that some good things happened on my watch. (Interview, November 2011)

Chancellor Tucker had ample reason to be careful in his approach to fundraising. With the financial distress of inflation, unemployment, and recession lingering for much of the

Brite began preparing to confront the governance relationship with TCU head-on.

***Institutional Change in Theological Education: A History of Brite Divinity School*, Toulouse et al., 180**

1980s, seeking financial support for major projects was not easy, and in fact The Next Frontier Campaign was delayed for several years while the economy recovered. It finally concluded in 1997 after raising $1,260,000. When thinking back on fundraising in the 1980s, Chancellor Tucker commented it was "a rather tortuous time in the economy of Texas (Interview, November 2011).

With the help of many people, both on and off campus, Chancellor Tucker and his administrative team accomplished much for TCU. After starting in Sadler when TCU was at a low point with budget deficits, low morale, and unstable enrollments, he and those he worked with redirected TCU on a steady, upward trajectory. All of TCU's later success and achievements were built on what was accomplished during the Tucker years, and there is no better barometer of these accomplishments than the endowment. Having made it a crucial priority when he started in 1979—when the total endowment was a little over $50 million—Chancellor Tucker made decisions that helped the endowment steadily grow. In 1983 the endowment had nearly doubled, reaching the $100 million mark, and six years later in 1989 it did double, topping $200 million. Four years later, in 1993, it doubled again, surpassing the $400 million mark. By the time he retired in 1998, the endowment was over $600 million.

Chancellor Tucker's final years in Sadler were not without stress, and undoubtedly one particular challenge caused him considerable concern and overshadowed both his retirement and Chancellor Mick Ferrari's transition. By the late 1990s, issues concerning Brite Divinity School's relationship with TCU were being discussed by some Brite board members and faculty who wanted greater autonomy for the school.

Ever since Brite had been incorporated in 1914 as a separately incorporated institution with its own board, there had been some confusion over its relationship with TCU. Having its own governing board, a different mission, and dissimilar students, Brite was not simply another college, yet in the university's organizational scheme its dean answered to the TCU Provost. During the divestment movement of the late 1980s and early 1990s, relations became particularly strained when Chancellor Tucker and both Brite and TCU boards refused to join the wave of schools and companies divesting their shares in South African stock. As the protests on the steps of Robert Carr Chapel failed to move TCU to divest, some Brite faculty, administrators, and trustees who favored divestiture thought that the divinity school's moral concerns were secondary to TCU's financial interests and were disappointed in Chancellor Tucker's leadership. Chancellor Tucker had deep connections with Brite. In 1953 he began his graduate studies at there, and in 1966 he returned to serve as the divinity school's assistant dean. Returning to TCU in 1979 as a national figure in the Disciples denomination, both he and members of the Brite community expected strong, reciprocal relationships from the start. Those expectations did not last long.

While there were many issues involved, particularly concerning Brite's governance structure, the construction of Leibrock Village, a new housing facility for Brite divinity students, became the tipping point in the relations between school and university. Relations were strained when Chancellor Tucker and the TCU Board of Trustees reversed an earlier decision about where the new Brite facility would be located, which at first had been planned for a site on Cantey street near the football stadium but had been moved to what then seemed a less attractive site east of campus on McCart. In response, a few Brite administrators and board members began to discuss options for redefining the school's relationship with TCU (*Institutional Change in Theological Education: A History of Brite Divinity School, Toulouse, et al., 180, 181).*

By November 1998 a confidential memo was circulated among some Brite board members questioning whether the school could remain in its current relationship with TCU. The memo argued that Brite, an independently incorporated Disciples' divinity school, was not in compliance with the recently revised standards of the national Association of Theological Schools. Those who circulated the memo contended that the divinity school's "chief executive leadership should come from within Brite rather than from TCU" (Toulouse et al., 183).

There is an apocryphal story that on Chancellor Tucker's last day in Sadler he received a letter from Brite board members declaring their intention to separate from TCU. While many have heard this story, it is not true. There is no mention of it in any documented sources. Clearly, some within the Brite community were discussing ideas to reconceive its relationship with TCU, but there is no source indicating that Chancellor Tucker was involved or even aware of these discussions. Yet the lack of direct discussions indicates that his relationship with Brite—once so close and cordial—had cooled.

Chancellor Bill Tucker is most remembered for his efforts building the endowment, and he is credited with launching TCU on an upward journey that continues to sustain its momentum. His vision of TCU becoming a major university while maintaining the atmosphere of a residential college has continued to characterize the best of what TCU offers. When looking back on his nineteen years guiding TCU forward, he was asked what motivated him, and his response revealed much about his character:

> I guess I was a driven person in terms of wanting to achieve . . . Why, I'm not sure I've ever known . . . You've asked me to look inside, and I can say the one thing I knew. I'm not sure I could out think anybody, but I've always felt I could outwork anybody . . . that's who I was. I may not out think, but I can outwork, and that served me well. (Interview, March 2012)

Lynn Guy, who worked closely with Chancellor Tucker, offered one anecdote about his work ethic:

> But Mary Nell and I [Mary Nell Kirk also worked in the Chancellor's Office] used to laugh that Chancellor Tucker's idea of a vacation was coming to the office in khakis. And so one day we figured that the only way we were going to keep him out of the office was to completely block the entrance to his office. We got butcher paper and we taped up the doorway to his office and marked on it "Do not enter until . . . " and it was the date of the last day of his vacation time. . . . He came up there and he saw it and said, "Well, maybe I really need to take a vacation." (Interview, November 2013)

When asked to describe Chancellor Tucker, she again referred to his constantly working as a defining characteristic but also mentioned his ability to work with others. Working constantly by no means meant working alone:

> Chancellor Tucker was probably considered a workaholic who appreciated that in others but didn't demand it of others. He had been a professor, so he knew what it was to be a faculty person. I think he had the ability to relate to anyone and everyone who worked here at the university, from the hourly workers to the endowed chairs . . . I think he was a very humble person and a brilliant person who didn't let either one of those define him. . . . [He] always had the ability of making you . . . feel like you were the most important person in that moment with him, and you were. (Interview, November 2013)

ABOVE
Chancellor Tucker with Bob Schieffer at commencement. Courtesy of Mary Couts Burnett Library.

ABOVE
Chancellor Tucker congratulates a new graduate at commencement. Courtesy of Mary Couts Burnett Library.

ABOVE
Chancellor Tucker celebrates with a student at commencement. Courtesy of Mary Couts Burnett Library.

Part 2
Action: The Ferrari Years

On March 26, 1998, Drake University President Michael (Mick) Ferrari was welcomed on campus as TCU's new Chancellor, and a day later the *Skiff*'s lead story, "Ferrari named newest frog," featured a photo of Chancellor Tucker pinning a horned frog pin on the university's new leader. Chancellor-elect Ferrari, however, needed little coaxing in transitioning to his new role and responsibilities. Trustee Denny Alexander, who chaired the search committee, was quoted as stating that "Ferrari has the talents and skills to keep the university moving full speed ahead" (*Skiff,* March, 1998).

LEFT
Chancellor Emeritus Michael R. Ferrari.
Courtesy of Texas Christian University.

There is no question that TCU is a jewel in higher education. This is a place making something happen.

Chancellor Emeritus
Mick Ferrari,
Skiff March 27, 1998

We went there [to visit TCU] and had time to walk around the campus, met some students and some of the staff, some of the board and search committee, and almost instantly I just said, "this is it." There's something about TCU, its energy, its potential to become even more widely respected and a more nationally recognized private university, indeed a leading private university in the country.

Chancellor Emeritus
Mick Ferrari,
Interview November 2012

Mick was more laid back. . . . He's just one of those leaders you don't even realize that is leading till he leaves.

Linda Moore, Interview,
November 2012

Ferrari named newest frog

Drake president chosen chancellor

By Kimberly Wilson
EDITOR-IN-CHIEF

"Ladies and gentlemen, the newest members of the Horned Frog family," said Chancellor William E. Tucker said as introduced his successor at a public announcement held shortly after 11 a.m. Thursday at the Dee J. Kelly Alumni & Visitors Center.

Michael "Mick" Ferrari, the current president of Drake University in Des Moines, Iowa, was named the next chancellor of TCU after he and his wife spent the week visiting with administrators, faculty, staff and students on campus.

"These past few days have been exhilirating," Ferrari said.

Between 75 and 100 students joined members of the TCU Board of Trustees, Chancellor Advisory Search Committee, faculty, staff, media and the community to welcome the man selected to lead the university beginning July 1.

"It's an overwhelming reaction and an overwhelming pleasure to be here today," he said. "I'm especially pleased to see so many students here today."

Denny Alexander, chairman of the 11-member search committee, said Ferrari has the talents and skills to keep the university "moving full speed ahead."

Ferrari said one of the reasons he decided to leave Drake to come to TCU was that he was impressed by TCU's "genuine commitment to excellence."

"There is no question that TCU is a jewel in American higher education," he said.

Ferrari said he plans to develop stronger relationships with the city of Fort Worth, which he said reflects a "can-do" attitude in the architecture, spirit and faces of the people.

"This is a place making something happen," he said.

Ferrari said he also plans to call on TCU alumni to assist the university more. He said he plans to improve technology at TCU and look for ways to bring the faculty and students together in planning.

In addition, he said having a shared vision among fac-

Please see FERRARI, Page 10

Philip Hawkins SKIFF STAFF

Chancellor William E. Tucker pins a gold Horned Frog on the lapel of Michael "Mick" Ferrari yesterday during the public announcement where Ferrari was named chancellor-elect.

ABOVE
Courtesy of the *Skiff*.
March 27, 1998.

His words were prescient. TCU's new chancellor wasted no time in moving the university forward, and the speed and energy of his plans astonished scores of people throughout the TCU community and Fort Worth.

Chancellor Ferrari was only at TCU for a short time, arriving on campus in the summer of 1998 and departing in the summer of 2003, but during these five years he accomplished an extraordinary amount of significant work and service that helped to propel TCU into the new century. Among the many accomplishments that occurred under his guidance are TCU's mission statement, The Commission on the Future of TCU, the reorganization of the colleges, the physical transformation of campus that included four major construction projects, the creation of the Staff Assembly, the resurgence of nationally respected athletic programs, the renovation of classrooms and labs with what were then state-of-the-art technology upgrades, and the revitalization of the core curriculum. Not the least of his efforts were his commitment to enhancing diversity on campus soon after his arrival, creating The Chancellor's Council on Diversity, establishing the Community Scholars Program, and inviting all TCU employees to the opening luncheon. Although he was TCU's first non-Disciple chancellor, he wanted to make sure that everyone had a place at the table.

At the March 26 welcoming ceremony, TCU's new chancellor-elect exclaimed: "There is no question that TCU is a jewel in American higher education . . . This is a place making something happen" (*Skiff*, March 27, 1998). Certainly, Chancellor Ferrari wasted no time in making a lot of things happen. When speaking to his first TCU audience, he signaled many of his ideas for building the university's future. While praising the "can-do" attitude in Texas, he introduced several of his ideas that soon became key components of his initiatives. He announced that he wanted to build stronger connections with Fort Worth, that he wanted TCU alumna to become more involved in the university, and that he wanted to improve technology on campus. More importantly, he announced his intention to involve everyone in the university community in a process of strategic planning. In his first appearance on campus, the new chancellor declared his intention to create a shared vision for the university's future.

Six months later, during his first convocation speech, Chancellor Ferrari opened TCU's 126th academic year by outlining ten areas of emphasis for the university's short and long-term goals, and among these ten areas were many of the initiatives that came to characterize his years at TCU. After stating that TCU is "a special place with an uncommonly bright future," he outlined his vision for moving TCU forward, and all his ideas, one way or another, involved inclusivity and sharing. In fact, his initial priority involved creating a shared vision of TCU's values and ideals. In order to distill its sense of purpose, TCU, he explained, needed a new mission statement: "A bold

From Chancellor Emeritus Mick Ferrari's Inauguration Speech, 1998

For more than a century, Texas Christian University has stood for what is valued and cherished in American independent higher education: a dedication to and love of sound learning; a commitment to tolerance, civility, and inclusiveness; an open and nondogmatic approach to matters of faith; and a pioneering, can-do spirit that has produced achievements and shaped aspirations that have brought honor and distinction to TCU.

AddRan Male and Female College, which later became Texas Christian University, was as its name boldly stated, coeducational from the outset. It was chartered to develop men and women for all walks of life, imbued with both faith and reason for the growing and promising frontier of Texas. As beneficiaries of this heritage, we now have the obligation and responsibility to develop leaders and responsible citizens for the uncertain frontiers of the global community in the twenty-first century. It is a noble and awesome challenge, but I believe it is one for which our university community is well prepared.

The genuine warmth and friendliness of faculty, staff, and students, long a hallmark of TCU, are attributes that we hope our students will take with them as they leave our campus and make a difference in the communities in which they reside.

We are indeed on the cusp of distinction, poised to seize this moment to establish a clear vision of the future in the midst of uncertainty and risk. I believe this is also a time to set ambitious goals that will accelerate movement to the next level of achievement.

To help realize that vision, we will soon launch a vigorous planning effort involving trustees, faculty, staff, and students as well as alumni and other friends from the community, state, and nation to help create a bold blueprint for the university we intend to become in the next decade.

ABOVE
Chancellor Mick Ferrari.
Courtesy of *TCU Magazine*.

I see many opportunities for the coming decade:

The opportunity to achieve greater prominence in American independent higher education . . .

The opportunity to attract students, faculty, and staff from a wider variety of backgrounds to ensure that our learning environment reflects the diversity of Texas and the nation as we educate students to be effective leaders and citizens in the next century.

The opportunity to strengthen our commitment to global education . . .

The opportunity to be a more involved partner in the intellectual, cultural, and economic development and progress of Fort Worth, our all-American hometown . . .

The opportunity to create a special university community, consistent with our inclusive and self-reliant heritage, in which each person is valued, each is treated with respect and dignity, and each can take justifiable pride in knowing that he or she is contributing to the building of a great university.

The Clark brothers and those who joined them had a grand dream and unbounded determination. Those of us who follow are the custodians of that heritage. Imagine what we can and shall make of this extraordinary university that has been entrusted to us!

Dr. Ferrari wanted to be called Mick. I was still an athletic trainer, and one day he was standing waiting for his press conference and . . . I walked out and introduced myself and said, "Hello Dr. Ferrari," and he said, "My name is Mick, just call me Mick." It's hard to call the Chancellor by his first name . . . a few weeks later I was in an elevator with him and his wife going to an event, and I went to introduce my wife to his wife, and he said, "I hate to tell you Mary, [but] your husband's a slow learner. I've had to tell him more than twice my first name's Mick."

Ross Bailey, Interview, December 2012

Dr. Ferrari came in and said, "Hi, I'm Mick Ferrari. What can you tell me about TCU?" He wandered [around] this campus talking to faculty, students, staff. He talked to groundskeepers . . . He was just out there meeting and greeting everybody. He wanted to see every nook and cranny of this campus and wanted to understand it . . . and he wanted it to be more collegial. He wanted it to be more inclusive. He didn't want just the straight-down approach where Daddy knows what's best and you children just sit.

Ann Sewell, Interview, October 2014

vision will lead to the university's increased academic stature and national visibility" (*Skiff*, September 18, 1998). A couple months later, when he presented his first Report to the Board of Trustees, he explained his desire "to clarify our mission and to develop a bold vision to guide TCU's move to another level of distinction." To accomplish this, he announced that a task force had been "appointed and charged with developing a clear, concise, and compelling statement that speaks to who we are, what we aspire to, and what distinguishes the outcomes of a TCU education from that provided at other colleges and universities" (Report to the Board, November 1998).

Chancellor Ferrari's second area of emphasis at Convocation was no less bold in sharing a vision for TCU. He declared that TCU needed to come together to create a strategic plan to map out its short and long-term priorities. When speaking later to the board in November, he explained that TCU needed "a comprehensive strategic planning process . . . to help formulate a blueprint for the future development of the university." What was unique about this initiative was its extensive inclusivity. He described his intention as "a vigorous planning effort that will involve a broad representation of constituents and stakeholders selected from across our campus, the community, state, and the nation." Such an all-inclusive, comprehensive, and long-range strategic plan, he declared, would help the university manage "the challenges and opportunities of higher education . . . to ensure that TCU is among the leaders in American higher education in the twenty-first century" (Report to the Board, November 1998).

While introducing further goals to strengthen TCU, he declared his intention to create a truly inclusive campus for all members of the TCU community. He called for "an improved working environment for the faculty and staff," and for "improving on-campus student life," which would include a renovated Student Center and an improved Rickel Building. To further promote the TCU community, he restated his commitment "to increase diversity on campus" and his intention to improve campus technology, which would literally improve university connections. Yet Chancellor Ferrrari's vision of what TCU could become was not limited to its physical campus. He not only expressed his hope that TCU could increase its "community involvement" in ways that would "enhance the quality of life in our neighborhoods and cities," but he also expressed his desire that TCU would become a "global university" (*Skiff*, September 18, 1998). In his first convocation address, Chancellor Ferrari shared his vision of TCU as a dynamic, comprehensive university active at home and abroad.

Proclaiming his plans to cultivate both mutual purpose and shared vision, Chancellor Ferrari's first all-campus address inspired many who attended that day. When she was interviewed soon after the event, Assistant to the Vice Chancellor for Academic Affairs Becky Roach noted that the attendance was "the highest at this convocation since former Vice President George Bush addressed TCU in the 1980s." Noting his desire to reach out to all members of the TCU community, she added: "Chancellor Ferrari spoke to every constituency of the university. It was uplifting and challenging for the future (*Skiff*, September 18, 1998).

When he was later interviewed in 2012, Chancellor Ferrari revealed that sharing a vision was based on a personal belief that the university needed to increase its inclusivity: "I was focused on TCU and what it could become and how we could create a shared vision. . . . I thought there were some aspects where we could become more inclusive" (Interview, November 2012):

> Leadership . . . is a process of engaging others in a way to share goals, to share dreams, and to work together to achieve those goals. . . . I subscribe more to a notion of servant-leadership, that you are really not here to direct the affairs of the institution as you are to create an environment where people's strength, the things they want to achieve, are to be maximized . . . the inclusiveness you have as a person in a leadership role . . . [is that] you're serving others . . . telling people who share a vision, we're all on the same page together, we all work together. That's leadership. It's a collaborative process. (Interview, November 2012)

To create collaboration, he described his community-building strategy as "more of a bottom-up approach, where you try to get as many ideas as possible from people" rather than a traditional "top-down approach" (Interview, November 2012).

By embracing inclusivity as a priority, Chancellor Ferrari wanted to stimulate TCU's momentum and unity. Effective collaboration required strong connections, and in various ways he worked at "creating a greater sense we are in this together." Some of his steps to bring about greater inclusivity were relatively uncomplicated. Soon after arriving on campus he learned that only faculty and a few selected administrators were invited to the opening lunch, and, without hesitating, he decided that everyone should be invited:

> Some of it [sharing vision and extending inclusivity] would be relatively simple, but very meaningful; for example, the opening lunches to start the new year. When I got there, only faculty were invited to this luncheon, and the staff were all sitting back in their offices wondering what people were having for lunch . . . we are a university, and we are all going to thrive together. (Interview, November 2012)

In his remembrance of the Ferrari years, long-time Professor of Religion and former Chair of the Faculty Senate Andrew Fort recalled:

> We would have a luncheon at the very beginning of the semester in the Fall, and it was for the faculty and certain key staff members. It was held in what was then the student center ballroom, and the argument was we couldn't make it any bigger because there's no room. Well, Ferrari said, "That has to change." And it was sent to the coliseum from his first year, and all the staff, the groundskeepers, everyone, came to sit and hear. (Interview, April 2014)

By inviting everyone to the opening luncheon, a significant and symbolic change, Chancellor Ferrari wanted everyone working on campus to feel valued and respected.

During Ferrari's tenure, more than 100 classrooms and laboratories were remodeled and equipped with state-of-the-art technology. The university refurbished residence halls and built three apartment-style residential communities. He oversaw four major construction projects—the William E. and Jean Jones Tucker Technology Center, the Steve and Sarah Smith Entrepreneurs Hall, the University Recreation Center, and the Charlie and Marie Lupton Baseball Stadium and Williams-Reilly Field.

"Man on a Mission," *TCU Magazine*, Summer 2015

The TCU Staff Assembly Bylaws

The TCU Staff Assembly was established in 1999 to provide an opportunity to discuss issues and address concerns of all staff. The Assembly consists of both exempt and nonexempt staff, representing all areas of the University. Meetings are held monthly from September to May. Elections are conducted in the spring and delegates are selected by their peers for two-year, renewable terms. Directed by an Executive Committee of officers, the Staff Assembly carries out most of its work through committees. Those committees include: elections, professional development, policy and advocacy, community service, committee on committees, media and communications, college resources, and constituency.

BYLAWS FOR THE CONSTITUTION OF THE TCU STAFF ASSEMBLY

I. MISSION AND VISION STATEMENTS

A. The mission of the Staff Assembly is to initiate communication among staff by providing a forum for expression and exchange of ideas and serve as an advocate for staff with administration.

B. The vision of the Staff Assembly is to foster a superior work environment with highly-motivated staff.

II. JURISDICTION, DUTIES, AND POWERS

A. The Staff Assembly shall study, consider, and exchange ideas concerning issues affecting Staff.

B. The Staff Assembly shall seek, devise, and propose to the Administration, as appropriate, new programs, modifications of current programs, or solutions to problems.

C. The Staff Assembly shall review proposed policies and/or programs referred by the Administration.

D. The Staff Assembly shall provide a communication channel between Staff and the University Administration.

(Staff Assembly website)

Inviting all employees to the opening luncheon was just the chancellor's first step, and he wasted little time taking further actions to bring the campus together in reciprocal effort and commitment. Another staff issue that Chancellor Ferrari soon identified was their lack of representation in the university's administrative process. Drake University had what he considered "a very strong staff council," and he was surprised there was nothing similar at TCU (Interview, November 2012). Consequently, not long after his start in

Chancellor Ferrari created the Community Scholars Program, and we are still much indebted to his leadership for bringing these students in from high schools in this region, where students are changing the experiences of their families and are living a dream that they never thought they could live.

Ann Louden, Interview, April 2013

Okay, that's enough. We're going to fix this.

Chancellor Emeritus Mick Ferrari

He challenged us to develop something that was not a jingle or a cliché, but a sentence that people could easily remember and rally around.

Barbara Herman, "Man on a Mission," *TCU Magazine*, Spring 2003

We had a commission, and what came out of the commission was superb.

Chancellor Emeritus Mick Ferrari

It's been years since I sat around and said, "How can I make TCU a better place?" . . . But then I started to do just that . . . and so did a whole lot of other people.

Bob Schieffer, Commission Chair, *TCU Magazine*, Winter 2000

ABOVE
Students from Barack Obama Male Leadership Academy find out that they have received TCU's Community Scholars scholarships, 2019. Courtesy of TCU Marketing and Communication. Photograph by Amy Peterson.

Sadler he appointed a committee to create a staff governance body similar to the Faculty Senate, which had been active on campus since the late 1960s. The committee moved quickly to propose a plan, and by his second year the Staff Assembly held its first meeting. "I felt the staff needed a voice in the affairs of the university," he said. "They've always been underappreciated . . . they weren't always directly involved in the process where they had a chance to think about major issues, major opportunities, and major concerns." Chancellor Ferrari believed that staff needed a forum to express their concerns and that broadening administrative participation "was something we just needed to have." When reflecting on creating the Staff Assembly, he noted that it quickly "made a big difference" in discussions about university policies, especially concerning benefits and compensation (Interview, November 2012).

Consequently, with strong support from the Staff Assembly, Chancellor Ferrari addressed another campus disparity by "equalizing benefits between faculty and staff." Formerly there had been a scale of lesser and greater benefits according to various pay levels and positions, with faculty being favored over staff, but Ferrari soon leveled the field for all university employees. When asked specifically about the advantages of having a Staff Assembly, he specifically referred to its recommendations for eliminating the hierarchy of compensation packages: "It gave them a voice in equalizing benefits." Enabling the Staff Assembly to contribute its collective voice, he concluded, ensured that everyone "had a seat at the table, which was a major victory for our staff" (Interview, November 2012).

Chancellor Ferrari's desire to build greater campus inclusivity included taking on one of TCU's most difficult challenges, its lack of racial diversity. In his November 1998 report to the Trustees, he announced that he had appointed The Chancellor's Council on Diversity, a committee made up of faculty, staff, and students who were charged with surveying current campus issues and making recommendations. With the support of the Council, Chancellor Ferrari launched one of his most significant initiatives a year later, the Community Scholars Program, which offered full-tuition scholarships to students of color at several area high schools. In recalling how the program evolved, former Dean of Admissions Ray Brown states:

> The Community Scholars Program . . . was established under Dr. Ferrari's watch . . . in my imagining of how this all unfolded, my sense is that Dr. Ferrari . . . knew that one of his missions was to change the complexion of this university . . . the face of our students. He established the Community Scholars Program, and . . . I've always described this as sort of a money-where-your-mouth-is kind of program. I think Dr. Ferrari . . . probably listened to our arguments about why we were so white and said, "Okay, that's enough. We're going to fix this." (Interview, December 2013)

The program started with four high schools hoping to recruit some of their best and brightest students of color, and within a short period of time the program expanded to more schools as the number of applications kept increasing, leading Ray Brown to conclude that the program "has become a bit of a jewel in the university's crown" (Interview, December, 2013). Without a doubt, the Community Scholars Program remains one of TCU's crown jewels. As of 2020, the program had forty students of underrepresented populations enrolled from a dozen area schools, and the Community Scholars graduation rate is one of the highest of any group on campus.

Though less tangible than creating the Staff Assembly or the Community Scholars Program, one of Chancellor Ferrari's most significant achievements was creating a collective sense of excitement about TCU's future. When he arrived on campus, he had ideas about how he could help TCU move forward, and he quickly succeeded in sharing his energy and vision. He urged everyone to "imagine the possibilities," which not only became a campaign slogan in strategic planning but also a call to action. The initiatives he outlined in his first Convocation address were all, in various ways, invitations to participate in transforming vision into reality. Symbolically, the first step he mentioned was "to develop a sharpened mission statement" (*Skiff*, September 9, 1998).

This is a university really poised to make another major step forward and move to another level of prominence in American higher education.

Chancellor Emeritus Mick Ferrari, *Star-Telegram*, March 25, 1998

Before TCU could elevate its position and reputation, he believed that the university first had to come together to define its principles and intentions. This crucial step of collective self-definition, he believed, was necessary to create a shared foundation for future growth. In explaining the purpose behind developing a new mission statement, he was quoted in the *Skiff* as saying: "A bold vision will lead to the university's increased academic stature and national visibility" (*Skiff*, September 9, 1998). In his 2012 interview, he clarified why he focused attention on developing a clear, concise mission statement:

> A mission statement is very important to me. I was captivated by trying to understand who we really are . . . in terms of what is our essence. What can we say about ourselves that is different from . . . the words you find at other places. Of course, I had catalogue statements three pages long, and so I suggested to some people [that] maybe it would be great if we clarified this mission statement, make it much more concise and really got it boiled down to what our essence really is. That would stand for forming a vision of what we aspire to become. (Interview, November 2012)

Yet the purpose of distilling the university's mission statement was not simply the product of a revised statement, but the process of uniting the campus community in discussions of what TCU was and what it could become.

In recalling Chancellor Ferrari's leadership in developing a new mission statement, Nowell Donovan, who in 1999 was then a member of the Faculty Senate Executive Committee, remarked that Chancellor Ferrari wanted the process to involve all areas of campus.

> Mick Ferrari decided he wanted a mission statement, and he wanted it to be inclusive. Therefore he set up an inclusive committee . . . he included members of the grounds staff, members of student affairs, he included faculty members, he included deans, [and he] put them all together and they came up with the famous phrase. (Interview, April 2014)

In a similar passage recalling the steps that led to the new mission statement, former dean of the business school Kirk Downey stated that Chancellor Ferrari "created an atmosphere where everybody understands it's our way and I'm not going to be mad if it's not my way." Extensive involvement was essential: "That was a community-wide project. There were committees of students, committees of faculty, committees of staff members, in all levels, retreating even if it was only to a classroom and sitting down and saying, what's our input to what the mission is going to be" (Interview, March 2013).

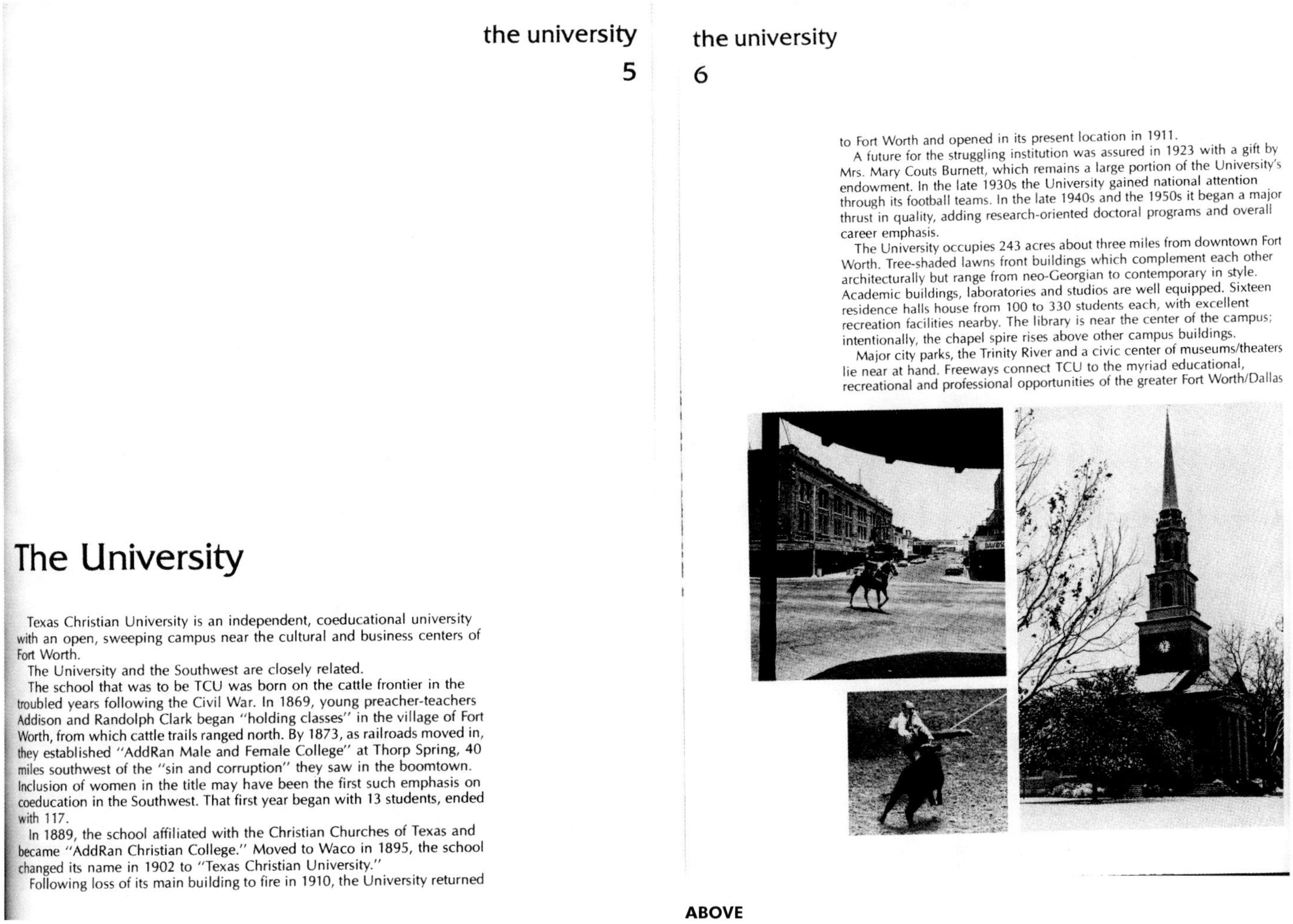

the university
5

The University

Texas Christian University is an independent, coeducational university with an open, sweeping campus near the cultural and business centers of Fort Worth.

The University and the Southwest are closely related.

The school that was to be TCU was born on the cattle frontier in the troubled years following the Civil War. In 1869, young preacher-teachers Addison and Randolph Clark began "holding classes" in the village of Fort Worth, from which cattle trails ranged north. By 1873, as railroads moved in, they established "AddRan Male and Female College" at Thorp Spring, 40 miles southwest of the "sin and corruption" they saw in the boomtown. Inclusion of women in the title may have been the first such emphasis on coeducation in the Southwest. That first year began with 13 students, ended with 117.

In 1889, the school affiliated with the Christian Churches of Texas and became "AddRan Christian College." Moved to Waco in 1895, the school changed its name in 1902 to "Texas Christian University."

Following loss of its main building to fire in 1910, the University returned

the university
6

to Fort Worth and opened in its present location in 1911.

A future for the struggling institution was assured in 1923 with a gift by Mrs. Mary Couts Burnett, which remains a large portion of the University's endowment. In the late 1930s the University gained national attention through its football teams. In the late 1940s and the 1950s it began a major thrust in quality, adding research-oriented doctoral programs and overall career emphasis.

The University occupies 243 acres about three miles from downtown Fort Worth. Tree-shaded lawns front buildings which complement each other architecturally but range from neo-Georgian to contemporary in style. Academic buildings, laboratories and studios are well equipped. Sixteen residence halls house from 100 to 330 students each, with excellent recreation facilities nearby. The library is near the center of the campus; intentionally, the chapel spire rises above other campus buildings.

Major city parks, the Trinity River and a civic center of museums/theaters lie near at hand. Freeways connect TCU to the myriad educational, recreational and professional opportunities of the greater Fort Worth/Dallas

ABOVE
Pages from TCU's 1980-1981 catalogue.
Courtesy of Mary Couts Burnett Library.

Ever since the Clark brothers had first established the AddRan Male and Female College, the university had continually published catalogues describing its curriculum and goals, and one way or another all of the catalogues commented on its purpose and goals. In 1965, after a formal university-wide process of adoption, TCU published its "Philosophy and Objectives of the University," a catalogue statement that ran two and a half pages. While celebrating its centennial, the TCU Priorities Committee added another two and a half pages of the university's "primary attributes," entitled "A View of Education at Texas Christian University." Not long after his appointment, Chancellor Tucker sought to revise the lengthy catalogue statements, and in March 1983 he submitted a series of revisions to the Board of Trustees, which were accepted and soon published in university catalogues as TCU's "Philosophy, Objectives, Goals," once again returning the university's declaration of its principles and purpose to a two-and-a-half-page statement. Among its "Specific Goals," Chancellor Tucker included a phrase that later would become quite well known: "To promote the development of mature individuals who respect others, who cherish a free and just society, and who are prepared to act as responsible citizens" (Board of Trustees Minutes, March 1983).

The problem with catalogue statements, however, is that they are read infrequently and rarely remembered. In recalling Chancellor Ferrari's interest in revising the mission statement, former Associate Provost and Dean of University Programs Bonnie Melhart stated: "When Dr. Ferrari came in, we probably had a mission statement . . . but it wasn't a mission statement that was a collective statement by the university. Nobody knew what the mission statement was unless you looked it up" (Interview, November 2013). Similarly, Vice Chancellor for Student Affairs Emeritus Don Mills declared: "One of the first things he [Chancellor Ferrari] wanted to do was to have us look at the mission of TCU, and when he got here the mission was two and a half pages long in a catalogue, so nobody knew what it was. It was nice, but really nobody knew what it was" (Interview, April 2014).

ABOVE
TCU mission statement. Courtesy of TCU Press.

To create a new mission statement, Chancellor Ferrari and his administrative team promoted a campus-wide discussion of the university's aspirations. They not only wanted a mission statement that could be remembered, but also one that would inspire, and everyone on campus was invited to reflect on TCU's purpose and goals. Yet such a broad, collaborative process required time and deliberation, which in turn caused some to question it. As he later recalled, Chancellor Ferrari noted that members of the Board of Trustees were at first not entirely enthusiastic: "I tried to describe this idea [creating a clear, concise mission statement] to members of the board, and they said, 'well, if you want to pursue it, that's fine, [but] we kind of like it the way it is'" (Interview, November 2012). Others around campus became impatient with the many meetings and slow process. When describing the process, Don Mills stated: "They held meetings and people would make suggestions and put things out for [other] people to comment on, and it was just taking a long time. People started to get impatient, and some of the executive officers said to him . . . just get on with it. And he said, 'No, trust the process'" (Interview, April 2014). While the year-long, campus-wide process did not quickly result in a clear, concise statement, it nevertheless succeeded in prompting all areas of the campus community to think about TCU's foundational principles and how it could achieve "the next level," which became a familiar catchphrase connected with many university plans and proposals.

Ultimately, the TCU mission statement—as most people know it today—resulted from Chancellor Ferrari's personal involvement. After gathering ideas from hundreds of students, faculty, staff, alumni, and community members, he scheduled a retreat in Glen Rose, Texas, for various campus leaders to work on the mission statement. Former Vice Chancellor Larry Adams attended the retreat and later described what happened:

> That planning process culminated in a retreat at Glen Rose with the leadership team . . . we debated . . . and Chancellor Ferrari listened to all of us go around the table. . . . But the sentence—after we debated all day . . . Chancellor Ferrari went back to his room, [saying] "Let me go work on this a little." And we came back the next morning following breakfast, and he said, "I want to try something on you folks . . . see what you think about this as a statement." He went to the chalkboard or to the flipboard and he wrote. . . . To educate individuals to act as responsible citizens and ethical leaders in the global community. As soon as he wrote that, we said, "Bingo!" We put it all together. (Interview, November 2011)

By combining responsible citizenship and ethical leadership in a global community, Chancellor Ferrari and the Glen Rose leadership team succeeded in connecting TCU's aspiration with what the Clark brothers had originally intended with their references to "character shaping": TCU's mission was to nurture responsible, conscientious citizens capable of making rational, thoughtful decisions for the good of their communities and the world at large.

After Chancellor Ferrari wrote the statement out for people to see, there was little discussion other than to add "to think" before "to act," since—as Nowell Donovan had suggested—thinking necessarily takes place before acting. For all those who were present, the new statement concisely captured the university's purpose. Concerning the statement, Don Mills concluded: "It certainly told people what TCU was about, that leadership was important to us, international was important to us, that community and ethics were all important parts of who we are. I don't think we

The effort was Herculean, to say the least. But Mick was determined to include individuals and groups that hadn't been affiliated with TCU previously. And what came out of that was a blueprint, pulled from everyone's ideas, that has changed TCU and, in the process, changed how Fort Worth sees TCU.

Bill Thornton, former CEO of the Fort Worth Chamber of Commerce, "Man on a Mission," *TCU Magazine*, Spring 2003

The Divinity School operated with the chancellor of TCU being the CEO of Brite. . . . [and with] the [TCU] vice chancellor for academic affairs being the chief academic officer at Brite."

Ann Sewell, Interview, October 2014

Mick Ferrari said, "Wait a minute, the guy that's out there planting flowers or the person that's cleaning your trash can is just as important in whether we're successful or not, so why shouldn't everybody come to the opening luncheon? We'll kick off the opening year together.

Ann Sewell, Interview, October 2014

MESSAGE FROM THE CHAIR

Looking Beyond the Obvious

Too often, universities spend their time constructing buildings and raising more money with no clear purpose in mind. *The Commission on the Future of TCU* looked beyond the obvious and the immediate. We paused to think about what the University is and where is it going. We questioned every assumption and took nothing for granted. This report outlines our results.

The golfer Lee Trevino once said, "Someone has to win these golf tournaments. Why shouldn't it be me?" There are going to be some great universities tomorrow. As we follow the blueprint for achievement that *The Commission on the Future* has provided, why shouldn't one of them be TCU?

Bob Schieffer
Chair
The Commission on the Future of TCU

"We questioned every assumption and took nothing for granted."

ABOVE
Courtesy of Mary Couts Burnett Library.

ABOVE
Courtesy of Mary Couts Burnett Library.

BELOW
Bob Schieffer. Courtesy of TCU Marketing and Communication.

> I think Ferrari saw a bigger picture and said, "Let's move out to a more national level" . . . he began a real push towards trying to get more scholarships, more academic concepts, more endowed professorships . . . He was the one that began to see these as larger steppingstones to get to a more national and international level. He was big on pushing international programs. . . . if I were to say one thing [he did], it would be changing the mindset of the Board of Trustees—that we're going to expand that academic push, and we're going to become a national university.
>
> **David Whillock, Interview 2014**

would have had that if Ferrari had allowed it [the process] to be short-circuited (Interview, April 2014). When asked about the mission statement, former Associate Vice Chancellor for Student Affairs Barbara Herman stated:

> It was during . . . the "Imagine the Possibilities" campaign and the strategic plan and we came up with the mission statement. I loved it because it involved students, parents, alumni, community members, faculty, staff, and we spent a year coming up with that mission statement. But I also love it because to me it is about helping students to become the best version of themselves, and then again, to make the world better. (Interview, December 2013)

Developing a mission statement that succinctly articulated TCU's purpose was only a preliminary step in imagining TCU's possibilities. As he had outlined in his first Convocation address, Chancellor Ferrari's next action was to launch a comprehensive strategic planning initiative, the Commission on the Future of TCU. Only after refining its aspirations could TCU then begin to identify its priorities, resources, and procedures to fulfill its mission. From the start, this undertaking was remarkably inclusive. To dream about TCU's future, Chancellor Ferrari encouraged input from all areas and levels of campus and beyond.

To help start the process, town hall meetings were held, and six "Background Committees" were appointed "to gather essential background information." These committees were tasked with "gathering documents and data concerning the university's Mission and Vision, Diversity, Physical Resources Analysis, Market Analysis, and Finance and Enrollment Issues" (VIA Report Card, 2004). While these committees were gathering information, seventeen task forces were created that not only represented each college and such academic programs as Ranch Management, but also crucial areas of growth and aspiration. These included:

Undergraduate Experience
Graduate Education
Technology
Distinctive Programs and New Directions
Community and Strategic Alliances
Global Positioning and Priorities
The Role of Athletics
Alumni Relationships

The task forces were given roughly one year, from November 2000 to the following October 2001, to report back with recommendations, and they ultimately concluded their work by submitting 386 recommendations. Yet one of the commission's most important achievements did not result from its recommendations, but from its inclusivity. Chancellor Ferrari not only involved students, faculty, staff, and administrators to take part, but he also invited alumni near and far as well community and corporate leaders, many of whom formerly had little or no connection to TCU. When reflecting back on the Commission's work, former Associate Provost Bonnie Melhart commented that Chancellor Ferrari was not shy about soliciting help: "I imagine that every person whose hand he shook, he [Chancellor Ferrari] asked them to be on one of those committees" (Interview, December 2013). When describing the full extent of campus and community involvement, former Vice Chancellor for Marketing and Communication Larry Lauer stated: "We know of no other university that has involved so many people in a serious and substantive conversation about its future. Half were from inside TCU, and others were supporters and friends representing virtually all of our constituents. I am confident that everyone who participated came away feeling that the future of TCU is extremely bright" (*TCU Magazine*, Winter 2000). By involving Fort Worth leaders in discussions about TCU's future, the Commission effectually created much deeper and more meaningful relationships between town and gown.

ABOVE
Larry Lauer. Courtesy of Texas Christian University.

ABOVE
Chancellor Emeritus Mick Ferrari.
Courtesy of *TCU Magazine*.

Emphasizing these connections, former Associate Dean of Admissions Janet Herald recalled:

> TCU really didn't have that strong of an image in Fort Worth . . . especially with the business community. That was something that was really lacking . . . [but the Commission] brought businesspeople and leaders . . . from all over the city and got them connected with TCU. I think that was . . . important. The concept of TCU being the home team of everybody that lives in Fort Worth, regardless of where they went to school, didn't exist [before the Commission]. (Interview, November 2012)

When describing how the Commission strengthened relationships between TCU and Fort Worth, Larry Lauer commented similarly: "It [the Commission] changed the dynamic of Fort Worth and TCU. . . . the interaction with the Commission on the Future began to shift the dynamic, and today you rarely hear people in the city say that TCU's not involved . . . we're very engaged in the city" (Interview, April 2012). In recalling his own efforts to build relationships between TCU and Fort Worth, Chancellor Ferrari concluded: "The city-university partnership is essential . . . You can't have a really great university without a really great city, and you can't have a really great city without a university" (Interview, November 2012).

In 2015, not long after Chancellor Ferrari passed away at the age of seventy-five, *TCU Magazine* republished an article from 2003 outlining his many accomplishments and enduring legacy. Quite appropriately, the article was titled "Man on a Mission," a reference to his energy and sense of purpose: "Ferrari brought a sense of urgency when he decided to make TCU the final stop in his career. His passion became so apparent that trustees and vice chancellors took to calling him 'a man on a mission.'"

In order to "move up" to the international stature it seeks, the Commission recommended that the University "shore up" certain areas of campus, Ferrari said. With that comes a university-wide plan to spend up to $100 million in the next few years, with funding to come from gifts, student and user fees, endowment income, and other institutional resources.

- Upgrade and improve classrooms, science laboratories, and studios across the University. Include equipment and technology used in instruction and research to benefit the learning process.

- Expand campus parking facilities on both the east and west campuses.

- Renovate and expand the Rickel Building, followed by the Brown-Lupton Student Center.

- Renovate and refurbish Waits and Milton Daniel residence halls. Expand teaching and research facilities for the MBA program in the M.J. Neeley School of Business, in concert with gifts focused on the James Ryffel Center for Entrepreneurial Studies and the construction of the Sarah and Steve Smith Entrepreneurs Hall.

- Complete the Tucker Technology Center.

"Realizing the Possibilities," *TCU Magazine*, Winter 2000

"Dr. Ferrari was a great educator, and one of his great strengths was connecting with people internally," said John V. Roach, who was chairman of the Board of Trustees during Ferrari's tenure. "He communicated so well with faculty and staff, and that spilled out into the community."

"Man on a Mission," *TCU Magazine*, Summer 2015

I felt the staff needed a voice in the affairs of the university. They've always been underappreciated.

Chancellor Emeritus Mick Ferrari, Interview, November 2012

ABOVE
Tucker Technology Center. Courtesy of TCU Marketing and Communication. Photograph by Amy Peterson.

ABOVE
Lupton Stadium, 2022. Courtesy of TCU Marketing and Communication. Photograph by James Anger.

ABOVE
Michael McCracken. Courtesy of Texas Christian University.

The mission statement and the Commission on the Future of TCU are two of the most significant results of Chancellor Ferrari's passion and mission. While both secured his TCU legacy, numerous other notable additions and adjustments came from them. According to the 2004 Report Card on the Commission, 43.6 percent of the 386 recommendations had been achieved and another 25.1 percent were still "proceeding," resulting in a nearly 70 percent completion rate. Among these are the Shore-Up Program, which upgraded teaching and learning technologies in over one hundred classrooms and labs around campus. According to the Report Card, this was the Commission's major accomplishment: "In many respects, the 'reshoring project' is the most important achievement that has arisen from the Commission; it has provided a shared teaching facility of considerable quality that encourages faculty to practice their art at a new level" (2004 Report Card). The thought then was that TCU could not move up if it did not first shore up.

Out of the 386 recommendations, there were, of course, dozens more Commission-related enhancements on campus. Residence hall renovations were started and Leibrock Village was completed, as were four other major new construction and renovation projects: The William E. and Jean Jones Tucker Technology Center, the Steve and Sarah Smith Entrepreneurs Hall, the University Recreation Center, and the Charles and Marie Lipton Baseball Stadium and Williams-Reilly Field. Such new and renovated buildings in a relatively short timeframe could not have been undertaken without considerable support from the Board of Trustees and, though less tangible than a new construction, clearly one of Chancellor Ferrari's more significant accomplishments was sharing his vision with the trustees, which encouraged them to move away from previous fiscally conservative restrictions and to spend around $150 million on campus building projects, some of which included endowment money.

Not all the new constructions on campus, however, were brick and mortar buildings. One of the most extensive changes that took place shortly after the commission was the reorganization of TCU's colleges. The AddRan College of Arts and Sciences was split into two colleges, the College of Science and Engineering and the AddRan College of Humanities and Social Sciences, and the College of Fine Arts and Communication was also split into two separate colleges. When reflecting back on the reorganization, Chancellor Ferrari simply stated that, while "looking into the schools and colleges [and] faculty opportunity, I thought we could do better if we had a different structure" (Interview, November 2012). Former Dean of the College of Science and Engineering, Mike McCracken—who was Dean of the AddRan College of Arts and Sciences at the time of the split—recalled being invited to a lunch meeting with the Chancellor and then Provost Bill Koehler: "What Mick and Bill were hoping to do is convince me that we should reorganize. Their perspective was that the AddRan was so large and so heterogeneous that

"The new core, and in particular that [HMVV] part of it, is the embodiment of our mission. It literally is the TCU mission come alive in a dynamic way," said economics professor Ed McNertney, director of the TCU Core Curriculum.

"Students, parents and everyone involved with the university from now on will know that these are the courses that make TCU what it is. They'll know that this is how we go about fulfilling our mission."

"The Core of a University," *TCU Magazine*, Winter 2005

What he [Ferrari] said to the Brite Board and the TCU board was: these are two corporations. It makes perfect sense for them to each have their own chief executive officer, but it would be a terribly pity if the historic relationship between these two schools were to be lost. We need to do the right thing, and we need to have a document that clarifies that we are related not by accident, not by coincidence, and not simply for the benefit of one party or the other, but because both institutions value the importance of a collaborative relationship between this university and this divinity school.

Newell Williams, Interview, March 2014

ABOVE
Newell Williams. Courtesy of Texas Christian University.

OPPOSITE
Leibrock Village. Courtesy of Texas Christian University.

LEFT
Robert Carr Chapel. Courtesy of TCU Marketing and Communication.

At that time Brite Divinity School operated with the chancellor of TCU being the CEO of Brite. . . . [and with] the [TCU] vice chancellor for academic affairs being the chief academic officer at Brite."

Ann Sewell, Interview, October 2014

We've had a positive working relationship. It's been distinctive . . . because of the organizational model that Mick Ferrari put in place for Brite and TCU. During the years Ferrari served as chancellor there was a significant evolution in the governance relationship between Brite and TCU . . . and the current form . . . owes everything to the decisions that were made while Ferrari was chancellor . . . he took significant leadership . . . [and] made it happen. If it had been another person, Brite could be off this campus now doing its own thing someplace else.

Newell Williams, Interview, March 2014

it was difficult to engage in any kind of meaningful planning, and actually I agreed with them" (Interview, November 2012).

Other Commission initiatives were equally bold and ambitious. In his October 2000 final report on the Commission, Chancellor Ferrari listed eleven broad steps that TCU needed to accomplish in order to "'move up' to another level of distinction," and "Enhancing the undergraduate experience with specific emphasis on revitalizing the core curriculum" topped his list. This was yet another extensive project that directly concerned TCU's core values and central aspirations, and consensus was at first difficult to achieve. Provost Koehler originally appointed a committee to make recommendations, but it quickly became apparent that wider input was required, and the Faculty Senate took the lead by appointing a Core Curriculum Committee, which after considerable discussion advanced the concept of connecting the new core with the recent mission statement. Through the Faculty Senate, the faculty collectively voiced its desire to create a new undergraduate core that would encourage TCU students to merge their learning and their lives with the mission to become ethical leaders and responsible citizens in the global community. The core committee urged faculty to adopt an academic core curriculum that would actuate the values TCU espoused—to walk the talk. In a December 2002 meeting, the Faculty Senate voted in favor of building the new core using an overlay of TCU's values.

Considerable work was still needed to identify the many different values, competencies, and outcomes of the new core's three primary areas: 1) Essential Competencies, 2) Human Experience and Endeavors, and 3) Heritage, Mission, Vision, and Values. A new Faculty Senate committee was formed, the Core Implementation Committee, with several smaller subset committees. Throughout the next two years the CIC regularly reported back to the Faculty Senate, and discussions were held to clarify the overlay of values and curriculum. Much back-and-forth discussion took place to define the specifics of cultural awareness, global awareness, religious traditions, and citizenship and social values. After these discussions and a final vote of approval by the Faculty Senate, the first students started under the new core in the summer of 2005. From that point on, TCU students were required to take courses that, one way or another, demonstrated TCU's most fundamental values of responsible citizenship and ethical leadership in the global community.

Chancellor Ferrari created greater areas of connection in every initiative he proposed, but soon after he arrived on campus he was challenged to help disconnect TCU and Brite. Although revising Brite's relationship with TCU is not often mentioned as one of Chancellor Ferrari's accomplishments, it remains one of his most significant achievements. At a time when some within the Brite community pushed for independence, he strengthened its connections with TCU by recognizing its differences.

By the time TCU's new chancellor began in August 1998, some Brite faculty and trustees were questioning their relationship with TCU and reviewing possibilities for their own governance. Historically, relations between Brite and TCU had always been generally close and cordial, but at times unclear. Brite College of the Bible had been incorporated in 1914 with its own Board of Trustees for the dual purpose of training students for the ministry and teaching Bible classes, and in 1939 Brite shifted its focus to become "a professional school for the ministry on a graduate level . . . a theological seminary" (Hall 220). Despite its quasi-independence and having its own governing board, Brite appeared in TCU's organizational structure similar to the other colleges. While its differences were respected, this meant that the Brite dean reported to the Provost, and that the Chancellor served as Brite's chief executive officer.

Such governance relations between Brite and TCU were acceptable at the start of Chancellor Tucker's days in Sadler, as he was not only closely associated with Brite but also with the Disciples of Christ. But the apartheid controversy provoked considerable tension between the divinity school and TCU. As questions concerning South African investments continued to smolder, the Brite faculty passed a resolution in 1987 "requesting the Brite board of trustees to divest funds from companies that support apartheid" (Toulouse 163). But Chancellor Tucker and the two governing boards held firm to their decision to take no action. Tensions between TCU and Brite again intensified in the later 1990s over the location and construction of Leibrock Village, a new divinity student housing facility, and once again Brite faculty and trustees questioned the university's priorities, believing that TCU had again prioritized its interests over those of Brite (Toulouse 180). As with the previous apartheid controversy, it seemed apparent to some people at Brite that in general TCU promoted its financial affairs over the divinity school's ethical concerns. As a result, Brite took its first steps for greater self-governance in 1998, when its board voted to remove Provost Bill Koehler from his role as its chief academic officer. A confidential document was soon circulated questioning governance relations between the two separately incorporated schools. Not long after he arrived on campus, in December 1998, Chancellor Ferrari met with several Brite representatives to initiate discussions on amending the formal association between the two schools.

Chancellor Ferrari was not opposed. In thinking back on his first months at TCU, he expressed surprise upon learning he was responsible for Brite as well as TCU.

> When I first got to TCU I was told that I was not only the chancellor of TCU, but I was also the chief executive officer of Brite Divinity School. I thought that was rather unusual . . . and so early on I questioned what the heck did it really mean. After I met the dean and some [Brite] trustees I realized . . . there may have been an organization issue. (Interview, November 2012)

After reviewing "some of the earlier documentation," Chancellor Ferrari agreed that Brite was entitled to its independence: "I was happy to work with the trustees and Brite trustees to bring about their independence . . . for Brite Divinity to be a school of its own authority and leadership . . . but at the same time still remain in our family." Rather than perceiving it as a cause for "obstacles, stresses, or crises," he viewed the separation as "an abundance of opportunity" (Interview, November 2012). With his help, a committee of both Brite and TCU board members was organized, and within a year a resolution was drafted and forwarded to both boards. Although supposedly some TCU trustees "expressed significant reservations relinquishing its control over the governance of Brite," Chancellor Ferrari and TCU Board of Trustees member Roy Snodgrass, who as well served on the Brite board and was widely respected by both groups, were able to persuade the trustees that the new agreement was beneficial for both school and university. In June 2000, the new governance agreement was implemented. According to the Brite history, *Institutional Change*, the new agreement "resolved the governance ambiguity that had clouded Brite for decades. Brite obtained the independence its original charter guaranteed and finally had the financial resources to carry out its mission (Toulouse 185).

ABOVE
Chancellor Ferrari sings the TCU alma mater at commencement, ca. 2000. Courtesy of Mary Couts Burnett Library.

RIGHT
Jean Walbridge, Chancellor Ferrari, and Mary Nell Kirk at commencement, 2000. Courtesy of Mary Couts Burnett Library.

Part 3
Achievment: The Boschini Years

After TCU had announced the appointment of its new chancellor, Dr. Victor J. Boschini Jr., Chancellor Mick Ferrari was asked to comment on the leadership transition. Referring to the changeover as a "highly personal time," he stated: "You want to get fully immersed in the institution on a personal basis. Establishing a style at the university is a chancellor's main goal from the beginning. You try not to be like the last chancellor and make your style apparent. The quicker that is done, the better" (*Skiff*, March 3, 2003).

LEFT
Chancellor Victor J. Boschini Jr., Courtesy of Texas Christian University.

I am excited about the future of TCU. Dr. Boschini has the energy and the skills to build on the important progress made by Dr. Ferrari. The [search] committee did an excellent job. I feel very confident that we got the best person to lead TCU in the future.

Denny Alexander, "A TCU Coup," *TCU Magazine*, Spring 2003

I am confident that TCU's future will be greater than its distinguished past.

Chancellor Victor Boschini, *Skiff*, September 10, 2003

I went to a really neat Disciples meeting once where the head administrator said, "Everybody has a place at the table." . . . I love that. That's TCU.

Chancellor Victor Boschini, Interview, July 2021

Everybody kept saying to me, "What's your vision?"

Chancellor Victor Boschini, Interview, March 2015

When asked what his style would be, Chancellor-select Boschini responded that it would include "management by walking around campus and understanding the people of TCU . . . I will be coming with a pen and paper, not with a sword" (*Skiff,* March 7, 2003).

Arriving with a pen and paper signified Chancellor Boschini's willingness to listen and learn. Once on campus, he immediately immersed himself in his new school by personally getting to know as many people as possible. Before indicating any directions or intentions, and in order to understand TCU's needs and issues, he committed himself to a nearly endless stream of personal engagements. From the beginning, he quickly became known as someone energetic, personable, and accessible.

A dozen years later, while responding to a question on how he perceived his leadership role, Chancellor Boschini commented on his commitment to personal engagement:

> I only do three things as chancellor of TCU. One, I try to look after student, faculty, and staff health, welfare, and safety. Two, I raise money for your good ideas . . . The third thing that I do is I try to set a tone, because I am a real big believer that leaders always set the tone for an organization. The tone I want to set for TCU is that there is room at the table for everyone. You may never get your way, although you probably will sometimes. I always want you to feel like you have a say and that you will be treated with respect. I'm a big believer in management by walking around. You could sit in this office all day and get isolated and not know what students experience, or not know what the cleaning staff really wants, if you don't get out there and talk to them. (Interview, March 2015)

Chancellor Boschini demonstrated at the outset that he valued all stakeholders. Management by walking around thus was a crucial part of his leadership style. To help TCU maintain its upward trajectory, he committed himself to discovering how his new colleagues—trustees, faculty, staff, alumni, and students—perceived their campus. When commenting on his first year in Sadler, Chancellor Boschini stated: "When you're new, people think you're going to make all these changes, but I didn't know what to change, so I tried to be a good listener that first year" (Interview, March 2015).

Yet management by walking around required extensive travel. In his first report to the Board of Trustees he included a "representative" two-page list of his meetings with trustees, faculty, staff, peers at other North Texas universities, city and community leaders, and alumni (Report to the Board, November 2003). Most of these meetings took place during an onerous summer tour that required him to attend a constant stream of breakfasts, lunches, and dinners, and appearances at local, regional, and national meetings and events.

One of his listening-tour stops, however, resulted in an unusual introduction into the TCU community's deep connections. While visiting TCU's alumni associations, he flew from New York City to Midland, Texas, not knowing much about his destination:

> I had never been to Midland, and I knew it wasn't New York City, but I thought it was, well, bigger. I didn't rent a car in advance, and when I arrived I went to rent a car, but there was only one booth in the airport, and I was told they were out of cars. I thought they were joking, but they said they really didn't have any cars, and I was going to be there three days. But this is what I love about TCU. Some kid walking by was a TCU student, and he came up to me and asked, "Are you the new Chancellor at TCU?" I said yes, but school hadn't even started yet, so I asked him how he knew that. He said he had seen my picture in the alumni magazine, and he then asked what was going on . . . and when I explained that I didn't have a car, he said, "my dad will give you a car." His father did and gave me a car for three days . . . I went back to my wife and said, "We're going to love this place."

As this story indicates, one of the primary lessons Chancellor Boschini first learned was the loyalty people had for TCU: "It was incredible to me how loyal they were to Texas Christian University. They all loved it." TCU—

From Chancellor Victor Boschini's Inauguration Speech

Every day I learn something new about this splendid university. I find more to admire, more to love. I firmly believe that TCU is an extraordinary place, too good not to be even better.

TCU is a place of academic challenge and intellectual excellence. Our faculty are changing the future with their scholarship and creative activity. They are changing the lives of our students as teachers and mentors.

TCU is a place of ideas and ideals. Where social responsibility and ethical behavior are the core of our mission and the center of our daily lives.

TCU is a place that provides a total college experience. Where learning extends from the laboratory and studio to the residence hall and playing field. This is a vibrant place where students are prepared to lead.

TCU is a place whose distinctive buff brick and architectural integrity reflect our strong sense of community. This is a place that connects with Fort Worth and with Texas not just geographically, but as a vibrant partner for progress.

TCU is a remarkable place whose achievements are exceeded only by its opportunities.

The 1887 catalogue described the college the Clarks founded as a "tree of unperishable riches." Transplanted a few times, it took root here and is strong. But it is not "unperishable." We must nurture the excellence of the academic enterprise and advance the teacher-scholar model that is the cornerstone of education at TCU.

TCU is unapologetically student centered. Our students are the source of our energy and the reason for our efforts.

ABOVE
Chancellor Victor Boschini at his inauguration, 2004. Courtesy of Mary Couts Burnett Library.

There is a spirit here unlike any I have ever seen. It is evidenced in our "can do" culture. Staff, students, and faculty do little things that make a big difference. They do great things that change people's lives. The people of TCU take enormous pride in our university and seek ways to advance TCU through their hard work and innovation.

We are a private university with a very public commitment to serve and to lead. Our campus is bounded only by our imagination and our spirit.

The VIA group is examining our aspirations in the context of today's realities, so that we can refine our focus and set goals that match our character with our capabilities. In short, we are setting a new strategic agenda for TCU that truly puts our vision in action.

Chancellor Victor Boschini, *Skiff*, April 1, 2004

I've never worked at a place where so many people thought they were the chancellor. And I mean that in a good sense. I love that. From students, staff, everybody, if they have an idea, they just jump out with the idea.

Chancellor Victor Boschini, Interview, March 2015

he quickly discovered—was a tight-knit community built around common values and reciprocal relationships (Interview, March, 2015).

Chancellor Boschini's signature initiative, the strategic planning process Vision in Action, resulted from listening to people. In describing how VIA started, he explained that the strategic-planning process developed from his desire to hear what people had to say:

> When I first came to TCU, we started a committee. Everybody kept saying to me, "What's your vision for TCU?" I responded that, first of all, it should be our vision, and second of all, I'm brand new here, and I have less of a vision than anyone here . . . and so I put together this committee of students, faculty, staff, community members, and alumni to look at a strategic vision for TCU, and we named it Vision in Action. Dr. Leo Munson and Dr. Nowell Donovan co-chaired it, and they're the people I really credit with starting everything. All these people got together, and they asked me my initial thoughts, which were too much blacktop and more green space, but I said let's talk to the faculty, students, and staff, the people that are going to live in these buildings, and see what they want. (Interview, March 2015)

Strategic planning began soon after Chancellor Boschini arrived and assumed his responsibilities on June 1, 2003. Within a few weeks he launched strategic planning discussions during a summer retreat, and from this meeting several priorities emerged: TCU would become ranked near the top of Tier II national universities; have a strong residential presence in and around its campus; seek modest increases in the number and types of . . . graduate programs; and work to enhance its national visibility. Although the earliest of VIA recommendations, these priorities have remained central to VIA's mission for two decades.

Chancellor Boschini publicly introduced a strategic planning initiative during his first convocation speech, but to give context he posed "five critical questions," whose answers would determine TCU's future: "TCU needs to consider the hallmarks of an undergraduate education and how best to achieve them, the future of graduate education, how academic programs and the new core curriculum can best fulfill the university's mission, how the physical campus can better reflect TCU's objectives, and the optimal size for the university" (*Skiff*, September 10, 2003). To respond to these questions, he stated the formation of a "planning committee" and identified its co-chairs, Drs. Donovan and Munson. The committee would first "assess the commission's work" and then "draft a plan to move the university forward" (*Skiff*, September 10, 2003).

When presenting his first report to the Board of Trustees two months later in November, Chancellor Boschini reiterated that the strategic planning committee would first review what the Commission on the Future of TCU had accomplished: "Among the University's most important tasks this academic year is reflecting upon our progress in realizing the goals set by the Commission" to "determine how best to continue to move forward." To "accelerate TCU's momentum," he also announced that the VIA committee would be working with Kaludis Consulting to identify "next level" projects (Report to the Board, November 2003). The Kaludis firm not only helped to manage the entire first phase of VIA, synthesizing hundreds of ideas and recommendations into an organized plan, but it was Kaludis that suggested the initiative's familiar name Vision in Action.

During a campus-wide symposium in January 2005, Provost Donovan gave a PowerPoint presentation to various groups around campus. Titled "Vision in Action: An Update," it succinctly stated the initiative's purpose was "to define TCU's preferred future." Although a vast, comprehensive process that eventually included over eight hundred students, faculty,

RIGHT
VIA PowerPoint, January 2005. Courtesy of TCU VIA archive.

Report Card

	Total	Achieved	Proceeding	Not Achieved	Not Relevant
Strategic Task Force					
1. Undergraduate Experience	24	8	12	4	-
2. Graduate Education	25	11	5	9	-
3. Technology	45	24	7	14	-
4. Distinctive Programs and New Directions	19	8	4	7	-
5. Community and Strategic Alliances	17	3	2	12	-
6. Global Positioning and Priorities	42	19	6	17	-
7. The Role of Athletics	14	14	-	-	-
College and School Task Force					
	Total	**Achieved**	**Proceeding**	**Not Achieved**	**Not Relevant**
8. Alumni Relationships	39	19	20	-	-
9. Addran College of Humanities & Social Sciences	17	8	2	5	2
10. College of Science & Engineering	20	7	3	10	-
11. College of Fine Arts	27	14	4	7	2
12. College of Communication	29	3	6	20	-
13. M.J. Neeley School of Business	14	10	1	3	-
14. School of Education	17	9	3	5	-
15. College of Health & Human Sciences	4	3	-	1	-
16. Brite Divinity School	23	-	22	1	-
17. Ranch Management	10	8	-	2	-
TOTALS	**386**	**168**	**97**	**117**	**4**
PERCENTAGES		**43.6%**	**25.1%**	**30.3%**	**1%**

COMMISSION ON THE FUTURE OF TCU
PROGRESS REPORT JANUARY 2004

LEFT
Report Card for the Commission on the Future. Courtesy of TCU VIA archive.

staff, alumni, trustees, and community members, and which involved countless meetings, events, and reports, VIA rapidly developed. The first step, assessing the Commission's progress, was not an easy task, since its seventeen task force committees ultimately made 386 recommendations, but throughout the fall Provost Donovan reviewed its achievements, and in January he submitted a "Report Card," concluding that "approximately 70 percent of the recommendations had been achieved or were proceeding" ("Report Card").

While the Commission's recommendations were being reviewed, several other initial steps were taken to launch VIA first phase. To provide "oversight and guidance for VIA throughout the project," the Strategic Planning Steering Committee was announced, and soon after, six "Strategy Work Groups"—later referred to as "the heart of VIA"—were appointed:

- Size, Mix, and Residentiality
- TCU Experience
- Academic Directions
- Connections to Communities
- Strategies for Athletics
- Learning Resources/Technology (VIA Project Report)

To imagine TCU's "preferred future" in their specific areas, each committee was given a specific set of "key strategic questions" to answer and were tasked with producing a "Strategic Work Report" by May 2004. Although areas and questions were quite different, there was an understanding that each group would work under the framework of "six key objectives":

- To build on the groundbreaking work of the Commission on the Future of TCU
- To more closely align strategic planning with budgeting cycles
- To identify short-range institutional priorities
- To fine-tune the case for the fundraising campaign
- To develop a long-range institutional worldview
- To create an active, ongoing university-wide planning process

This last "key objective" is significant. For the first time in TCU's history, strategic planning was established as a continuous institutional process that would continually assess the university's goals and progress.

The Strategy Work Groups were required to involve diverse areas across campus, including students, faculty, staff, alumni, and community members, which they variously accomplished using interviews, surveys, forums, focus groups, and especially townhall meetings. Held throughout the spring, these latter events were well-attended, averaging around three hundred at each event. The gathering of responses and research required nearly weekly meetings throughout the academic year, but by the end of May 2004 the six groups submitted their reports to the Steering Committee.

While the six committees were working, four other major VIA components were initiated: an Environmental Scan Conference, an Economic Scan Seminar, the Campus Master Plan, and the Information Technology Plan. The Environmental Scan Conference was held in March 2004 and "ninety faculty, staff, students, trustees, and alumni attended . . . to discuss trends in society and higher education and their impact on TCU" (VIA Project Report, Fall 2005). The following month the Economic Scan Seminar reviewed "the essential elements and trends of the TCU economy" (VIA Project Report). Charged with establishing "a standard for continued development of a physically attractive and stimulating campus environment," the Campus Master Plan Committee also convened in April to reconsider and update the original TCU Master Plan, which had been first developed in 1991 and then updated in 1998 (VIA Project Report, Fall 2005). In May, after working throughout the year, the Computing and Technology Committee submitted its final "Technology Planning Document," recommending "a range of suggestions covering topics from the implementation of quality standards in all aspects of the university to enhancing the living and learning environment of the institution" (VIA Project Report, Fall 2005).

After updating the chancellor and cabinet on VIA's progress in early June, the Steering Committee forwarded the six Strategy Work Reports to Kaludis, and within three weeks the consultants sent back their "Synthesis Document," which provided "the basis for a beginning strategic agenda for TCU" (VIA Project Report). While the committee reports were quite different in their recommendations, the Kaludis synthesis found "fairly broad agreement on several points":

- Importance of doing everything at the highest standards of quality, defined by national criteria and implemented through TCU-specific definitions
- Primacy of undergraduate education as the building block for increasing the national recognition of TCU
- Importance of retaining and enhancing TCU's position as a national university
- Desire for increased residentiality and creation of true living and learning environment in and outside the classroom, with access to this experience for all undergraduate students
- Physical, academic, and support infrastructures have been stretched beyond normal limits
- Need for more explicit criteria for resource allocation and a more open (transparent) process
- Need for growth in graduate enrollment through the addition of new graduate programs
- Value of interdisciplinary/multidisciplinary programs
- Increasing intra-institutional collaboration/synergy (undergraduate/graduate; across units; Centers/Institutes
- Requirement to maintain an environment rich in personal interaction
- Need to recognize and value Fort Worth communities as an important resource for TCU and for the communities to see TCU as a valued neighbor and resource
- Importance of building and integrating strategy across the University's critical priority areas to make the best use of available current and future resources
- Need for increased availability and utilization of technology in teaching and learning
- Requirement to deliver on the TCU Promise
  The commitment to renewing the TCU Promise finds consensus as an organizing principle in many of the committee reports
  (Synthesis Report, Summer 2004)

Throughout summer the "Synthesis Report" was discussed, and in early September more than two hundred students, faculty, staff, alumni, administrators, and trustees gathered on a Saturday to establish preliminary pathways for moving VIA into a series of strategic decisions. The Saturday symposium, "Putting Our Vision into Action: The TCU Promise," was a crucial point in TCU's strategic planning. By the end of the symposium "Major points of discussion were recorded and distilled," resulting in several "VIA Strategic Goals":

- Recruit and retain students, faculty, and staff who can achieve their full potential at TCU
- Design a vibrant learning community characterized by distinctive curricular, co-curricular, and residential programs
- Sustain an environment in which rich personal interaction is enhanced by outstanding facilities and appropriate technology
- Accelerate our connection with the greater community: Fort Worth, Texas, the nation, and the world. Couple wise financial stewardship with a well-planned entrepreneurial approach to academic opportunities
  (VIA Project Report, Fall 2005)

These five "VIA Strategic Goals," which eventually became known as the "Five Cardinal Principles," were used to define and determine all subsequent VIA action steps.

Considered "a critical factor in strengthening TCU's distinction and quality," graduate education was next discussed when Provost Donovan "convened a Graduate Education Vision and Strategy Group" to review current programs and then "propose a vision and strategic goals" for future growth. (VIA Project Report, Appendix N). One of the "key points" that the group stressed was the essential synergy between graduate studies and undergraduate learning, and this understanding was based on "TCU's core educational paradigm, namely the role of faculty as teachers and scholars": "Ultimately, excellence in research and creative activity among faculty is the best way to ensure the quality of undergraduate education at TCU" (VIA Project Report, Appendix N). Graduate education growth, the report concluded, should "fit the needs of the undergraduate program" and that it should also be "responsive to . . . [the] needs of the Metroplex." Rather than attempting to model "graduate programs after large research institutions," which tend to separate research and labs from undergraduates, the report stressed that TCU's graduate programs should maintain a "high level of student-faculty interaction that is a hallmark of TCU" (VIA Project Report, Appendix N).

Having quickly evolved with considerable consensus and momentum, VIA developed into an extensive university-wide undertaking that one way or another affected everyone on campus. Early in the Fall 2004 semester, Provost Donovan further expanded VIA's reach and impact when he charged the deans to draft their own individual school or college strategic plans that would further "enhance TCU's reputation as a national and international university" (VIA Project Report, Fall 2005).

Intended to "give substance and texture to the TCU Strategic Agenda," the various charges were based on several central VIA assumptions:

- that TCU would develop undergraduate programs "that provide distinction and distinctiveness in the marketplace"
- that much of its financial aid would be used to attract students with exceptionally strong academic backgrounds and/or increase "the geographic diversity of the student body"
- that TCU would continue to develop as a residential campus
- that it would increase its retention rates
- and that it would increase its graduate and professional enrollments while maintaining stable undergraduate numbers

In addition to examining discipline-specific issues, the colleges and schools were also asked to imagine their "desired destinations" (VIA Project Report, Appendix O).

Once the school and college plans were submitted in late December, the Kaludis consultants again merged the various recommendations into a synthesis that outlined "five major elements":

- Refining the undergraduate and graduate program portfolios
- Making TCU the university "of Fort Worth" [and] not just "in Fort Worth"
- Increasing the opportunities for interdisciplinary activity across the TCU curriculum
- Strengthening learning in the global community
- Continuing reshoring of the academic infrastructure (Kaludis Synthesis Report II)

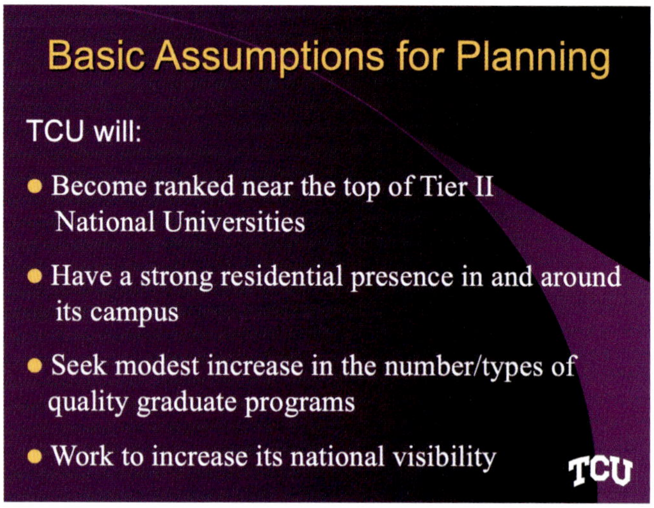

ABOVE
VIA PowerPoint, January 2005.
Courtesy of TCU VIA archive.

Some of the more innovative recommendations that emerged from the plans involved enriched learning programs, the creation of interdisciplinary institutes and centers, and the development of experiential learning opportunities.

During the January 2005 symposium, students, faculty, staff, and community members were not only informed of VIA's progress in the previous year but also how TCU's strategic vision would develop into a series of decisions related to undergraduate and graduate enrollments, capital campaigns, and resource allocations. Much of the presentation focused on "Points of Congruence" gathered from previous reports and responses. Among these were several familiar VIA premises:

- The importance of doing everything at the highest standards of quality
- The primacy of undergraduate education as the building block for increasing national recognition
- The importance of retaining and enhancing TCU's position as a national university
- The desire for increased residentiality
- The requirement to maintain an environment rich in personal interaction
- The requirement to deliver on the TCU Promise (VIA Report Appendix P)

The January report acknowledged that the physical, academic, and support infrastructures had become "stretched beyond normal limits," an institutional strain that—if not addressed—not only threatened TCU's growth but also what Provost Donovan articulated as The TCU Promise. As it was later expressed in a 2011 VIA brochure, The TCU Promise was "a reciprocal commitment to excellence through discovery and achievement that unites the TCU community." Ultimately, the university's effectiveness could only be measured by its ability to honor its commitments (TCU Looking Forward: 2011 and Beyond).

> The TCU faculty and staff commit to providing:
> Relevant and challenging curricula
> Energetic and innovative learning opportunities
> An invigorating social milieu
>
> TCU students commit to:
> Investing in intellectual curiosity and active learning
> Practicing high standards of personal behavior
> Maintaining a vigorous engagement with their community and the world around them
>
> The University commits to:
> Nurturing a safe and diverse environment
> The free exchange of ideas
> The discovery and dissemination of knowledge
> The encouragement and recognition of creative and scholarly distinction
> (TCU Looking Forward: 2011 and Beyond)

When imagining TCU's preferred future, members of the TCU community were encouraged not to limit their aspirations, and in visualizing what the school could become they did not worry about the costs or funding. Consequently, many of the recommendations had substantial price tags. Yet TCU's Board of Trustees never hesitated in its support for VIA, and trustees were as much a part of the process as were TCU students, faculty, staff, and administrators.

During its November 2004 meeting, the trustees took direct action by approving a resolution to allow "facility planning design and financing plans for:

- A new student center
- A related parking structure
- A new student residence facility
- Conversion of the existing student center for academic space
- Remodeling/Renovation of Milton Daniel Residence Hall
  (Trustee Minutes, November 2004)

While these plans evolved over time, they demonstrate the board's initial advocacy for VIA, which remained constant as TCU's physical campus underwent a major makeover. At the board's next meeting in April, the trustees attended a pre-meeting VIA update, and the following day Board Chair John V. Roach and the trustees formally adopted "three strategic decisions" to cap undergraduate enrollments, enhance campus residentiality, and increase graduate enrollment (Trustee Minutes, April 2005).

The board's most decisive actions to support VIA, however, were financial. In their Fall 2005 discussion of TCU's annual budget, the trustees made a fourth crucial strategic decision when they approved designating $1,800,000 specifically for VIA activities during the 2005-2006 academic year. This was the first of several installments over a five-year period that eventually totaled approximately $8.4 million. This Strategic Initiative Fund (SIF), as it became known, was a grant-funding source "designed to provide 'seed' money to seize opportunities to create new programs that further the goals of VIA" (VIA Project Report, Fall 2005). Unleashing an entrepreneurial spirit across campus, and quickly transforming the physical appearance and layout of campus, the Strategic Initiative Fund became a significant source for achieving VIA's most ambitious goals. Working collaboratively, faculty and staff were encouraged to submit proposals for creative, innovative endeavors that closely aligned with one of the five Cardinal Principles and that directly promoted VIA's ultimate vision: "TCU will become an increasingly significant internationally known private university. This requires raising the academic profile of the university" (VIA Strategic Initiative Fund Grant Proposal Guidelines).

Our goals are, and should be, lofty. We don't want to limit our aspirations.

Chancellor Victor Boschini, *TCU Magazine*, Summer 2006

Over the next five years, around one hundred proposals were submitted, and sixty-one were funded in one of two categories: "Pathways to transformation—smaller tactical grants," and "Transformational grants—larger strategic projects expected to significantly improve the University" (Strategic Initiative Fund Assessment). Several of the funded projects attracted considerable external funding, such as the Institute for Child Development, the Neeley leadership program, and the Oxford Sustainable Futures Project. At the end of five years, SIF-funded projects were assessed, and a total of $7.5 million in external funding had come back to TCU, which was used to support further VIA initiatives.

By providing a host of new programs and opportunities for students, faculty, and staff, SIF notably enhanced VIA's commitment "to deliver on the TCU Promise." SIF projects improved retention and graduation rates, enhanced undergraduate advising, supported undergraduate research, created several interdisciplinary centers, lowered the faculty-student ratio, increased financial support for graduate students; nurtured opportunities for professional growth for both faculty and staff; initiated planning for the renovation of existing buildings and the construction of new buildings; updated classrooms and labs; established outreach programs in several areas, including health, fine arts, business, communication, science, and the liberal arts; brought distinguished speakers to campus; inaugurated and strengthened global connections; developed new student internships and summer

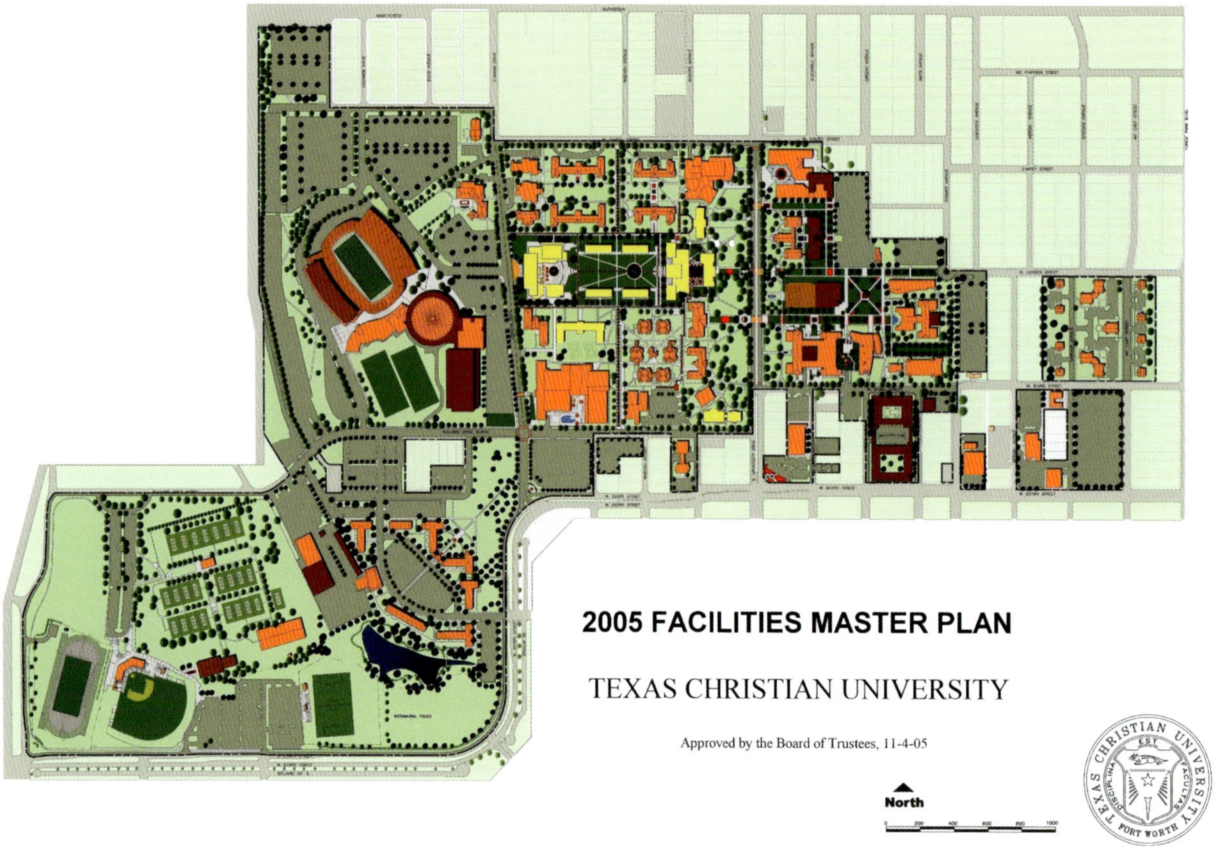

programs; and overall "acted as a catalyst that has encouraged creativity, collaboration, and communication across campus" (Strategic Initiative Fund Assessment).

The willingness of the trustees to fund major construction projects totaling millions of dollars not only gave substance to their commitment to VIA's goals but also underscored their confidence that the combined efforts of the TCU community could achieve these goals. Such confidence was shared by most of TCU's campus community, as there is no better indication of a university's shared belief in progress than new construction. For a decade and a half, TCU experienced so much construction and renovation that faculty, staff, and students alike wryly began referring to it as Texas Construction University. From 2004 to 2020 TCU continuously underwent either new construction or major renovation. Entire cohorts of students came and graduated without ever experiencing a campus without construction crews, cranes, trucks, noise, and disruption. There were over twenty new buildings added to campus and over fifty renovations of existing buildings. In addition, the reshoring of classrooms and labs continued. There was so much new construction that returning alumni often had difficulty navigating their way around campus. Yet the result was transformative. Within a short period, the center of campus—formerly a parking lot—had become "the heart of the university" (*TCU Magazine*, Summer 2006).

Building activity began with the renovation of Landreth Hall in 2005, but the tsunami of construction that transformed campus was launched in 2007, when six new buildings were erected and one existing building refurbished. Of these, Education was notably enhanced when the Bailey Building was renovated and Palko Hall built, creating the J.E. and L.E. Mabee Foundation Education Complex. The Sam Baugh Indoor Practice Facility and its adjoining Cox Field were also completed. The most significant change, however, came with the construction of four new residence halls—Amon G. Carter Hall, Teresa and Luther King Hall, Kellye Wright Samuelson Hall, and Mary and Robert J. Wright Hall—and the Campus Commons. The impact was immediate and meaningful—student interactions, connections, and activities replaced a parking lot and cars in the center of campus. Vision had been literally transformed into action.

The construction and renovation projects in 2007 and 2008 accomplished several central VIA goals by increasing residential space, green space, and academic space. Perhaps the most symbolic campus change occurred in 2008 when the old student union was demolished, and the new Brown Lupton University Union was completed. This year also saw the completion of TCU's new bookstore and the renovations of Jarvis Hall (one of TCU's oldest buildings), Starpoint and KinderFrogs, Clark Hall, and the Art Gallery. A year later the center of campus was fully framed when Scharbauer Hall was completed on the site of the former student union.

RIGHT
Campus Commons during construction, 2006. Courtesy of TCU Marketing and Communication.

OPPOSITE
2005 Facilities Master Plan. Courtesy TCU Facilities.

BELOW
Campus Commons during construction, 2008. Courtesy of TCU Marketing and Communication.

RIGHT
The BLUU (Brown-Lupton University Union), 2019. Courtesy of TCU Marketing and Communication. Photograph by Juan Ojeda Mendoza.

BELOW
TCU Campus Commons during the commencement reception for the class of 2022. Courtesy of TCU Marketing and Communication. Photograph by James Anger.

ABOVE
Skyway and patio area between Mary Couts Burnett Library and Rees-Jones Hall. Courtesy of TCU Marketing and Communication. Photograph by Jeff McWhorter.

Also in 2009 Sherley Hall was renovated, followed by the renovations of Reed, Milton Daniel, and Montcrief halls, quickly followed by a new construction, the Mary Wright Admissions Center, in 2010.

As VIA moved into its second phase, VIA: The Academy of Tomorrow, construction steadily continued on the west side of campus. In 2012 the first of two renovations and additions to the stadium was completed, and two new residence halls, Pamela and Edward Clark Hall and Marion Hall, were added to Worth Hills in 2013, followed by Marlene Moss Hays Hall in 2014. But the center and east side of campus were not neglected. What had been built as the university gym in 1921, then converted into the Ballet and Modern Dance Building in 1973, was completely transformed into Erma Lowe Hall in 2011, and in 2014 the construction of the technology-rich Rees-Jones Hall was completed, symbolically launching TCU's Academy of Tomorrow. Described as "an incubator facility designed to maximize social and intellectual connectivity," Rees-Jones Hall was constructed to promote active learning and facilitate multidisciplinary collaboration (*TCU Magazine*, Spring 2015). Its completion was soon followed by the major renovation of the Mary Couts Burnett Library in 2016, which included substantial new space and bridge hallways connecting it to Rees-Jones, the demolition of the old entrance, and the construction of two new entrances. Linking past and present, the new front entrance, facing University Drive, was reminiscent of the library's original entrance, which had been torn down in a 1960s renovation. With the widening and redevelopment of the pedestrian zone from Tandy to University Drive, TCU established an Intellectual Commons to complement its Campus Commons.

Strikingly, during the years from 2015 to 2020, over thirty major projects were undertaken all across campus. In 2015, Frog Alley Garage, TCU's first parking structure, was completed, soon followed by a second, Worth Hills Garage, in 2016. The King Family Commons, a new student-services center serving the Worth Hills area, also opened in 2015, and the Bass Building was completely renovated and significantly enlarged with a new addition. In 2016 both Schollmaier Arena and Carr Chapel were enhanced with extensive renovations, and in the next two years the entire Greek Village was reconstructed, creating a total of eleven new buildings. While the Greek Village was being rebuilt, the Kelly Alumni and Visitors Center was renovated and expanded, and Human Resources and IT moved into a newly renovated building on the south side of Berry. Two new residence halls, Ashley and Greg Arnold Hall and Richards Hall, appeared on the east side of campus in 2019, and on the west side of campus, Fine Arts was extended in a new wing connected to Moudy North. In 2020 two major new constructions significantly altered TCU's operations, design, and traffic patterns. The Harrison replaced Sadler as the new administration building, and the Van Cliburn Concert Hall was built north of the library and east of Brite.

New and newly renovated buildings were, of course, not the only additions to TCU's campus. Streets had to be rerouted, new green spaces and landscaping added, and several new facility structures had to be built to accommodate the campus's enlarged footprint. In further enhancements, over a dozen new landmarks appeared on campus, beginning with Froghenge in 2004, sponsored by former Provost Nowell Donovan, followed by the Ray Gates in 2005, the King Entrance in 2007, Education's *Teaching to Change the World* statue in 2008, the Charles D. Tandy statue in 2009, and the *Range Duty* statue in 2010. The City of Fort Worth worked closely with TCU to improve both the appearance and flow of the streets surrounding campus, especially enhancing University and Berry Streets.

Establishing strategic planning as a continuous and continually self-assessing process was one of VIA's most significant accomplishments. Rather than submit a one-time single-document report, VIA continued to adjust its focus as TCU grew. To evaluate what progress had occurred, VIA: The Sequel was launched in December 2009 when Chancellor Boschini appointed a Steering Committee to undertake the review of VIA's five-year impact and then recommend future directions in terms of TCU's mission and values, vision, TCU Promise, and Cardinal Goals. Within a year's time, focus groups were held, SIF funding was reviewed, previous goals were re-evaluated and adjusted in a VIA Progress report, and academic plans for all departments and programs were updated and merged to create TCU's first "Academic Master Plan."

Promoted by Provost Donovan, The Academy of Tomorrow—the academic portion of VIA's second phase—was an ambitious plan to involve students and faculty in relevant, real-world dialogues anticipating a future of population growth and waning resources. Designed to encourage interdisciplinary collaboration and innovative investigation, the Academy of Tomorrow was intended to merge state-of-the-art technology and pedagogy with TCU's traditional emphasis on student-centered curricula and the teacher-scholar model to bring students and faculty together in discussions examining critical world challenges ("The Academy of Tomorrow," *TCU Magazine*, Spring 2012).

We developed the second phase of our strategic plan, Vision in Action: the Academy of Tomorrow. The University's future is unfolding with a new Intellectual Commons, a crossroads for academic minds. Students will be surrounded by amazing technology, courses that examine the world's most significant challenges, and unprecedented opportunities to find solutions to critical problems in an environment characterized by diversity of thought.

Chancellor Victor Boschini, *TCU Magazine*, Spring 2014

The Academy of Tomorrow will revolutionize the learning experience and elevate TCU's people and programs. This is an exciting time to be a Horned Frog!

TCU Facebook on Academy of Tomorrow

The library is not going to be bigger, it's not going to be smaller, but it's going to look completely different inside and out. It will have less stacks of books, more interactive study places. Less quiet; more noisy. It'll have food. It'll be a place people go 24/7.

Chancellor Victor Boschini,
VIA website, The Academy of Tomorrow

We've seen the results of our commitment to strategy. These ambitious dreams have resulted in innovative academic programs, an optimal campus environment, and increasingly impressive faculty, staff, and students from all over the world.

It's now time to Lead On. The next three to five years represent the third phase of our strategic plan for TCU with Vision in Action: Lead On.

Chancellor Victor Boschini,
***TCU Magazine*, Fall 2017**

ABOVE
The Harrison, built in 2020. Courtesy of TCU Marketing and Communication. Photograph by Andrew Emery.

LEFT
TCU Music Center and Van Cliburn Concert Hall, completed in 2022. Courtesy of *TCU Magazine*. Photograph by James Anger.

ABOVE
Froghenge. Courtesy of TCU Marketing and Communication. Photograph by James Anger.

OPPOSITE
Sculpture outside the Bailey Building, entitled "Teaching to Change the World." Sculpture by Angela Mia de la Vega, donated by the Malcolm and Ann Louden family, installed in 2008. Courtesy of TCU Marketing and Communication. Photograph by Jeffrey McWhorter.

ABOVE
Winthrop Rockefeller Building, home to TCU's Ranch Management program. Courtesy of TCU Marketing and Communication. Photograph by Carolyn Cruz.

While focusing on critical issues and creative solutions, the Academy of Tomorrow continued to identify TCU's academic profile and reputation, its size and balance, and its optimal campus environment as its overall objectives. At a two-day retreat in February 2012, Chancellor Boschini and the Board of Trustees discussed the university's future and resolved that the Academy of Tomorrow would enhance TCU's capacities to offer "person-centered academic excellence housed in extraordinary facilities built for 21st century education." While describing TCU's future, Chancellor Boschini recalled its past: "The hallmark of TCU since 1873 is that the students have a real opportunity to know the faculty and staff, both inside and outside the classroom. These plans will guarantee that for the foreseeable future that will continue to happen. TCU will remain student-centered" ("The Academy of Tomorrow," *TCU Magazine*, Spring 2012).

Much of the construction and renovation from 2012 to 2020 was aligned with TCU's identified focus areas, especially the creation of TCU's Intellectual Commons with the library and Rees-Jones at its center. With its incubator lab and interactive classrooms, Rees-Jones Hall particularly welcomed innovation. While the library was renovated and enlarged, its internal changes were equally important. To reshape the building to better serve the needs of its patrons and the goals of the Academy of Tomorrow, a large portion of its book collection—books seldom checked out—were relocated to an off-campus site, while new spaces and services for student learning were added. Equally important were the additional residential opportunities for students to live on campus as constructions continued in Worth Hills.

To maintain its forward focus, VIA continued to transition as circumstances on and off campus changed and as the university continued to grow. At a 2017 retreat, the Board of Trustees "charged the chancellor to refresh the *Vision in Action* planning process by implementing a new phase . . . *Vision in Action: Lead On*." Initially, four charges were identified as goals for the TCU community, all of which connected with VIA's core outcomes:

- Strengthen Academic Profile and Reputation
- Strengthen Endowment
- Strengthen TCU Experience and Campus Culture
- Strengthen Workforce

While familiar objectives throughout VIA, these goals were established in response to two pervasive challenges that, to continue its momentum, TCU needed to anticipate. The first was how TCU would "respond to the changing, increasingly diverse demographics of the nation and in particular Texas," while the second concerned the need to develop strategies to "counter changing public and political perceptions of higher education . . . that question the relevance, cost, and . . . basic fairness of a university education ("Report to the Board," Trustee Minutes, April 2017).

We've seen the results of our commitment to strategy. These ambitious dreams have resulted in innovative academic programs, an optimal campus environment, and increasingly impressive faculty, staff, and students from all over the world.

It's now time to Lead On. The next three to five years represent the third phase of our strategic plan for TCU with Vision in Action: Lead On.

Chancellor Victor Boschini, *TCU Magazine*, Fall 2017

To respond to these issues, *Vision in Action: Lead On* was launched with the four primary goals and four teams. Each team was charged by the chancellor and trustees to propose recommendations, identify resource requirements, and deliver their reports in spring 2018. The many and various responses were then consolidated into one report, which was presented back to the trustees in April 2019. Strengthening the academic profile, for example, resulted in seven overall recommendations with over forty more specific suggestions for achieving its primary objective, all supporting one fundamental assumption: "It is important to realize that, in the long view, the academic profile is the most true and important component of the front door of the university" (Vision in Action: Lead On, A Report to the Board of Trustees, April 2019). Strengthening the teacher-scholar model was viewed as a building block for all further recommendations for boosting TCU academic profile.

Despite numerous plans and approaches, there was significant overlap in the report's many recommendations, and in several instances specific wording was repeated in each of the four overall goals. One way or another, each of the goals offered similar recommendations in response to social demographics and external perceptions:

- Provide a highly engaging and inclusive TCU student experience
- Foster a diverse and inclusive university for all
- Encourage student success through an integrated and holistic student-support model
- Tell the compelling stories of TCU and its students, faculty, and staff

In reviewing the four reports, the central committee acknowledged that each of the four "emphasized DEI," and thus the third goal, improving campus culture, came to focus specifically on "Diversity, Equity, and Inclusion" (Vision in Action: Lead On, A Report to the Board of Trustees, April 2019). Drawing on TCU's Disciples tradition of inclusion and embracing diversity, and in response to national "dialogues of race and gender, with their themes of privilege, wealth disparity, and unequal opportunity," the report for improving campus culture based its recommendations on another fundamental assumption: "An inclusive TCU will be a place where all are welcome and no one is excluded" (Vision in Action: Lead On, A Report to the Board of Trustees, April 2019).

With so many worthy ideas, the April 2019 report to the Board of Trustees necessarily recognized that "there is, of course, a price tag" (Vision in Action: Lead On, A Report to the Board of Trustees, April 2019). In less than two decades, VIA not only physically transformed campus but was also transformative in numerous areas, growing notably in applications, enrollments, scholarships, faculty and staff, athletics, academics, and ultimately national recognition. Yet none of TCU's many advances could have occurred without philanthropic investment facilitated by University Advancement.

The teacher-scholar model is, therefore, that part of our culture of which we are most proud, enabling us to integrate our scholarly activity, our students, and our service to society at large.

Goal 1 Recommendation, Strengthen the Academic Profile and Reputation of TCU, Vision in Action: Lead On, A Report to the Board of Trustees, April 2019

But you have to admit that Athletics is a window . . . through which many people see a university. I mean look at how most of us view other universities, often through the window of athletics.

Larry Adams, Interview, November 2011

Dr. Tucker said Athletics was the window through which the university was viewed. Whether that's right or wrong, that's the part that makes the headlines. And so we have to be willing to live up to those expectations in the community, in the athletic world, which means competing at a higher level, and minding your business.

Ross Bailey, Interview, December 2012

I've always felt . . . that it [Athletics] is the window to the university . . . The publicity that is received free is better than you can get if you hired an outside national agency to do your public relations.

Leo Munson, Interview, April 2013

Bill Tucker said that athletics were the window through which the university was viewed. I've always thought that was true and that with Chancellor Boschini we've gone from the window to the front porch.

Laura Miller, Interview, April 2013

LEFT
Alejandro Saucedo '22, Kynnedi Rone '22, and Trustee Ron Parker at the 2022 scholarship dinner. Courtesy of University Advancement.

LEFT
Lead On: A Campaign for TCU Launch, 2019. Trustees and Co-Chairs Dee Kelly, Jr. and Ron Parker. Courtesy of University Advancement.

LEFT
Hays Business Commons Dedication, 2020. Courtesy of University Advancement.

ABOVE
Campaign for TCU celebration, 2008.
Courtesy of University Advancement.

New construction, new programs, and new positions required fundraising. Beginning in 2003, one of VIA's basic objectives had always been to closely align strategic planning with budgeting and fundraising, and the primary intention of the 2004 economic review at VIA's outset had been to review TCU's financial opportunities and resources. With its successful fundraising efforts, first with the Campaign for TCU and then with Lead On: A Campaign for TCU, Advancement played a continuous key role throughout the VIA process and the university's progress.

Philanthropy, of course, is as old as the university. Money was always scarce during the early years, and fundraising was continual. During the lean years of the late 1890s, it was T. E. Shirley's fundraising efforts that saved TCU after "the Trustees were of a mind to give up the struggle" (Hall 85). Since the centennial, however, there have been several specific, comprehensive campaigns. Although he preferred his rifle approach—as opposed to a shotgun approach—Chancellor Tucker had developed plans for a "Commission on TCU and the Future" and connected it to a strategic planning process, which he introduced to the Board of Trustees in November 1984 as "The 1990s Project" (Report to the Board, November 1984). But with the energy crisis and a national recession, plans were postponed for several years until the Next Frontier campaign was launched, and from 1992 to 1997 more than $126 million was raised, funding which helped finance the construction of the Mary D. and F. Howard Walsh Center for Performing Arts, the Dee J. Kelly Alumni and Visitors Center, and the Walsh Physical Performance Complex for Athletics.

VIA and The Campaign for TCU developed together and for nearly a decade were closely intertwined. The campaign officially was launched in June 2005 with a goal of raising $250 million and concluded seven years later in June 2012 after raising over $434 million. Except for one year (2009, following the 2008 financial crash), the campaign averaged well over $60 million each year. The original goal was passed during the silent phase and nearly doubled during the public phase. All funding initiatives were met, which included academic programs, endowed scholarships, faculty positions, and facilities (including athletics). During the campaign's final two years, the Board of Trustees requested that $100 million be raised in scholarship support, and as the campaign concluded, over $108 million had been acquired to bolster financial aid. While $100 million went into the endowment, the remainder was evenly split between academics and athletics, with a majority on each side helping to fund new constructions and renovations, including the Amon Carter Stadium renovation that cost a total of $140 million.

ABOVE
Dee J. Kelly Alumni Center, built in 1997. Courtesy of Linbeck Group, LLC. Photograph by Leo Wesson.

ABOVE
Walsh Center for Performing Arts, built in 1998. Courtesy of TCU Marketing and Communication. Photograph by Rodger Mallison.

TCU's Rose Bowl victory calls for a celebration in Fort Worth.

***Fort Worth Star-Telegram* headline, January 1, 2011**

Building for the future requires continual effort, and soon after the Campaign for TCU successfully concluded, Advancement began an even more ambitious philanthropic initiative for TCU's sesquicentennial celebration, Lead On: A Campaign for TCU, with a goal of raising $1 billion by 2023. The funds raised will be used to support two primary areas: (1) people and programs and (2) facilities. At this writing, the Lead On campaign was on track to reach its goal by May 31, 2023, having raised over $940 million with over fifty-five thousand donors. Since 2012 the campaign has averaged $84 million a year, a significant increase over the Campaign for TCU.

Another one of Advancement's successes has been its annual Faculty/Staff Campaign. In the past decade the campaign has averaged nearly a 75 percent participation of TCU faculty and staff. For several years before the pandemic, the campus fundraising drive had topped over 80 percent participation, a significant indication of faculty and staff willingness to support TCU. All major university areas participate and some, such as Facilities, have continually contributed at higher rates than the campaign averages. In the past ten years Facilities averaged a participation rate exceeding 85 percent.

In July 2011, *Fort Worth Magazine* published an article on recent TCU successes, "Why TCU Is the Hottest School in Texas," and its opening lines contrasted admission applications in 2000 with those in 2011. The differences are remarkable. In 2000 the number of applications set a new school record at over 4500. In 2011 the number of applications set another new record at 19,000 applications. Written by Nancy Bartosek, former editor of *TCU Magazine*, the article examines the reasons behind TCU's "explosive growth" in applications, which is described as "a 300 percent increase in applicants in only 10 years—a leap unheard of in the education industry" (*Fort Worth Magazine*, July 2011).

A quick explanation for the substantial jump might be TCU's memorable Rose Bowl victory on January 1, 2011. Certainly the win and national coverage of the game helped attract the interest of prospective students and their parents. Over 20 million people watched the Frogs win on New Year's Day 2011, and more than 100,000 visited TCU's website—tcu.edu—that day, during and after the game. Notably, these online visitors were not checking out TCU's football program, which has a separate website, gofrogs.com. They were exploring TCU as a university.

Yet winning the 2011 Rose Bowl is not the only reason for TCU's remarkable growth. With considerable depth, the article explores TCU's development in all areas, with athletics

I think every chancellor since I've been here has really had . . . to grow . . . the Athletic Department. I know that . . . Dr. Tucker and Dr. Ferrari and specifically Chancellor Boschini have had more and more and more involvement . . . I think they understand that it's a huge part of the university and it's a huge marketing window that [provides] publicity for the entire school.

Richard Sybesma, Interview, May 2013

Two, four, six, eight, we hope TCU wins before we graduate.

Student cheer during losing football seasons

I decided we needed to stabilize our fan base and started . . . the Committee of 100, and [it] was just a hundred people that I could round up that were interested in saving the football program . . . we actually ended up with two hundred.

John V. Roach, Interview, March 2012

But they didn't care a bit about what was happening in tennis and women's golf. They wanted football.

Chancellor Emeritus Bill Tucker, Interview 2011

LEFT
Demolition of the Amon G. Carter Stadium, 2010. Courtesy of Steven J. Meyers.

OPPOSITE
Front cover of *Fort Worth Magazine*, July 2011. Courtesy of *Fort Worth Magazine*.

BELOW
Amon G. Carter Stadium, 2022. Courtesy of TCU Marketing and Communication. Photograph by James Anger.

being only one of them. The Rose Bowl win was part of an extensive concerted movement that began decades earlier. While both understood the importance of college athletics and were committed to developing TCU's programs, Chancellors Tucker and Ferrari made TCU's upward growth possible in numerous pivotal areas well beyond sports. With the help and support of the trustees, their administrative teams, and numerous faculty, staff, and alumni, they significantly contributed to raising the endowment, enhancing academics, improving campus appeal, increasing diversity, connecting with Fort Worth, upgrading the master plan, identifying institutional priorities, initiating strategic marketing programs, and sharing a vision of TCU's potential to generate excitement and optimism.

The article quoted Chancellor Boschini stating that the prospective students and their parents "want the whole package," a holistic bundle of student-centered opportunities, services, programs, and facilities. In addition to great academics and a nationally competitive football program, they look for a commitment to provide "an extraordinary residential experience," what former Provost Nowell Donovan described as "a place where living and learning intersect." In 2011, newly admitted students were surveyed on why they chose TCU. They listed "personal attention and the campus environment" first, followed by "availability of majors, academic reputation, and value for the price" (*Fort Worth Magazine*, July 2011).

The visibility that results from TCU's athletic successes, however, cannot be overstated. When he was interviewed, former Football Head Coach Gary Patterson described himself as "not just a football coach" but also as "an ambassador of the university." Coach Patterson often remarked that "athletics is the front porch of a house. It's not the most important, but it's the most visible" (Interview, April 2015). When describing the significant "exposure of intercollegiate athletics," former Athletics Director Chris Del Conte stated that athletics is "the ultimate marketing tool for the university." Echoing Coach Patterson's familiar statement that "we are the front porch," he added that the publicity generated by athletic success, while significant, means nothing if there is not a great university behind the porch. In his words:

> You can go buy a lemonade stand, and it can be the greatest lemonade stand, but if it is bad lemonade, you'll never go back . . . We are the ultimate lemonade stand. You come take a sip, and you walk on campus, and everything is pretty. The flowers look great, the classrooms are clean, the new dorms looks great, the new BLUU . . . everything looks fantastic . . . what athletics has done is just open the door for people to come visit. (Interview, April 2017)

In a similar strain, former Athletics Director Danny Morrison credited Chancellor Boschini for understanding that athletic success was not enough, that all parts of the university had to move forward together:

ABOVE
Gary Patterson. Courtesy of TCU Athletics.

ABOVE
Former Athletics Director Danny Morrison. Courtesy of Texas Christian University. Photograph by Glen E. Ellman.

ABOVE
TCU wins the Rose Bowl, 2011. Courtesy of Texas Christian University.

RIGHT
Former Athletics Director Chris Del Conte. Courtesy of Texas Christian University. Photograph by Glen E. Ellman.

> He recognized that athletics brings great visibility to the institution, done in the right way. He also realized that it can't be by itself. All parts of the university have to get better and improve, or otherwise things get out of whack. What was great about TCU, and has continued to be great over the last fifteen years . . . has been that TCU has been moving forward on all fronts, not just in the athletic program. I think that when that happens it creates this sense of momentum and also a sense of pride in all areas of the campus. I think it is dangerous when one part of campus gets out of whack. (Interview, November 2014)

Bringing invaluable visibility to the university and raising interest levels across the country, success on the gridiron has helped to create a synergy of TCU athletics, academics, and residential life. Momentum in one generates similar energy and interest in the others. When speaking on the relationship between athletics and academics, former Associate Athletic Director for Operations Ross Bailey stated:

> The university has always been great academically, but unfortunately 42,000 people don't show up to watch a chemistry experiment. That really may be more important in some cases, but Athletics becomes that window . . . I think we've been able to elevate the desirability of the university, which has then let us elevate the admission standards, which lets us bring more students in, which helps being in more financial resources to the university. Maybe it makes alumni a little bit more willing to give back. (Interview, December 2012)

Unquestionably, athletics is a crucial part of TCU's remarkable story. Since the mid-1990s, TCU athletic successes increased the university's visibility and desirability. But there were times in the 1970s and 1980s when there were few successes and little momentum. Football reached a low point, going over a decade unable to win more than a couple games in a season. In 1976, the football team lost every game it played. After several seasons of losing games and losing money, the stands were half filled at home football games, and at times there were more people cheering for visiting teams than for TCU. Resulting in severe sanctions that limited scholarships and recruitment, the 1985 football scandal further added to losses and lost enthusiasm. Some people in the campus community began to question whether TCU, winner of two national championships in the 1930s, should continue to compete in Division I athletics.

In 1994, former Board Chair John V. Roach organized a group of people committed to rescuing TCU football, which became known as the Committee of 100. In recalling how the committee got started, he stated:

> We were having a board dinner one night downtown at the Fort Worth Club, and during the board meeting I just was talking to the people that happened to be sitting at the same table and said, "You know, we've got to do something to really solidify our fan base if we want to continue to be in football . . . I was chairman at the time, so after dinner when I got up to speak, I announced that we were to start the Committee of 100. (Interview, March 2012)

Made up of alumni and businesspeople from the area and across the state who "were interested in saving the football program," the Committee of 100 functioned to expand TCU's fan base by promoting athletics, and specifically football, as Fort Worth's home team. Committee members not only contributed funds but also developed strategies to build excitement about TCU football. To further explain how the group functioned, John V. Roach commented that the committee came together as the Southwestern Conference was breaking up, and there was considerable discussion about what TCU should do: "We studied whether or not we ought to continue football and concluded that it was going to cost us more not to do football than it was to play football." The committee then resolved that Amon Carter Stadium had to be filled with enthusiastic fans: "We really built our fan base . . . [the Committee of 100 began] to really significantly help to sell tickets, get fans in the stands . . . and make us competitive" (Interview, March 2012).

Two years later, in February 1996, the *Skiff* ran an article about the Committee of 100 under an eye-catching banner title in bold, "Committee of 100 betters ticket sales," and quoted Glenn Stone, former TCU Sports Information Director, stating that, "As far as I'm concerned, the [football team's] MVP is the Committee of 100." Stone had several

Committee of 100 betters ticket sales

Boosters strive for 'warm and fuzzy fans'

By Rob Sherwin
TCU Daily Skiff

Who has been TCU football's most valuable player over the past two years? Andre Davis? Max Knake?

Not according to Glen Stone, TCU sports information director. "As far as I'm concerned, the MVP is the Committee of 100," he said.

Formed in May 1994, the committee is a coalition of about 200 business and community leaders from across the state who share the goal of promoting TCU athletics.

Larry Teis, TCU athletics marketing and promotions director, said, "The committee was initially designed to be a group of 100 business leaders, members of the community and friends of TCU that would come together and sell TCU athletics. It's really one big public awareness campaign."

Whether it is simple public awareness or intensive scientific marketing, many are praising the results.

Stone said, "The committee has added to the overall excitement of game day. I'm not just talking about crowds, which is obviously a big factor, but the goings on, events, and atmosphere that prevails. They'll do whatever it takes to keep a crowd feeling warm and fuzzy."

For Stone, warm and fuzzy fans mean an increase in ticket sales.

"As far as attendance goes, we've had two consecutive record breaking years," he said. "The numbers speak for themselves."

Stone said that he expects the committee to extend more of its efforts to TCU's other sports.

"If you and I were going to start a new business, we'd have to devote all our time and energy to one aspect to begin with, and once we felt comfortable, then we could broaden our horizons," he said. "That's what they did.

"They didn't turn their backs on the other sports, but they wanted to make sure that football got off on solid footing, and then they'd come back this year and really start working on the other sports."

Stone said the improvements in the basketball program are already visible.

"Just go to a basketball game and look around," he said. "Look at all the image enhancements that have been made.

see **Boosters**, *page 2*

ABOVE

Courtesy of the *Skiff*. February 2, 1996.

ABOVE
TCU's 2011 Rose Bowl trophy. Courtesy of TCU Marketing and Communication. Photograph by Andrew Emery.

reasons to cite the committee as the team's most valuable player. In quoting the rise in attendance, he added: "As far as attendance goes, we've had two consecutive record-breaking years. The numbers speak for themselves." But Stone explained that higher attendance numbers were not the only results of the committee's work: "The committee added to the overall excitement of game day. I'm not just talking about the crowds, which is obviously a big factor, but the goings-on, events, and the atmosphere that prevails" (*Skiff*, February 2, 1996). In recalling the committee's work, former Associate Dean of Admissions Janet Herald stated that much of what seems familiar now, such as Frog Alley, the Frog horn, and the giant Frog inflatables, was developed by the committee:

> The concept of TCU being the home team of everybody that lives in Fort Worth . . . didn't exist. It really came later, when John Roach was chairman of the Board of Trustees, and he started the Committee of 100. That was to help season ticket sales, to get . . . the community involved with TCU, and to make TCU your home team. There were a lot of things you almost take for granted now because they've just been part of the university now for so long, but they weren't there . . . back then. (Interview, March 2013)

While there are many other integral chapters in TCU's remarkable story, clearly the exceptional football seasons of 2010 and most recently 2022, capped by winning the Rose Bowl in 2011 and the Fiesta Bowl in 2022, have caused thousands of people to perceive TCU through football's window.

All of TCU's former and current Athletics Directors—Frank Windegger, Eric Hyman, Danny Morrison, Chris Del Conte, and Jeremiah Donati—and their staffs were committed to making TCU football successful. Despite setbacks and hurdles, their combined efforts have helped to fulfill the high expectations of the TCU community and, since the late 1990s, have helped make bowl game appearances fairly common.

Football, however, is not TCU's only athletic success story. In previous decades TCU achieved considerable success in nearly all of its athletic programs. After responding to several alumni dissatisfied with losing football seasons, Chancellor Tucker complained that they did not want to hear about such success in other sports:

> I'd write back and say, look at what our record was in tennis this year, look at what our record was in women's golf, look at what our record was in men's golf. (Interview, November 2011)

Chancellor Tucker had good reason to praise TCU's other sports. During the low years of football, TCU men's and women's golf and tennis teams were being nationally ranked and winning conference championships. More recently, TCU baseball, men's basketball, women's basketball, rifle, equestrian, track and field, and women's soccer all have attained similar successes. Altogether, TCU athletics have achieved 128 conference championships, with men's tennis (27) and baseball (25) leading the way. Nationwide, TCU sports have earned fourteen national championships, with the Rifle team earning nine national titles. Thanks to the commitment of TCU Athletic staffs, TCU has competed at the highest levels of collegiate sports, despite being one of the smallest Division I schools.

I think the biggest changes have been in technology.

Phil Hartman, Interview, 2011

One of TCU's most indispensable programs is also one of its most invisible. Often what is ubiquitous is overlooked. Yet TCU's phenomenal growth over the past half century could not have occurred without the constant support of technology. Since the 2000s, every person and every service on campus has been in daily contact with Information Technology. While computers started appearing in the 1950s, and TCU's first computers—exceptionally large mainframes—arrived on campus in the early 1960s, their general use—first with desktops and then with laptops, cell phones, and tablets—expanded in the 1990s and has exploded since the 2000s. Computers are now essential tools everywhere on campus and for every person on campus. To serve the needs of so many areas and people, IT had to develop an extended infrastructure of networks, cables, servers, routers, services, software programs, file storage, printing access, phones, computer lab support, live support, firewalls, and applications, nearly all of which remains invisible to users. Today IT makes work productivity and connectivity possible on campus. All university offices, programs, and departments—as well as all students, faculty, staff, and administrators—rely on IT technology and infrastructure to work efficiently and collaborate effectively. Whenever anyone has a computer or technology issue or question, they call the Help Desk, chat online, or attend training webinars. From AddRan to Women and Gender Studies, from campus classrooms to collaborators across the globe, computers and technology are omnipresent, and IT is responsible for maintaining the systems that make such capacities possible.

ABOVE
Former Athletics Director Eric Hyman.
Courtesy of Mary Couts Burnett Library.
Photograph by Linda Kaye.

ABOVE
Athletics Director Jeremiah Donati.
Courtesy of TCU Media Relations.
Photograph by Michael Clements.

ABOVE
The TCU rifle team celebrates their NCAA National Championship win, 2012.

ABOVE
TCU Women's Soccer wins the Big XII championship, 2020. Courtesy of TCU Athletics.

BELOW
TCU Baseball at the 2017 College World Series in Omaha, Nebraska. Courtesy of TCU Media Relations. Photograph by Michael Clements.

Our goal is to provide the TCU campus with superior technology and a robust infrastructure that will meet the needs of a growing student and employee population. We are dedicated to securing, supporting, and assisting users with the technology services that we provide.

IT website

There is a great perception from the budget office, the finance team, the chancellor, and everyone about the importance of technology. They make sure that it is a well planned for, well-funded resource, and that they treat it like a strategic asset.

Bryan Lucas, Interview, February 2018

ABOVE
IBM 1401, photographed in the Computer History Museum. TCU bought the IBM 1401 in 1964, and it was the second computer acquired by TCU. Courtesy of wikimedia commons.

Although IT today is everywhere on campus, it started out in the basement of Sid Richardson in an area known as the Machine Room, which housed several IBM mainframes; nearby was a separate, specially designated keypunch room. Students and faculty punched their cards, turned them in at the desk, and then waited while the mainframe operators ran their simulation programs and returned both the cards and output. Faculty from the School of Education and the Neeley School of Business were some of the early users, as were Leigh Secrest and Bill Koehler.

The first computer science courses were taught within the Mathematics Department, but in 1981 the Management Information Systems was created, followed a year later by the Computer Science Department. In 1987 the first campus Ethernet network, using a "Thick Wire" cable and "Vampire" taps, connected Sid Richardson, Sadler Hall, Dan Rogers Hall, and the Library. In 1987 the Computer Center and Management Information Systems merged to become Information Services, and a year later TCU connected to UTA, the university's first connection to the outside world. In 2006 Information Services changed to Technology Resources, and Bryan Lucas was appointed its Executive Director. Continuing to expand, Technology Resources then became Information Technology in 2012, and Bryan Lucas became its Chief Technology Officer.

ABOVE
Students working on computers, 1980s. Courtesy of TCU Marketing and Communication.

Information Technology has been a vital part of TCU since the first emails began to be transmitted across campus, but once COVID-19 appeared as a serious threat, IT's functions and responsibilities became not only an indispensable part of

Technology Updates: Zoom-enabling classrooms

Space	Covid >10	A/V	Percent
Scheduled Teaching	217	202	93%
Dept Scheduled	3	3	100%
Meeting/Event	27	15	56%
Conference Rooms	6	6	100%
Other	8	1	13%
Performance	11	1	9%
Unscheduled Teaching	45	30	67%
Totals	**317**	**258**	**81%**

- Enabled 93% of scheduled teaching
- Enabled non-traditional spaces
- Completed in 60 days
- $1.7m cost

LEFT
PowerPoint slides in technology presentation to the Board of Trustees, August 2020. Courtesy of Bryan Lucas.

the TCU pandemic response but also its primary means for all communication. Administrators, faculty, staff, and students all relied on IT services once campus closed in mid-March 2020. Working and teaching from home could not have happened without the continuous effort of IT personnel, who provided both the connections and the training that made the sudden transition possible.

Throughout the pandemic, faculty and staff had to learn new software and skills, and during the summer of 2020, extra effort was necessary to prepare for the fall semester. Faculty were required to take special Hybrid Certification training offered by the Koehler Center that provided instruction in distance-learning pedagogy as well as information concerning various federal, state, and local regulations for online instruction. To assist with the training, each college had an eTrainer to help faculty complete their assignments and receive their certification. With well over six hundred faculty members, the task was immense, but both the Koehler Center and IT made the training possible and ultimately successful.

Although the summer training was over as the semester started in August, online instruction continued. IT launched two websites filled with helpful information, webinars, and software access: the Keep Learning site for students and Keep Teaching site for faculty. Students were provided with the resources and tools for virtual learning and all areas of campus support, including health information, advising, counseling, and career preparation. Faculty were provided with instruction into online best practices for teaching, including content delivery, student engagement, learning evaluation, and student feedback. Moreover, IT's Help Desk continued to offer real-time technical advice on all areas of TCU Online.

To make the online transition possible, IT retrofitted 258 classrooms and meeting rooms with cameras, microphones, and related technology to enable faculty to make use of Zoom for instruction within a narrow sixty-day window during the 2020 summer. During a typical pre-pandemic summer, IT usually upgraded the technology in thirty to forty classrooms within a ninety-day window. Once IT had negotiated a new site license, the number of Zoom meetings rapidly multiplied from roughly one thousand per month to a peak of 40,288 during April 2020. While making classrooms and meeting rooms Zoom capable, IT also implemented new hardware and configured network access to allow students to remotely access 102 computer labs across campus, and additionally added a laptop loaner program to help students, faculty, and staff participate in Zoom classes and meetings.

TCU's commitment to students and its confidence in the future are evident in the physical transformation of campus, increased endowment dollars, higher admission applications and enrollments, campus growth, expanded student services and programs, and improved rankings. Less apparent but ultimately more significant are the additions, augmentations, and innovations of TCU's academic programs. From the start, VIA recognized that raising TCU's academic profile was an essential step in gaining greater national and international recognition, and much of the strategic planning had been directed toward repositioning TCU academics for learning in the twenty-first century. In addition to TCU's values-driven new core that promoted the university's mission, plans were quickly developed to invigorate existing areas and majors, add new programs, expand support for research and creativity, create innovative interdisciplinary centers, increase international learning experiences, and improve classroom technologies. In various ways, all SIF-funded projects strengthened TCU's academic culture.

Several large-scale academic additions were also a part of TCU's recent developments. One of the most apparent was Honors transitioning from program to college in 2009. As a means of competing for the best students in the country, elevating Honors had been considered for several years. When she directed the Honors Program in the 1990s, Kathryn McDorman had circulated a proposal of Honors becoming a college, and, after taking over as director in 2003, Peggy Watson raised similar possibilities. But constructing a college required generous funding, and without it no steps were taken.

In 2008, however, Associate Vice Chancellor for Advancement David Nolan approached Professor Watson with the tantalizing possibility of donors who might be willing to fund an Honors College, and he asked if she could submit a proposal in less than a week. Without knowing who the potential donors were,

When I was in school, it was just the Honors Program, but to see the transformation to a full-fledged college with a dean, and what that does to strengthen our academic reputation, is key.

Brenda Cline, Interview, May 2018

With the addition of the Honors College, there's been a good focus on academic achievement and interest in interdisciplinary thinking, cross-sharing across campus and across disciplines.

Sharon Fairchild, Interview, November 2013

In the late fall of 2008, I was in the small Honors Program Office in Sadler when David Nolan from Advancement paid a surprise visit to let me know that there were possible donors for the long-awaited creation of an Honors College.

To this day, when I mention to parents that the Honors College offers outstanding housing in Milton Daniel, a father is likely to chuckle and say, "Is that the Milton Daniel that I lived in as a freshman? The one that smelled so?"

Peggy Watson, Interview, April 2013

ABOVE
Peggy Watson, founding dean of the John V. Roach Honors College, at the college's dedication, 2009. Courtesy of John V. Roach Honors College.

ABOVE
David Grant, former Director of the TCU Honors Program and Emeritus Professor of Religion, plays the banjo—as he used to do for Honors students—during the 2009 John V. Roach Honors College dedication. Courtesy of John V. Roach Honors College.

LEFT
Paul and Judy Andrews with Jean and John V. Roach at the Honors College dedication in 2009. Courtesy of John V. Roach Honors College.

and knowing only that they were admirers of the economist Thomas Friedman and his recent book, *The World Is Flat*, she quickly wrote and submitted a proposal quoting Friedman, and only later learned that the benefactors were Paul and Judy Andrews, two of TCU's most philanthropic patrons. The Andrews were not only interested in supporting an Honors college, but they also wanted it to be named for their good friend, former Board of Trustees chair and TCU benefactor, John V. Roach. With funding suddenly in place, plans were announced, and in a little over a year the founding of the TCU John V. Roach Honors College was celebrated.

Creating a college is not an easy task, particularly from the ground up, and especially when significant funding is needed, but within a half-dozen years TCU announced uniquely ambitious plans to create a new medical school in partnership with the University of North Texas Health Science Center. In July 2015, both schools issued public announcements of their intention to create a shared medical school, and within a few months joint committees had been formed to search for a dean, develop a curriculum, create policies for admissions, and assess financial issues. In less than a year the dean search had been completed, and Dr. Stuart D. Flynn had been named the school's founding dean. An ideal choice, Dr. Flynn had received his medical training at the University of Michigan and Stanford University and taught medicine at the Yale University School of Medicine before moving to Phoenix, where he became the founding dean of the University of Arizona College of Medicine—Phoenix. After his appointment, he signaled his intentions "to develop a cutting-edge MD school with national aspirations" (*TCU Magazine*, March 2016).

Traditionally, medical school curricula start with two years of pre-clinical, lecture-based classes with little or no student/patient contact or one-on-one mentoring between students and doctors. Dr. Flynn and his staff immediately developed plans for a school that would offer students a "more patient-focused training and patient-centric education." In describing the school's unique curriculum, he stated: "We will maintain what they [entering students] start medical school with, which is a high level of empathy, and which traditionally disappears in medical school . . . we will train empathetic scholars" (*TCU 360*, August 24, 2017). In explaining how the new school would "change the training paradigm in those pre-clinical years," he affirmed: "Our pre-clinical is a hundred-percent-flipped classroom model," where faculty would not be lecturing at the podium but instead working more closely with students to develop a "four-year research project" (Interview, March 2018).

Medical school tuition is notoriously expensive, and students often graduate with enormous debts running into hundreds of thousands of dollars. Yet plans for the new school were given a major boost in 2017 when Paul Dorman, a Fort Worth pharmaceutical executive, business investor, and philanthropist, committed to providing full first-year tuition for the inaugural class. As a result, when the first

ABOVE
Stuart Flynn. Courtesy of TCU Marketing and Communication. Photograph by Amy Peterson.

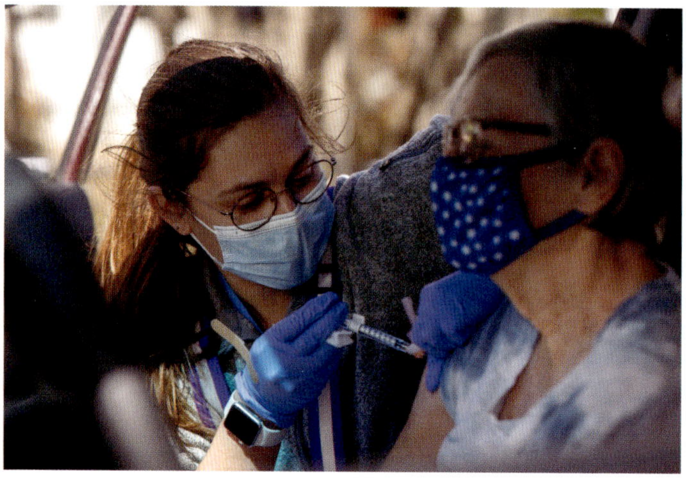

ABOVE
Med school student Quinn Losefsky administers a COVID-19 vaccine during a drive-through vaccine clinic held at TCU, 2021. Courtesy of *TCU Magazine*. Photograph by Mark Graham.

cohort of sixty students arrived in July 2019, they were able to begin their studies without the usual financial burden, and Dr. Flynn and his staff straightaway introduced them to the school's "unique curriculum—a patient-centered approach that will produce compassionate, innovative . . . life-long learners." Rather than passively listening to lectures, students began working with patients while receiving "one-on-one mentoring sessions with faculty clinicians" (*TCU 360*, September 23, 2019).

The TCU and UNT medical school started with great excitement and enthusiasm, but no one could have possibly anticipated that within eight months the unique curriculum based on personal interaction would be severely tested when the COVID-19 pandemic spread across the globe, causing unprecedented disruptions and deaths everywhere. Along with the rest of TCU, the medical school suspended in-person classes and went entirely online. Although unable to meet with mentors and patients in person, and yet wanting to contribute, the students volunteered their time in a variety of ways, assisting local care centers, collecting protective equipment for local physicians, answering hotlines, and tracing coronavirus contacts, ultimately gaining a greater awareness of disease and death than most previous cohorts of first-year medical students.

On January 12, 2022, Chancellor Boschini sent an email to the TCU community announcing that, going forward, the medical school would "move into its next phase of development and growth solely as the TCU School of Medicine" (January 12, 2022). The following day *TCU 360* followed the Chancellor's announcement with a brief report stating that "TCU has taken full control of the medical school" and that "it would be "the sole degree-granting university of the TCU School of Medicine" (*TCU 360*, January 13, 2022). The announcements publicly concluded the joint venture with the UNT Health Science Center that began in 2015. While praising the "groundbreaking collaboration," the chancellor and the announcements that followed expressed gratitude for UNT Health Center's help in establishing the medical school.

Yet from the 2015 beginning there were unresolved issues over management, resources, and support that worried both sides, and in the seven years that followed the initial announcements these issues continued to cause concern until Dean Flynn and his team believed the medical school would best thrive under TCU's single leadership. Once the collaboration ended, there were immediate questions concerning fees for UNT space and services. Two months later TCU announced plans to construct a new home for the medical school on the corner of South Henderson and West Rosedale streets in the Fort Worth Medical District. Anticipating growth, former Vice Chancellor Brian Gutierrez had been purchasing property through a third party for several years until TCU had acquired five acres in one of Fort Worth's most valuable areas. The location is ideal for the many clinical partnerships the medical school had developed in the Medical District. Current plans call for a four-story medical

Having Dr. Flynn join us in this ambitious project is a tremendous step forward. His expertise in navigating the complexities of a new medical school, combined with his passion for mentoring the leaders and critical thinkers who will drive health care transformation, fully aligns with the mission of Fort Worth's MD school. We're so happy to welcome him to campus and to our community.

Chancellor Victor Boschini, *TCU Magazine*, March 2016

I think Nowell's greatest gift is his ability to work with a broad range of professors. I mean when you've got Business School professors, English professors and Philosophy professors—that's a broad range of people with a lot of needs and a lot of wants. Talk about a good listener. He is an exceptionally good listener. He is generally softspoken except when he needs to speak up. I love listening to the man. It's like eating candy. . . . We're going miss him. He's a really great man.

Brenda Cline, Interview, May 2018

I would like people to remember the fact that I tried very hard to create a compassionate and congenial university.

Nowell Donovan, *Skiff*, April 24, 2019

The Chancellor is always willing to participate. . . . he's always been available. When we hand him reports, he listens to our suggestions. We have informal and formal meetings, so we are in constant communication. He wants to listen. He wants to take in information and then make decisions based on that. Our relationship has been good because he has been an advocate for DEI.

Aisha Torrey-Sawyer, Interview, July 2020

Our University community is imperfect, but I have not experienced another that cares for its members like TCU. We have work to do, and I ask that we engage in this important work with respect for each other, openness to change, and a desire for a more inclusive community.

Victor Boschini, Email, October 18, 2016

ABOVE
Architectural drawing of the Burnett School of Medicine. Courtesy of Texas Christian University.

RIGHT
Nowell Donovan. Courtesy of TCU Marketing and Communication. Courtesy of Glen E. Ellman.

LEFT
Teresa Abi-Nader Dahlberg. Courtesy of TCU Marketing and Communication. Photograph by Amy Peterson.

education complex of approximately 100,000 square feet. Construction is currently underway, and until it is finished the TCU Medical School is using temporary space near the TCU campus.

Building on the momentum, TCU and the medical school announced in July 2022 one of the university's "most generous gifts . . . [given] in support of the TCU School of Medicine operations in perpetuity"—a $50 million gift from the Anne W. Marion Endowment (TCU Medical School Press Release). To honor the late Anne Burnett Marion's extraordinary support, the school was named the Anne Burnett Marion School of Medicine (more generally known as the Burnett School of Medicine). In announcing the gift, Dr. Flynn stated:

> The Anne W. Marion Endowment will provide funds to support our students, faculty, and programming for the medical school and continue to fuel our mission of transforming health care by inspiring Empathetic Scholars. This generosity empowers us to continue recruiting and nurturing talented and diverse students who are shaping the future of medicine and health care in an abundance of ways. We continue to carry out the vision of creating physicians who are knowledgeable and compassionate caregivers. (TCU Medical School Press Release).

As Mary Couts Burnett had in 1923, the Burnett family once again provided TCU with an extraordinary gift to fund its most ardent aspirations.

In 2019 another significant academic change occurred when Nowell Donovan retired at the end of the spring semester, and Dr. Teresa Abi-Nader Dahlberg took over as Provost. After fifteen years as TCU's chief academic officer, Nowell Donovan had established a substantial legacy. Throughout VIA he had been a central participant, and he had been one of the chief architects behind one of its principal tenets, the TCU Promise, and one of its major platforms, the Academy for Tomorrow. While his contributions are evident throughout campus, from Froghenge to Rees-Jones, his shaping of academic policies is less visible but deeply felt. Typical of his collaborative spirit, two of his final gestures had been to urge the TCU Faculty Senate to formally define, and thus perpetuate, both shared governance and the teacher-scholar model. Before retiring, Provost Donovan took on the extensive task of reorganizing TCU's academic structure.

In its synthesis of academic recommendations, the 2004 Kaludis report had noted that there was strong campus interest in actively facilitating "interdisciplinary and multidisciplinary program development" as a means of strengthening TCU's academic profile and its disciplinary connections across campus. Not long after, VIA's Cardinal Principle 2, which was a call to foster "a vibrant learning community," specifically listed "interdisciplinary centers and institutes" as one of its strategic action steps (Vision in Action: Defining the Next Decade and Beyond, VIA Brochure). Once the Strategic Initiative Fund was announced, several interdisciplinary centers were proposed and supported, resulting in the creation of the Center for Texas Studies, the Center for Urban Studies, the Center for Digital Expression, and the Energy Institute. TCU already had, however, a campus culture of promoting interdepartmental collaborations. The Karen Purvis Institute for Child Development, Women and Gender Studies, and Latinx Studies had already been established on campus, and as innovative and boundary-breaking programs they offered students greater depth and coverage by linking related courses across the curriculum and by supporting related campus events and community outreach.

Launched in 2018, the School for Interdisciplinary Studies was originally established to further strengthen connections and collaborations. Intended to promote "diverse perspectives, disciplines, and methods of inquiry," SIS was created as the academic home for several interdisciplinary programs that focused on the experiences of marginalized groups. In addition to Women and Gender and Latinx studies, it housed African American and Africana Studies and a recently developed innovative program, Critical Race and Ethnic Studies, or CRES as it came to be called. Initiated to promote intercultural competency, CRES brought interested students and faculty together from across campus and, by connecting several fields of disciplinary inquiry, generated synergy and impact in overlooked, undervalued racial and ethnic areas. While it began as an area of emphasis, by 2018 CRES had become an academic program offering a major and minor.

The School for Interdisciplinary Studies had been established to add weight and value through consolidation, but in 2022, after four years, Provost Dahlberg announced that, "to strengthen Texas Christian University's academic excellence, scholarship and student support for disciplines," SIS's various programs would "benefit from the foundational support . . . [of] long-standing, well-established colleges." Women and Gender Studies, Comparative Race and Ethnic Studies, African American and Africana Studies, and Latinx Studies were relocated to the AddRan College of Liberal Arts, while other interdisciplinary programs were distributed elsewhere on campus, with the University Life program going to the College of Science and Engineering, the Idea Factory to the Neeley School of Business, and Interdisciplinary Inquiry to the College of Education. These moves were announced as a means of strengthening "Texas Christian University's academic excellence, scholarship, and student support for disciplines central to our mission *to educate individuals to think and act as ethical leaders and responsible citizens in a global community* (Provost Teresa Dalberg, Email, July 27, 2022).

Much of the motivation for nurturing diverse perspectives, however, had developed earlier in 2016, when a series of events took place on campus and around the country. After the presidential election and the silent protests of NFL players taking a knee during the national anthem, discussions concerning issues of racial injustice had increasingly become pervasive on a national level, and both students and faculty on campus similarly began to question what TCU was doing to promote diversity, equity, and inclusiveness. Chancellor Boschini became personally involved when three African American students sent him a letter during the fall semester requesting quick action on racial issues. His response was immediate and vigorous. After meeting with the students, he sent out a campus-wide email announcing several actions and recommendations. These included a new "Cabinet-level position to lead our efforts regarding diversity and inclusion," training for all students, faculty, and staff "so that they may better partner with us to effect culture change," active recruitment of a more diverse campus community, development of greater diversity in disciplinary curricula, and establishment of a Bias Response Team (Email, October 18, 2016).

About the same time, Chancellor Boschini also received a copy of a resignation letter written by an African American faculty member, citing several instances of bias and neglect he had encountered on campus. The chancellor's response was again immediate and forceful. He met with the former professor's chair, Karen Steele, and—calling on the Disciples tradition of inclusiveness—proposed appointing a new standing university committee, the Diversity, Equity, and Inclusion Committee. Organized in Fall 2016 and formally launched in January 2017, the DEI Committee soon became a transformative force on campus. Chaired by Karen Steele and Aisha Torrey-Sawyer, then Director of the Neeley Academic Advising Center, the committee's agenda was to review what was being done—and not being done—in terms of TCU's campus culture, and then make recommendations for promoting greater diversity, equity, and inclusion. Although first appointed as an ad hoc committee, DEI's importance was soon acknowledged when the TCU Faculty Senate approved it as a permanent university standing committee.

After spending its first year reviewing TCU's campus culture, the DEI Committee presented a list of recommendations to Chancellor Boschini, nearly all of which were immediately approved:

Recently, three students shared with me their concerns about the culture of our community, specifically the culture surrounding the issue of race in campus. They presented to me a list of ideas to help address some of the issues they believe black students sometimes face as members of the TCU community.

I'd like to acknowledge these students for bringing their concerns forward. TCU has enjoyed a long-standing commitment to shared governance, and students have an important voice in discussions involving their quality of life on campus. At the core of our university is our mission to educate individuals to think and act as ethical leaders and responsible citizens in a global community. If we are to live out this mission, then our University must create space for its members to express their apprehensions, along with their ideas for positive change. I appreciate the effort it must have taken for these students to act on their concerns.

Victor Boschini, Email, October 18, 2016

Some things haven't changed. There is still definitely a feeling of family, community, and student-centeredness.

Barbara Herman, Interview, December 2013

TCU is just a great university. I'm really excited to see it continue to grow and move forward, and it is because of the people who work in the physical plant on up through the administration. There's such a sense of family here and such a sense of camaraderie and wanting to see this university succeed.

Tracy Syler-Jones, Interview, December 2014

We don't want to lose that sense of family that we have right now and that perfect idea of "we're not too big, we're not too small." We can still love what we do and enjoy coming to work and enjoying the people we work with. I think that's one of the university's challenges for the present time.

Scott Sullivan, Interview, March 2014

- Establishment of Faculty Diversity Advocates in each College/School
- Establishment of the Chancellor's Postdoctoral Fellowship Program
- Launch of an annual Diversity, Equity, and Inclusion Award
- Increase number of incoming Community Scholars
- Establishment of STEM Scholar Program
- The hiring of Director of Diversity and Inclusion Initiatives
- Establishment of a commemorative plaque to acknowledge and pay respect to Wichita and Affiliated Tribes upon whose historical lands TCU is located
- University membership in National Center for Faculty Development and Diversity Faculty Success Program

Shortly after meeting with the chancellor, the DEI Committee presented its work and recommendations at an open campus meeting attended by over 250 people.

The DEI Committee's impact on campus has been extensive, particularly in creating connections, initiating dialogues, and increasing awareness of crucial campus issues. It brought speakers and consultants to TCU, held dozens of trainings on campus, organized a university-wide structure for promoting inclusive-excellence programs, and effected substantive change on campus through scholarship and recruitment support. Each college and school on campus developed and implemented a DEI plan with specific goals and appointed College Diversity Advocates to help achieve those goals. Yet perhaps DEI's most significant achievement has been to promote diversity, equity, and inclusion as an "Esssential Competency" in the core curriculum, giving it the same weight as "Mathematical Reasoning, Oral Communication, and Writing Communication." The Faculty Senate, which supervises the Core, unanimously endorsed the proposal, and once the final details of funding and staffing are worked out, all TCU students will be required to take at least three hours of a DEI-vetted course. Once fully launched in the Core, DEI outcomes will become a central part of TCU's commitment to realizing its mission of educating students as ethical leaders and responsible citizens in the global community.

TCU's all-inclusive commitment to students was clearly enunciated after an April 2022 Board retreat that reaffirmed Vision in Action: Lead On's four primary outcomes of strengthening TCU's academic profile, endowment, campus culture, and workforce. Concerning students and high levels of postpandemic anxiety on campus, the trustees "directed the administration" to bolster TCU's campus culture by promoting a "Comprehensive Collaborative Care Model," a holistic program specifically focused "on student well-being" (April 2022 Outcomes).

Yet the Clark Brothers had always been focused on student well-being. After the devastations of the Civil War, helping students develop into capable, responsible citizens to rebuild Texas had been their primary motivation. Back in Thorp Spring, TCU had literally started as a family affair, and for much of its early history the Clark families and their close associates had continually expressed a concern for students that extended well beyond classrooms. In their desire to promote responsible citizenship, they had continually been concerned with both curricular and cocurricular areas of student experience. The AddRan Male and Female College had been set up as an extended family.

Since those early days in Thorp Spring, TCU has continually demonstrated a deep commitment to student well-being. Yet what is remarkably different one hundred and fifty years later is the extensive organizational structure that solely concentrates on student welfare. Student Affairs evolved from a set of student conduct policies and a couple of housing offices in the 1970s into a comprehensive system of programs and services that "support student success and enhance the collegiate experience" (TCU Student Affairs website). Starting in the 1980s, Student Affairs increased its responsibilities by developing a variety of cocurricular activities intended to help students engage with their campus community and enrich their campus experiences.

Connecting cocurricular activities with curricular learning had always been deeply embedded in TCU's culture. From the beginning, faculty engaged with students outside the classroom as well as within. Addison Clark enjoyed taking students on long walks around the Thorp Spring countryside. When he revised the philosophy statement in 1983, Chancellor Tucker carefully used the phrase "curricular and extra-curricular activities" when citing TCU's "Particular Goals," and he clearly announced an important aim was "to support extra-curricular as well as curricular opportunities" for students. While the wording has slightly changed—extra-curricular becoming co-curricular and then cocurricular—Chancellor Tucker's words not only remain in the *Faculty/Staff Handbook* but also central to TCU's core mission.

More recently, during VIA's early discussions, the Undergraduate Experience strategy group identified both "Interaction" and "Curricular/Co-Curricular" as two of the essential dimensions of the TCU student experience. When listing the ideal characteristics for each area, the Undergraduate Experience report identified two areas: "Close interaction between students, faculty, and staff in order to foster an academically stimulating learning environment" and "A total, seamless learning experience in curricular and co-curricular settings"—as epitomizing student experiences on campus ("The Undergraduate Experience Strategic Group Report," VIA Archive website).

When speaking about the relations between curricular and cocurricular, TCU's first female vice chancellor, Margaret (Peggy) Barr, stated that concern for student welfare crossed organizational boundaries: "TCU is not a place where you

ABOVE
Margaret (Peggy) Barr. Courtesy of Mary Couts Burnett Library.

have fiefdoms where people do not cross lines and barriers. The academic deans understood that the out-of-class life of students was as important as their academic work in terms of their growth and development." In recalling her decades of experience helping to develop several of TCU's signature cocurricular programs, former Associate Vice Chancellor for Student Affairs and Dean of Student Development Dr. Barbara Herman similarly stated that TCU offered "an integrated education, a holistic education, linking Student Affairs to academic affairs and making sure that students understood the interrelations between what they do out of class and what they do in class, and between the here and now and their future." When reflecting further on these vital associations, she added: "Sometimes people get hung up on what department they are in, or what program or division. I think we are all educators regardless of our role or title at the university. We should all be about educating future citizens" (Interview, December 2013).

Student Affairs, however, had not always had the capacity to respond quickly to student needs. When former Vice Chancellor for Student Affairs Peggy Barr first arrived on campus in 1985, she was expected "to make things work better for students," but one of her first tasks had been making things better for staff working in student support areas. When starting out, she recalled having to "bring together a diverse group of people who had not worked together in what now is recognized as a traditional division of student affairs." Back in the mid-1980s, "it was more isolated departments that all reported to the same person" than a cohesive team (Interview, November 2012). Vice Chancellor for Student Affairs Emeritus Don Mills, who worked with both former Dean of Students Libby Proffer and Peggy Barr in various roles, stated that when he started working as a program adviser in Student Activities, he "had no clue what Student Affairs was," adding that "in those days the total Student Affairs staff including hall directors—although they were house mothers back then—was only thirty-two or thirty-three people" (Interview, April 2012).

In the 1970s, Student Affairs had primarily promoted responsible citizenship by enforcing conduct policies. When recalling TCU's extremely "conservative lifestyle on campus," Don Mills commented that the year he started "was the first year women could wear pants on campus." Curfews and visitation were huge issues. "Women had to be in their residence halls at ten o'clock at night," he recalled. "There was no co-ed housing," and "boys were not allowed to visit in the women's residence halls except in the lobbies" (Interview, April 2012).

Student Affairs grew by focusing on what would "make residence hall life more significant for students" and thus keep them from "moving off campus as quickly as possible." Curfews and visitation policies gradually gave way, though the first step in the latter was to allow male students to visit females in their rooms—but only on Sunday afternoons with the doors open. As new policies were developed, Student Affairs widened its focus to enhancing student life by implementing programs designed to "engage with students" in multiple areas. Adding front line personnel was essential in its development. There were not enough staff, and responsibilities were often massed together. In the 1980s, when he became Associate Dean of Student Affairs, Don Mills stated that his extended responsibilities included "housing, the student center, orientation, student activities, fraternities and sororities, and recreation" (Interview, April 2012).

Thanks to the dedication of people committed to improving student life, Student Affairs kept pace not only with campus growth but

TCU is not a place where you have fiefdoms.

Margaret (Peggy) Barr

I had no clue what Student Affairs was.

Don Mills, Interview, April 2012

There was no co-ed housing . . . boys were not allowed to visit in the women's residence halls except in the lobbies.

Don Mills, Interview, April 2012

I think in general we are a community, how we continue to be . . . a family-like community . . . If I have a problem, I know from experience which office and which person I need to contact in order to resolve something, and I am always sure that I can get good service. It's a personal relationship.

Magnus Rittby, Interview, March 2018

What I tell parents at Orientation is the priceless part of a TCU education is the cocurricular and curricular union . . . we do that integration well.

Kay Higgins, Interview, October 2013

also with national developments in the emerging field of student services. Not long after she arrived as a Brite divinity student in 1977, Kay Higgins started working part time as the apartment manager for Graduate Housing but quickly moved into a full-time position and ultimately spent seventeen years in Housing. By the late 1980s she "took up Orientation," and for sixteen years served as the Director of New Student Orientation, working closely with students and their families. In the early 1990s, not long after Don Mills became Vice Chancellor for Student Affairs and created Student Development Services, she added another role as the first director of the Women's Resource Center. In reflecting back on her four decades of service, she stated:

> When I came to TCU, the whole field of Student Affairs . . . had really only begun. . . . There were no national norms for what should happen in college . . . and when I started hiring and training staff, nobody opened a file drawer and said, here are all the files and creative ideas for programming . . . it was life from scratch in so many ways. (Interview, October 2013)

When asked about Student Affairs programming, she stressed the importance of a holistic campus:

> If you want to go to a classroom and have information poured in so that you can regurgitate it . . . there's schools that do that. But if you want a quality academic experience, you can get it here . . . what I tell parents at orientation is the priceless part of a TCU education is the cocurricular and curricular union . . . we do that integration well. (Interview, October 2013)

Equally committed to building student-centered programs, Barbara Herman worked over three decades in Student Affairs, dedicating much of her time to "creating community at TCU." Her work included several of TCU's most significant community-building programs. Frog Camp was created to help students build a network of connections before they arrived on campus and the semester got underway. While describing Frog Camp's origins, she stated: "One of the reasons I wanted to start Frog Camp was to have students bond to each other and to TCU before classes started." Commenting further on its origins, she added: "I was concerned that, when students came to campus, the first thing they did was go through recruitment . . . and then there was a divide between Greek and non-Greek students, and that divide was reflected in many ways." Frog Camp, she concluded, "has made a difference at TCU": "Our first Frog Camp had 101 campers, and we now have over 1,800 . . . when we started Frog Camp, the first to second year retention was maybe 78 percent, and now it's almost twenty points higher" (Interview, December 2013).

ABOVE
Barbara Herman. Courtesy of Texas Christian University

> There's an excitement and a bonding that happens at Frog Camp that has been very helpful.
>
> **Barbara Herman, Interview, December 2013**

> When I got here, it was . . . like being on the front burner for construction.
>
> **Kathy Cavins-Tull, Interview, March 2015**

In addition to Frog Camp, Barbara Herman also helped to launch several other successful programs, including the Model UN Program, Connections, LEAPs, Common Reading, House Calls, Chancellor Ferrari's Council on Diversity, Leadership for Life, the TCU Challenge Course, Allies, Community Scholars, and the Wassenich Mentoring Award. While a couple of these initiatives have come and gone, all of them were started to help Student Affairs build bridges and create community.

When she arrived on campus in 2011, Vice Chancellor for Student Affairs Kathy Cavins-Tull became immediately—and literally—involved in building campus. Plans for rebuilding the Greek Village and adding new residence halls for first- and second-year students in the Worth Hills area were already underway when she arrived, and for a half-dozen years or so she helped manage the construction of more than two dozen buildings. She quickly learned—as she later commented—what it was like to be "on the front burner for construction" (Interview, March 2015).

Yet her primary charge was to help students build their lives. In commenting on her areas of interest, Kathy Cavins-Tull stated: "I'm a Student Affairs person. That's what I love and what I'm passionate about." When asked about her leadership style, she offered further insight into her passionate commitment to students:

> I don't pull any punches, and I wouldn't ask anyone to do something that I would not do. I like to be where the students are, and I expect that of my own staff. I want us to be close to our students, and that means you can't clock in at eight and out at five. There's stuff that happens here all the time, and we have to be available to students. I like to get in the weeds and roll up my sleeves. (Interview, March 2015)

While overseeing all areas of student life outside the classroom and a staff of over 250 people, Kathy Cavins-Tull responds quickly to all urgent situations dealing with students, which sometimes sadly includes serious health issues, accidents, and deaths. She takes "hard phone calls from parents who are upset," and she also visits students in "the hospital when they're hurting and their parents are six states away." Her great concern for students is evident in areas of mental health and well-being that she has particularly promoted, such as suicide awareness and prevention and also alcohol and substance abuse intervention. Two programs that she advocated soon after her arrival were Question, Persuade, Refer, a suicide awareness program, and R U OK, a depression awareness program.

Police round up 16 TCU students in drug-dealing arrests; one at large
Skiff headline, February 15, 2012

Today's events have forever changed the lives of the involved students, and we hope they will find a healthy way to move forward. Also, the next couple of weeks will be tough for the TCU family. There is no doubt that it will hurt to see our name associated with this type of behavior. But we must not allow this moment to define us. We must remember that we are overwhelmingly a community of dedicated students, faculty, and staff and focused on changing the world through our collective work and commitment to leadership. (Victor Boschini, Skiff, *February 15, 2012)*

In describing her need to react quickly, she stated: "Students are risk-takers, and, like risk-taking behavior, sometimes you add impulsive behavior. Under the influence of something, you can get into a lot of difficulty . . . I'm very concerned about sexual assault and . . . student mental health" (Interview, March 2015). One of the first difficulties occurred in 2012 when TCU made national headlines for a campus drug bust involving sixteen students for possession and distribution. Chancellor Boschini, Vice Chancellor for Student Affairs Cavins-Tull, and other administrators reacted immediately. In his press release, the Chancellor declared:

> While this news is certainly shocking and disappointing, it is important to remember that TCU has clear expectations for its students: that they behave in an ethical manner, abide by campus policies, and adhere to state and federal law. These students are charged with acting in a manner that is incompatible with TCU values and against the law. That is simply unacceptable, and such reported behavior is not tolerated at this university. We have a responsibility to ensure our campus environment is free of such behavior. (*TCU Magazine*, Spring 2012)

In reflecting on the drug bust, Kathy Cavins-Tull stated:

> We took a hard stand and said, "These students are not going to be associated with our campus." In further explaining the immediate dismissal of the students involved. We knew from the police . . . that TCU was a hotspot because we had all these students that had a lot of disposable income and were a huge market, and we didn't want that. We had to protect our school. . . . The arrest of sixteen students was unfortunate for us, but . . . it's my responsibility to protect our student body. (Interview, March 2015)

The university's immediate and forceful response was impressive, and soon after the arrests and national headlines, the TCU Faculty Senate passed a resolution commending the administration's swift and transparent actions:

> The Faculty Senate commends Chancellor Victor Boschini, Provost Nowell Donovan, Vice Chancellor Kathy Cavins-Tull, Vice Chancellor Tracy Syler-Jones, TCU Chief of Police Steve McGee, Athletic Director Chris Del Conte, and Football Coach Gary Patterson for their forthright, transparent, and timely response to the arrests made this February. They brought respect to TCU during a difficult time; they demonstrated their deep commitment to the mission of the university; and they strengthened the national regard for our institutional integrity. The obvious concern for the well-being of all students allowed TCU to garner approval across the region, state, and nation for their efforts handling this unfortunate situation. The Faculty Senate appreciates their efforts.

TCU student leaders were also quick to respond. During

the spring the Student Government Association and Intercom, a group of student organization leaders, held meetings to discuss how they could respond, and their discussions resulted in a student creed: "As students we commit to excellence by serving with respect, learning with passion, and leading with integrity" (*TCU Magazine*, Fall 2014). Once passed by the SGA, the creed was introduced to first-year students at Frog Camps and at the Chancellor's Assembly.

Without a doubt, responding to the COVID-19 pandemic has been the most difficult challenge TCU has faced in decades. Yet in recent history Chancellor Boschini, the cabinet, and the trustees responded to numerous issues that required considerable tact, dialogue, and foresight. One of the problematic issues has always been negotiating the cost of a TCU education during times of inflation and recession. As TCU grew, so too did its expenses.

During the early 2000s, not long after VIA was underway, the Board of Trustees agreed to administrative recommendations to raise tuition rates annually, and both students and parents complained. Previously, to make the university affordable for most students, Chancellor Tucker had intentionally kept tuition low to make sure that middle-income families could afford TCU. By the end of the twentieth century, however, the university was underpriced compared to its peer and aspirant universities. While a great bargain in higher education, TCU's tuition could not keep pace with rising costs, particularly in such areas as health insurance, health care, and energy. Prior to 2002, tuition costs were priced by the number credit hours with a base rate of $420 per hour; thus a twelve-hour load was $10,089. In 2003 TCU adopted a packaged tuition plan, and the total for tuition rose to $15,740 for the academic year, which was still quite low compared to most other private schools.

To offset expense increases, TCU has continuously raised tuition, if only by modest amounts, nearly every year over the past half century. But beginning in 2004 the Board of Trustees approved higher tuition increases to bring TCU more in line with its peer and aspirant schools, and for the next several years these increases averaged around 8 percent. After four years, students and their parents saw tuition go up by around 30 percent, and such annual increases were not well received and resulted in several front-page headlines in the *Skiff*. Many in the campus community were worried that tuition costs would become a barrier for students wanting to attend TCU. In a front-page *Skiff* article on rising tuition rates, former SGA President Jace Thompson stated: "I am concerned TCU will outprice prospective students in future years" (*Skiff*, November 13, 2007).

As an inclusive institution, TCU acted quickly to mitigate financial barriers by matching tuition hikes with sizeable increases in financial aid. During the 2000s, increasing financial aid became a significant goal in The Campaign for TCU, which ultimately raised over a million dollars for scholarships. In commenting on TCU's increases in tuition

"As students, we commit to excellence by serving with respect, learning with passion, and leading with integrity."

TCU Student Creed

I am concerned TCU will outprice prospective students in future years.

Jace Thompson, Student Government Association President, *Skiff*, March 11, 2007

My commitment is, if any student feels like they can't afford the extra amount, to come into financial aid, and we'll reassess your financial packet, and if you have needs we'll definitely make sure you come back next semester.

Chancellor Victor Boschini, *Skiff*, March 11, 2007

A firestorm of angst and objection.

TCU Faculty Senate Minutes, March 2013

The TCU Faculty Senate commends Chancellor Boschini for his exemplary leadership and expresses its profound gratitude and esteem.

A Resolution Honoring Chancellor Victor J. Boschini, Jr.

and financial aid, Chancellor Boschini emphasized that TCU was committed to helping families concerned about tuition increases: "My commitment is, if any student feels like they can't afford the extra amount, to come into financial aid, and we'll reassess your financial packet, and if you have needs we'll definitely make sure you come back next semester" (*Skiff,* November 13, 2007).

Prepared in 2007, the 2008 budget had called for a tuition increase of 8.4 percent. But no one preparing that budget knew what would happen in 2008. Despite numerous warning signs, no one on campus, nor around the world, anticipated the severe economic distress on the horizon. The financial crisis of 2008 began when the United States housing bubble burst after years of excessive risk-taking, and securities tied to real estate collapsed in value. Many homeowners found themselves owing more on their mortgages than their homes were worth, and many lost their homes, their savings, and in some cases their jobs. The economic chaos spread worldwide, and the Great Recession, as it came to be known, was the most serious financial crisis since the Great Depression. Within the year, banks and investment firms collapsed around the globe, including Lehman Brothers in September 2008, and governments were forced to make massive bailouts to financial institutions burdened with toxic assets and bad loans. Stock and commodity prices plunged in value, and both investor confidence and public support for federal financial policies declined (The 2007-2008 Financial Crisis in Review, Investopedia).

TCU's response to the Great Recession was quick and proactive. Previous to the sudden downturns, scholarships had been increased by 8.4 percent to match the tuition increase, but in 2009 TCU "financial aid was increased by 18 percent." When asked about the university's response to the financial crisis, former Vice Chancellor for Financial Affairs Brian Gutierrez commented: "That commitment to financial aid represents approximately 21 percent of the university budget. Our desire is to make sure we have sufficient financial aid for our students." More importantly, TCU's endowment remained strong compared to most other universities around the country, thanks to a stable regional economy and the foresight of TCU's investment team led by Jim Hille. When asked about TCU's financial situation, he stated: "Last summer, before the economic downturn, the endowment was earning a 5.1 percent return, which was rated No. 1 in performance among similar-sized universities . . . We were one of the best-performing endowments last year . . . so we had a good deal of momentum before the downturn" (*TCU Magazine*, Spring 2009).

Yet TCU still had to immediately reduce its expenses, as the endowment inevitably dropped in value as stocks plunged. When asked if TCU would "have to cut back on its planned growth," and thus stall its upward momentum, Chancellor Boschini responded: "We have to reduce travel, goods, and service expenses by 8 percent to make the budget work. And we will also need to conserve our use of energy, go paperless wherever possible, and reduce expenses every other way we can. All of this will result in no reduction of faculty and staff." In addition to austerity measures, as well as a 5 percent tuition increase, the Board of Trustees took decisive action when it approved a higher payout from the endowment, effectively allowing TCU to borrow against itself to cover its budget and maintain its momentum and morale rather than resort to layoffs and program cancellations. While explaining the board's decision, Chancellor Boschini stated: "For the foreseeable future the trustees approved raising the effective payout rate of the endowment modestly in order to assist us in dealing with increasing expenses. The well-being of our students, faculty, and staff in this uncertain economic climate comes first" (*TCU Magazine,* Spring 2009).

The Board's decision to free up more endowment money eased the financial burden on TCU faculty and staff and helped TCU move past the immediate setbacks of the Great Recession, but economic uncertainly continued. At the first Faculty Senate meeting in 2012, Chancellor Boschini stated that TCU's budget was "rich in benefits," which—he added—were "quite high compared to many other universities." Citing the millions the university spent on benefits such as the tuition remission program and the retirement contribution, and citing the need to be "prudent . . . stewards of TCU resources," he encouraged those present at the meeting to examine the TCU benefits package "before there's a crisis" (Faculty Senate Minutes, September 6, 2012).

A few months later, in March, there was something of a crisis, which—according to the Faculty Senate minutes—resulted in "a firestorm of angst and objection, based on the perception that benefits were about to be changed for the worse" (Faculty Senate Minutes, March 2013). Still interested in having faculty review their benefits package, Chancellor Boschini had requested that the Faculty Senate and the Staff Assembly send out surveys to all fulltime employees, asking them to rank which of the benefits they most preferred. The survey was not well received. Many across campus refused to fill it out and asked why, if "the university is currently in the best financial position it has ever been in," a discussion on benefits was even needed (*TCU 360*, March 22, 2013).

In response to the unease across campus, Chancellor Boschini assured members of both Faculty Senate and Staff Assembly that he was only interested in starting a conversation and that no actions to reduce faculty/staff benefits were planned. Yet one change had already occurred. While reassuring faculty and staff, the chancellor mentioned "that the only real change in faculty benefits is that retirees can now pick their own health plan" (*TCU 360*, March 22, 2013). This change, however, heightened the angst not only among the retirees but also among faculty and staff. Up to this point, retirees had been able to continue participating in the TCU medical insurance program, which greatly increased the university's liability and limited its borrowing capacity. To reduce TCU's liability, which was projected to reach $100 million in a few years, retirees received a monthly stipend of $202 to cover the cost of their own individual plans. While some retirees welcomed the change, others felt insecure about leaving TCU's coverage. Faculty and staff maintained that there had been no prior notice or discussion before the change was announced. On a deeper level, their anxiety resulted from concern that further cuts lay ahead.

On March 28, 2013, a campus-wide town hall was held, nearly filling the BLUU Auditorium, and the Chancellor stressed that "improvements need to be made to save money because the university cannot keep increasing tuition every year." He stated that "the Board of Trustees is looking at benefits because they are $60 to $80 million of the $512 million budget." Many of those in attendance were not mollified, especially those who remained anxious about the decision to remove the retirees from the university's health care plan. Although TCU was supplementing their independent health care coverage, many retirees remained resentful of the change, while others were worried that the retiree supplement was "a fixed monthly contribution . . . that is not expected to increase in the future," although medical costs inevitably would continue to rise ("Report of the Faculty Senate Task Force on the TCU Promise" 1).

In a chorus of voices over the next months, many faculty and staff members argued that no changes to benefits should occur without prior discussion among those involved. To this end, the Faculty Senate unanimously passed a resolution declaring "that any reductions to faculty compensation, including benefits, be discussed in the Faculty Senate before any steps toward implementation are taken." The resolution further stated that the Faculty Senate be allowed to formally vote on any increases and that "designated representatives of the TCU Faculty Senate take part in cabinet-level budget discussions when changes to compensation are being discussed" ("Faculty Senate Resolution on TCU Employee Benefits"). To demonstrate a vigorous, unified response, both the Staff Assembly and the Retirees Association passed nearly identical resolutions.

Despite anxious discussions of benefits, faculty and staff generally remained happy with their work and content with TCU and the administration. At the same time the benefits resolution was passed, the Faculty Senate also approved a resolution thanking Chancellor Boschini for ten years of leadership and service at TCU. While citing many of TCU's achievements and initiatives, such as VIA, the rise in rankings, increases in applications, retention, and financial aid, and the many new and newly renovated buildings, the resolution concluded "The TCU Faculty Senate commends Chancellor Boschini for his exemplary leadership and expresses its profound gratitude and esteem" (A Resolution Honoring Chancellor Victor J. Boschini Jr.).

Resolution on TCU Employee Benefits

The TCU Faculty Senate
May 2013

Whereas the TCU Faculty Senate recognizes the need of the Board of Trustees and senior administrators to practice fiscal responsibility, and that prudent oversight of such responsibility ensures the longevity, competitiveness, and well-being of the institution, and

Whereas the TCU Faculty Senate believes that robust benefits are a vital part of employee compensation and thus crucial in attracting top faculty and staff, fostering long-term employee commitment to the institution, and promoting its national and international reputation, and
Whereas the TCU Faculty Senate further believes that robust benefits are crucial in sustaining institutional momentum, maintaining faculty and staff morale, and preserving the Teacher-Scholar model that distinguishes TCU's excellence, and

Whereas the TCU Faculty Senate is proud to contribute to TCU's momentum, distinction, and excellence, and is fully committed to protecting the overall health of the university,

Therefore, be it resolved, that the TCU Faculty Senate recommends that employee compensation, including benefits, either be maintained at current levels, or increased when appropriate;

Be it also resolved, that reductions to employee compensation, including benefits, should only be considered in the event of a severe budget crisis that clearly threatens TCU's institutional health and well- being; that, if such financial exigency occurs, employee compensation should only be considered for reduction as part of a larger campus-wide effort to reduce costs; and that, if such budget cutbacks become necessary, all employees be grandfathered in at their current levels;

Finally, be it further resolved, that any reductions to faculty compensation, including benefits, be discussed in the Faculty Senate before any steps toward implementation are taken; that, as a means of declaring its position, the Faculty Senate take a formal vote on such reductions; and that designated representatives of the TCU Faculty Senate take part in Cabinet-level budget discussions when changes in employee compensation are discussed.

Resolution Honoring Chancellor Victor J. Boschini Jr.

The TCU Faculty Senate
May 2013

Whereas, Dr. Victor J. Boschini, Jr. has provided exemplary leadership and service as Texas Christian University's Chancellor since 2003;

Whereas, he has encouraged new strategic initiatives that have raised TCU's reputation while positively impacting the community, nation, and world, such as Vision in Action and Vision in Action: The Academy of Tomorrow;

Whereas, under his leadership the student-faculty ratio has improved to 13:1; the freshman-to-sophomore retention rate has reached 90 percent; undergraduate financial aid has doubled; and applications for admission have soared to more than 19,000;

Whereas, under his leadership TCU has been consistently listed among the nation's top 100 universities, its schools, colleges, and programs highly ranked; and its reputation enhanced with the recognition it has received for its promising and innovative changes in the areas of academics and campus life;

Whereas, under his leadership a dozen chairs and professorships have been created, so that now 11 percent of the faculty hold endowed positions;

Whereas, under his leadership the physical campus has been transformed by continual improvements; TCU's facility space has increased by 24 percent; $573 million has been invested in 25 new facilities and renovation projects, including Scharbauer, Palko, Reed and Lowe halls; and classrooms and laboratories have been universally upgraded;

Therefore, be it resolved, that the TCU Faculty Senate commends Chancellor Boschini for his exemplary leadership and expresses its profound gratitude and esteem;

Be it further resolved, that this resolution be made a part of the official minutes of the TCU Faculty Senate and that a copy be presented to him.

Given the lingering unease over benefits, the Faculty Senate Executive Committee appointed an ad hoc task force to review TCU's financial outlook and its health care package, with a special focus on the decision to remove the retirees from university coverage. Publicly distributed in February 2015, the "Report of the Faculty Senate Task Force on the TCU Promise" acknowledged that the change to retiree benefits was made to reduce the university's financial liability, which by the end of the 2012 fiscal year "had grown to $78 million and was projected to reach $100 million within a few years," thereby weakening TCU's financial position (Report of the Faculty Senate Task Force on the TCU Promise 1). The report further acknowledged that "rising medical costs create a serious economic burden" and that "the Administration's decision to reduce retiree medical benefits was a good-faith effort to deal with this issue." Yet the report concluded that the decision "was made without adequate consideration of its consequences" and "was made with no significant consultation with faculty, staff, or retirees" (Report of the Faculty Senate Task Force on the TCU Promise 3).

ABOVE
The campus is virtually empty after classes are moved online to protect the community from the spread of COVID-19, March 23, 2020. Courtesy of TCU Marketing and Communication. Photograph by Amy Peterson.

In response to the campus disquiet, and to demonstrate its commitment to support those working and retired, Human Resources developed and adopted several programs to support retirees, and created a new position, a Retiree Program Manager, to help retirees with all questions and issues. Additionally, a new cabinet-level position was created, the Vice Chancellor for Human Resources, which was filled by Karen Baker.

Concern for TCU's financial outlook and benefits continued, and in October 2019 the Chancellor held another town hall where he declared that TCU's current benefits package was "too rich to be sustainable" and stated that the Board of Trustees had "asked him to prepare a package of options for them to consider instead." According to the chancellor, "compensation and benefits must be addressed because they account for more than 60 percent of the university's operating budget." TCU's healthcare costs were steadily rising, and such increases appeared inescapable, having "increased by 145 percent" since 2010. In addition to healthcare, Chancellor Boschini asked that all benefits be carefully examined, including TCU's retirement, tuition, and reimbursement plans. Citing a possible drop in future enrollments and the Board's plan to keep tuition increases at four percent, he added that many universities, such as Baylor, SMU, Vanderbilt, and Tulane, "have already restructured their benefits packages" (*TCU 360*, October 24, 2019).

Response from faculty and staff was predictably unenthusiastic. Many complained that benefit reductions would harm recruitment, while others expressed their fear that ultimately such reductions would lower—rather than raise—TCU's academic profile. When members of the University Compensation Advisory Committee were specifically charged to make recommendations on benefits, several of its members, including Professor Andrew Ledbetter in the College of Communication, challenged the assertion that current benefits levels were "too rich to be sustainable." After reviewing TCU's 990 tax forms since 2017 and publishing his findings in a report distributed not long after the town hall meeting, he concluded: "It doesn't appear that they are unsustainable" (*TCU 360*, December 12, 2019).

As the Fall 2019 semester ended, disquiet over benefit reductions continued, but a far more ominous threat was on the horizon. COVID-19 was spreading across the world, and nothing could stop its transmission or mitigate its virulence. By the start of the 2020 spring semester, countries across the globe had closed their borders, cities were quarantined, and people were being ordered to isolate. With its arrival on campus inevitable, campus preparations were already underway to respond to the life-threatening medical crisis. In the DFW area, the number of infections and deaths were already being reported as the new semester got underway, and by mid-March TCU had made the difficult decision to close campus.

As soon as the viral contagion's spread became inexorable, TCU took immediate action in dozens of areas, and a central Campus Readiness Committee, chaired by Vice Chancellor for Student Affairs Kathy Cavins-Tull and Vice Chancellor for Human Resources Yohna Chambers, were appointed to coordinate the university's multifaceted responses. With student, faculty, and staff well-being the highest priority, and TCU's most fundamental mission and commitments at stake, campus health protocols had to be quickly developed and disseminated; classes immediately had to transition to online learning; policies and procedures for working remotely had to be devised; a new technological infrastructure had to be constructed for faculty and staff working from home; a constant flow of anxious queries had to be answered; difficult decisions, contingency plans, and cancellations for TCU's athletic programs had to be made; and the entire TCU budget had to be restructured.

No one had ever faced a medical crisis like COVID-19 before, and no one on campus was fully prepared. But the Campus Readiness Committee, and especially Student Affairs, reacted quickly to the numerous pandemic issues that had to be immediately confronted as the news repeatedly related

ABOVE
Kathy Cavins-Tull. Courtesy of Texas Christian University. Photograph by Glen E. Ellman.

stories of the virus's unstoppable spread. As borders began to close and international flights began to shut down, Kathy Cavins-Tull, Sandra Callaghan, Director of TCU Global, and many others on campus confronted a host of issues related to TCU students studying abroad. But the difficult challenges of bringing TCU students back to the US was only the start of a logistical, mental, and physical ordeal that followed when campus was closed. By spring break, March 2020, students were told that their break was being extended and not to return to campus.

This necessary but difficult decision caused endless issues everywhere on campus, and sudden major decisions were required in every area and program. Student Affairs had to quickly respond to student needs. Most students had left for their break taking little with them and leaving everything else behind in their residences. When classes quickly moved online, students who had been living on campus had few, if any, of their course materials, and Student Affairs had to devise a system for them to speak directly with their hall directors on FaceTime and identify what they needed sent to their homes. In describing this initial set of challenges, Kathy Cavins-Tull stated: "When you're talking about almost 5,000 students, that was a humongous undertaking" (Interview, May 2022).

As the spring semester ended, Student Affairs confronted another logistical chaos. Since they were isolating at home, students living in TCU residence halls could not move out of their rooms, nor could new students move in, making it nearly impossible to get ready for the fall semester. Yet the logistical challenges of moving out and moving in were nothing compared to the urgent issues concerning student health when the fall semester started. Kathy Cavins-Tull explained: "We set up really huge protocols in Student Affairs on how to take care of those who were diagnosed positive, how to provide testing and make that available to students, how to quarantine and isolate people—and we had full residence halls at the time." To accommodate crucial student needs, TCU rented space in a hotel and an apartment complex "so that students could use that as isolation space . . . we probably had about 250 isolation spaces" (Interview, May 2022).

While some campuses around the country again shut down in the fall as COVID case numbers quickly rose when students returned, Student Affairs focused on responding to student needs, especially for those diagnosed and those in quarantine. In recalling the sudden increase in TCU cases, Kathy Cavins-Tull commented: "Our number in the fall just spiked right away, and we were getting 100 a day—our highest rate was 105 cases in one day." In addition to the urgent medical needs of students with COVID-19, Student Affairs, the Campus Readiness Committee, and the Emergency Management Office, headed by Sean Taylor, continually had to trace and quarantine anyone who had been in close contact with those diagnosed, and who often had to isolate for a week or more. In summing up TCU's activities managing student pandemic issues, Kathy Cavins-Tull stated, "It really felt like we were running an infirmary" (Interview, May 2022).

Student Affairs looked for ways to help students withstand the strains and tensions of the pandemic, and one of the most helpful responses was actually one of the simplest to effect—creating a safe place where students could gather. Kathy Cavins-Tull and her team created a comfortable outdoor space in the Campus Commons where students could interact with each other in relative safety. In recalling this outdoor initiative, she stated:

> We just needed to give students opportunities to gather because, if we didn't do it, they were doing it at off-campus parties, so we decided to do some low-risk kinds of programming out in the Commons. We put some furniture out there; we had a huge TV out there; and we did some light programming. This was all during the election stuff too, so it was kind of a bizarre time . . . in the spring we added another space in Worth Hills because it was well received in the Commons. (Interview, May 2022)

In summing up her pandemic experiences both in Student Affairs and the Campus Readiness Committee, Kathy Cavins-Tull stated: "I feel like I haven't had a day off in two years" (Interview, May 2022).

Not long into the pandemic the emotional and psychological suffering caused by COVID-19 became unmistakable. People were anxious, and stress levels were high. To respond to student anxiety and depression, Student Affairs set up opportunities for students to have Zoom counseling sessions, and the Counseling and Mental Health Center, directed by Dr. Eric Wood, sponsored several presentations around campus describing the pandemic as a mass trauma and then suggesting ways students, faculty, and staff could reduce their stress levels.

ABOVE
Eric Wood. Courtesy of Texas Christian University. Photograph by Glen E. Ellman.

TCU also saw a significant increase in the number of telehealth calls related to stress and depression. While commenting on her concern for mental health issues among TCU employees, Vice Chancellor for Human Resources Yohna Chambers stated: "In 2019 there were 298 telehealth calls of employees or their covered family members . . . in 2020 there were 5,465 telehealth calls. That is a 1,734% increase in the use of telehealth. In 2020 40% of the calls were mental health related compared to 10 percent in 2019. This demonstrates a 300% increase in mental health related calls from 2019 to 2020." (Interview, May 2022)

Reducing stress was difficult. On campus, relations between faculty and staff and the administration became particularly strained when Chancellor Boschini announced several decisions in response to the pandemic's financial fallout. Like so many other universities around the country, TCU soon made the decision to discount tuition and refund money for online learning. Since TCU's budget is primarily tuition-driven, the chancellor, board, and cabinet had to decide how to make up the huge loss of revenue, and immediate budget reductions became inescapable. During the 2020 spring and summer, temporary budget cuts were made across campus, and no program or area was excluded. To help students and their families during the pandemic, the following year's budget called for a reallocation of recurring funds to raise TCU's average tuition discount from 38 percent to as much as 48 percent. Despite the pandemic's financial burden, TCU reallocated funds to improve diversity on campus, which included recruiting students from underrepresented groups.

Inevitably, the issue that really sparked tensions between faculty and staff on one side and the administration on the other was the chancellor's announcement in April 2020 that TCU's retirement contribution was being immediately

ABOVE
The Campus Commons is transformed with outdoor furniture, lights, and an outdoor television as a place for students to interact safely in-person, bringing a sense of community and energy to the Commons, 2020. Courtesy of TCU Marketing and Communication. Photograph by Eric Sasadeusz.

ABOVE
Rob Rhodes. Courtesy of Neeley School of Business.

ABOVE
Beto Cruz. Courtesy of the Cruz family.

TCU Faculty Discussing Vote of No Confidence of Leadership

***Fort Worth Star-Telegram* headline, June 25, 2020**

Then there was a motion about a vote for no confidence that was seconded. Afterwards, there was a discussion about a vote of no confidence against the Chancellor, Provost, Vice Chancellor for Finance and Administration, Board of Trustees, and Vice Chancellor for Human Resources. Many wanted such a vote to happen while others were asking to exercise caution.

Faculty Senate Minutes, June 2020

I don't think we want to change what we are in our heart, our core, and that is this personalized, connected culture

Provost Teresa Abi-Nader Dahlberg, Interview, May 2022

You do what you've got to do because it's what you are supposed to do. You just do the right thing.

Yohna Chambers, Interview, May 2022

Success was our only option.

Todd Waldvogel, Interview, April 2022

I watched with gratitude as a new normal unfolded for a spirited Horned Frog family that can never truly be separated, even when apart.

Chancellor Victor Boschini, *TCU Magazine*, Winter 2020

ABOVE
Yohna Chambers. Courtesy of Texas Christian University.

reduced from 11.5 percent to 8 percent. Responses were immediate. Some protested that the reduction was a permanent response to a temporary financial situation, citing other universities that reduced employee benefits temporarily until their financial situations improved. Signed by over three hundred TCU employees, an open letter to the board of trustees, the chancellor, and the cabinet requested that the 11.5 percent contribution be restored once the pandemic had passed. Professor Sean Atkinson, Chair of the Faculty Senate, stated that the administration had failed to uphold the principle of shared governance, while Professor Andrew Ledbetter, Chair of the Faculty Relations Committee and UCAC member, distributed a lengthy financial report contending that, with the reduction in the retirement benefit, TCU faculty/staff compensation dropped to near the bottom of its peer and aspirant schools. The low point came when the Faculty Senate discussed holding a vote of no confidence on the administration. Although no vote was taken, the discussion was publicized, resulting in newspaper headlines, and—despite a general acknowledgment that the pandemic had raised stress levels—both sides believed there had been a breach of trust.

There were many low points during the pandemic. Sadly, TCU lost two of its campus community when Robert Rhodes, a faculty member from Neeley, and José (Beto) Alberto Cruz, a Facilities employee, succumbed to COVID. Both were widely esteemed and greatly missed. To commemorate their passing and honor their lives, the TCU Faculty Senate took two actions. Rob Rhodes was posthumously awarded an honorary doctorate, and in Beto Cruz's remembrance, and to acknowledge the contributions of Facilities employees, the Faculty Senate created an annual award to be given to a Facilities employee—The Beto Cruz Award.

One way or another, COVID-19 taxed everyone on campus. Every area, every program, and every person were affected. Yet despite the travail and stress, and despite the risk of infection, TCU had been able to uphold its mission and operations and maintain its extensive commitments to students, faculty, and staff. As an institution committed to high levels of engagement with students, TCU was challenged to find ways to preserve its culture of close interpersonal contact when most students, faculty, and staff were isolating at home. Continuity was a major concern.

When asked to reflect on the pandemic's impact on TCU, Provost Dahlberg expressed her worry that COVID-19's endless separations and interruptions would tear the fabric of TCU's culture of connections. While isolating at home and worrying about their families, faculty and staff inevitably experienced some level of tension between professional and personal lives, which in turn diminished their links with others: "Because of COVID and our inability to do much on campus," Provost Dahlberg stated, "I am worried about us losing what is our key ethos, our connected campus culture. . . . we can do stuff online, but our goal is not to be best online campus. I don't think we want to change what we are in our heart, in our core, and that is this personalized connected culture. That's one of my greatest worries" (Interview May 2022).

Similarly, Kathy Cavins-Tull expressed concern that students, forced to isolate at home, were missing the TCU essential experience of learning in a community:

> I think we learn in community, and that's the best way to learn. I feel like our students are not only learning the knowledge and content for what they're going to go on and do . . . they do that in a community of diversity. Taking that community aspect out of learning, to me, only gives you one hand to clap, and to clap is to be here having those conversations that maybe you didn't expect after class or in the hallway or sitting in your residence hall late at night, where some of those important value questions come to be . . . If they're sitting in their bedrooms at home, tuning into their class, they're sitting in the same place where all of their values have been shaped. Part of going to college is to broaden perspectives and to challenge values. (Interview, May 2022)

When commenting on COVID-19's impact, Vice Chancellor for Human Resources Yohna Chambers stated that Human Resources had two critical areas of concern, campus safety and continuity. "The safety of our campus community was critical to us. It's number one that our students and employees are safe, that we're providing a safe environment for them. And then number two is continuity of operations." As Student Affairs had done with students, Human Resources worked to reassure TCU faculty and staff its services were continuing and that it was "doing everything we could to ensure a safe campus." With everyone on campus anxious, Human Resources increased its efforts to support TCU. When asked about HR's efforts, she described their efforts in terms of resilience:

ABOVE
Todd Waldvogel. Courtesy of Todd Waldvogel.

> We were shooting YouTube videos. We were printing information and pushing information out in English and Spanish. All of that took time. It's so bizarre to reflect now because it's making my shoulders a little tense thinking about it. Because when you're in it, you're just doing it. You just do what you've got to do. It's resilience. It's commitment. You do what you've got to do because it's what you are supposed to do. You just do the right thing. (Interview, May 2022)

Although campus was mostly deserted, Facilities still had to continue caring for its buildings and grounds. In reflecting on how his more than three hundred staff members kept working during the pandemic, Associate Vice Chancellor for Facilities and Campus Planning Todd Waldvogel stated:

> Success was our only option, and then the execution, the work in the teams. The work and the leadership of the teams in the field can't be overstated. They might not have been in boardrooms as we were making decisions, but . . . some of the most important people on campus were our housekeepers who were keeping the spaces that we were using disinfected . . . Our team didn't go home. (Interview, April 2022)

When asked further about the pandemic's impact, he described the difficulties of dealing with both reduced budgets and reduced staff. After the early retirement program for staff was announced, he stated that "we lost about 570 years of service in one day . . . we lost twenty-seven employees in essentially one day, so that's almost 10 percent of my team." Mirroring national issues concerning job vacancies, Facilities had difficulty fillings its open positions. "This was a tough time to go find employees." When asked how Facilities responded to the challenges of reduced budgets and reduced staff, he declared:

> We had to stop doing stuff. We work really hard to be as efficient as we can, but in some cases we stopped doing things. One of our largest curtailments . . . [was that] we changed our housekeeping standards . . . we withdrew some of our daily support within individual offices, and we made that more of a weekly thing . . . we don't go into every single office every single day and pull trash. (Interview, April 2022)

Mentioning that Facilities is responsible for taking care of 5.2 million square feet of space, he added: "It was a great concession because it doesn't affect the student experience. It doesn't affect the mission" (Interview, April 2022).

Some of the most poignant breaks and disruptions occurred when student athletes were no longer able to practice and compete. One of the first such disruptions occurred when the TCU women's basketball team, which had been projected to earn a March Madness appearance, abruptly had their season cancelled. While practicing in Kansas City, Missouri, for the Big XII championship, they learned that the conference tournament had been called off, and then during their flight home they learned that the NCAA had cancelled March Madness, a particularly bitter disappointment for seniors like Kianna Ray, whose outstanding TCU basketball career was suddenly cut short.

Financially, TCU Athletics suffered acutely during the pandemic. Resulting from losses in ticket sales, parking fees, and concession revenue, it was down $30 million, and "80 percent to 90 percent of that loss was directly attributed to football" (Jeremiah Donati, Interview, May 2022). But TCU Athletics Director Donati and the coaches were more worried about TCU's student athletes than budget losses:

> I think the biggest thing that I worried about more than kids getting sick from COVID was the mental health aspect of it. We saw that has ultimately been much, much more challenging than the actual sickness . . . this is not a TCU Athletics issue. This is happening everywhere. The mental health aspect of the pandemic was probably much more damaging to the younger college-level group. (Interview, May 2022)

On looking back at how TCU Athletics responded to the pandemic, Jeremiah Donati stated: "We had decision-making fatigue because we had to rewrite the rules on how you prepared, how you practiced, and how you competed, and you had to do that for every sport, and you had to do it with medical guidance changing by the week . . . it was all these moving targets. Overall, I am really proud of the way we managed" (Interview, May 2022).

While causing massive disruptions, the pandemic paradoxically also brought people together. In his "Chancellor's Message," published in *TCU Magazine's* Winter 2020 issue, Chancellor Boschini declared that, despite COVID "radically altering the way we relate to each other," TCU was strengthened by the way people on and off campus came together:

> What sustained me through the worst of these unprecedented times was the incredible way the TCU community came together. Alumni instantly flooded my inbox with offers of assistance. I witnessed parents—total strangers from different parts of the country—reaching out to help other people's children. Employees organized free meals for essential personnel as the campus prepared for the uncertain days ahead. Our faculty sprang into action to prepare for a new way of teaching, supported by dedicated staff to making sure the university didn't miss a beat in fulfilling its mission. (*TCU Magazine*, Winter 2020)

This sense of community is pervasive among students, alumni, faculty, and staff. Our connection culture is an essential part of who we are as a Horned Frog family.

Chancellor Victor Boschini, *TCU Magazine*, Summer 2021

We are at a crossroads of racial equity and justice.

Chancellor Victor Boschini, *TCU Magazine*, Winter Redux 2020

You must be the change you wish to see in the world.

Mahatma Gandhi

When asked about the pandemic's impact on people, Chancellor Boschini acknowledged it fractured connections, but he also stressed it also made people more responsive and sensitive toward others. With so much sickness and disruption, people—especially young people—started to feel greater levels of empathy: "Because of people getting sick and all the news . . . I think it made younger people, who don't really think about those things . . . more empathetic" (Interview, August 2021).

Similarly, in another *TCU Magazine* column, Chancellor Boschini described how COVID-19, while isolating people, also created greater connections: "The pandemic brought into focus the power of connecting with people who live in our local community, making us appreciate our campus and hometown relationships even more. In a year of uncertainty and separation, Horned Frogs repeatedly came together and stepped up to serve the people around us" (*TCU Magazine,* Summer 2021).

Ironically, one of 2020's greatest disturbances was also one of its greatest unifiers. What brought people across the country together like never before was the Black Lives Matter protests that erupted when a handcuffed African American man, George Floyd, died in Minneapolis with a policeman's knee pressed against his neck. His death on May 26, 2020, in the midst of the pandemic, followed the deaths of two other African Americans—Ahmaud Arbery, who was killed by three white men while he was jogging in February, and Breonna Taylor, who was shot when police raided her apartment in March. Immediately, massive outrage swept across the country as a bystander's video of Floyd's death went viral, and over the course of the next few months, millions of people worldwide took part in Black Lives Matter protests. That shock and horror were equally evident at TCU. Just days after George Floyd's death, Chancellor Boschini sent out campus-wide email acknowledging the hurt on campus: "Our campus is bewildered, angered, outraged, and sorrowful over the tragic death of George Floyd" (Email, June 1, 2020).

Thanks to the efforts of students, faculty, staff, and administrators committed to making campus more diverse and inclusive, DEI and CRES had already been at work to help TCU live up to its mission and values since 2016, but the Black Lives Matter movement triggered deep campus responses. Spearheaded by Kellton Hollins, a senior TCU football player, and supported by the chancellor and other campus leaders, the End Racism mural project near the Coliseum and stadium quickly gathered hundreds of signatures in support of its emphatic message. At the same time, the chancellor, trustees, provost, and others across campus conferred about how TCU could make a decisive response.

Two weeks after his first all-campus message, on June 18, 2020, Chancellor Boschini sent out another email to close campus the following day, Juneteenth, "to commemorate that historic day." Everyone in the TCU community was encouraged—"out of respect and love for our Black colleagues, friends, and acquaintances"—to use the time "as a day of peace and reflection." The Chancellor's message clearly announced TCU's commitment: "We remain committed to actively seek and create solutions that will result in the inclusive and diverse community we all desire" (Email, June 18, 2020).

Seeking solutions was fully implemented not long after when the chancellor, together with Trustee Chair Mark Johnson and "the unanimous support of the entire Board of Trustees," sent out a joint email announcing the creation of "an initiative to study TCU's own experiences with racism, slavery, and the Confederacy." Addison and Randolph Clark had both served in the Confederate army, and while neither had ever owned slaves, their father had. As Confederate statues were pulled down or removed across the country during BLM protests, questions arose on campus about TCU's own origins and past. A student group, the Coalition for University Justice and Equity, had requested that TCU acknowledge its founders' Confederate history, while some called for the removal of Addison and Randolph Clark's statue.

A joint project sponsored by Women and Gender Studies and CRES—the TCU Diverse History Project—was already underway to "research, engage, and learn from histories of race, gender, sexuality, and other social identities." Several faculty who were involved, such as Professors Nino Testa and Jacqueline Lambiase, were invited to meet with Provost Dahlberg, along with Aisha Sawyer-Torrey, Co-Chair of the DEI Committee, and Timeka Gordon, Director for Inclusiveness and

OPPOSITE
TCU graduate student Kellton Hollins next to the END RACISM mural on Frog Alley, a project he spearheaded with the cooperation of the Chancellor's Office and campus leaders, 2020. Photo courtesy of TCU Athletics.

Intercultural Services, to discuss "researching race and history at TCU" (*TCU360*, July 15, 2020). As a result of these discussions, TCU's Race and Reconciliation Initiative was launched.

In their message, Chancellor Boschini and Chair Mark Johnson announced that greater diversity and inclusivity were irrevocably part of "the University's strategic plans" and that TCU's mission and values clearly "repudiate all forms of racism." Declaring that "racism has been consistently present for far too long," and acknowledging that "the deaths of George Floyd and many others have awakened a passion for true equity and justice," the message proclaimed: "the Board of Trustees and Office of the Chancellor are jointly commissioning an initiative to study TCU's own experiences with racism, slavery, and the Confederacy. . . . reviewing, understanding, and transparently sharing information about our history will make us a stronger institution as we plan for the years ahead." The statement added that Provost Dahlberg would lead the initiative and create the charge that not only would study TCU's past but also make recommendations about its future (Email, July 15, 2020).

Following the announcement, Chancellor Boschini used his *TCU Magazine* column in the delayed Winter Redux 2020 issue to assert, as his column's title proclaimed, that TCU was at a pivotal point in its history: "We're at a Crossroads of Racial Equity and Justice":

> As Americans and Horned Frogs, we find ourselves at a crossroads in terms of racial equity and justice. Our community journey into an inclusive future includes an academic and honest reckoning with the past . . . we want to examine how the legacy of racial hierarchy affects today's Texas Christian University.

After announcing that the Race and Reconciliation Initiative had been recently launched and that Professor Frederick Gooding (Dr. G), Associate Professor of African American Studies in the John V. Roach Honors College, would chair the committee, the chancellor concluded:

> This is an academic endeavor that will spend its first year on research, focusing on Black Americans and the University's experiences with racism, slavery, and the Confederacy. . . . Through a new understanding, we can—and must—take action that will lead to healing of any inequality here and more broadly in our world. (*TCU Magazine*, Winter Redux 2020)

The chancellor stressed that, although the past cannot be undone, its lessons can be learned.

By August, plans were underway for the RRI Committee to begin its work of reconciling TCU's past with its present. To be transparent and start "a continuous ongoing conversation," town hall meetings were scheduled and a RRI website was constructed. When asked about how RRI would move forward, Professor Gooding responded: "I can't make any promises to you or anyone as to what we will find and what we will do, but at the very least I can make the commitment to find and discover the history so that we can continue to have these conversations and honor that history as we look to making a new legacy for ourselves." To express his optimism for RRI, he added: "What I've been saying to those who will listen is that we should be prepared to embrace our past and not erase it. There is nothing to be afraid of; knowing our history and acknowledging it makes us stronger in terms of our foundation for moving forward in the future" (*TCU 360*, August 26, 2020).

Professor Gooding and the RRI Committee were given a short nine-month period to conduct all the necessary research to produce a conclusive report on TCU's links to racism, slavery, and the Confederacy, yet that is exactly what the committee accomplished. On April 21, 2021, TCU celebrated its first Race and Reconciliation Day, a program that included music, prayer, reports from RRI committee members, and messages from campus leaders, including Chancellor Boschini, Board of Trustees Chair Mark Johnson, Provost Dahlberg, Vice Chancellor for Student Affairs Kathy Cavins-Tull, Dean of Admissions Heath Einstein, and Athletic Director Jeremiah Donati. A significant part of the program included a public announcement—accompanied by publication—of seven RRI recommendations:

> **Slavery**
> We recommend that TCU develop and implement a comprehensive strategic plan to promote equity and inclusion in graduate and undergraduate student admissions, faculty and staff recruitment and retention, and the illumination of TCU's full history through curricula programs such as Frog Camp and UNLF.
>
> **Confederacy**
> We recommend providing more robust contextual information near the Clark Brothers' statue and memorialize a more complete story of TCU, commemorating the efforts of underrepresented or marginalized groups who contributed to TCU's development, and highlighting racist attitudes and behaviors from earlier years as an educational step toward creating an anti-racist community.
>
> **Segregation**
> We recommend the development and maintenance of an online digital depository specifically focused upon Race & Reconciliation, which all members of the TCU community are able to access to understand the collective histories that contribute to TCU's legacy.
>
> **Desegregation**
> We recommend more consistently recognizing the contributions of our Black, Indigenous and other alumni

of color, more specifically through the ongoing funding, development, and maintenance of the RRI Oral History Project designed to capture key alumni experiences.

Voice
We recommend the perpetual and continued observance of "TCU Reconciliation Day" as a means to maintain open forums of communication and expression on the topic of race and reconciliation, while deliberately, intentionally and strategically increasing access to existing TCU media channels (i.e., student-run television, print and radio) to amplify multiple voices and perspectives on campus.

Good Neighbor?
We recommend conducting a comprehensive inventory of all official vendors conducting business with TCU to qualitatively measure and assess equitable representation by diverse members of our business community.

Repair
We recommend continuing this Race & Reconciliation Initiative beyond the initial one-year time frame originally set for this committee's investigation by continuing to make the modest investment in the human capital necessary to carry out the work of research and reconciliation as part and parcel of TCU's efforts to lead on.

ABOVE
Frederick Gooding. Courtesy of TCU Marketing and Communication. Photograph by Jeffrey McWhorter.

As Chancellor Boschini mentioned in his prefatory remarks, RRI's "First Year Survey Report" offered "a more complete telling of TCU's history, told humbly and in truth" (4). To emphasize its veracity and candor, the chancellor followed his opening remarks with a "Statement of Acknowledgment": "TCU acknowledges its ties to slavery, racism, and the Confederacy by virtue of the Clark family's ownership of enslaved persons and by virtue of Addison and Randolph Clark both picking up arms as Confederate soldiers." While expressing gratitude for the "founders' vision in fostering the world-class university with which we are proud to be associated," and then adding that appreciating this vision "does not require that we agree with every action or belief held by our founders," he continued:

Yet, as an institution of education, where truth and knowledge remain our hallowed pursuits, we reserve the right to do better once we learn better. The stated values of TCU include personal freedom and integrity, the dignity and respect for the individual, a heritage of service in pursuit of the greater good, and active appreciation for the array of human experience, and the potential of every human being. While these values are inconsistent with racism in any form, they also provide a solid foundation upon which to pursue racial healing. (First Year Survey Report 5)

In its thirty-seven pages, the RRI report did not attempt a definitive examination of TCU's past. Instead, it offered three "windows" into the university's history: the formative years after the turbulence of the Civil War (1861-1891), the integration years (1941-1971), and recent times (1998-present). Despite the brief looks offered by the windows, significant recoveries presented.

In addition to exploring the Clark family history, Addison and Randolph Clark's actions and intentions, and TCU's origins in Thorp Spring, the first "Founding Years" window recounted the roles and contributions of two emancipated African Americans, Charley and Kate Thorp, both of whom made significant contributions during the early years of the AddRan Male and Female College. While Kate was an invaluable member of the Clark family, taking responsibility for many of the daily domestic tasks and care for family members, she also served the Thorp Spring community as a midwife and nurse. Charley was instrumental in keeping the new school functioning. Although he was first "occasionally employed for janitorial service," Charley soon became indispensable, accepting responsibility

> for practically every detail, aside from academic activities, not specifically belonging to someone else. He saw that the buildings were kept in repair. He advised on improvement. He repaired frozen water pipes. He made winter fires in the classroom stoves, and filled

> What I've been saying to those who will listen is that we should be prepared to embrace our past and not erase it.
>
> **Frederick Gooding, *TCU 360*, August 16, 2020**
>
> TCU acknowledges its ties to slavery, racism, and the Confederacy. . . . Yet, as an institution of education, where truth and knowledge remain our hallowed pursuits, we reserve the right to do better once we have learned better.
>
> **Chancellor Victor Boschini**
>
> It is imperative that we, as stewards of TCU, do everything we can to instill, and live, very real change.
>
> **Chancellor Victor Boschini and Board of Trustees Chair Mark Johnson, Email, July 15, 2020**

> the oil lamps, and when the duty was not assigned to a reliable student, he rang the big bell which regulated the school's daily schedule. (Joseph L. Clark, *Thank God We Made It* 361)

TCU's early history cannot be told without recognizing the remarkable stories of both Charley and Kate Thorp.

On April 21, 2022, TCU celebrated its second Reconciliation Day, a day which included the distribution of RRI's second report. In its embrace of the past, the program started with Professor Greg Cantrell, the Erma and Ralph Lowe Chair in Texas History, enumerating a series of shamefully racist jokes and cartoons from early twentieth-century *Skiffs* and yearbooks, which prompted Chancellor Boschini to state in his closing remarks: "You can't go somewhere if you don't know where you've been" (*TCU 360*, June 10, 2022). A significant—and equally powerful—part of the program included recognizing several descendants of Charley and Kate Thorp.

A sixty-page document, "The Second Year Survey Report: TCU and Race, the First Fifty Years, 1873-1923" offered "a deeper dive into TCU's first half-century," tracing the university's history from its years in Thorp Spring, its fourteen years in Waco, and its move to Fort Worth. In addition to providing

Who is responsible for this waste?

Randolph Clark, Eulogy on Charley Thorp

greater depth and scope than RRI's first report, the Second Year Survey Report also focused on "TCU and Race," giving numerous, well-documented examples of how racism was not only embedded in TCU's cultural contexts but also on TCU's campus. The report, however, concluded with a tribute written by Randolph Clark in 1927 upon Charley Thorp's passing:

> Charles Thorp was born in slavery and his 78 years was a life of slavery. After emancipation he was told he was free, but he never realized the freedom. If any difference it was harder work. He was not allowed to get an education . . . Charlie was endowed with far more than ordinary intellect. He would have made the equal of Booker Washington, or the successful business men of his race, yet he was not allowed to have a vision of that life.

Without acknowledging his or his family's responsibility, Clark concluded his tribute with a simple rhetorical question: "Who is responsible for this waste?" In the early twentieth century, Clark, eighty-three years old at the time, in poor health and nearly blind, made no attempt to answer the question he posed. Though he and everyone listening knew the answer, no one there dared to utter it, given the pervasive cultural racism of the early twentieth century. Nearly a century later, the work of the Race and Reconciliation Initiative Committee and its reports answered Randolph Clark's question.

> I want to make sure we leave [TCU] in better shape than when we got it—and we got it in great shape . . . I'm a big believer that I'm just a placeholder. I'm the tenth chancellor, and there will be an eleventh one, and no one will know my name in six months.
>
> And that's how it should be, because this is way bigger than me. I hope that the people who were here when I was here will say, "He did a good job." I'm trying to make it so that the next person in here is on a good financial base, and then also that when they come in there's a good zeitgeist on campus.
>
> **Chancellor Victor Boschini**

ABOVE
A possible photo of Charley Thorp. Courtesy of TCU Race and Reconciliation Initiative.

LEFT
Randolph Clark, 1920s. Courtesy of Mary Couts Burnett Library.

ABOVE
Fireworks over the campus commons to celebrate the spring 2022 graduates. Courtesy of TCU Marketing and Communication. Photograph by Glen E. Ellman.

ABOVE
Chancellor Boschini celebrates with a graduate from the class of 2020 at the delayed commencement ceremony in May 2021. Courtesy of Mary Couts Burnett Library. Photograph by Glen E. Ellman.

RIGHT
Chancellor Boschini and Provost Donovan at at spring commencement, 2019. Courtesy of TCU Marketing and Communication. Photograph by Glen E. Ellman.

ABOVE
Chancellor Boschini hands a degree to a new graduate, 2021. Courtesy of TCU Marketing and Communication. Photograph by Glen E. Ellman.

LEFT
Chancellor Boschini with Carson Huey-Yu, TCU's youngest graduate, 2017. Courtesy of TCU Marketing and Communication. Photograph by Glen E. Ellman.

IV.

Voices and Images: Perceptions of Our History

**Selections from
TCU Oral History Project Interviews
2011-2023**

1.
The 1970s

Chancellor Moudy led the University to higher academic levels during his tenure. He was widely regarded as an intellectual with solid grounding in philosophy, religion, Christian theology, economics, and university administration. During the 1970s several areas and majors were added, research capabilities were enhanced, and PhD programs were started. A major university push resulted in a Phi Beta Kappa chapter being established on campus in 1971. In the context of cultural turbulence, a more collaborative form of management evolved with administrative staff and the trustees meeting with faculty on key policies and issues. Through the recently established Faculty Senate, faculty brought proposals to the administration on matters including formalized administrative search committees, improved personnel benefits, grade guidelines, improved processes concerning academic dishonesty and student relations, and improved scheduling for classes and finals. While salaries were low for faculty and staff, improved retirement benefits were instituted, which resulted in creating long-term institutional commitments to working at TCU.

I actually started working at TCU in 1969, when we underwent some interesting changes. That was the first year women could wear pants on campus. You would see lots of girls wearing raincoats because they had shorts or pants underneath. They would roll their jeans up so it wouldn't look like they were wearing pants. We changed the role of Resident Assistants to make them less police officers and more of a support for students. It's a difficult job because they have to do both. Back then we had one RA for every 110 students. We still had housemothers, and we eventually changed the housemothers to graduate students. When we changed that, some people thought the world was coming to an end. Now all hall directors have MA degrees.

There was a woman, Katie DePlata, who was the housemother in Colby for years and years. The students just loved her. One day she came into my office almost in tears, saying she was afraid she was going to have to quit.

"Why Katie? You're doing a great job!" I said.

She said, "For the first time, I found some boy sneaking into Colby, and I chased him and I couldn't catch him. I think I must be too old."

Women had to be in their residence halls at 10 p.m. at night, and they could stay out until midnight on weekends. That wasn't true for boys, which aroused the ire of the women. Of course, there was no coed housing at all. The boys were not allowed to visit in the women's residence halls except in the lobbies. That changed slowly when visitation was allowed, first on Sunday afternoons with the doors open. It was a conservative lifestyle on the campus. We began to think a little bit more about what would make residence hall life more significant for students, so that students wouldn't be moving off campus as quickly. Ultimately, by the mid-1980s, every residence hall had regular visitation, and now it's pretty open. We continued to have traditional residence halls, but early on I thought we needed to diversify the type of housing that we had. Many years later we were able to do that.

The student body in 1970 was only about half the size it is now, so getting to know students was a little easier. Not everyone had cars, and many students worked on campus. At TCU the "front line" people engaged with students and got to know all the students as best they could. The importance with me, for staff, is knowing that a lot of staff are working a lot of hours, and they are not paid particularly well. They do it because they love what they're doing. It was important for leadership to support staff as much as possible, and in whatever way possible.

In the 1970s, the chancellor had to approve which speakers came to campus. Jane Fonda [controversial actress and activist] was banned from campus. There were no R-rated movies on campus. It was very much a top-down administration. Students, with some faculty and staff, put together the Bill of Student Rights and Responsibilities, which remains in the back of the student handbook. It has never been amended. Chancellor Moudy and trustees were leery of that because they just didn't know what would happen. A lot of what I did was negotiate between administration and students. We

OPPOSITE
Aerial view of the TCU campus, late 1960s.
Courtesy of Mary Couts Burnett Library.

ABOVE
Students on move-in day, 1975. Courtesy of Mary Couts Burnett Library. Photograph by Linda Kaye.

ABOVE
Sorority annual rush, 1963. Courtesy of Mary Couts Burnett Library.

ABOVE
Student Government Association Programming Council, 1978. Courtesy of Mary Couts Burnett Library.

created committees to review speaker and film requests. I think I gained a lot of trust on both sides. The administration knew that I wasn't trying to overthrow anything, and students knew that I would take their case forward.

Later, when we wanted to make some changes, like the first coed residence hall, there was an amount of trust. I was able to assure them that we could move forward and it would be okay, and they accepted it.

— **Don Mills, Vice Chancellor for Student Affairs Emeritus, at TCU 1969-2022**

TCU is very different now. When I first came here in the 1970s the best students were PKs, Preachers' Kids. They were sons or daughters of Disciples Ministers who were here on scholarship. It was a different time.

— **Don Jackson, Emeritus Professor of Political Science, at TCU 1975-2010**

In 1972 I was asked if I would consider going on the TCU board. I was only twenty-six at the time. The TCU board was predominately older members, and I think they were looking for someone who was younger because they had recently formed a Student Relations Committee. At the time, Dr. James Moudy was chancellor of the university, and there were a lot of differences in the school back then compared to right now. I remember going to the student leadership retreat not long after I joined the board, and I was confronted with an issue about visitation in the residence hall. There weren't any coed dorms, and the issue was whether or not males could visit females in dorms. It was interesting for me to get to know some of the student leadership at that time. The purpose of that committee was to develop a relationship between the board and the student leadership.

— **Denny Alexander, Trustee Emeritus, served 1972-2005**

When I was dean of students, the Vietnam War came along. We had ROTC on the campus and we had anti-war sympathizers on campus, and they were clashing. There were times when we would be giving out awards to the ROTC and they'd be marching out where the old fraternities and sororities were, and these anti-war guys would come out and run through the lines. Chancellor Moudy would nudge me and say, "Wible! Get that man!"

I was honored to receive the student faculty of the year award, and I felt close to the students. I think that's why I had good luck during the Vietnam years with the anti-war guys and the ROTC guys.

Obscenity Rules May Be Cleared (See Page 5)

The Skiff

Volume 69, Number 30 Tuesday, November 10, 1970

Texas Christian University • • • • Fort Worth, Texas 76129

Question: Is This 'Wholesome' Entertainment?

ABOVE
Skiff front page, November 10, 1970, with photo of Jefferson Airplane. Controversy over concert-goers smoking pot nearly resulted in a ban of all rock concerts on campus, but a year later the Grateful Dead concert provoked little consternation. Courtesy of Mary Couts Burnett Library.

One young man had been drinking and whatnot, and I said, "I'm sorry, but we're going to have to put you on probation." He got mad, and one night he filled a Coke bottle with gasoline and threw it under the ROTC building and set it on fire. That was one of the temporary buildings. That brought in the FBI and the whole works because it involved military property during the Vietnam War. I had to set up an office for the FBI, and they started bringing in kids to interrogate. I would overhear some of that, and I thought they were being hard on these guys. They never did find this guy, and in fact I didn't know who did it. The funny thing is that many years later when I was the vice chancellor there was a knock on my door and in walks this man.

"Do you remember me?" he asked.

"I sure do."

And then he said, "I'm the one who set the fire."

"What are you doing now?"

"I'm a priest," he said.

He was a Catholic priest. That's how it goes!

— **Howard Wible, Vice Chancellor for Student Life, at TCU 1958-1985**

ABOVE
Men's dorm room, ca. 1970. Courtesy of Mary Couts Burnett Library.

LEFT
ROTC building fire, 1969. Courtesy of Mary Couts Burnett Library. Photograph by Clyde Moore.

TEXAS CHRISTIAN UNIVERSITY
Fort Worth, Texas 76129
817-926-2461

House of Student Representatives

February 5, 1976

Chancellor James Moudy
Texas Christian University

Dear Chancellor Moudy:

On behalf of the Executive Board, I wish to express our support of Dr. Henry Hammock's production of "Hot l Baltimore". The Executive Board after investigation and consideration feels that the play director and students are qualified to judge a production's appropriateness. We hope that the concerned parties will be able to communicate and clarify what must be done for the play to be put into production.

Further, we hope that after this situation is concluded the matter will be studied so that such future confrontations do not arise. Perhaps a committee in the School of Fine Arts composed of impartial faculty and students should be formed to advise in future questions.

At this point, direct personal communication, guideline clarification in writing, and compromise is essential. However, we stand firm that censorship is inappropriate in a major university.

Respectfully yours,

James L. Case

James L. Case
Student Body President

JC/bh

CC: George Tade, Dean of Fine Arts
✓Bill Hall, President of the Faculty Senate
George Sorenson, Chairman of the Theater Department
Henry Hammock, Director of Theater Productions

ABOVE

Letter from Student Body President James Case to Chancellor Moudy, February 5, 1976. Courtesy of Texas Christian University.

Debate . . . centered on the question of censorship. . . . The chair read a communication from James L. Case, Student Body President, regarding the production of *Hot L Baltimore*. The administration had not canceled the play [in the Theatre Department], but certain changes had been requested.

— **Faculty Senate Minutes, February 5, 1976**

Resolution offered to the Faculty Senate, February 5, 1976, by Senator Neil Daniel:

There are few situations, perhaps none, that justify censorship of the arts. Among the institutions of society, the liberal arts university has a most solemn calling to defend freedom of expression.

Any action on the part of Texas Christian University to cancel the production of *Hot L Baltimore* or to impose modification of the play against the judgment of its director is a betrayal of its nature as a university and of the personal and professional rights of its students and faculty.

Be it therefore resolved that the Faculty Senate of Texas Christian University opposes censorship and that the Faculty Senate favors freedom of expression for all members of the university community, and most particularly freedom from censorship of the arts.

— **Faculty Senate Archive, February 5, 1976**

Chancellor Moudy was a traditional southern academic and very much a gentleman. He went blind before he left office, but he remembered people by their voice. It was amazing [that] if you went into a room and he heard you greeting other people, he would turn and welcome you. While he had all these rules students hated, he cared deeply about the quality of life for students. He brought the first PhD programs to TCU and helped the process to have TCU admitted into Phi Beta Kappa. He focused on academic excellence.

— **Don Mills**

Probably one of Dr. Moudy's greatest contributions to TCU was that he was instrumental in starting doctoral programs. He had hired Leigh Secrest to develop PhD programs in Physics, Chemistry, and English.

— **Ann Sewell, Associate Provost for Academic Affairs, at TCU 1978-2016**

One of the most important things that happened at TCU was the start of several PhD programs in the early sixties. A lot of the work was done by Dr. Moudy when he was a vice chancellor, and then he became chancellor in 1965. This was the Sputnik era, and it was a time when the space program was just starting. There was a lot of impetus from the government to get science education developed in this country. There was no PhD program in the metroplex. There were discussions between TCU and SMU as the two major private schools. SMU opted to have a law school, and we started the graduate prgrams.

— **Manfred Reinecke, Professor of Chemistry, at TCU 1964-2006**

[With the addition of doctoral programs, TCU became a Tier One school but had the lowest salaries among all 149 Tier One schools]

When I was on the faculty senate, I did a salary study comparing TCU with all the other Tier One schools in the country. We were proud of the fact that we had become a Tier One school. I presented a report at the senate meeting, and Dr. Moudy was there. I remember saying, "There are 149 [Tier I] schools and TCU ranks 149th in salaries at all levels...."

I think that made him aware of how serious the problem was and probably was the impetus that started the salary discussion.

— **Manfred Reinecke**

When I came to TCU, I wrote a guest article in the *Skiff* which I called "The Secret Shame of TCU." This was probably 1977 or 1978. I was referring to the fact that at that time TCU was heavily dominated by fraternities and sororities, and there were virtually no Black members in fraternities and sororities. I thought that was absolutely awful. I thought that we shouldn't put up with that. We're dealing with racism. We can do better than that because we ought to have transcended that and left it behind.

— **Don Jackson**

ABOVE
Students on campus, 1972. Courtesy of Mary Couts Burnett Library.

When I came here in 1961, the trees were little; it was really hot. The buildings weren't air-conditioned, the dorms weren't air-conditioned. I would guess there were four to five thousand students. Over the years, the culture has built on itself. TCU survived the 1970s, which was a terrible time I think for any university. Then in the 1980s, when Bill Tucker became chancellor, I think the school had a solid foundation education-wise and culture-wise. But they were still on shaky grounds financially.

—Jean Walbridge, Administrative Assistant to the Chancellor, at TCU 1994-2004

When I became chancellor in 1979, higher education in America was at a time of low tide. All ships rise, or most of them do, when the tide turns high, and a lot of ships are really quite low when the tide is low. It was especially low tide at TCU. Those were difficult times. Enrollment was a struggle—enrollment had declined at TCU. Morale was low . . . the mood at TCU was gloomy. In fact, the year I began my work, TCU was in the red.

— Chancellor Emeritus Bill Tucker, at TCU 1979-1998

It was a time of change, and not only at TCU. This was the hippie time. Some students I knew were streakers. But that sort of thing just seemed to disappear when Tucker came in. It was a changing era.

— Manfred Reinecke

2.
Leadership

Leaders may see a vision and say, "We can do that, and that, and that," but you must then know how to understand and align people and communicate that vision, and gain colleagues if you're going to make changes. It's the nature of leadership. My view of leadership has never been one that it's simply one or two people at the top.

— Larry Adams, Emeritus Associate Provost and Professor of Sociology, at TCU 1969-2011

I don't see the students over here, and the administration over there. I see us all in this for the same common goals, and that's to graduate students who are impacting the community in a positive way. I think that's one of the best definitions of leadership.

— Susan Adams, Associate Vice Chancellor for Student Affairs, at TCU 1975-2014

Leadership comes in many forms. It can come in big things that people do and small things that people do, but leadership is seeing a pathway that needs to be trod and breaking that pathway. We think of leadership and sometimes make it a mystical thing.

— Margaret "Peggy" Barr, Vice Chancellor for Student Affairs, at TCU 1985-1992

To be a good leader you have to care about people. You have to care about those people that you're trying to lead even if you ask them to do hard things.

— Kirk Downey, Emeritus Professor of Management and Dean, at TCU 1983-2001

LEFT
Kirk Downey. From TCU 1998 yearbook. Courtesy of Mary Couts Burnett Library.

One characteristic of a good leader is being a good listener, not just hearing the words but understanding enough to know the root cause behind what is said. There also has to be a core vision—what you think really matters about higher education. I'm not sure you can teach that, since it comes from experience as much as anything else. Leaders are sometimes thrust into circumstances and learn from experience. You learn what works, and you learn how to persuade people to move in your direction.

— Paul Hartman, Vice Chancellor for University Relations and Development, at TCU 1972-1988

Leadership is a process of engaging others in a way to share goals, to share dreams, and to work together to achieve those goals. It's a collaborative process.

— Chancellor Emeritus Mick Ferrari, at TCU 1998-2003

Leadership, like empathy, is being able to put yourself in the shoes of others. Leadership includes listening, collaborating, and trying to collect as much information as possible. I think leading is the art of getting all that information together, getting all the perspectives together, and making people feel like they are a part of the discussion and part of the decision. We might not always agree with a decision, but we certainly understand why something needs to happen.

— Richard Gipson, Emeritus Professor of Music and Drama, at TCU 2002-2023

You have to have a good sense of humor [to work in the Chancellor's Cabinet]. You can't take yourself seriously because we tease each other a lot. We poke fun at each other. We know the parts of our personalities that are quirky and funny, so there is a lot of give-and-take. I think that just keeps the group loose, and nobody gets too full of themselves. The leadership becomes more genuine, more sincere, and much more fun.

— Brian Gutierrez, Vice Chancellor for Finance, at TCU 2006-2022

We've been lucky over the years because of the leadership of our trustees and all of our chancellors. We've been [financially] conservative, and we've diversified our portfolio a great deal. In different periods over the years, in the eighties and nineties, there were tough economic times, but we continued to succeed and build because of our leadership.

— Kristi Hoban, Associate Vice Chancellor for Alumni Relations, at TCU 1980-2019

ABOVE
Don Jackson. Courtesy of *TCU Magazine*. Photograph by Gary Logan.

[As a leader] you have to do what your personal integrity tells you is the right thing. You have to stand up for that. A leader has to think carefully and determine what the right thing is to do and have the courage to accomplish that, even if it's unpopular or against the grain. . . . Saying the popular thing is the easiest thing to do. I think leadership is the ability to stand up and say the right thing even when people disagree with you.

— **Don Jackson, Emeritus Professor of Political Science, at TCU 1975-2010**

LEFT
Allene Parks Jones. Courtesy of *TCU Magazine*. Photograph by Jill Johnson.

I didn't want to lead people in negativism. I like people to make up their own minds. Leadership is guiding people in a direction that they should go, a direction that is going to have a positive effect on their lives. If a student hasn't learned how to think for herself, she's going to be in trouble.

— **Allene Jones, Emeritus Professor of Nursing, at TCU 1968-1998**

You need to have positive people taking leadership positions. I don't remember a year I was on the board that I didn't feel like we had wonderful leadership on the board, especially with the chancellors. I think we've been extremely fortunate with them.

— **Dee J. Kelly, Trustee Emeritus, served 1971-2007**

Based on a person's age, leadership styles change a lot. When you're twenty-five, thirty, or forty, you view the world and managing staff one way, and when you're nearly seventy you view managing staff in an entirely different way. . . with age comes maturity and wisdom.

— **Roby Key, Vice Chancellor for Development Operations, at TCU 1988-2016**

ABOVE
J. Luther King. Courtesy of Texas Christian University. Photograph by Glen E. Ellman.

I define a leader as someone you want to emulate, someone that people look up to. It's important to have intelligence and skill sets, but it's also important to have personal characteristics that attract people to you. Don't be self-aggrandizing, don't be loud and boisterous, don't be condescending. Instead, be constantly building and supporting. Visionaries are important, but somebody who's fought the battle can also be a visionary. A leader is somebody that you want to go with. A leader has to be constantly listening and learning. You want to surround yourself with young people because of their intellect and their energy. It's hard to be successful unless you can listen. You have to be receptive to disagreement. You need to be fair, and being fair isn't treating everybody the same. A leader needs to see what's at stake five years from now. . . .

As a trustee, you're part of the governing body of the university. Your involvement as a trustee can range from hearing reports about the university and offering your advice to exercising leadership at the board level, impacting things that you think are important to the university. What do you want the university to be? How selective do you want it to be? How do you want to position the university from a marketing standpoint? . . . It's important as a trustee to give your time, your talents, or your financial resources. Good trustees will do at least one of those things, if not all three of them.

—J. Luther King, Trustee Emeritus and former Chair, served 1992-2021

There may have been more books written on leadership than on any other topic. To me, leadership involves understanding and meeting a need. Typically, it will involve building a consensus about that need, motivating people and keeping them on track, and finally, after successfully fulfilling the need, moving to the next need. Leadership is a process.

— Bill Koehler, Provost Emeritus, at TCU 1969-2005

Leadership is communicating a shared vision and marshalling the forces towards it.

— Laura Miller, former President of the National TCU Alumni Board and ex officio Board of Trustees member, served 2000-2006

Leadership styles hopefully mature and change. I've always tried to hire people around me who look at the world a bit differently than I do, but who have the same motivations of quality and getting ahead. I do a lot of listening, and I have a lot of discussions. I'll change my opinion, and sometimes the managers will change their opinions. But when we leave we're all on the same page and we work toward one conclusion.

As long as the conversation is civil, and as long as it doesn't involve someone saying, "I'm right and you're wrong," it's always better to listen to the other person's disagreement rather than put up a wall.

—Leo Munson, Associate Provost for Academic Support, at TCU 1983-2018

I was really impressed with the leadership when I came here, with Chancellor Tucker, who is a high-quality individual. I worked primarily with Provost Koehler, Dean McCracken, and Vice Chancellor of Financial Affairs Leigh Secrest. Those three people were just absolutely outstanding to work with, and they were dedicated to TCU. They were decisive if I needed assistance. If I had some idea, they would give me an answer almost immediately. I thought the leadership here was just amazing.

— Harold Nelson, Chair of the Department of Engineering, at TCU 1991-1998

What makes a good leader? Passion. Passion and feeling that you want to make a difference. Leadership comes because you really care about something. You really want to lead, and you have ideas and thoughts, and you're not afraid. There's one thing you have to understand. You're not the smartest guy in the room. You never will be. . . . Leadership is getting a room full of people who may have diverse ideas, listening to them, and having everybody come together for a common goal. I think a true leader is the person who can take a room full of those folks and get the talents that they are best at and put them on the table, one pile, and everybody shapes it into something, and be the one who says, "Let's go, let's make something happen." Leadership is surrounding yourself with people who want to pull the wagon.

— Clarence Scharbauer III, Trustee Emeritus and former Chair, served 1990-2017

It's significant that what we're talking about now was talked about ten years ago, was talked about twenty years ago—the same topics over and over again. Sometimes, it just takes the right time, the right groups, the right resources, and the right leadership to change the outcomes. I think the individuals in the past had the same passion and the same goals. We're just in a different time.

— Aisha Torrey-Sawyer, Director of the Office of Diversity and Inclusion

LEFT
Darron Turner. Courtesy of *TCU Magazine*. Photograph by Glen E. Ellman.

There were times around campus when we got really stuck into thinking that leadership was a position. The only people we called leaders were the individuals like the chancellor and executive team. We lost the whole idea that there are a lot of people who offer something to the organization, that move the organization, and that lead the organization without ever making a big fuss about it. A person is still a leader within the organization even if we don't want to recognize that person as a leader.

— **Darron Turner, Chief Inclusion Officer and Title IX Coordinator, at TCU 1994-2021**

ABOVE
Art Ehlman holding a meteorite.

My leadership style? When I was chair I always taught the same course load that I did when I was not chair, because the best leadership is to be a model for the other people. You can't expect other people to do things that you're not willing to do.

— **Art Ehlmann, Chair and Professor of Geology, at TCU 1958-1993**

My leadership style is to be inclusive and to really try to build a consensus. I recognize, of course, that there are some times when I make the final decision, but I like to think I'm doing that with the input I really need. The best thing I can do in my job is to provide an environment that makes the faculty productive and then basically to get out of their way. When I sit around the room with nine departmental chairs, I know that the collective wisdom's a lot greater than sitting in my office by myself.

— **Phil Hartman, Emeritus Professor of Biology and Dean, at TCU 1981-2022**

When I started, there were not a lot of women in leadership positions, and there were comments made about appearance. Sometimes women would feel that they were being patted on their heads rather than taken seriously.

— **Barbara Herman, Associate Vice Chancellor for Student Affairs, at TCU 1986-2021**

Unfortunately, there aren't that many women in academic leadership, so we need to keep working on that.

— **Bonnie Melhart, Emeritus Dean of University Programs and Associate Provost, at TCU 1990-2019**

I believe that the [Board of Trustees] chair should provide good support for the chancellors and help them when difficult times come along. I believe strongly that it is the chancellor's job to run the school, and the chair shouldn't get involved below the chancellor.

—John V. Roach, Trustee Emeritus and former Chair, served 1981-2005

I saw administration as a form of not just leadership but as a form of service—service to the faculty, staff, students, and professional community. For some people, service is an old, antiquated notion, but I think we're all better off when we help one another, assist one another, when we put extra time and energy and thought into something to enable others.

— Douglas Simpson, Dean of the College of Education, at TCU 1988-1999

It's a cliche, but it's what I've found that works: hire good people and get out of the way. Give them the resources they need to do a good job. The most important thing a dean can do is to be fair. This is easy to say but hard to do. Be fair in your allocation of resources, be fair in your decisions, be fair in how you treat people. You have to be approachable. You have to feel comfortable about people coming to talk to you about anything and also listening to them.

— Scott Sullivan, Emeritus Professor of Art History and Dean, at TCU 2000-2016

Don't assume that people are paying attention, or buying into what you're saying, just because you are standing up in front of them. You really have to make sure that you're meeting their needs in order to move forward. If you're just out there espousing ideas and you think everyone's going to run behind you, you are wrong. I spend a lot of my time now just talking to students or talking to staff, trying to make sure I'm hearing what they're saying before I respond.

— Darron Turner

LEFT
Susan Weeks. Courtesy of TCU Marketing and Communications. Photograph by Amy Peterson.

I have adopted a motto from a colleague here at TCU: blessed are the flexible, for they shall not be bent out of shape. The ability to be competent as a leader involves the confidence that you can handle whatever is thrown at you and that you can make a meaningful difference.

— Susan Weeks, Vice Provost

ABOVE
Howard Wible, 1969. Courtesy of Mary Couts Burnett Library.

My style is to listen, to encourage, and to try to see ideas from another person's perspective. I've been told by other vice chancellors that I don't make up my mind fast enough, and I tell them that I have to hear what other people have to say, so I can reflect a collective mind.

— Howard Wible, Vice Chancellor for Student Life, at TCU 1958-1985

Reflections on Three Chancellors

ABOVE
Chancellor Emeritus Tucker, 1990s. Courtesy of Mary Couts Burnett Library.

ABOVE
Chancellor Emeritus Mick Ferrari, 1999. Published in TCU yearbook. Courtesy of Mary Couts Burnett Library.

ABOVE
Chancellor Victor Boschini, 2009. Courtesy of TCU Marketing and Communication.

I frame my thinking about TCU in the context of our three chancellors. I came in under Bill Tucker. His greatest legacy was to build the endowment to the point that enabled a lot of the things we're doing now. I think when I arrived at TCU the endowment was about 57 million dollars and when Chancellor Tucker retired it was about 750 million dollars. My math may be off, but the point is the huge endowment increases set TCU to aspire to be the institution that it is now. Mick Ferrari came in as chancellor, and he was here a relatively short time, but he basically said, "You know, TCU's a great institution; I think it can even be better." He really started the momentum that Victor Boschini seized on and really accentuated to build TCU beyond an institution that was a nice little regional Christian school to the juggernaut that it is now. Each of those chancellors played slightly different roles, and I see them almost as a sort of perfect storm in terms of complementing each other to make TCU what it is now.

— **Phil Hartman**

ABOVE
Chancellor Bill Tucker with students at a pep rally, 1985. Published in TCU yearbook. Courtesy of Mary Couts Burnett Library.

I had the privilege of working with all three chancellors. Bill Tucker to me was an inspirational person. He genuinely cared about others and about serving. He loved TCU so deeply. He also was an ordained minister in the Disciples of Christ, and he solidified that relationship. Chancellor Ferrari was in many ways visionary. He put a lot of emphasis on the employees as well as the students. He started all of the strategic planning, and that was really an exciting time for us to think about the possibilities for the future. When Dr. Boschini came here, he was just a ball of fire and a really hard worker. He has done a fabulous job of fundraising, of transforming the campus, of being student oriented, being really energetic. Each of them had great leadership qualities but in different ways.

— **Barbara Herman**

I have always thought that when Bill [Tucker] made a decision, it was based on logic, fact, and a very deliberative process. He was not one who would just shoot from the hip, so to speak.

—**Bill Koehler, Provost Emeritus, at TCU 1969-2005**

Chancellor Tucker was always out there on opening day moving people into residence halls, and it just blew my mind. I thought he was just going to walk around in a suit, but he came with sleeves rolled up and carried boxes. I think that epitomized people who really wanted to create an environment where students felt at home and felt welcomed.

— **Peggy Barr**

LEFT
Chancellor Ferrari with students, 1999. Published in TCU yearbook. Courtesy of Mary Couts Burnett Library.

Ferrari wanted to make sure everybody had a voice, everybody had a place at TCU. We knew what he wanted us to do, and we did it because we believed in it.

— **Linda Moore, Emeritus Professor of Social Work, at TCU 1977-2017**

Mick Ferrari—I learned a lot from him. He's a very process-oriented person; if you put the process in place, you will come to a good end result. He wanted to see every nook and cranny of this campus and wanted to understand it, what made it tick, and he wanted it to be more collegial, he wanted it to be more inclusive. Mick would go out say "What do you need? If I could give you that, what would you do with it?" Mick Ferrari had an open door policy and started the open email policy with students. He wanted to involve a lot of people. He might not take your advice, but he wanted to know what everyone thought and that energized everybody.

— **Ann Sewell, Associate Provost for Academic Affairs, at TCU 1978-2016**

ABOVE
Chancellor Boschini answers student questions at his Chat with the Chancellor, 2021. Courtesy of TCU Marketing and Communication. Photograph by Amy Peterson.

When Chancellor Boschini arrived, probably the biggest thing that people noticed was his genuine love and appreciation for students. I think Boschini is a classic example of servant leadership. I think he brings out the best in the people that work for him. He is empathetic. He lets people make their own mistakes. He does not hold a grudge. If there's a difference of opinion, he says, "Let's talk about it," then it's over. I think he always wants the best for people, particularly students.

— **Karen Baker, Chief of Staff and Vice Chancellor for Human Resources, at TCU 1992-2016**

Chancellor Boschini has done an amazing job with embracing the culture of the campus, and he models how we should engage with each other, treat each other, respect each other, and just enjoy being around each other. I'm honored to get to work under the leadership of Chancellor Boschini.

— **Cheryl Wilson, Associate Vice Chancellor and Controller, at TCU 2001-2019**

I think each of the chancellors has their love for TCU and their desire to take TCU to the next level. They've all been wonderful and built on the strengths of each other. And each of them has been able to carry the university forward using their own unique styles and gifts.

— **Cheryl Wilson**

Each chancellor has done different things during his tenure at TCU. Chancellor Tucker built up the endowment for TCU, so that we could achieve financial stability. Chancellor Ferrari started a new strategic planning program called the Commission of the Future of TCU, which allowed Chancellor Boschini to come in and to start Vision in Action and do miraculous things. Dr. Ferrari helped start the Staff Assembly which partners with the Faculty Senate in governing the university. Chancellor Ferrari was also responsible for making retirement benefits equal for exempt and non-exempt staff, which was a huge thing. Chancellor Boschini has continued the commitment to a vital community, and under his leadership TCU has received recognition as one of the greatest colleges to work for. All three have been visionaries and big on guarding TCU's history. All three have had the ability to wear many hats at once and juggle the many demands on their time. All three have been especially interested in students, which is the main reason we are here at TCU.

— **Mary Nell Kirk, Executive Assistant to the Chancellor, at TCU 1989-2021**

As I look back at the thirty years that I've been here, each chancellor came at exactly the time that we needed the form of leadership that he had—and they've all done what was needed to be done to propel us to the next step. That's extraordinary.

— **Leo Munson, Associate Provost for Academic Support, at TCU 1983-2018**

ABOVE
Chancellors Emeriti Mick Ferrari and Bill Tucker, 2003. Courtesy of *TCU Magazine*.

ABOVE
Chancellor Boschini and Cabinet members celebrating on stage at the 2013 commencement. Courtesy of TCU Marketing and Communication. Photograph by Glen E. Ellman.

I think that you often hear the example of one person stands on another's shoulder and continues to build. While I was board chair we had three great chancellors, and each one of them had their own strengths, but they all kept us in the right direction; so we've been lucky, and hopefully we can continue to be lucky.

—John V. Roach, Trustee Emeritus and former Chair, served 1981-2005

These last three chancellors have really brought TCU into the modem age.

— Bob Schieffer, Honorary Trustee

I thought Dr. Tucker, Dr. Ferrari, and later Dr. Boschini [were] all different kinds of leaders, but they all cared about TCU tremendously and did whatever they could to make it a better place—whether it was bringing in new faculty, starting new academic programs, constructing new buildings—everything they did made TCU a better place. I was lucky to work under three very strong leaders.

—Robert Seal, University Librarian, at TCU 1994-2005

I think all of them had the same focus on providing a good education for the students and to create better citizens and leaders of the community.

— Buddy Dike, Trustee Emeritus, served 1985-2016

3.
SuperFrog

ABOVE
Addie the Fighting Frog, 1966. The Horned Frog mascot debuted in 1949 and was named Addie the Fighting Frog. The costume was purple and gray and made of fabric with a paper-mache head. Courtesy of Mary Couts Burnett Library.

RIGHT
Addie the Fighting Frog, 1966. Courtesy of Mary Couts Burnett Library.

RIGHT
Addie the Fighting Frog with cheerleaders, 1967. Courtesy of Mary Couts Burnett Library.

ABOVE
Cheerleaders pose with Addie the Fighting Frog, 1973. Courtesy of Mary Couts Burnett Library.

LEFT
SuperFrog, 1979. In 1979, the TCU student government purchased a new mascot costume and gave the mascot a new name—SuperFrog. Courtesy of Mary Couts Burnett Library.

ABOVE
SuperFrog, 1990. Courtesy of Mary Couts Burnett Library. Photograph by Linda Kaye.

RIGHT
SuperFrog, 1990. Courtesy of Mary Couts Burnett Library. Photograph by Linda Kaye.

RIGHT
In 1999, the SuperFrog mascot was updated and looked similar to the mascot today. Courtesy of Mary Couts Burnett Library. Photograph by Linda Kaye.

LEFT
SuperFrog, 2003. Courtesy of Mary Couts Burnett Library. Photograph by Linda Kaye.

ABOVE
SuperFrog, 2006. For a brief period, SuperFrog had a toothy sneer but was soon changed back to a smile. Courtesy of Mary Couts Burnett Library. Photograph by Linda Kaye.

LEFT
SuperFrog, 2014. Courtesy of TCU Marketing and Communication. Photograph by Michael Clements.

RIGHT
SuperFrog, 2022. Courtesy of TCU Marketing and Communication. Photograph by James Anger.

LEFT
SuperFrog greets Horned Frogs fans who have gathered at the Santa Monica pier before the College Football Playoff National Championship, January 2023. Courtesy of TCU Marketing and Communication. Photograph by Amy Peterson.

4.

The Teacher-Scholar Model

LEFT
Students in a physics class, ca.1970. Courtesy of Mary Couts Burnett Library.

BELOW
Professor Sarah Quebec Fuentes and students in the College of Education, 2018. Courtesy of TCU Marketing and Communication.

Teaching has been something that I've been interested in since I was a teenager. I found teaching to be a delightful and stimulating experience. Once I was introduced to the whole universe of research and scholarship, I continued to maintain my commitment to teaching, but in the context of being a balanced, well-rounded scholar. Research, scholarship, and teaching were equally part of the profession.

As time passed, I found that I had unintentionally integrated myself into the environment [at the University of Wisconsin at Madison], which had a heavy focus on research. Teaching and being involved with students was becoming an interference. One day I was walking to class and there were students everywhere. I was completely lost in thought, engrossed in planning my day. I was walking quite fast and so, as I was charging along, I literally ran into a student. I paused and apologized and started on, but then I stopped and looked around and there were students everywhere, and I realized I had reached a point that I no longer saw the students.

I went straight to the phone, called Durward Smith [at TCU] and I said, "Dur, you got to get me down for an interview. I'm turning into that thing I never wanted to be." When I arrived at TCU in the spring of 1970, what I found at that time [was a university] that was relatively small, probably fewer than six thousand students, with a heavy focus on teaching and student welfare—those things I liked. The university was beginning to move from the heavy emphasis on teaching with less focus on research and scholarship and more toward a balanced model.

So we began to look for those faculty that we felt would be teacher-scholars. That teaching would be of paramount importance to them, but they would develop and conduct research programs as well, and they would involve students in that research. When I talk about research and scholarship, I consider that teaching. Because anybody that is doing research at a university, particularly at a university like TCU, should be involving students. This was kind of the way things got started.

— **Michael McCracken, Emeritus Associate Professor of Biology and Dean, at TCU 1971-2010**

One of TCU's defining characteristics is its teacher-scholar model.

— **Chancellor Victor Boschini, Address to the TCU Board of Trustees, November 2003**

We must nurture the excellence of the academic enterprise and advance the teacher-scholar model that is the cornerstone of education at TCU.

— **Chancellor Victor Boschini, Inauguration Speech, 2004**

ABOVE
Dr. Amanda Hale and students conduct research on the effects of wind turbines on birds and bats in Muenster, Texas, 2008. Courtesy of TCU Marketing and Communication.

We believe that the cornerstone of Goal # 1—Strengthen Academic Profile and Reputation—is through enriching the Teacher-Scholar paradigm at TCU. The Teacher-Scholar becomes . . . both the starting point and also the denominator or foundation upon which all subsequent recommendations are offered. The Teacher-Scholar will personify . . . the faculty's role in the TCU Mission and Vision

— **The Academic Mission: The Highest Strategic Priority of the University, Vision in Action Subcommittee Report, 2004**

ABOVE
Chancellor Boschini teaching Introduction to University Life, 2018. Courtesy of TCU Marketing and Communication. Photograph by Amy Peterson.

Our distinctive character derives from our capacity to unite scholarship with teaching. Given TCU's strong commitment to the teacher-scholar model, it is imperative that we place a high value both on scholarship that has an impact on the learning experience of students and on teaching that is informed by scholarly activities.

— **Graduate Education Vision and Strategy at TCU: A Position Paper Prepared by the Committee on Graduate Education, 2004**

LEFT
Faculty in academic regalia for Fall Convocation, 2012. Courtesy of Texas Christian University. Photograph by Glen E. Ellman.

Since I've been at TCU, I've met graduates from Manhattan to Midland and from the classes of 1945 to 2005. What is truly remarkable is the value that they place on the relationships that they have had with their professors. These connections have been—and will continue to be—at the center of the TCU experience and differentiate us from so many other universities where teaching isn't highly prized. These relationships result from TCU's teacher-scholar model, through which we seek out professors who have a passion for teaching as well as for conducting research that keeps them at the top of their fields.

— **Chancellor Victor Boschini, 2005 Convocation Address**

One thing I see that's very similar from when I was a student here is the emphasis on the teacher-scholar model.

— Cheryl Wilson, Associate Vice Chancellor and Controller, at TCU 2001-2019

ABOVE
Students in an engineering lab in the Tucker Technology Center, 2018. Courtesy of TCU Marketing and Communication. Photograph by Jeffrey McWhorter.

I think that is one of the things that is real special about TCU—getting students involved in research. That was always a selling point. As an undergraduate you could be involved in research activities with your professors.

—Janet Herald, Associate Dean of Admissions, at TCU 1974-1989

LEFT
Richard Enos receiving the 2008 Chancellor's Award for Distinguished Achievement as a Creative Teacher and Scholar. Courtesy of TCU Marketing and Communication.

TCU strives to embody the ideal of the teacher-scholar model, a model whereby faculty engage in serious . . . research and creative activities [and] rapidly and energetically translate that knowledge into the classroom. Virtually all faculty members should be solid contributors to both teaching and research/creative activities. . . . Synergy is most evident with the teacher-scholar model, the cornerstone of Texas Christian University's vibrant intellectual community. TCU faculty members are considered teacher-scholars because they integrate instruction and scholarship—defined as research and creative activity—in ways beneficial to students and professors. This academic model entails dedicated, engaging, and innovative teaching, serious academic investigation, and real contributions to academic and professional fields.

Highly ranked academic programs are characterized by mentoring teacher-scholars who enjoy being in the classroom as well as conducting leading-edge research.

— Chancellor Victor Boschini, *TCU Magazine*, Spring 2014

ABOVE
Students in Brian Clinnin's Drawing for Theater class sketch the BLUU in the Campus Commons. Courtesy of TCU Marketing and Communication. Photograph by Jeffery McWhorter.

I think TCU has had as its mission to improve itself, and it has done that. For the first time, I think we have students who are interested in coming here to work with a particular faculty member because of that person's research.

— Rhonda Keen, Emeritus Professor of Nursing and Dean, at TCU 1982-2020

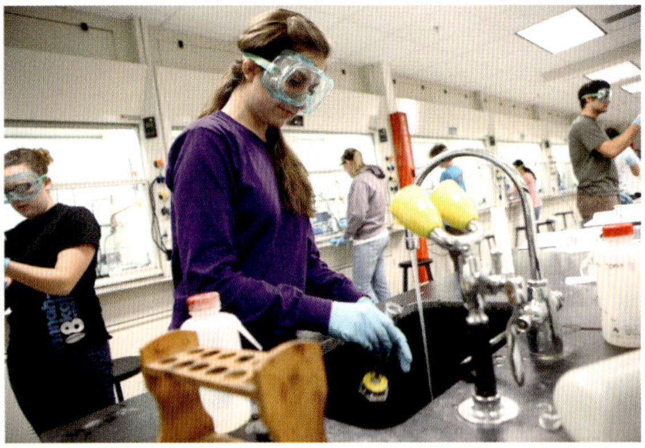

ABOVE
Students in Dr. Jean-Luc Montchamp's chemistry lab, 2008. Courtesy of Texas Christian University. Photograph by Glen E. Ellman.

TCU's strength is the teacher-scholar model. We've hired faculty that want to teach and want to do research . . . they were people that were in front of you, could inspire you with ideas, and could relate to you as a student. That's who we are, that's our culture.

— Ann Louden, Chancellor's Associate for Strategic Partnerships, at TCU 1978-2017

I discovered that I really like the teacher-scholar model. I have a history of scholarship, and it has been a part of me and the way I teach. But I also love teaching, and I love being with students in the classroom. Probably, the most difficult part of becoming a dean is that I no longer have that constant interaction with students. I think that that teacher-scholar model works well at TCU.

— Peggy Watson, Emeritus Professor in the John V. Roach Honors College and Dean, at TCU 1984-2015

We continue to support our teacher-scholar model, which places great emphasis upon faculty doing an exceptional job using their scholarship to help inform their teaching.

— Andrew Schoolmaster, Emeritus Professor of Geography and Dean, at TCU 2007-2021

ABOVE
Students and Professor Tatiana Arguello from the Department of Spanish and Hispanic Studies gather in the Campus Commons to hold a class discussion, 2019. Courtesy of TCU Marketing and Communication. Photograph by Jeffrey McWhorter.

TCU views teaching and scholarship as a dynamic, symbiotic interchange in which excellence in each improves both. Both are important in and of themselves, but the essence of TCU academic culture is founded on the premise that they are complementary. We recognize that our students benefit strongly from interacting with faculty who actively engage with the world through scholarly activity . . . The teacher-scholar model is, therefore, that part of our culture of which we are most proud. It enables us to integrate our scholarly activity, our students, and our service to society at large.

— VIA Recommendation to the TCU Board of Trustees, 2017

Faculty Senate Teacher-Scholar Resolution, 2019

Encompassing all faculty, the teacher-scholar model serves as a foundation for academic life at TCU. . . . Teaching and scholarly activity are mutually compatible and reciprocal, and exceptional performance in one inspires equal merit in the other. Students benefit when faculty engage in scholarly activity and share their zeal and insights in the classroom. . . . The teacher-scholar model thus integrates faculty productivity and student learning, enhancing both and facilitating awareness of, and service to, the world.

5.

TCU and Fort Worth

ABOVE
Campus and downtown Fort Worth skyline, August 19, 2012. Courtesy of TCU Marketing and Communication. Photograph by Epic Helicopters.

Fort Worth is as friendly as they say it is. I came from the South, which is also supposed to be friendly, but it was nothing like Fort Worth. There had been a small article in the newspaper about the new Dean of Education at TCU and a picture, and I walked into a grocery store, and a young lady looked at me said, "Oh you're the new Dean of Education at TCU." And I thought that in Atlanta nobody would notice.

— Sam Deitz, Emeritus Professor of Education and Dean, at TCU 2000-2009

[For any former TCU coaches] that I ever talked to when I was an assistant coach, TCU was always in the top two schools because of the way the town and the administration treated them. I've been here for three chancellors and three athletic directors in my time. Everybody's different, but they all have the same basic motive: to move forward and make TCU be the best it can be. I think Fort Worth has a great level of quality of life.

— Gary Patterson, Head Football Coach, at TCU 1998-2021

ABOVE
Unveiling of the TCU historical marker in downtown Fort Worth, August 30, 2010. Courtesy of TCU Marketing and Communication. Photograph by Glen E. Ellman.

Fort Worth won a contest basically to get TCU here. They realized the economic, social, and conscience engine that a university is. The attitude in Fort Worth is "sky's the limit."

— Chancellor Victor Boschini

I couldn't ask for a better city. You look around the country and where would you rather be? They are great cities for business laboratories such as Chicago and LA, but they're not going to support one school because they have multiple universities there. But Fort Worth is TCU, and it's a huge advantage. People tend to want to stay here after they graduate. Job recruiters have had a hard time convincing students that they might try New York or Chicago or LA. They really like staying in this area, in Fort Worth or Dallas.

— **Bill Moncrief, Emeritus Professor of Marketing, at TCU 1982-2023**

ABOVE
Big Tex and SuperFrog at a pep rally in downtown Fort Worth, September 13, 1996. Courtesy of Mary Couts Burnett Library. Photograph by Linda Kaye.

There's an awful lot of pride in being a horned frog, and some of that stems from being in Fort Worth, Texas. Being at TCU is being a part of the community. People walk out of here and they're proud to be bleed purple, and they're proud of being a horned frog.

— **Richard Sybesma, Swimming and Diving Coach, at TCU 1979-2017**

The university matches the culture here. It's a really great environment, and it is nice to see how the two connect on that personal level and that friendliness level because it is a culture definitely embedded not only at the university but also in Fort Worth.

— **Tracy Syler-Jones, Vice Chancellor for Marketing and Communication**

One of the things I still believe to this day is that as TCU goes, so goes Fort Worth. All the incredible academic changes and facility changes and changes in every possible area of TCU have helped facilitate the changes in Fort Worth. In my mind, they've gone hand in hand.

— **Peggy Watson, Emeritus Professor in the John V. Roach Honors College and Dean, at TCU 1984-2015**

ABOVE
Young TCU fans at the homcoming parade, 2009. Courtesy of TCU Marketing and Communication.

When I got here, you never saw a purple flag in this community. There was a saying, "TCU is Fort Worth's hometown team," but it was hollow. There was no college town, there was no commitment. I remember one time I had some donors get upset with me because the stores, like WalMart or Kroger, would never carry TCU paraphernalia, clothing, attire. If the fans didn't demand it, why would they carry it? As time has progressed, the visibility of TCU has been elevated. One of the greatest little smidges of excitement that I got was when I went to a mall one time, and there was TCU stuff all over.

— **Eric Hyman, Athletics Director, at TCU 1998-2005**

ABOVE
TCU football crowd. Courtesy of TCU Marketing and Communication.

Something that has been apparent in the last ten to twelve years is the involvement of the city of Fort Worth with TCU. Way back, when I was in school in the fifties, we had some support from people who had gone to the University of Texas, Oklahoma, and A&M, but nothing like we have today. We always had 8,000 to 10,000 people who attended TCU games, and this year [2013] we sold over 30,000 season tickets and filled the stadium several times.

Gary Patterson has done a good job with communications and goodwill with the community and outreach. He's recruited a lot of the local talent and does a radio show that is communicated through the city and the surrounding areas. TCU has also done outreach to get the community more involved, by bringing students who can't afford to come to games. There's been a lot of programs that try to get the community involved, and they've been well received by the community. The community is behind our athletic program.

— **Buddy Dike, Trustee Emeritus, served 1985-2016**

ABOVE
Families support TCU football, 2003. Courtesy of TCU Marketing and Communication.

When I came in, TCU was the university on the hill, kind of the ivory castle. There weren't too many connections with the Fort Worth community. Now in Fort Worth it's become so cool to wear a TCU shirt, and it's important to be at a TCU athletic event. It's thrilling to think your child would get to come to TCU, where in the past we were viewed as "Froggy High." That was the nickname. You didn't go to TCU if you lived in Fort Worth.

— **Ann Louden, Chancellor's Associate for Strategic Partnerships, at TCU 1978-2017**

LEFT
TCU flags lining University Drive, October 17, 1995. Courtesy of Mary Couts Burnett Library. Photograph by Linda Kaye.

I've really seen the relationship between TCU and Fort Worth grow. I've been lucky to be here for that. Now we have "Purple Fridays." They never had that before. When I first came here, you couldn't buy TCU stuff anywhere. Now they have it in grocery stores. People on my staff say, "We want to be the university of Fort Worth, not just a university that happens to be in Fort Worth."

— **Chancellor Victor Boschini**

Fort Worth has been a part of TCU's shift from an outstanding regional university to a national university of promise. Fort Worth is much more of an "in" city today than it was twenty years ago. It's a city that's prospering and growing, and all cities like Fort Worth . . . need a good local university . . . It's been a collaborative effort to move the school forward and to make it better known.

—J. Luther King, Trustee Emeritus and former Chair, served 1992-2021

TCU and Fort Worth ISD

ABOVE
Caylin Moore, TCU S.P.A.R.K. (Strong Players Are Reaching Kids) founder, speaks to students at a pep rally at Harlean Beal elementary school. May 30, 2017. Courtesy of TCU Marketing and Communication. Photograph by Glen E Ellman.

The Fort Worth community has been tremendously embracing. Philanthropy has been phenomenal . . . They're very community centric, they're very proud of their own and now I think that we are part of the community. I have been excited about some of the initiatives with Paschal High School because long ago one of the grant proposals that I was involved in was about having our students mentor Paschal students and helping Paschal students mentor middle school students, and having middle school students going into the elementary school . . . Starting with young children is the key to helping improve access for college. . . . One of my dreams has been to have more opportunities to have students use their majors, like for Spanish majors to go out and help families in the Spanish-speaking community with whatever needs they might have, or for our nursing students to provide basic health services to the surrounding community, or our accounting students to help with tax returns for people who need it. There is a lot of practical knowledge and experience that students can provide . . . it is a reciprocal thing, and it is learning and becoming a part of the community and uplifting each other. . . . I think that is so exciting for our students so they are not just learning in a vacuum.

I hope that we will continue to be a part of the larger community, to learn from our fellow citizens to work together for the common good, to look at what could be better. We have such talent in our student body, and our students are hungry to make a difference.

— Barbara Herman, Associate Vice Chancellor for Student Affairs, at TCU 1986-2021

LEFT
Oak tree symbolizing educational partnership between TCU and R.L Paschal High School, 2012. Courtesy of TCU Marketing and Communication. Photograph by Glen E. Ellman.

If you don't understand just some basic tenets of Hispanic culture, you're going to struggle. You don't learn it in lectures—you learn it by being in that environment, and that environment starts when your student body has that kind of diversity. It's a big hill for every medical school to climb, and a lot of it has to do with pipeline. Everything is local. For us it's a big deal to work closely with the Fort Worth ISD and Tarrant County community colleges . . . The medical school will be a role model. . . . You have to build the pipeline all the way back almost to kindergarten. You can't wait until they're in college because you've already weeded out a whole bunch of the population that you really need.

We should graduate very talented young people that residency programs want wherever they land to practice, but we already know the majority will practice right here. . . . The region already loves TCU, and they'll start to see a return on this investment. They'll see young people who are great citizens. They're out in Fort Worth ISD teaching. They're all working in homeless clinics. That's a beautiful thing. That's a give-back from these young people to the community.

— **Stuart Flynn, Dean of the Burnett School of Medicine**

ABOVE
Westpark Elementary fourth graders visit TCU for the College of Education's Bryant Bridge of Hope Math & Science Trail. November 15, 2019. Courtesy of TCU Marketing and Communication. Photograph by Tim Coles.

I was really proud of the partnerships that we developed with local school districts, particularly the Fort Worth Independent School District. What we did was offer courses to their teachers right in their schools. In addition to offering courses there, we got our undergraduates to have pre-graduation experiences. Rather than just theory, we put them in schools where they were with real live people. The other thing I was real proud of was the research. If a school couldn't understand why in fifth grade mathematics their kids were dropping performance-wise, we did the research for them that could tell them why.

— **John Mangieri, Dean of the School of Education, at TCU 1982-1989**

TCU and Fort Worth Working Together

When I was first here, there were physical changes needed that were more easily detected on the campus. But there were other needs that proved to be more profound. One of them had to do with the relationship between the university and the city. Fort Worth was already taking pride in TCU. The question was how do we become more fully partners in the progress of this region and community. What resources and programs at the university did we have that could make a difference for this city? . . . There were enormous issues just getting that baseball stadium located where it is, and without getting civic leaders involved . . . we probably would not have gotten that done. . . . I think the city-university partnership is essential. You can't have a really great university without a really great city, and you can't have a really great city without a university.

— **Chancellor Emeritus Mick Ferrari, at TCU 1998-2003**

ABOVE
Fort Worth shows support for TCU along the Trinity River, 2009. Courtesy of TCU Marketing and Communication. Photograph by Keith Robinson.

For a long time, TCU was known as the city on the hill. There was really not a lot of interaction between the Fort Worth residents and the campus. The first meeting where I was the representative of TCU to the community, people just didn't trust TCU. We were going to rebuild housing down on McCart. It was a drug-infested apartment, it was falling down, it was nasty. That project was one of the most important things we did. When that was finished, people said, "Wow, okay, TCU is serious. This is really nice; this really does enhance our neighborhood."

Berry Street was turning into a pretty scary place where students were told not to go at night. Admissions told people when coming to campus, instead of taking Berry Street, to swing around and come up on the Hulen side. TCU became a part of the Berry Street initiative.

We got involved with city planning boards, academic departments adopted schools, and we had faculty out in the schools. We had more internships in Fort Worth agencies and with Fort Worth businesses. We began to see a turn in the way the city looked at us.

— **Don Mills, Vice Chancellor for Student Affairs, Emeritus, at TCU 1969-2022**

ABOVE
Mayor Betsy Price and Chancellor Victor Boschini, alongside others, cut the ribbon celebrating the newly finished construction of West Berry Street. Courtesy of TCU Marketing and Communication. Photograph by Glen E. Ellman.

We work with the city closely, virtually every project that we do. We take care of the landscaping along Berry Street and University Drive for the city. We helped design the new drainage where the Brite housing is because when it rained heavily, cars actually floated down the street. I'm on several commissions committees with the city, as are a number of other people on campus.

— **Will Stallworth, Associate Vice Chancellor for Facilities, at TCU 1989-2012**

When they were doing some remodeling over at Sadler Hall, the fire department wanted to have access right up to the back door, and the school wanted to keep cars from driving there. After negotiating, TCU ended up getting permission for the poles that the fire departments can pull from the ground. Now Mayor Price will be here off and on because of zoning and other things. TCU is one of the largest institutions in the city, similar to a large business. It's a big player in the city. In addition, TCU is turning out the very people we need, generally, to get new jobs in this area.

— **Bob Bolen, former Fort Worth Mayor and Senior Advisor to the Chancellor, at TCU 1991-2014**

We have a relationship with the Fort Worth Police; we have a lot of officers on our staff, we have the former SWAT Commander, former homicide and sexual assault commander, and five former sergeants. A lot of the young Fort Worth officers have worked for the officers that are now working for TCU. Because of our great relationship with the Fort Worth Police Department, we can work together to solve cases.

— **Steve McGee, Chief of TCU Police, at TCU 1995-2020**

When I got here, I was involved in the development of the urban institute and providing internships and students to work on projects that are important to the community. We worked with the city and took an old derelict property, and we created the Fairmont Community Garden. I think every college here realizes the importance of strong relationships with the Fort Worth community and do what they can to cultivate that.

— **Andrew Schoolmaster, Emeritus Professor of Geography and Dean, at TCU 2007-2021**

ABOVE
Liz Schmitt, a nursing student, helps prepare a bed for a garden at the YWCA in downtown Fort Worth. March 17, 2011. Courtesy of TCU Marketing and Communication. Photograph by Kathryn Hopper.

I take the position that, if something is good for Fort Worth, it is likely to be good for TCU.

— **Chancellor Emeritus Bill Tucker**

The Commission on the Future of TCU reinforced the value of the integrated process. We had the opinion leaders from inside the university talking with the opinion leaders outside the university, developing a unified idea about where we were, where we needed to go, and developing a shared language when they went out in the community. It changed the dynamic of Fort Worth and TCU. Up until then, people in Fort Worth were saying, "You're out on the hill, we don't see you involved in a lot of things." It seemed like a contradiction because the Van Cliburn competition started here and many theaters started here, but that began the process of resolving it. We put more money in advertising in the city. I got myself on the board of the Convention and Visitors Bureau and the task force on marketing the city because we had to develop this synergy with the city. Today you rarely hear people in the city saying that TCU's not involved. The perception is that we're very engaged in the city.

— **Larry Lauer, Emeritus Vice Chancellor for Government Affairs, at TCU 1966-2014**

I had a goal to connect more to the community as well and to work with agencies in the community, and I think we met that goal by having people on boards in the community, by working with places like Easter Seal and Goodwill—providing for people who might otherwise not have jobs and the underemployed.

— **Shari Barnes, Director of Employee Relations, at TCU 1983-2014**

ABOVE
TCU student with children from Butler Elementary at the Boys and Girls Club repairing the basketball court. Courtesy of Texas Christian University.

Receiving the Spirit of Enterprise Award had to do with the Commission on the Future. It was the first recognition that we were really engaged in the city and that we looked like we were an efficient operation.

— **Larry Lauer**

ABOVE
TCU colors displayed in downtown Fort Worth, 2009.
Courtesy of TCU Marketing and Communication

Fifteen years ago [1999], it was a cordial relationship between TCU and Fort Worth . . . but it was not as close as it is today. Fortunately, the leadership in both TCU and the city recognized that by working together we could build an incredible name for the city. For a long time, former mayor Bob Bolen was at TCU, and he was a conduit between the university and the city, making sure there was cooperation. I think it's at a point now where the relationship is good, and you can do just about anything you want to solve any problem you want to solve.

I think that TCU and the City of Fort Worth have grown together. The improvement downtown basically helped some of the economic development in and around TCU, and [the change at] the whole Berry Street corner took a partnership to make happen.

— **Vernell Sturns, Trustee Emeritus, served 1992-2002**

TCU is Fort Worth's university, and we are growing with Fort Worth. As Fort Worth develops, TCU develops. That's a great thing.

— **Scott Sullivan, Emeritus Professor of Art History and Dean, at TCU 2000-2016**

TCU and Fort Worth share a rich history of working today to create a better tomorrow, or turning obstacles into opportunity, of rejecting the way things are so that we can make things the way they should be—for the next 100 years and beyond

Michael J. Moncrief, former mayor, 2011

6.
Athletics

For the first three years I was here [1974-1976], the football record was 2-31. The coach then was Jim Shoffner, and he was fired after three seasons. The new head coach, F. A. Dry, had six seasons here, and his best record was the last year in 1982, and they were 3-8 that year. We were in the Southwest Conference then. In 1982 Jim Wacker was hired as the head coach, and he had some immediate success. He was a charismatic person, a larger-than-life kind of guy. In 1984 we went 8-3. We were ranked as high as twelve and went to the Bluebonnet Bowl in Houston. We hadn't been to a bowl game in a long, long time, so that was pretty exciting. Kenneth Davis, who was our running back, was a finalist for the Heisman that year as a junior. He was expected to be a strong candidate his senior year in 1985. After the first game Coach Wacker found out that some players were being paid by alumni, and they were all kicked off the team. That was a huge blow to the program, needless to say. During the Wacker time, especially in 1983 and 1984 when we were having some success, we got a lot of publicity. He was named Coach of the Year. I remember seeing the *Wall Street Journal*, and there was a story that day on the sports page about Coach Wacker and this phenomenon that was going on at TCU. You can't pay for that kind of publicity.

—Janet Herald, Associate Dean of Admissions, at TCU 1974-1989

ABOVE
Coach Jim Wacker with John Denton, 1984.
Courtesy of TCU Marketing and Communication.

I remember TCU basketball caught fire when a fellow by the name of Jim Killingsworth became the men's basketball coach [1979]. The team became known as the "Killer Frogs." It generated a lot of enthusiasm.

The first national championship we won was in women's golf in the eighties, and every year we were a top-ten team in men's tennis under coach Ted Barson, who was one of the great tennis men of his time. He was a great player too.

— Chancellor Emeritus Bill Tucker, at TCU 1979-1998

ABOVE
TCU women's golf NCAA Championship team, 1983.
Marci Bozarth, Jenny Lidback, Rae Rothfelder, Rita Moore, Anne Kelly, and Coach Fred Warren. Courtesy of TCU Marketing and Communication.

ABOVE
Students sunbathe in the bleachers during a TCU baseball game, 1978. Courtesy of Mary Couts Burnett Library. Photograph by Linda Kaye.

Probably one of the biggest steps forward is the baseball program. At one time, back there where the practice fields are for football, was our baseball stadium. There were wooden bleachers, maybe seats for three hundred people. Some sat on the grass field. The concessions stands were in Daniel-Meyer . . . The baseball team locker room was an old track locker on the south end of the stadium. The games would start at 3 p.m. on Fridays, so if you were at work you couldn't get there. The Saturday games were always a double header starting at noon. Sometimes they were suspended because of darkness.

There was some discussion of what to do with baseball because obviously the revenue was minimal. Some key people who were baseball players raised the money for a new stadium. The venue was so nice. As the team started winning, the crowds grew. It's just taken off. Every year there's been an NCAA appearance or a college world series. This year's class [2012] was ranked eleventh in recruiting. Little kids grow up and want to play for TCU.

—Jack Hesselbrock, Associate Athletics Director, at TCU 1988-2018

ABOVE
TCU baseball, 2022. Courtesy of TCU Marketing and Communication. Photograph by James Anger.

ABOVE
TCU volleyball, 2022. Courtesy of TCU Marketing and Communication.

When Lance Brown was here, we built the new stadium. Coach Brown had been in the stadium for a year, and then Coach Schlossnagel came in and really embraced the community. He started doing a lot of camps, formed the Diamond Club, and interacted with the former players and university alums and donors. He brought a lot of energy to the table.

I think the university also had more resources that they started devoting to the baseball program. Baseball was suddenly important. I think it was sort of a declaration. You either raise the money for this stadium and show that you have the support for baseball here, or baseball may be done with here.

— **Ross Bailey, Associate Athletics Director, at TCU 1977-2021**

ABOVE
TCU women's basketball takes home the Mountain West Conference championship after a win against the University of New Mexico, 2010. Courtesy of TCU Marketing and Communications. Photograph by Michael Clements.

ABOVE
TCU women's soccer vs UNT, 2013. Courtesy of TCU Media Relations. Photograph by Michael Clements.

I think once Coach Peterson came into women's basketball, we started recruiting a different type of athlete. Then when we added volleyball in the mid-nineties, and when we scholarshipped women's soccer, you started seeing the high school and club players from out of state visiting TCU. Mr. Rosenthal and the Garveys and the Justin Foundation believed in the women's soccer program and invested in it, funding the stadium and field house. I've known all these people for years and run into them and they say, "You hear how the women's soccer is doing?" I mean, that's cool.

— **Jack Hesselbrock**

Committee of 100

Your image starts in your backyard, and TCU really didn't have that strong of an image in Fort Worth, especially with the business community. The concept of TCU being the home team of everybody that lives in Fort Worth, regardless of where they went to school, didn't exist. It came when John Roach was Chairman of the Board of Trustees and started the Committee of 100.

—**Janet Herald**

The Southwest Conference breakup was pretty traumatic. We studied whether or not we ought to continue football and concluded that it was really going to cost us more not to do football that it was to play football, and so we continued.

At the same time, I decided we needed to really stabilize our fan base and started an organization called the Committee of 100. And the Committee of 100 was just a hundred people that I could round up that were interested in saving the football program. Before, when we had a football game, about half the fans were for TCU and about half the fans were for the opposing school. As the years went along, we developed as much fan base as we had before but with fans in support of TCU.

—**John V. Roach, Trustee Emeritus and former Chair, served 1981-2005**

When the Southwest Conference fell apart, Texas Tech and Baylor were going off to the Big XII; SMU, Rice, TCU were left without a conference. The press was beating us up. We were national champions in 1938, and now we didn't even have a conference to play in. As a university, we were trying to figure out how to fix this no-conference problem, and we didn't know what to do.

— **Larry Lauer, Emeritus Vice Chancellor for Government Affairs, at TCU 1966-2014**

We created the first marketing position in athletics. John Roach then came up with the idea of the Committee of 100. Eventually it became three or four hundred, but it was always called the Committee of 100. The idea was to try to mobilize the city of Fort Worth to help us solve this problem, getting business people to start buying season tickets to support us, and to get them to take ownership with us and to see us as Fort Worth's team. We developed a theme—TCU, your home team. It was Committee of 100 that created Frog Alley to see if we could get whole families to come out and have fun before going to the game. We did fireworks almost every game; we had parachutists and helicopters coming it at halftime. We wanted the city to see this as a social event for them and their families. Even if they weren't football fanatics, this was an event, an experience. The Committee of 100 was the architect of getting the city involved in athletics. Then we found Conference USA and several conferences after that, and the Committee of 100 became just a moment in history.

—**Larry Lauer**

The idea was to enhance athletic attendance, and their slogan was "the home team." Former coach Jim Wacker in the eighties used to say he was perfectly happy to have 10-1 fans when we played eleven games. You can be for us ten times and be against us when we play your school.

—**Don Mills, Vice Chancellor for Student Affairs Emeritus, at TCU 1969-2022**

ABOVE
Homecoming game, 1994. Courtesy of Mary Couts Burnett Library. Photograph by Linda Kaye.

As it worked out, losing our conference affiliation is probably one of the best things that ever happened to us, because during those few years we were playing schools across the country in different conferences, we got much better known. We realized that our athletic facilities weren't up to par, so we built the baseball stadium, the track, the women's soccer stadium, the Justin Center, and the indoor practice field to make ourselves look more attractive to other conferences.

— **Bronson Davis, Vice Chancellor of University Advancement, at TCU 1990-2006**

Sun Bowl

- December 31, 1998
- TCU's first bowl victory in forty-one years
- TCU vs. University of Southern California
- Played in El Paso, Texas, on the campus of the University of Texas at El Paso
- TCU wins 28 to 19
- First-Year Coach Dennis Franchione

On New Year's Eve of 1998 the Sun Bowl lived up to its name with a bright, almost scorching sun shining both literally and figuratively on the TCU Horned Frogs and their fans. The game opened with local sky divers who parachuted into the stadium to deliver the game balls (photo 1).

The Frogs came out of the chute running, scoring on their first possession, led by senior running back Basil Mitchell (3, photos 2 and 3), who gained 185 yards for the game and was named the Most Valuable Player.

TCU's defense also stepped up behind players such as senior defensive end Kam Hunt (48, photo 4) and junior safety Reggie Hunt(2, photo 5) leaving the Trojans with -23 yards rushing in the game.

After leading in the third quarter by as much as 28-3, the Frogs held off a late Trojan surge to win the game 28-19 and celebrate their upset victory (photo 6).

ABOVE
Skiff, January 20, 1999. Courtesy of *Skiff*.

Coach Franchione was the one that started moving us forward. The most exciting thing, however, the big turnaround game, was when we were in the Sun Bowl against USC. We were the underdog. People couldn't believe that we were even going. USC almost seemed humiliated that they were having to play this team. "TCU, who?" But we won that game. We made three touchdowns bam, bam, bam, before they even knew what was going on. A lot of people see that Sun Bowl game as a turning point. From that point, people started realizing who we were.

— Kristi Hoban, Associate Vice Chancellor for Alumni Relations, at TCU 1980-2019

One year we went to the Sun Bowl in El Paso, one of the most beautiful football stadiums I've ever seen. It was built in the side of the mountain. We were playing USC, which was a well-known football program that was invited to bowl games every year. And then we beat them.

— Roby Key, Associate Vice Chancellor for Advancement Operations, at TCU 1988-2016

USC was stunned because we beat them. That was the first big step to getting back to where we wanted to go with football—beating Southern Cal. That woke up a lot of kids to TCU.

— Frank Windegger, Athletics Director Emeritus, at TCU 1959-1999

For most of my early years at TCU, we had a weak football program. Our losing record was holding us back and made TCU a sleepy backwater school. Dennis Franchione turned that around and made TCU a winner . . . he took our team to the Sun Bowl, and they beat USC. That was so huge for the program, for the university. He didn't stay long after that, but he was here to recruit LaDainian Tomlinson and brought Gary Patterson to campus.

We give a lot of credit to the Rose Bowl, and we should, but that Sun Bowl team was really the match that lit the wick.

— Dick Hoban, Assistant Treasurer, at TCU 1981-2019

We were like 24-25 point underdogs. Clarence Scharbauer, who was the chair of the board, went to the game, but he was so nervous about how TCU would do, he didn't even wear purple. I never let him forget it. TCU at the time had vulnerable self-esteem, and what Coach Fran did was build up that self-esteem.

— Eric Hyman, Athletics Director, at TCU 1998-2005

Starting in 1998, when Dennis Franchione and Gary Patterson came in, we went to the Sun Bowl against the University of Southern California, and that was the beginning of the current football era, and we've been to a bowl practically every year since. That has raised the recognition of the university. We started to see the rankings come up right after that.

— Bill Moncrief, Emeritus Professor of Marketing, at TCU 1982-2023

Rose Bowl

- January 1, 2011
- 97th Rose Bowl
- Pasadena, California
- TCU beats Wisconsin 21-19
- This game marked the first time a team from a non-Automatic Qualifying Conference won the Rose Bowl since 1934, when Columbia beat Stanford, 7-0.
- TCU finished the regular season with a 12-0 record and the Mountain West Conference title.

The year Coach Fran left, I think we had more football players sign pro contracts than any school in the country besides Florida State. People began to be intrigued by TCU. In 2010 TCU was undefeated, and we were the darlings of the country.

— **Eric Hyman**

What happened of significance in 2011? We won the Rose Bowl. Our applications went from about 14,000 a year to 19,000 a year in one year. A big event in TCU's history.

— **Dick Hoban**

Whenever there are really ambitious goals, you are rarely going to be able to achieve those in a single incident or flash. Many are ongoing, and it's a continuing process. Football is like that. You don't go from where we were in 1998 to being in the Rose Bowl without a lot of things moving forward and falling into place.

— **Chancellor Emeritus Mick Ferrari, at TCU 1998-2003**

The changes here have been phenomenal. I knew Dutch Meyer and Davey O'Brien when he played in the 1939 Sugar Bowl. I watched the Rose Bowl on TV. Not many people saw both those games.

— **Bob Bolen, former Fort Worth Mayor and Senior Advisor to the Chancellor, at TCU 1991-2014**

Athletics have been incredibly fun. I would have to say that one of the peak experiences I'll ever have was going to the Rose Bowl—well that's a lie—winning the Rose Bowl. Being there in that moment was so cool.

— **Chancellor Victor Boschini**

ABOVE
The TCU football team celebrates a momentus victory at the 2011 Rose Bowl. Courtesy of Texas Christian University. Photograph by Glen Ellman.

We did a thank-you ad in the *Los Angeles Times* that we were going to run win or lose, [which included] a Quick Response Code at the bottom. When you [followed the link] it sent you to a video that showed different images of TCU. A reader of the *LA Times* emailed the Chancellor right after seeing it and said, "It was great to see this thank you ad." No one had ever done a thank you ad after the Rose Bowl [before]. He said, "I don't have any children, but I have friends who have college-age children, and I am going to tell them about TCU." That was worth the price of that ad. Now I'm told that whoever plays in the Rose Bowl has been doing thank-you ads. It was great to set that standard.

— **Tracy Syler-Jones, Vice Chancellor for Marketing and Communication**

Winning the Rose Bowl had a major impact that still continues. You couldn't market the school in a better way. Athletics and academics work together in teams, bringing people to the school, educating them, helping raise funds, and [promoting] development.

— **Mark Johnson, Member of the TCU Board of Trustees and former Chair**

ABOVE
Rose Bowl, 2011. Courtesy of Texas Christian University. Photograph by Glen E. Ellman.

ABOVE
Amon G. Carter Stadium, 2012. Courtesy of TCU Marketing and Communication. Photograph by Sharon Ellman.

Chancellor Tucker used to call athletics the window through which people viewed the university. Before the Rose Bowl, we never could directly contribute any increase in giving to a bowl game. But when we won the Rose Bowl it changed everything. There was just a huge change in attitude and mentality about TCU in a lot of places. Winning the Rose Bowl really put TCU in the minds of many people who didn't know the school. It put us in a new class.

—**Roby Key**

In the second big campaign we started, Vision in Action, we were going to raise $250 million. The big exciting thing in that campaign that wasn't anticipated was the new football stadium. We were talking about renovating it, and we couldn't touch the football stadium without bringing it up to ADA (American Disability Act) compliance. The university wanted to do that to be ADA compliant, but it required a whole lot more than just a little fixer-upper. It was going to be a major renovation, $160 million or so for the project. The university said we would do it in phases, the west side first, and if we raised the money for that, then the east side. Then we went to the Rose Bowl, and there was a lot of enthusiasm and support. Before we knew it we raised $142 million just for the stadium. The Chancellor said, "Let's just do it," so the university financed the difference. If you go to the games, you know how wonderful the stadium is compared to the old one.

For us to go to the Rose Bowl, it's quality with integrity.

—**Larry Adams, Emeritus Associate Provost and Associate Professor of Sociology, at TCU 1969-2011**

We've become coast to coast. Now everyone knows about TCU. Athletics is the ultimate marketing tool for the university. We are the front porch. Going to Omaha in baseball, Peach Bowl, Rose Bowl, Fiesta Bowl in football, you can't buy that exposure. And after every bowl game we run an ad that says, "Great season, thanks for having us," and everyone talks about TCU.

— **Chris Del Conte, Athletics Director, at TCU 2009-2017**

A greater number of people know more about TCU now. And it's partly because of athletics, no question about it. It's successful athletics in baseball, football, equestrian—and our rifle team is tremendous.

— **Jim Atwood, Professor of Religion and Assistant to the Dean of Admissions, at TCU 1979-2020**

ABOVE
TCU rifle team wins the NCAA 2013 National Championship. Courtesy of TCU Marketing and Communications.

The applications really rose because of recognition of the athletic programs. It was a positive change to see so much purple in the stadium, the community support of TCU, our sports fans filling the seats, and the pride students have in their college.

— **Edward G. "Ned" Boehm, Dean of Admissions and Associate Vice Chancellor for Academic Programs, at TCU 1979-1989**

ABOVE
Brandon Parrish and teammates hold the NIT trophy high after defeating Georgia Tech in the championship game, 2017. Courtesy of Texas Christian Univeristy. Photograph by Glen E. Ellman.

There have been some monumental things that have happened. We went to the Fiesta Bowl, Rose Bowl, twice to Omaha, and we've had countless individual national championships and NCAA tournament appearances. We have a new soccer stadium, new football stadium, new basketball stadium, and improvements to track and field and the baseball stadium. We're growing, and it has been a whirlwind. We joined three different conferences. We went from the Mountain West to the Big East to the Big XII. Our ultimate goal is to graduate 100 percent of our student athletes and for us to win championships in every sport, and to do it all with class, honor, and pride.

— **Chris Del Conte, Athletics Director, at TCU 2009-2017**

TCU Championships

Conference Championships

- Men's Tennis – 27
- Baseball – 25
- Football – 18
- Men's Basketball – 13
- Men's Golf – 9
- Women's Tennis – 8
- Rifle – 7
- Women's Basketball – 6
- Women's Golf – 6
- Track and Field/Cross Country – 6
- Women's Soccer – 3

Total – 128

National Championships

- Rifle – 9
- Football – 2
- Equestrian – 1
- Women's Golf – 1
- Men's Tennis – 1

Total – 14

We're going to win a national championship—football, basketball, baseball—it's going to happen. We already did it in rifle and equestrian. Why not do it in the others?

— **Clarence Scharbauer III, Trustee Emeritus and former Chair, served 1990-2017**

ABOVE
TCU equestrian team at the Varsity Equestrian Western National Championship, 2008. Courtesy of TCU Marketing and Communication.

ABOVE
TCU rifle team member, Mindy Miles, who received the 2016 NCAA Sportsmanship Award after self-reporting a misfire during the 2016 NCAA National Championship. Courtesy of TCU Athletics. Photograph by Sharon Ellman.

As we moved into 2007-2008, a lot of good things happened that year. A lot of sports did well, and equestrian won the national championship. From a facilities standpoint, the construction of the end zone project got completed that year. It was wonderful that they named it after two legendary coaches at TCU, Dutch Meyer and Abe Martin, just as the indoor practice facility was named after Sammy Baugh, the Hall of Fame football player at TCU. Also that year we had a student javelin thrower who also played football, a guy named Joe Brown, and he was the Mountain West Conference Student Athlete of the Year.

Then in 2008-2009, we hosted the rifle national championship, and one of the members of our rifle team was cited for her sportsmanship when she called a misfire on herself, which I think spoke well for TCU. There was a young quarterback that year named Andy Dalton, who did a lot of nice things, and then led a win over Boise State in the Poinsettia Bowl.

— **Danny Morrison, Athletics Director, at TCU 2005-2009**

For us to get where we wanted to be at TCU, there was no such thing as being comfortable. I think you have to be comfortable being uncomfortable, because that means we have to keep pushing. We're at a point getting in the Big XII Conference where you'll say, "Well, we've arrived." No, not really. What we've done is we just got to where now the real work begins.

I've always felt like you get to a point where you're also an ambassador of the university. Athletics is the front porch of a house. It's not the most important, but it's the most visible. Whether it be admissions or any other aspect of the university, I think that we play a part in that. We've been very fortunate to have really good assistants all the way down through the ranks of our trainers, equipment people, strength coaches, everyone. Good people, hard workers.

Going to the Big XII, financial formation has never been like this at TCU in however many years that it's been in existence. We sit on top of a rock now. It's been an unbelievable journey, and it's taken a lot of people to be successful.

— **Gary Patterson, Head Football Coach, at TCU 1998-2021**

ABOVE
TCU men's tennis, Jerry Lopez, 2016. Courtesy of TCU Marketing and Communication.

It would be hard not to recognize the visibility that our athletic teams have had. I do believe that that has been an impetus for this upward trajectory because we got more national attention when TCU competed in the Rose Bowl several years ago. There was a direct correlation to the number of applications we got that year.

—Jean Pickett, Chief of Staff

In a lot of institutions you see the athletic programs and the institution growing apart from each other. They not only have their own identity, but they have their own values, their own culture, and it doesn't match very much the institution's values and culture. We set out to say that the athletic program has to look like athletics . . . but it also has to look like TCU's message and has to be connected to leadership, vitality, all of those qualities that bring value to the total community experience.

— Larry Lauer

When you're hiring a coach, it is critical that they fit your culture, fit your mold of what you want young people to be around—that they fit what you're trying to do.

—Chris Del Conte

I think we've got a really good team of head coaches. We need to get better in our strength and condition efforts, and we've got an initiative underway there. We've got to get better in our recovery and nutrition. Those are big priorities of mine. We're starting a new program in triathlon that will come online in 2023.

—Jeremiah Donati, Athletics Director

ABOVE
TCU swimming and diving, 2015. Courtesy of TCU Marketing and Communication.

Each sport has had its high points throughout the years, and different programs have really excelled. We've been known for tremendous tennis, golf, and track teams. We've seen some success over the years in our swimming program, and we won the Mountain West championship one year with the men. We won five actually—four men and one women's Conference USA title. We've beat some big schools head-to-head. Recently, baseball has really come on, and I think that's a tribute to the type of people that those coaches recruited. Equestrian and rifle, holy cow, those have been some of our most successful in recent years too. The Big XII has been fun for us to join. I think you see all sports have contributed to the wellbeing of TCU and its athletic program.

— Richard Sybesma, Swimming and Diving Coach, at TCU 1979-2017

ABOVE
TCU rifle team, 2022. Courtesy of TCU Athletics.

ABOVE
TCU women's soccer wins the Big XII championship, 2020. Courtesy of TCU Athletics.

ABOVE
Clara Cargile from the TCU equestrian team, riding White Indian, 2017. Courtesy of TCU Marketing and Communication.

Women's Soccer—After tying 0-0 in a defensive battle with Baylor in their first game, the Frogs won eight straight games to end the 2020 season, cruising through the season without much pushback and winning their first-ever Big 12 Championship.

—*TCU 360*, March 14, 2021

It's a pretty cool moment in history for the women's soccer team. We needed that moment. Since March 11, the day the pandemic dropped on us, it had just been so hard. Then women's soccer goes on this incredible run. They were undefeated. I'll always remember that moment when people were so happy. They were smiling and crying, and it was so uplifting to have that energy back. I think about what the team went through, the pandemic and the BLM movement, to then have a perfect season—just a really special time in our history.

—Jeremiah Donati

Fiesta Bowl 2022

TCU is the first school from the state of Texas to make the College Football Playoff, and just the second team to be in the CFP after starting the season unranked.

— TCU Athletics, Press Release

[Max Duggan] attended the Heisman ceremony. He was unanimously awarded Big XII Offensive Player of the Year. The only winner of the Heisman in TCU's history was Davey O'Brien in 1938, which was the year the Frogs won their second national championship. The last finalist TCU had for the Heisman Trophy was running back LaDainian Tomlinson in 2000.

— *TCU 360*, Dec. 5, 2022

ABOVE
TCU football players celebrate the Horned Frogs' victory in the Fiesta Bowl, 2022. Courtesy of TCU Marketing and Communication. Photograph by Amy Peterson.

ABOVE
TCU football players celebrate the Horned Frogs' victory in the Fiesta Bowl, 2022. Courtesy of TCU Marketing and Communication. Photograph by Amy Peterson.

Our student-athletes, coaching staff, and entire football team represent the very best of college athletics—their character, determination, and grit are hard at work every day. What I love most—and what I want everyone to see—is that this team represents all of us, our academic mission and the values-based TCU community that has been built over 150 years.

— **Chancellor Victor Boschini**

We cannot thank you enough for the incredible support and showing in Los Angeles for our College Football National Championship game (2023). We turned Southern California into a sea of purple. While the game did not go our way, it was still a magical season and your appreciation of Head Coach Sonny Dykes and his program was truly felt. During my twelve years on campus, I have never seen our fans and city bond with a team as much as we saw this season. It meant a lot to our student-athletes, coaches, and staff to be greeted by so many of you upon our return to campus the night after the game.

—**Jeremiah Donati**

ABOVE
Horned Frogs and members of the Fort Worth community gather to send off the football team as they depart for Los Angeles to play in the College Football Playoff National Championship, 2023. Courtesy of TCU Marketing and Communication. Photograph by Amy Peterson.

7.

Students and Student Life

ABOVE
Students making music together, 1973. Courtesy of Mary Couts Burnett Library. Photograph by Linda Kaye.

ABOVE
Students with motorcycles, 1972. Courtesy of Mary Couts Burnett Library.

RIGHT
Student government officers, 1978. Courtesy of Mary Couts Burnett Library.

RIGHT
Student pauses outside of Sadler Hall to pet a dog, 1971. Courtesy of Mary Couts Burnett Library.

ABOVE
Students celebrate at graduation, 1986. Courtesy of Mary Couts Burnett Library.

LEFT
Student, 1980. Courtesy of Mary Couts Burnett Library.

ABOVE
Students playing frisbee in front of Sadler Hall, 1971. Courtesy of Mary Couts Burnett Library.

LEFT
Voices United gospel choir, 1976. Courtesy of Mary Couts Burnett Library. Photograph by Linda Kaye

ABOVE
Homecoming parade, 1995. Published in TCU yearbook. Courtesy of Mary Couts Burnett Library.

RIGHT
Students play hockey in Clark Hall, 1995. Published in TCU yearbook. Courtesy of Mary Couts Burnett Library.

ABOVE (RIGHT)
Student playing with hackey sack, 1999. Published in TCU yearbook. Courtesy of Mary Couts Burnett Library.

ABOVE
A student takes a spin on the TCU Time Machine at the 2005 homecoming parade. Courtesy of Mary Couts Burnett Library. Photograph by Linda Kaye.

RIGHT
Homecoming king and queen with Chancellor Boschini, 2005. Courtesy of Mary Couts Burnett Library. Photograph by Linda Kaye.

ABOVE
Students play a game of soccer on the lawn, 2007. Courtesy of *TCU Magazine*.

LEFT
Outside in the spring sun, Atisha Thomas takes a ride on Daryl Stafford's back while he attempts to catch a grape in his mouth, 2009. Courtesy of TCU Marketing and Communication. Photograph by Amy Peterson.

OPPOSITE
Students enjoy the record-breaking snowfall on campus, 2010. Courtesy of Texas Christian University.

ABOVE
Carols by Candlelight at Robert Carr Chapel, 2019. Courtesy of TCU Marketing and Communication. Photograph by Amy Peterson.

ABOVE
Farmers Market in the Commons, hosted by the Crew. Courtesy of TCU Marketing and Communication. Photograph by James Anger.

BELOW
Graduates celebrate at the fall commencement ceremony, 2021. Courtesy of Texas Christian University. Photograph by Peter Matthews.

ABOVE
Students set up their hammocks outside to study and socialize, 2019. Courtesy of TCU Marketing and Communication. Photograph by Jeffrey McWhorter.

RIGHT
Student scales the climbing wall at the Recreation Center, 2022. Courtesy of TCU Marketing and Communication. Photograph by James Anger.

LEFT
Students play frisbee on the Campus Commons, 2019. Courtesy of TCU Marketing and Communication. Photograph by Jeffrey McWhorter.

The students have just written a creed [2011]. "Learning with passion, serving with respect, and leading with integrity." This is what the students want to own. This is not in place of the mission statement. It's what student leaders are going to teach other students. It's what TCU students want to be known for. I think students of today are saying what the founders would be real proud of, so we've got this great big circle.

— **Larry Adams, Emeritus Associate Provost and Associate Professor of Sociology, at TCU 1969-2011**

I think what I liked most about the school was the size of TCU. And some of the things that an undergraduate can do there. My daughter said, "One of the things I like about TCU is that I can go into the breakfast commons and I know everyone there."

— **Fred Heath, University Librarian, at TCU 1987-1993**

The division between students in fraternities and sororities and those not is diminishing. A reason for that is Frog Camp, Frogs First, and then orientation—emphasizing TCU as a body first.

— **Michael Russel, Associate Vice Chancellor for Student Affairs**

This has always been a relatively sophisticated student body. In the past we were a little less broad-minded. Today we are a little more cosmopolitan. We are clearly more national, we are more international. The students are an interesting mix. On average they are pretty politically conservative and socially liberal. It's a brighter student body than it used to be, much more intellectually engaged. They are much more serious students. I think that goes along with the increasing prominence of the school. I would like to see a little more diversity—diversity of thought, diversity of race, diversity of socio-economic status. This is about the politest student body I have ever seen. People are holding doors open and I really like that. I find myself doing that as well.

— **Michael Russel**

One of the things that's changed rather dramatically within the last several years is the rigor and quality required to get into TCU, and the admissions standards have gone way up. It doesn't mean that everyone is an academic whirlwind here, but generally speaking the quality of preparedness and propensity for academic studies has gone up at TCU. There's no question about that.

— **Jim Atwood, Professor of Religion and Assistant to the Dean Of Admissions, at TCU 1979-2020**

If there's one thing I would urge all students to do, it's to become compassionate about your fellow students in everything that you do, because they are very vulnerable human beings at this time in their lives. People drinking and driving, fraternities not taking their responsibilities seriously, those kinds of things I wish never happened, but they do. They're a part of the human condition. Our hope is that students can move forward with having more concern for their fellow students and be willing to say "no" to the danger, or "I'm concerned about my friend who is depressed," so that we can stop needless harm to students.

— **Peggy Barr, Vice Chancellor for Student Affairs, at TCU 1985-1992**

For students we promote lots of things. You don't have to be president of something to be a leader, but get involved. In a lot of ways, I wish the United States government functioned the way our student government does, because we have limits on how much you can spend on a campaign. It's not about who spends the most money, it's about who gets out there and learns what your issues are as students, what you care about, and what you should do as student leaders. I see students learning their own leadership style.

Administrators have always listened to student leaders here. I think it's because they're very careful with how they put things together. They don't demand things; they request things after doing a lot of homework to find out what's reasonable and how best to go about it. When students point out a problem, they want to be part of the solution, and that to me is one of the best leadership skills you can have. We coach them on how to do that, but [they go by] their own sense of what they're going to do and how they're going to do it.

— **Susan Adams, Associate Vice Chancellor for Student Affairs, at TCU 1975-2014**

Student finances are always an issue. Only yesterday, I heard the chair of the Board of Trustees say that the next great financial campaign will be for scholarships. We really want to make sure that TCU does not become a rich kid's college only. They realize, given the size of tuition, that there has to be more scholarship money to attract people from all economic backgrounds. A student body that is more heterogeneous is better than a student body all from the same socioeconomic status.

— **Ron Flowers, Professor of Religion, at TCU 1996-2021**

At the smaller, private schools, commitment to the individual directly correlates to performance of the students as leaders and their cooperation with the university. It's a little harder to get lost here. I hear that from students. "I'm not going to do something if my friend won't let me, if my faculty won't let me. If I don't show up for class, I'll be missed. Faculty are going to notice that, and somebody's going to be calling to ask, "What's up?" and, "Is something going on that you need help with?" Now some people really want to be more solo and concentrate on their academic work, and that's fine. We just want to make sure everybody's doing well in that process and that they are interacting. Hence, the design of the new Student Union. Everyone eats in one big place. That's an intentional design, so that it can create interaction.

— **Susan Adams**

Fraternity and sorority life has evolved over the last twenty years. When I came here twenty-one years ago, it was clearly southern Texas style with only a certain way of doing that. The amount of money that the young women were spending on their clothes for day one, their clothes for day two, for day three, I think was divisive and not very helpful. They felt like they had to look a certain way and act a certain way.

There were national guidelines and norms that we tended not to follow. The national guidelines for the Panhellenic sororities are to go "no frills." It becomes less a beauty contest and more of who you are. . . . I think they hear us loud and clear that you've got to be a TCU student first and an XYZ second. There were times when I first got here that this group would not talk to that group, and that has diminished. I don't see people not getting along because of the groups they are in. We are certainly keeping the same percentages of Greeks, and the numbers are staggering. I think our average membership for each women's chapter is 220 to 240. Most chapters across the country have 110 members.

— **Michael Russel**

There is still definitely a feeling of family and community and definitely a student centeredness. But, oh my goodness, the campus has totally changed. The size is close to double; it is a more diverse population. I think that when I first came it was primarily Texas, mostly West Texas, and now we have students from all over the world. We did then too, but not as many. I also think that our students are even brighter than they used to be. But there is still a feeling of being more down to earth and polite and nice that maybe comes with the Texas vibe, I don't know. We have great students.

— **Barbara Herman, Associate Vice Chancellor for Student Affairs, at TCU 1986-2021**

8.
Frog Camp

ABOVE
Team challenge during Frog Camp, 2014. Courtesy of TCU Marketing and Communication.

LEFT
Frog Camp attendees volunteering with Habitat for Humanity, 1998. Courtesy of Mary Couts Burnett Library. Photograph by Linda Kaye.

One of the reasons I wanted to start Frog Camp was to have students bond to each other and to TCU before classes started and before they joined any organizations. I was concerned that the first thing students did was to go through Greek recruitment and to choose or be chosen for their social groups. Then there was a divide between Greek and non-Greek students, and I thought that the first student experiences should be bringing everyone together.

If you can get rid of the phones and the distractions and be totally present, listening to each other, sharing fears and concerns and excitements and learning about what college life is going to be, that has made a difference at TCU. I know when we started Frog Camp, the first to second year retention was maybe 78 percent, and now it's over 90 percent.

I think bonding to the university has been pretty successful. Learning the songs and the chants and the traditions and being with upper-level students who love TCU. I think there's an excitement and a bonding that happens at Frog Camp that has been extremely helpful.

The first year we had right around one hundred campers, and now we have almost fourteen hundred a year. So that has been thrilling. I'm pretty proud of the fact that the Frog Camp model has stayed exactly the same. From the very first camp we had small groups of twelve to fourteen with a faculty or staff facilitator and two upper-level student facilitators. It emphasizes our unique identities, what we bring, how we are different yet all looking for many of the same things, and so celebrating that diversity and that community has been a part from the beginning.

Frog Camp was an attempt to find ways to value every identity. We've changed that in recent years, and that was something that I promoted—being more cognizant of how many discussions can be triggering, and so finding ways to make sure that as we celebrate diversity, it doesn't create division—and so again putting the emphasis on connectedness and community and sharing and respect.

And the heart of Frog Camp has always been the student leaders. If people ask me what's unique about TCU, I always talk about that relationship between faculty, staff, and students. I think that having student-led programs is one of our hallmarks. That it's the job of staff to stand in the background and cheer on our student leaders. They're the ones up front, they're the ones making decisions, they're the ones creating relationships, and to me that's so exciting. It gets back to that idea of mentoring, that you see that student leaders blossom, and it's important for us from the beginning to have student leaders who reflect every part of student life, every part of student interest, every part of student identity.

— Barbara Herman, Associate Vice Chancellor for Student Affairs, at TCU 1986-2021

ABOVE
Frog Camp, 2014. Courtesy of TCU Marketing and Communication.

ABOVE
Frog Camp, 2011. Courtesy of TCU Marketing and Communication.

ABOVE
Frog Camp Challenge in Bruceville, Texas, 2022. Courtesy of TCU Marketing and Communication. Photograph by Roxanne Odiorne.

ABOVE
Frog Camp, 2011. Courtesy of TCU Marketing and Communication.

LEFT
A member of the incoming class of 2020 works on painting a mural during Frog Camp, 2016. Courtesy of Texas Christian University. Photograph by Glen E. Ellman.

RIGHT
Campers cheer each other on during Frog Camp All-Stars at Burger's Lake, 2022. Courtesy of TCU Marketing and Communication. Photograph by James Anger.

Frog camp has changed the way TCU looks. When I came here twenty-one years ago, people did wear TCU shirts, but not very often. Now every other person has some sort of purple on. And fortunately, purple is a good color.

— **Michael Russel, Associate Vice Chancellor for Student Affairs**

ABOVE
Incoming students at Sundance Square in downtown Fort Worth with Frog Camp, 2021. Courtesy of TCU Marketing and Communication. Photograph by Andrew Emery.

We are interested in being sure that we are a community that is vitally interested in one another. We have always worked at ways in which we kept the incoming student connected: student activities, student life, Frog Camp, welcome week, Howdy Week, as it's traditionally called at TCU. There are a number of organizations that students may join for connectedness, because the more connected we are, the more beneficial that the community will be to us.

— **Larry Adams, Emeritus Associate Provost and Associate Professor of Sociology, at TCU 1969-2011**

ABOVE
Incoming first-year Horned Frogs tackle the ropes course during Frog Camp Alpine, 2022. Courtesy of TCU Marketing and Communication. Photograph by Amy Peterson.

ABOVE
Students in Frog Camp Alpine amidst the Colorado Rockies, 2022. Courtesy of TCU Marketing and Communication. Photograph by Amy Peterson.

9.

Community Scholars

LEFT
Students don TCU hats at a Community Scholars scholarship event, 2018. Courtesy of *TCU Magazine*. Photograph by Leo Wesson.

BELOW (LEFT)
Community Scholars pose by Frog Fountain. Courtesy of TCU Marketing and Communication.

The Community Scholars program champions dreams. TCU provides Community Scholars with outstanding leadership skills and the necessary support to be successful members of the TCU community. The long-term goal is to help students attain their full potential, including advanced degrees, to help them become the next generation of community and business leaders.

Approximately forty of the best applicants join our first-year class each year. These students receive academic and career support, and opportunities to participate in leadership and social activities. The Community Scholars program was created to further the belief that a diverse community is essential to a quality education. This program has grown to include thirteen underrepresented public high schools where top students are recruited for full-ride scholarships to TCU.

— **TCU Community Scholars website**

The Community Scholars program is really brilliant. It acknowledges that there are high school students in Fort Worth who come from families that never thought about college. There were students going to high school who had dreams way bigger than their parents' dreams, or their parent's dreams were just as big but they couldn't support them—TCU was totally out of reach, with tuition that couldn't even be touched with academic scholarships. Chancellor Ferrari created the Community Scholars program, and we are still very much indebted to his leadership for bringing these students to campus. These students are changing the experiences of their families and are living their dreams.

— **Ann Louden, Chancellor's Associate for Strategic Partnerships, at TCU 1978-2017**

The Community Scholars program was established on Dr. Ferrari's watch. He listened to our arguments about why we were so white, and said "Okay, that's enough. We're going to fix this." We started with four eligible high schools, and these were four schools where we said in essence, "Give us your best and your brightest and we'll take care of them," and so it's just continued to build over time to where that program has become a bit of a jewel in this university's crown.

Mick Ferrari set out as one of his goals to begin the change of making this very white institution more reflective of the environment where we find ourselves. At that time, in the year 2000, we were 9 percent students of color. Today [in 2014], we've more than doubled that. We cracked 20 percent in the first-year class this past year, which is nice. We've made a great deal of headway on that front, but it's not where we need to be. One of the things that has changed dramatically is that when I got here, we could go to some of these city schools that are now a part of the program and ask the kids there, "Would you consider TCU?" Often their response would be, "Oh no, wrong color." We don't hear that anymore.

— **Ray Brown, Dean of Admissions, at TCU 2000-2016**

LEFT
Students from Trimble Tech High School with their Community Scholars acceptance letters. Courtesy of FWISD.

Darron Turner was the one who took the lead in running the program, but the program was actually initiated by Sandy Ware in admissions and Cornell Thomas, who was the chancellor's assistant for diversity. We knew how important it was to be more reflective of diversity, so the design was created to target certain high schools that were diverse. I think it's a model that [provides] attention and support and creates leaders for life. These are fabulous, amazing students, and we are lucky to get them—look at what they bring to our campus.

— **Barbara Herman, Associate Vice Chancellor for Student Affairs, at TCU 1986-2021**

Community Scholars

The program started in 2000 with twelve students from four underserved Fort Worth high schools. By 2020, TCU welcomed 40 students from thirteen high schools from throughout the Metroplex. These include Diamond Hill-Jarvis, Dunbar, North Side, O. D. Wyatt, Polytechnic, South Hills, Trimble Technical, Young Men's Leadership Academy, Sam Houston, Lincoln, DeSoto, Barack Obama Male Leadership Academy, and David W. Carter.

One hundred percent of tuition and housing is paid. There is a ninety-plus percent graduation rate, and more than forty percent continue to graduate study.

ABOVE
Caitlin Reed, a junior studio art major is part of TCU's Community Scholars program, 2018. Courtesy of *TCU Magazine*. Photograph by Leo Wesson.

When I first started at TCU, the Community Scholars Program was just beginning. The program attracts local students from urban high schools. A lot of students from those schools, tended to think, "Oh, I could never go to TCU." I was really proud to see TCU put that initiative in place and aggressively do outreach. These students have done tremendously well at the university. We get fantastic students here at TCU.

— **Tracy Syler-Jones, Vice Chancellor for Marketing and Communication**

ABOVE
From L-R, Victoria Garcia, Brandon Carrasco Ballinas, and Cecilia Esparza from Polytechnic High School in Fort Worth have received the TCU Community Scholars scholarship, 2018. Courtesy of TCU Marketing and Communication. Photograph by Leo Wesson.

I know we have more scholarships intentionally targeted to attract students from a wider range of economic backgrounds. The Community Scholars program has really grown over the past ten years to become an important way of bringing economic diversity to campus. We are certainly getting to be a more expensive school. The chancellor and administration are committed to keeping the financial aid growing at the same rate, or better than, tuition increases.

— **Michael Russel, Associate Vice Chancellor for Student Affairs**

To see them [Community Scholars] want to go abroad and to make that work, and for TCU to have made that possible for them, has been one of the great breakthroughs. It has been terrific to hear Community Scholars come back and say, "If I can do it, you can do it."

— **Susan Layne, Advisor in the Center for International Studies, at TCU 1987-2018**

ABOVE
Students receive the news of being named Community Scholars for the incoming Class of 2022. Courtesy of TCU Marketing and Communication. Photograph by Amy Peterson.

ABOVE
Students at O. D. Wyatt High School awarded TCU's Community Scholars scholarship, 2018. Courtesy of TCU Marketing and Communication. Photograph by Amy Peterson.

10.
Academics

ABOVE
Violinst from the School of Music, 2016.
Courtesy of TCU Marketing and Communication.
Photograph by Dixie Dixon.

RIGHT
Student in the Neeley School of Business, 2019.
Courtesy of TCU Marketing and Communication.
Photograph by Jeffrey McWhorter

Admissions

When I started in the admissions office in 1974, we had no clear image of what defined TCU. The university was just whatever you wanted it to be to all people. In 1979, after Dr. Tucker became chancellor, Larry Lauer convened a committee, which I served on, to discuss what made TCU what it was, and out of that discussion we came up with what we called the "case points" for TCU. The overarching theme was that TCU had the advantages of a large university with the environment of a small college. There was finally some consistency to our message, and we hammered it in publications, in discussions and interviews with students, and while visiting with high school counselors. There were a lot of things that began at the university at that time that have honed our image as we have gone forward.

We began in about 1983 to focus more on quality and on changing the profile of the first-year class. In 1985 we finally cracked 3,000 applications. We thought, "Oh my gosh, we have arrived."

In terms of admission strategy, we added recruitment staff over time, and in the 1980s we had superb recruitment support staff. We were concerned about our demographic picture, so in 1979, Ann Louden, who was then Director of Alumni Affairs, and I started a program that involved alumni with the recruitment process. We started with ten target areas, some out of state and some in state, including committees in Connecticut; Washington, DC; Chicago; Kansas City; and in multiple cities in Texas.

In terms of awareness, football made a big difference. While I don't give the football program credit for all our success in the eighties, it did generate some national publicity that I think helped us with local publicity as well. There was definitely a correlation between good teams and number of applications. By 1987 we really had gained some ground with the SAT; we finally got it back up to where it needed to be, where we were at least in line with SMU, Baylor, UT, and A&M.

—Janet Herald

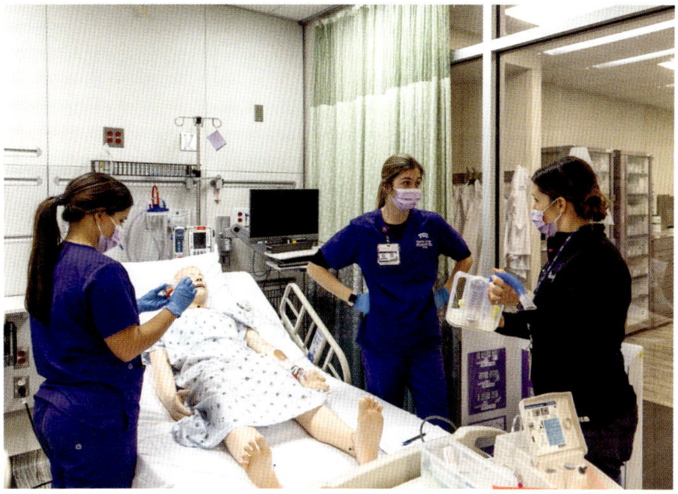

ABOVE
Students in Harris College's nursing program learn skills in the Basic Care Lab, 2022. Courtesy of TCU Marketing and Communication. Photograph by James Anger.

The opinion back in 1983 was that TCU was a regional university that didn't have the academic respect, even within the region, that it desired. The longer-term vision that TCU maintained, however, was that of a national university with academic respect. To go to a national university was what really intrigued me about TCU.

It was in 1985 or 1986 that we made the decision to close admissions for the first time, which was a stunning thing for this university. That had never happened before, and that decision charted us on the course that we're on today. People began to believe that we did have some academic merit.

We had, and we still have, a university faculty and staff that back the admissions office and that were willing to be ambassadors, be emissaries, and we were able to do some pilot projects to try to bring in a different caliber of student.

—Leo Munson, Associate Provost for Academic Support, at TCU 1983-2018

Closing admissions really got people around the state at least talking about what was going on at TCU. It was a risk on the Chancellor's part which he took on to improve the university. I think it sent a signal to the larger community and to students that were going to apply that the university was serious about setting standards for applicants. It sent a signal to the faculty and students here that things were changing and evolving. I think we went from being on everyone's lists as perhaps a safe school to being first on many people's lists for being a great school.

—Bill Koehler, Provost Emeritus, at TCU 1969-2005

ABOVE
Theatre TCU performs *Babette's Feast* at the Hays Theatre, 2022. Courtesy of TCU Marketing and Communication. Photo by Amy Peterson.

ABOVE
Westpark Elementary fourth graders visit TCU for the College of Education's Bryant Bridge of Hope Math & Science Trail, 2019. Courtesy of TCU Marketing and Communication. Photograph by Tim Coles.

I think athletics has helped academics because it has raised the profile of the university. The university has always been great academically, but unfortunately, 42,000 people don't show up to watch a chemistry experiment.

— **Ross Bailey, Associate Athletics Director, at TCU 1977-2021**

If you go back and look at how the admissions jumped after TCU went to the Rose Bowl, you will understand that in America today, sports is one of the best ways to promote your school. I have to say that we don't want to just be a place known only for its football team, but having a good football program, and a football program where you are educating young people and not just bringing them there to play football, is important.

— **Bob Schieffer, Honorary TCU Trustee**

Of the 4,500 applications we had in 2000, everybody who could have done well academically was offered admission. Today, in 2014, it's not nearly the case. We expect that we will have at least 18,000 applications this year. My guess is that of those 18,000, 17,000 of them, maybe more, could reasonably do the academic work and graduate. But fewer than half of those are going to be offered admission to TCU. The institution has gotten much more selective.

With respect to the makeup of the student body, Chancellor Ferrari had a very important role in moving this university to start becoming more closely reflective of our environment. Dr. Boschini has been the captain of the ship that has led us through this surge in national attention. All of that has gone to make our lives wonderfully complex in the Office of Admission—instead of having 5,000 applications to deal with, we now have nearly quadruple that, and we're happy to do it.

We have an interesting practice here at TCU that predates me. We want to have as many countries in the freshman class represented as we possibly can. We have between sixty and seventy nations represented in the university as a whole. In every freshman class, we generally have seventy-five freshmen from international addresses that generally come from about twenty-five different nations. The mix is pretty broad there, and that is intentional. We really would like to have as broad a mix as we possibly can muster here. We don't want every student to come from one type of high school or one type of metropolitan area or one state, and the same holds true with international students.

— **Ray Brown, Dean of Admissions, at TCU 2000-2016**

I think that putting more emphasis on trying to improve the student body—in other words, making this a school people want to attend—has impacted TCU the most. The number of admissions you have compared to the number of students that qualify to get into the university is raising the level of the institution. It's definitely the students that make the school.

— **Bob Schieffer**

ABOVE
Frog Corps, 2016. Courtesy of TCU Marketing and Communication. Photograph by Leo Wesson.

Creating an Engineering Program

1992

Bill Koehler and I both really felt that we ought to bring engineering into the TCU curriculum, so we decided to pursue the idea. We knew that one of the things we would have to contend with was a perspective that existed that engineering doesn't fit in a liberal arts university, so we felt like we needed to move with some degree of care.

We put together a committee of around fifteen people from the different schools and colleges to help us study the issue. We tried to get some sense of what having engineering cost. And if we decided to have engineering, should we have multiple disciplines? Should we offer degrees in civil, mechanical, and petroleum? Or should we go with general engineering? I visited several universities to try to get a sense of how they were set up. Everywhere from Baylor which is pretty similar to TCU, to A&M, which is the largest college of engineering in the country, and all kinds of places in between. I spent time in New York visiting with the ABET [Accreditation Board of Engineering and Technology], [which is] the accrediting body for all engineering programs in the country.

We knew that we wanted a general engineering program that had a strong union with the liberal arts, and they [ABET] thought that was ideal. In their judgment, one of the real weaknesses of engineering education in this country was that it had become too specialized, and they thought that engineers needed the broad training that would come from being part of a college or a university that had a commitment to liberal arts. And so a proposal was made and submitted, and Bill and I began to work with Chancellor Tucker.

Bill Tucker was not completely convinced that we could afford a program in engineering. Interestingly enough, the two universities that provided the greatest support to us as we were developing our concepts were Texas A&M and Baylor.

The program at Baylor was a general engineering program, which was the model we had decided on, so Bill Koehler and I persuaded Bill Tucker and Leigh Secrest, the chief financial officer of the university, to go down and visit, and the folks down at Baylor devoted a whole day to meeting with us and explaining how they had come to make all the decisions they made. As we were driving back, Bill Tucker said, "If Baylor can do it, TCU can do it."

The program actually came into existence in 1991. Our first step, then, was to find a department chair, someone to develop a curriculum and hire faculty. Hal Nelson, [our new Engineering Department Chair] was really the man for the job. He was very committed to the idea that a successful program of engineering should be like a successful program in any of our other disciplines—one with a lot of focus on students and a lot of opportunity for personal interaction from students to faculty.

— **Michael McCracken, Emeritus Associate Professor of Biology and Dean, at TCU 1971-2010**

ABOVE
Harold Nelson. Courtesy of the TCU Department of Engineering.

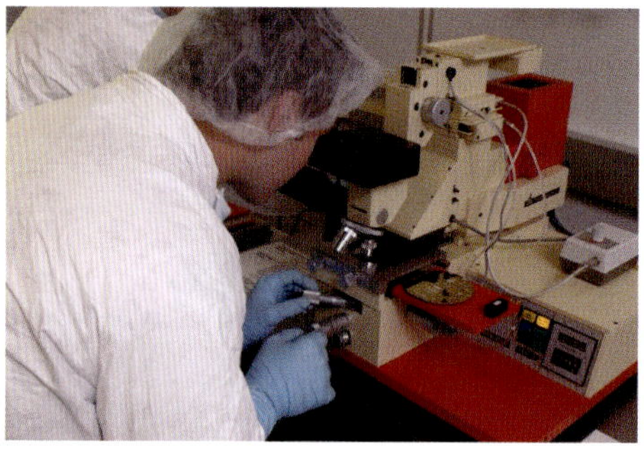

ABOVE
Engineering lab in Tucker Technology Center, 2007. Courtesy of TCU Marketing and Communication.

A major goal of ours [was] to be accredited at the earliest date that we could be. Being accredited is particularly important in engineering because various forms of licensure and becoming a professional engineer and many job opportunities depend upon being a graduate of an accredited program, but you cannot be accredited by ABET until you graduate your first class. In 1996 we graduated the first group; I think there were seven in that first class. ABET spent a lot of time with those students and made a lot of judgments on whether the program was successful or not. In the spring of 1996, the accreditation team came on campus, and we didn't know quite what to expect. Baylor, for example, was turned down the first time that they sought accreditation. So we put our best foot forward and went right through with flying colors, and a lot of it was due to the fact that the first group was so outstanding. I still have very fond memories and feelings for that first group of seven. After that accreditation visit, Dr. Tucker said he had sat in on a lot of accreditation visits in various departments, and he had never sat in one where there were no deficiencies. A short time later, he hand-delivered to us a dozen roses, which I thought was very high class.

— **Harold Nelson, Chair of the Department of Engineering, at TCU 1991-1998**

The next thing we began to push for was for a building. We occupied space in Bass Hall, Sid Richardson, and Winton Scott. A department occupying many different buildings is not an ideal situation. We got the Tucker Technology Center in 2002. And the program to this day continues to be very successful.

— **Michael McCracken**

When I arrived, Koehler and McCracken had already obtained approval from the Board of Trustees to start the program and funding for the program. They also formed a board of advisers of faculty members on campus. If I needed something done—courses approved or whatever—they knew what the process was because they'd been here for a long period of time. When I arrived here, I met Dean McCracken; he gave me the budget, a budget stamp, and the key to my office. I walked in [the office], and there was a single desk and a telephone, my nameplate was on the door, no chair—that was it. That's how we started. With absolutely nothing except a desk and a telephone and a nameplate, and the budget.

— **Harold Nelson**

We chose to offer a fairly general engineering degree—Bachelor of Science in engineering—with options in mechanical and electrical. We didn't have any space, so we had to steal space from other [departments] on campus. The first year I was here we were developing freshman courses for the next year, and then during the freshman year we would design and construct laboratories and courses for the sophomore year, and so forth. And then we would hire faculty members sequentially as [we] would need them. So it was a four-year step process. Almost everyone at TCU was extremely helpful, which was probably the nicest feature of my being here, that I could go to anyone and get assistance and they'd offer willingly.

[Recruiting students] was probably the most difficult aspect of the whole process of developing an engineering program. Prospective students would come and talk to me, and I would try to sell them on an engineering program that we didn't even have. We didn't have any labs; we didn't have any faculty. We didn't even have a program of study written down. We had [around] thirty students that originally signed up for engineering, and I think they came because they trusted TCU. They liked the campus, they liked the environment, and so they took a chance.

— **Harold Nelson**

ABOVE
Engineering students at work in a lab in the Tucker Technology Center, 2018. Courtesy of TCU Marketing and Communication. Photograph by Jeffrey McWhorter.

One of the hallmarks of the program is the senior research project. All the seniors devote their final year to solving a problem that we get from industry, and the industry pays for it. We produce a product for them as any group of engineers would, and over all these years every class has been successful. They have solved the problem, and the company has taken it and incorporated it. That continues to be a unique feature of the program.

— **Michael McCracken**

The engineering program has been a success. And what they have to do, I think, is take a look at whether they want to keep the present arrangement of degrees–which is the Bachelor of Science in engineering with electrical or mechanical emphasis–or whether they want to add other majors. Those are big decisions, because they involve a lot of money, they involve space, laboratories, equipment. So TCU has to decide: Do we want to stay where we are and try to be as good as we can here, or do we want to enlarge a little bit?

— **Harold Nelson**

The creation of an engineering program at TCU was a dream that the dean of the college of sciences, Michael McCracken, and I both shared. On several occasions, we tried to start an engineering program and were not successful, and it finally seemed like the right time, and we were able to start an engineering program. It was a really significant and important program. It was the one that other universities offered but TCU didn't. We were missing some good students because we lacked the program. There have been many positive things that I enjoyed, but given the fact that the engineering program took ten, maybe fifteen years coming to fruition, the wait made it that much more fulfilling when we finally got to do it.

— **Bill Koehler, Provost Emeritus**

Reorganization of Colleges

2000

There were several colleges that reorganized at the same time. Harris College of Nursing, for example, was combined with Kinesiology, Communication Disorders, and Social Work. Fine Arts and Communications split into separate colleges. My sense is that part of the reason for the split was that the old AddRan was so big that it became administratively unwieldy. Now that we've split into our current AddRan College of Humanities and Social Sciences [now AddRan College of Liberal Arts], and Science and Engineering, everything is a little bit easier and less unwieldy.

— **Phil Hartman, Emeritus Professor of Biology and Dean, at TCU 1981-2022**

ABOVE
Chinese class in AddRan College of Liberal Arts, 2019. Courtesy of TCU Marketing and Communication. Photograph by Jeffrey McWhorter

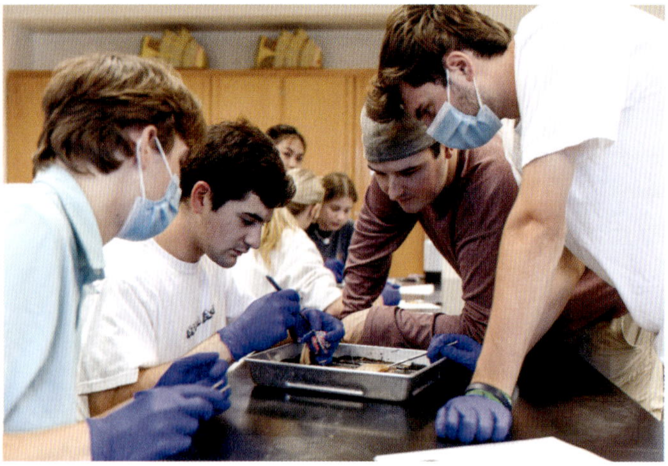

ABOVE
Biology students dissect a squid, 2022. Courtesy of TCU Marketing and Communication. Photograph by James Anger.

Before AddRan was divided into two colleges, the college was large with diverse perspectives. We were trying to develop goals, plans, and criteria for departments, and it was a challenge to decide how to proceed when you have some programs that are strictly undergraduate, some programs heavily into graduate studies, and just about everything in between. Restructuring AddRan was something I'd been personally thinking about, because I felt that the area in which I had not been as successful as I'd hoped was planning and establishing goals, because so much of my time was spent just reacting. And I thought that it would make more sense to have smaller, more homogenous groups, and maybe we could all engage in meaningful planning and goal setting. In 2000 we eliminated AddRan College of Arts and Sciences and created the College of Science and Engineering and what's now the AddRan College of Liberal Arts. It made my job easier, to be honest, although I was sorry to leave the people because I really enjoyed working with the folks in social sciences and the folks in humanities.

— **Michael McCracken**

There was an opportunity to restructure, mostly because science and engineering were splitting off from the liberal arts. Even though the School of Nursing was a decent-sized department, adding the other departments [Communication Sciences and Disorders, Kinesiology, and Nurse Anesthesia] has given us more personnel, more money, more students, more everything. My real strategic objective was to be able to work with the department chairs. It was not only learning what these people do, what they teach, what they are studying, but also who I could work with on a committee. We spent a lot of time in department chair meetings getting to know each other, and then people were able to start saying, "We've had that problem, this is what worked for us." We really wanted to be seen as a resource for one another, rather than in competition for limited resources.

— **Rhonda Keen, Emeritus Professor of Nursing and Dean, at TCU 1982-2020**

ABOVE
A Schieffer College student produces the News Now newscast in Moudy South, 2019. Courtesy of TCU Marketing and Communication. Photograph by Jefrey McWhorter.

ABOVE
Interior design class, 2020. Courtesy of TCU Marketing and Communication. Photograph by Andrew Emery.

I was the dean of AddRan College of Arts and Sciences, which at that time was loosely organized into three divisions. We had natural sciences, and then the humanities, and then we had the social sciences. Social work at that time was in the College of Arts and Sciences. And initially when I became dean, journalism was in the College of Arts and Sciences. George Tate was the dean of Fine Arts and Communication for several years, and in fact he was really interested in moving towards [separating] the College of Fine Arts and the College of Communication.

Home Economics was in the College of Arts and Sciences. It never really fit. This was a large and complex department, too complex to be a department. We had the traditional home economists, who believed that every student should take a course in sewing and construction and cooking. And then we had, for example, the folks in nutrition, who couldn't see any use in a nutrition major taking a course in sewing. And we also had a child development program. Ultimately, I found it necessary to separate those programs and create three departments. There was a lot of shifting around.

— **Michael McCracken**

Creating KinderFrogs

2000

KinderFrogs, founded in 2000, is a family-focused, early intervention program for young children with Down Syndrome and other developmental delays. The Starpoint School is a laboratory school (founded in 1966), which offers an individualized curriculum for elementary-age children with learning differences and/or attention deficits that interfere with academic progress. It provides children the opportunity to reach their educational potential with the help of TCU faculty, staff, and students.

My wife, Jean, was one of the people that convinced the university that there was a huge need in the community, and the university responded. I know it's not been a huge moneymaker to the university, but it's been a huge benefit to the community.

—**John V. Roach, Trustee Emeritus and former Chair, served 1981-2005**

ABOVE
Mary Patton with children in TCU's KinderFrogs program, 2014. Courtesy of TCU College of Education.

A group of parents made the case that there were too many children in Fort Worth that had no options if they were born with developmental disabilities. So I flew to Alabama with another faculty member and two parents, and we looked at the program there on the University of Alabama campus, and then we came back and we converted a few college of education classrooms into the space where Kinderfrogs is now. We started on a shoestring, with two classrooms and about fifteen kids. Our goal with Kinderfrogs children is to get them [into] mainstream [schools]. Many of them come to us at eighteen months, and they are not talking, not walking, not feeding themselves, and they leave and go into regular kindergarten programs. I just ran into the father of one of our graduates who's in fifth grade now, and he was telling me how his son is in Aledo in a regular fifth-grade classroom. It's a really wonderful success story.

— **Mary Patton, Dean of the College of Education, at TCU 1994-2020**

ABOVE
Student teacher working with pupils in the Starpoint School, 2016. Courtesy of TCU Marketing and Communication. Photograph by Carolyn Cruz.

ABOVE
KinderFrogs student, 2018. Courtesy of TCU Marketing and Communication. Photograph by Amy Peterson.

When I came, Starpoint and KinderFrogs didn't have enough money to really run a school. We spent a lot of time with [those programs], and now they are both on good financial footing.

— **Sam Deitz, Emeritus Professor of Education and Dean, at TCU 2000-2009**

Undergraduate Student Research and Scholarship

The percentage of undergraduates who have a substantive research experience has gone up dramatically. It was not that many years ago that we implemented an academic activity we call the Student Research Symposium, or SRS. That occurs typically the third week in April, and students present their research findings in a poster-session format. Those opportunities were fewer and farther between in my first ten to twenty years at TCU than they are now.

— **Phil Hartman**

ABOVE
Michael and Sally McCracken Student Research Symposium in the Tucker Technology Center, 2017. Courtesy of TCU Marketing and Communication. Photograph by Leo Wesson.

One thing that I'm very proud of is that we now have the student research symposium in the College of Science and Engineering. This was in 2003, and my belief was that students having involvement in scholarship is a very important part of the learning process. I thought that we should formalize that to some degree, and in particular give students the opportunity to actually organize their research and to present it, and to present it in a format where it could be shared throughout the college. Scientists have a tendency, and I'm as guilty of this as anybody, to get a little isolated in their labs, so we had a program where the students from all across the college were making research presentations, and we involved the majority of the faculty. The faculty in physics would find out what's going on in psychology and so forth and so forth and so on. And the students would have experiences that many students don't have until they are well into a graduate program. It was an easy concept to sell, and we were successful from the first time we had the program. It has gotten more and more successful, larger, with more presentations. The quality of the work that has been presented still blows me away. I think, boy, when I was a junior or a senior I don't think I could have come close to doing something like this, and you know we got these undergraduates that are engaged in very meaningful scholarship. It's such a prime example of how learning, research, teaching, all fit together. After a couple of years, the model in various forms has been adopted pretty much across the university.

— **Michael McCracken**

This year [2018] we just started something in AddRan called SURF (Summer Undergraduate Research Fellowship). It's a program to help our students get prepared to possibly go on and do graduate studies. They work collaboratively with a faculty member. It helps them learn how to do research.

— **Andrew Schoolmaster, Emeritus Professor of Geography and Dean, at TCU 2007-2021**

That notion of involving an undergraduate in the laboratory, that's a core value. There's a little bit of Bill Koehler in that, and there's a little bit of Bill Tucker in that. But that notion that one can learn outside the classroom in the laboratory and the association with the faculty—that came from Bill Koehler.

— **Fred Heath, University Librarian, at TCU 1987-1993**

LEFT
Bill Koehler. Published in the TCU 1983 yearbook. Courtesy of Mary Couts Burnett Library

But the other thing here which you don't often see at large schools is an undergraduate student doing research. Just about every faculty member here has undergrads doing research in their labs. That's something that TCU really excels in.

Our SERC (Science and Engineering Research Center) grants for research started when we realized that we should engage undergrad students in research more. Undergrads are capable of doing much more than what we had expected of them earlier. So we wanted to raise the bar. I think that undergrad research is one of our core values at the university, and being able to communicate that research is also important.

— **Manfred Reinecke, Professor of Chemistry, at TCU 1964-2006**

For an undergraduate student to be able to say that he or she researched alongside a professor or in some cases, as has happened, an undergraduate student to be published in a refereed journal with the professor's name on the same line—those things happen to most people in their graduate programs without any possibility of them having it at an undergraduate level.

— **Kay Higgins, Associate Dean of Student Development, at TCU 1977-2021**

ABOVE
Students do research in Dean Williams's Biology lab, 2008. Courtesy of TCU Marketing and Communication. Photograph by Amy Peterson.

ABOVE
TCU student Carson Huey-You in the Department of Physics & Astronomy's optical spectroscopy lab, 2016. Courtesy of TCU Marketing and Communication. Photograph by Amy Peterson.

One thing that I really loved about TCU was the commitment to undergraduate student education and how they are very intentional about involving TCU undergraduate students in research activities, scholarly efforts, and creative activities at the university. It was because of that excellence in the area of undergraduate scholarship and studies that I wanted to come to a university to pursue that excellence at the graduate level and also build the research activities within the university.

What I loved about the university is that I did not see them losing focus on that mission in training students, but I also saw an opportunity to help grow their research infrastructure. When I was a student, one of the most pivotal parts of my career was getting that hands-on research time in a laboratory, working on projects, talking to the professors. There's a lot to be gained outside of what we call the formal classroom.

I think that enhancing the research infrastructure and bringing in external support of research programs at the university will only help to enhance the scholarship and the hands-on teaching of the students. What I've also learned is when undergraduate students get that training and that experience, they not only are better students, they also have a much better opportunity to pursue graduate education, professional education, or to get jobs.

— **Floyd Wormley, Associate Provost for Research and Dean of Graduate Studies**

The deans took great pride in involving their undergraduate students in their laboratories. When I graduated from Tulane, I had never been inside a lab, but at TCU there was an effort to involve students not just in the classroom, but in their labs, and in the work professors were doing, if they wanted to do that. And that chance to prepare for life's work, or going to graduate school early, and getting a head start on those in that way. So I think those were parts of the strengths of TCU then and they are part of the strengths now. The scale and the involvement and the association of students and faculty was very strong and very close.

— **Fred Heath**

ABOVE
Students in Kayla Green's chemistry lab, 2018. Courtesy of TCU Marketing & Communication. Photograph by Jeffrey McWhorter.

There's a certain vision people have of TCU, and we need to turn that ship a little bit. Marketing did a study recently about what kind of words people associate with TCU: fun, friendly, and athletics. There's nothing wrong with being fun, friendly and have interesting athletics to watch or participate in, but I don't think that's the vision of a great university. We need to talk more about the research that we do and how our students contribute to solutions of big world problems. We have some cancer researchers over in Sid Richardson Hall that are contributing to major cures that we'll see in clinical trials in a few years. We need to talk about that more. I don't think that that makes us unfun or unfriendly, we just need to embrace that part of what we do. So we need to find ways to get that in people's minds.

— **Bonnie Melhart, Emeritus Dean of University Programs and Associate Provost, at TCU 1990-2019**

New Core Curriculum 2003

To my understanding, the first look at whether we should revise the core came in the [faculty] senate around 1996. Then around 1999 Bill Koehler appointed three committees who were not supposed to talk to each other and were supposed to come up with three different proposals that they were going to look at, but none of the three proposals came to fruition. The fall of 2001 a committee produced the Common Undergraduate Experience, (CUE), [and] that was presented to faculty as a done deal, that it was going to go into effect and you had to take it or leave it.

— **Ed McNertney, Emeritus Associate Professor of Economics and Director of the TCU Core Curriculum, at TCU 1977-2022**

There were requirements in the prior curriculum that had disappeared, and we didn't ever have a chance to argue for them . . . it was just seemingly decided. There was a wide array of disgruntled people. About a week later there was a Faculty Assembly; this was the only time in my over thirty-year career here that a room was completely filled with faculty. The core curriculum [proposal] was clearly going down in flames. I felt a little bad that a small number of people had put in an enormous amount of work, but it was clear that there wasn't enough input.

— **Andrew Fort, Emeritus Professor of Religion, at TCU 1982-2017**

Chancellor Ferrari finally just said to the chair of the senate, "Okay. It's yours. Come up with a core," and walked out. And so the senate did. The senate set up an ad hoc committee. I agreed to be on the committee as long as we'd come to a vote, because I wanted to be able to vote against it if I didn't like what came out of it. Nowell was sort of the unofficial chair. We met every Monday at 5:00 p.m. One night we were there until nine o'clock at night.

Not only were we coming up with the design, but also it was going to result in learning outcomes for each of the fourteen categories in the core. It took a year before we got the design approved by the senate, the faculty assembly, and the board of trustees, and then the next year was spent getting all the learning outcomes. We finally came up with a good design. And then we had to implement.

Setting up that operational implementation committee of all the associate deans was absolutely essential to getting it to work. I am still amazed at what the registrar's office did creating that grid, where all the courses fit in for advising. Anyway, that's a short history. That was the most bottom-up process I think was possible. It didn't start off that way, but it ended up that way.

— **Ed McNertney**

When we re-did the core curriculum, I learned a lot about how slow that process is, because if you change the number of required religion hours from six to three, you're impacting some department, you're impacting some faculty member. That was a slow process, but we got it done.

—**J. Luther King, Trustee Emeritus and former Chair, at TCU 1992-2021**

The current curriculum is a result of the input from all the different interest groups in the university. If something was going to be dropped or altered, we would ask the stakeholders who were affected to argue for why they wanted it.

— **Andrew Fort**

I was chair of the Faculty Senate the year we passed the new core curriculum, and it was a pretty big deal. It was a very complicated process and was handed over to faculty through the Faculty Senate. These faculty were empowered and given the responsibility to look at the old core and decide what should stay, what should go, what fits in with the mission statement of TCU, what fits in with the historical values of TCU. It's a really interesting example of shared governance. A huge amount of discussion and disagreement and people having different opinions went into all that. A lot of people really wanted a requirement on ethics, but nobody could agree on what that was. Is it how you apply your personal values? Is it a philosophical discussion on what values really are? Is it a religious discussion? Could it be a class in Neeley where you're talking about ethics in business? I was privileged to be a part of the discussion, even though we couldn't solve that one. It was left out. We thought a little bit broader, but still included ethics and values, and that's how we ended up with the citizenship and social values requirement. That was our compromise.

A radical thing at the time, an idea that we had never had before, was that there are multiple departments on campus that offer classes that could satisfy a requirement; for example, you could satisfy the religion requirement with an anthropology class. Oh, the discussions that went into all of that. We felt like that was freeing for students.

At the end of our discussion, we, the Faculty Senate, approved the new core curriculum unanimously. I don't know how we did that. I think maybe it was because everybody had a say. I was a spokesperson for having a foreign language requirement for all students, and everybody wouldn't agree on it, so we had to leave that out, but I still voted yes for the core curriculum because I had had a say and I was listened to. It struck me as a great process and an example of how things can be done well. Nobody got exactly what they wanted, but we've been pleased with it. When I look back on my professional life, that was one of the most difficult things that I ever did, because I was so afraid that faculty was going to vote it down. But somehow everybody voted yes, and I just walked out and drove my car around town because I was just so happy.

I think in the next five years or so we'll look again at the core, and the first thing we will do is ask for input from the students.

— **Peggy Watson, Emeritus Professor in the John V. Roach Honors College and Dean, at TCU 1984-2012**

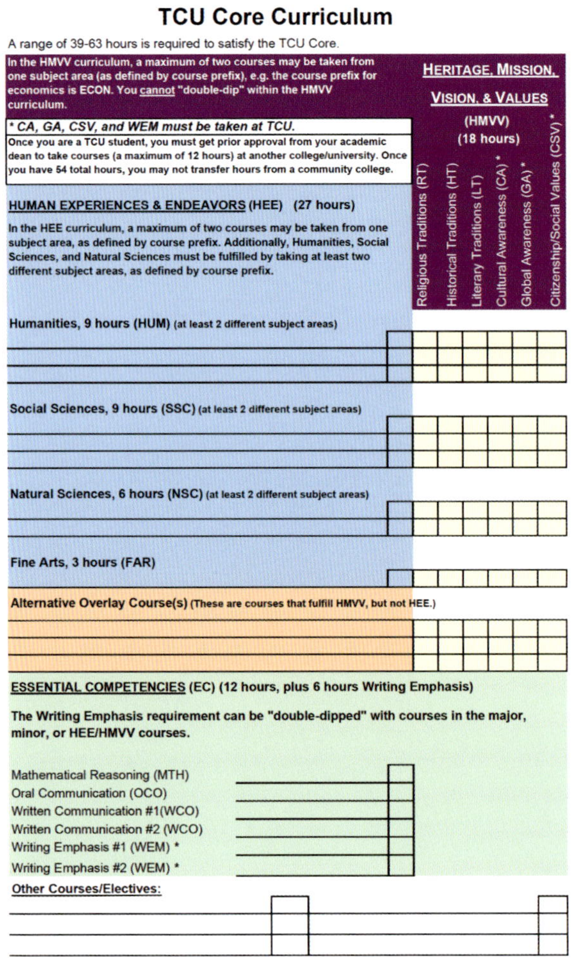
TCU Core Curriculum

A range of 39-63 hours is required to satisfy the TCU Core.

In the HMVV curriculum, a maximum of two courses may be taken from one subject area (as defined by course prefix), e.g. the course prefix for economics is ECON. You cannot "double-dip" within the HMVV curriculum.

HERITAGE, MISSION, VISION, & VALUES (HMVV) (18 hours)

Religious Traditions (RT) | Historical Traditions (HT) | Literary Traditions (LT) | Cultural Awareness (CA) * | Global Awareness (GA) * | Citizenship/Social Values (CSV) *

* CA, GA, CSV, and WEM must be taken at TCU.

Once you are a TCU student, you must get prior approval from your academic dean to take courses (a maximum of 12 hours) at another college/university. Once you have 54 total hours, you may not transfer hours from a community college.

HUMAN EXPERIENCES & ENDEAVORS (HEE) (27 hours)

In the HEE curriculum, a maximum of two courses may be taken from one subject area, as defined by course prefix. Additionally, Humanities, Social Sciences, and Natural Sciences must be fulfilled by taking at least two different subject areas, as defined by course prefix.

Humanities, 9 hours (HUM) (at least 2 different subject areas)

Social Sciences, 9 hours (SSC) (at least 2 different subject areas)

Natural Sciences, 6 hours (NSC) (at least 2 different subject areas)

Fine Arts, 3 hours (FAR)

Alternative Overlay Course(s) (These are courses that fulfill HMVV, but not HEE.)

ESSENTIAL COMPETENCIES (EC) (12 hours, plus 6 hours Writing Emphasis)

The Writing Emphasis requirement can be "double-dipped" with courses in the major, minor, or HEE/HMVV courses.

Mathematical Reasoning (MTH)
Oral Communication (OCO)
Written Communication #1(WCO)
Written Communication #2 (WCO)
Writing Emphasis #1 (WEM) *
Writing Emphasis #2 (WEM) *

Other Courses/Electives:

ABOVE

TCU Core Curriculum grid, 2022. Courtesy of the Office of the Registrar.

Now DEI [Diversity, Equity, and Inclusion] is going into the core. It came from students to the chancellor, then to a group of faculty that wanted to bring DEI into the core. My role in that was to make sure they were following the emendation policy that we have in place, and they have done a great job. It's been really nice to see something similar to what happened almost twenty years ago, a bottom-up change to the core without having to blow the whole core up again. It's been approved by a faculty assembly. Now it's going to go into the implementation stage. That's a nice kind of ending, a follow-up to the core process.

— **Ed McNertney**

The university decided to embark on its formal efforts of diversity, equity, and inclusion beginning spring of 2016. The DEI Committee came into being, and Aisha Torrey-Sawyer and Ariane Balizet asked me if I would participate on that committee on the curriculum piece, because one of the charges was to figure out how to embed diversity, equity, and inclusion into the core curriculum. Faculty, a few staff, and some students pulled together to create a proposal that we took to Faculty Senate. In the fall of 2017, we learned that the Faculty Senate was working on a similar project. So at that moment, we began to work collaboratively with the Faculty Senate Academic Excellence Committee (AEC).

And so, initially, the proposal for the DEI component of the core committee came out of AEC. What came out was very different from what we had sent in. What came out was the proposal to do something rather than the proposal for the core piece itself. So that sent us into round two in fall of 2018. The critical juncture there is Teresa Dahlberg, and she was hired as provost. I was sitting at my computer and up pops this email from Teresa Dahlberg, and it's one of those freeze-frame moments in my memory. She offered me the position of Provost Faculty Fellow for Diversity, Equity, and Inclusion and Diversity Advocate for Academic Affairs. I mean, it was just amazing. One of the things she said to me was, "As I began to talk to other people about this position, your name came up in every conversation." I knew that I knew people across campus, but what I didn't realize was the way in which people saw or see the work I have done or the work I'm doing. And then she said, "Faculty Senate is going to create an ad hoc committee for the implementation to move forward the DEI Essential Competency, and they're going to ask you to co-chair."

So it was fortuitous in many ways that the DEI Essential Competency requirement in the core curriculum was my priority project for this academic year in the provost office, which meant I had the support of the provost.

— **Claire Sanders, Provost's Faculty Fellow for Diversity, Equity, and Inclusion**

I've been here through three different common curriculums. One of the things I think TCU has done a good job at is maintaining in its core requirements some requirement that students be exposed to the liberal arts. That has been a central anchor to support increasing professionalism.

— **David Grant, Emeritus Professor of Religion, at TCU 1981-2022**

We have a curriculum that requires students to be exposed to a broad spectrum of education materials. We have been through several different versions of a core curriculum in my time here, and they all have more or less the same things in common.

If three of us sat down and said this is what makes up an educated person, we would share the expectation to be able to do some math and to write and to be able to communicate in ways in addition to writing. That you are going to have some ability to understand and appreciate science and humanities. In general, those things are in our core curriculum and always have been.

We are a liberal arts university, but most of our graduates are not liberal arts graduates and they haven't been for quite some time. We have many graduates coming out with professional and pre-professional degrees. I think the transition has to do with a core that creates a liberal arts background and gives students the opportunity to become educated in the broadest sense of the word. At the same time, they move right into professional and pre-professional programs of their choice. Part of the difficulty for the university has been creating a resource base that supports all of that.

I think students in general look at the core as something they have to get through in order to get to their major, and I think that's a shame, because I'd like to think that the core would be a place where students would play intellectually, that the core would be a place where they would have the chance to broaden their experience, learn and see and do things that may pay out for you for the rest of their lives.

—**Patrick Miller, Registrar, at TCU 1981-2016**

Creation of the John V. Roach Honors College

2009

When I was in school, it was just an Honors program, but to see the transformation to a full-fledged college with a dean, and what that does to strengthen our academic reputation and our profile, is key.

— **Brenda Cline, Member of the TCU Board of Trustees**

We have the ability to create an Honors College and to devote resources to giving students an excellent academic experience.

— **Patrick Miller**

LEFT
Peggy Watson, founding dean of the John V. Roach Honors College. Courtesy of Texas Christian University.

In late fall of 2008, I was in the small Honors Program office in Sadler when David Nolan from Advancement paid a surprise visit to let me know that there were possible donors for the long-awaited creation of an Honors College. I had spent the last two years working with Provost Nowell Donovan on how we might create such a college, and Dr. Kathy McDorman, the previous director of the Honors Program, had also strongly championed the idea.

I agreed to write a narrative about Honors to include with the proposal. The only information I had about the donors—who were later to be identified as Paul and Judy Andrews—was that they were influenced by the writings of commentator and author Thomas Friedman. Friedman portrayed himself as deeply idealistic, believing that young people could change the world for the better. He talked about the power of studying multiple worldviews and of being immersed in other cultures. These ideas, along with the importance of interdisciplinary study and undergraduate research, were a perfect fit with the priorities of Honors and served as the basis for the proposal.

— **Peggy Watson**

After officially opening the new college in the fall of 2009, we were able to add some talented faculty within the next few years. Ron Pitcock, known for his highly engaging teaching and mentoring, had recently become the second full-time Honors faculty member, and he was followed by Dan Williams, who also maintained his position as Director of TCU Press and created multiple opportunities for Honors students to participate in publishing and editing, including designing and producing most of the interviews for this sesquicentennial history of TCU. Wendy Williams, a recent PhD in English, published a well-received monograph her second year in Honors, while also being recognized for her multidisciplinary courses and inclusive teaching style. We were also able to add an Honors Faculty Fellow appointment for Beata Jones, who was responsible for designing an innovative program called Neeley Fellows that, for the first time, created a path for business students to participate in Honors.

— **Peggy Watson**

ABOVE
Ron Pitcock's Cultural Memory class in the John V. Roach Honors College, 2019. Courtesy of TCU Marketing and Communication. Photograph by Jeffrey McWhorter.

When I started with the Honors Program, Honors housing had just recently been established, and it was just a few students on one floor in Moncrief. The students who lived there had loved it. It was powerful for them. So I went to Housing to see what we could do to move more students into Honors housing. The process of turning Milton Daniel residence hall into the Honors House was daunting and involved multiple meetings and a lot of convincing on my part. Built in 1956, Milton Daniel traditionally served as first-year housing for men, and in the past had been athletic housing. At one point there was even a fraternity house in Milton Daniel. To this day, when I mention to parents that the Honors College offers outstanding housing in Milton Daniel, a father is likely to chuckle and say: "Is that the Milton Daniel that I lived in as a freshman? The one that smelled so bad? The one where they pulled the water fountain out of the wall?"

Our complicated plan started with some basic renovations during the summer of 2007 to allow both women and men to move in for the fall semester. The complete renovations were accomplished during the 2009-2010 academic year, while many first-year Honors students resided in Clark Hall. We were able to open the beautiful and carefully redesigned building to incoming Honors students in the fall of 2010.

The odors and broken water fountains are now gone, replaced by multiple student meeting places and study niches. I always tell people yes, it is a beautiful building, but students move there for the community. The new Milton Daniel was built to foster communities for students and ideally to provide support to student scholars.

I have always wanted for students, and for myself, and for everybody, to know that it is okay to have real conversations about real things at random moments. For students, it's great to talk about the party last Saturday night, or to speculate what you want to do next weekend, but also to have more complicated conversations about growing thoughts and ideas. The idea that you do not have to hide that part of yourself wanting to grapple with issues, even though you know you don't have all the solutions and you don't know all the facts. I think living in Milton frees students to be who they are and to be leaders.

— **Peggy Watson**

One highlight from the college's dedication was watching Dr. David Grant energetically play the banjo with students singing along. It echoed past Honors fall retreats, where learning took place in not only intellectual discussions but also light, fun-filled moments. Seeing the Roach and Andrews family interactions represents a second highlight. Their close friendship, shaped by years of reciprocal mentorship and support, emphasized the importance of giving, accountability, and sacrifice—hallmarks of honors teaching and learning.

Moving from a program to a college allowed Honors at TCU to build a stronger national presence. This had an immediate impact on the college's admission and retention data; students come to campus expecting the John V. Roach Honors College to challenge them intellectually and help them grow. Over the past decade, another impact of the shift is evidenced within the curriculum, where faculty have developed new honors courses and received national attention for their pedagogical approaches.

— **Ron Pitcock, Dean of the John V. Roach Honors College**

With the addition of the Honors College, there's been a good focus on academic achievement and interest in interdisciplinary thinking, cross-sharing across campus and across disciplines. It seems that academic areas are less isolated.

The Honors College has been completely transformed from a relatively small program with a director. I always associated it with AddRan, with liberal arts, because basically the students in the Honors program were liberal arts students. As the program grew and then became a college, it had to be more inclusive of all disciplines, and it has been. Many students in the sciences and in business are in my colloquium. I think the student participation, not only the number of students, but the broad reach of the types of majors and types of students, has grown tremendously in the Honors College.

— **Sharon Fairchild, Emeritus Professor of Modern Languages, at TCU 1978-2017**

ABOVE
Milton Daniel Hall, 2022. Courtesy of TCU Marketing and Communication. Photograph by James Anger.

The Honors College has admitted to TCU one of the best possible incoming classes, better than most of its competitors. The Honors College fits in with all the university and is growing well.

—John V. Roach

Just this semester, I have added co-teaching an Honors colloquium on identity and transformation in the college years. The Honors students have been fantastic. It's been a great experience, and I was sad to have the last class last week. Hopefully, I will be able to do that again.

— Barbara Herman, Associate Vice Chancellor for Student Affairs, at TCU 1986-2021

Once we got going on the Honors College, the quality of the students got better.

— Ed Schollmaier, Trustee Emeritus, served 1996-2021

Comparative Race and Ethnic Studies

2007

We started Comparative Race and Ethnic Studies (CRES) as a program. Now it is a department. An email went out to all faculty and staff, asking anybody who was interested in participating in this effort to show up. I was acutely aware of the challenges that people of color on this campus have faced and, to some extent, still face today. I was aware of the way in which students could sometimes feel isolated or alienated, and I've heard a number of horror stories about experiences that students have had. So, I showed up and ended up being part of that leadership team that was critical to the creation of CRES, which would've been Max Krochmal, Emily Farris in Poli Sci, David Colón in English, and myself. Melanie Harris decided to create the African American and Africana Studies minor. I had a much more tangential role in the creation of that minor, although I'm now the co-director of it. And then, of course, the university decided to embark on its formal efforts of diversity, equity, and inclusion beginning the spring of 2016. The university created one more committee, DEI.

— Claire Sanders

Like Honors, we rely heavily on faculty across the curriculum to deliver our coursework. We have a lot of faculty who are field experts in our areas of comparative race and ethnic studies or women and gender studies or LatinX studies who are housed in other departments like History or Anthropology or Social Work. One of our signature course offerings in comparative race and ethnic studies is called the "justice journey," which includes a site-based or high-impact learning that happens during spring break, when they tour social justice and civil rights sites. This focuses alternately on African-American civil rights and LatinX civil rights, and the students meet with community leaders, people who have been in this fight since the 1960s, who are now quite old, who are still doing the work or really sharing their knowledge, and that's extraordinarily impactful for our students. That's one of the examples of the way that we're really trying to give students the sense of the Long March.

— Karen Steele, Special Assistant to the Provost

We are moving forward with our plans and our strategies for diversity, equity, and inclusion, and the DEI inventory we had in the fall of 2019 has helped people think about approaching diversity, equity, and inclusion from an organic level. It's not something that the administration, the Provost Office, the dean's office, or CRES is imposing on the campus—this is something that we, as a campus, are going to undertake to improve the campus itself. And I think CRES also helps people see that the diversity, equity, and inclusion in higher education does have a disciplinary reality, a disciplinary anchor. It really is something substantive.

— Claire Sanders

ABOVE
Class in the Women and Gender Studies program, 2009. Courtesy of TCU Marketing and Communication. Photograph by Amy Peterson.

11.

The Mary Couts Burnett Library

ABOVE
Mary Couts Burnett Library, ca. 1930s. (Original building 1924-1958.) Courtesy of Mary Couts Burnett Library.

RIGHT
Expansion remodeling in process, ca. 1958. Courtesy of Mary Couts Burnett Library.

ABOVE
Library renovation and expansion, 1959.
Courtesy of Mary Couts Burnett Library.

RIGHT
1983 renovation, new south entrance.
Courtesy of Mary Couts Burnett Library.

There have been a lot of changes. Years ago there was something called a card catalogue. It consisted of three-by-five-inch cards, and they were in many drawers and were alphabetical. In the late 1980s, TCU went from a card catalogue system to a database. At that time we had hundreds of thousands of books on the shelves, so someone had to create a computer record for every single book. Every book had to be pulled off the shelf and have a barcode put in the book. That was the library automation project, and that was a big deal. It was expensive; it took a lot of people. We had a lot of student helpers, a lot of staff. We came in and worked over Christmas; we worked for a lot of time to get all this done. We had t-shirts for everyone on the staff, "I survived the barcode."

ABOVE
Librarian's office and card catalogue, 1930. Courtesy of Mary Couts Burnett Library.

ABOVE
Mary Couts Burnett Library card catalogue, 1958. Courtesy of Mary Couts Burnett Library.

We still use the word *catalogue*. You can search that catalogue database for all the titles or for the authors. And it has a lot of other things. For example, you can add into a database additional information beyond what the book actually tells you. With the card catalogue, you could only look it up by the author or the title or subject heading that was supplied. You spent a lot of time looking through the cards. Today you may not know the exact title or the author, but you can put in key words. So the database is a very important part of the library.

Something new that we've added just a couple years ago in the library database is "browse shelf." We have purchased thumbnail images of book jackets, and you can see the book titles in the same sequence as if they were on a shelf, and of course the books are arranged by subject, so you are getting books related to the subject you are on. It's not the same thing as being in the stacks and pulling the book out and looking at it, but you can virtually browse. The beauty of that is that hundreds of thousands of books are now stored off site in facilities two miles from campus, and so in many cases when you go to the shelves now, you are seeing a selection of the books, and we deliberately chose the ones that were more frequently used [to] stay on campus. If you are choosing one that is not in the building, you fill out a short form, and then we get the book like in a day and bring it to the library.

There's now a lot of links to the eBooks, so there is no call number, there is no barcode, because there is no physical book. If you click on the link, you will then see full-text eBooks. So the database is not limited to physical things anymore.

—**June Koelker, Dean of the Library, at TCU 1988-2020**

We, in those days, had sort of a mid-twentieth century library, the card catalogues. But what I liked was that I had the support to automate the library. Bill [Tucker] moved it to first priority, called in the foundations he knew that would support that, and lined up sessions with me to outline this idea of automating the library to potential corporate donors. Bill would readily support the increases in the costs of library operations. The dollar fell badly in the late eighties, and journal prices skyrocketed forty percent in a year. Most libraries around the country cancelled journals like mad. Bill Koehler and Bill Tucker stood by and kept those resources for the faculty and students. Chancellor Tucker was very careful and measured in the risks that he took, but in the commitments he made, he had the resources to stand by them, and that's important.

—**Fred Heath, University Librarian, at TCU 1987-1993**

ABOVE
Reading room, 2009. Courtesy of Texas Christian University. Photograph by Glen E. Ellman.

In 1981, when I was chair of Faculty Senate, one of the privileges that I had was to turn the soil for the additions to the library. The old library is what is now just the reading room.

— **Bob Frye, Emeritus Professor of English, at TCU 1966-2003**

ABOVE
Periodical stacks, 1950s. Courtesy of Mary Couts Burnett Library.

Another large, large, area of change—the computer became widespread in the 1980s. The library started having computer labs. Back before the computing, in most cases you went to a library, you found a journal article, you found a book, and you took the items back to a dorm room or apartment. You didn't necessarily write your paper in the library. You could, but in most cases it was sequential; you did the research, and then you went off and did the paper.

— **June Koelker**

We were on that first little edge of the Internet and the World Wide Web. The library still had print collections. You had to come in and use a printed guide to the literature, and then go back to the periodicals in front and articles you needed for your research. And it was a laborious process. We were able to do the electronic catalog, to bind the collections in an electronic file so that the research could be done in a very efficient way. But even in that day, you still came into the library to look at the electronic resources and you would download electronic files to something. We weren't yet pumping electronic articles to your dorm, to your apartment, to your home. But we were laying that groundwork, just changing from a pen and ink situation to an electronic situation, and the ability to see that and send that was a part of TCU.

— **Fred Heath**

ABOVE
Information Commons in the Mary Couts Burnett Library, 2009. Courtesy of Texas Christian University. Photograph by Glen E. Ellman.

Today we've got a computer lab in the Information Commons. The information commons is the name that we use here at TCU for really large computer labs. You can get to the things like Microsoft word, Excel, PowerPoint that enable students to work on their assignments, so the library now is a place where you can get things, but you can also get the work done in the same place. We've deliberately done something with staffing. The people who work in the Information Commons have information technology expertise and library research database expertise.

—**June Koelker**

[On moving the computer lab from the basement to the main floor]. It was clear there was a greater demand to access to computers, and so we had the idea of creating an Information Commons in the reference room, starting out with a computer lab but then expanding that computer lab to include the help desk, which included people from information technology services. When students have a need for information help it might be from a librarian, but it might also be from a tech person.

Later, we put the frog pods in as an additional feature of that area. I think the students really appreciated it, and certainly from our gate counts to the library it was getting used more and more. It didn't hurt either that we put a cafe in the lobby, which also helped attract students.

When I suggested having a cafe in the library, the administration kind of raised their eyebrows. I had seen the model at Barnes and Noble years before and how popular that was. I thought, why couldn't we do that in the TCU library? We raised some money and got some funding from the university as well, and we were able to put in a cafe. Everyone loves it.

— **Robert Seal, University Librarian, at TCU 1994-2005**

When I was an undergraduate, I always thought libraries were stiff. And I got to thinking, why can't libraries be comfortable? And while libraries shouldn't be noisy, they don't have to be quiet. Why can't they be inviting? Have nice big comfortable stuffy chairs. And literally, as I talked with our librarian then, he wrote a paper on "the Barnes and Noble effect on libraries." A number of us worked on that, and the good leadership of the library also helped put that in place. But there was a notion that libraries could be inviting, comfortable, attractive, and well-appointed. And they didn't have to be stuffy.

— **Larry Adams, Emeritus Associate Provost and Associate Professor of Sociology, at TCU 1969-2011**

The change in the library is one of my personal favorites. I love the way in which the library has become almost really like a student union. I am old enough to remember that when you went to the library, you had to be quiet, and you could not take any food or drink into the library. And now, this library is a hub of activity. There are still quiet spaces. And I really like that about the library—that students feel that the library is their space. I like to think they're studying, and I think, most of the time, they are, but there's a certain amount of socializing that goes on in the library as well.

I also appreciate the fact that one of the changes that the library made in terms of the way it functions, interacts with faculty and students, is the dedicated research librarians. Every discipline has a dedicated librarian, like a dedicated librarian for business, a dedicated librarian for social sciences, a dedicated librarian for fine arts. And for me, that's phenomenal because I have a point person that I go to for anything library-related, but she's also the point person when my students have a research project. We go twice to the library as a class. And so, the students know Robyn Reid and how to use the library resources. I know that's been a huge help for me in terms of the way I teach and the way I work to guide students through their research projects.

— **Claire Sanders, Provost's Faculty Fellow for Diversity, Equity, and Inclusion**

ABOVE
Students protest the library's limited hours on weekends, requesting that the library be open on Sundays, 1963. This request was granted. Courtesy of Mary Couts Burnett Library.

ABOVE
Reading Room, 1972. Courtesy of Mary Couts Burnett Library.

Years ago, in general if you were a college student and you had research to do, you tended to go to the library, and there was a distinction between research material in a library and everything else outside of the library. My generation grew up knowing the difference, because the scholarly things were in libraries and the other things that are worth reading and interesting but weren't necessarily scholarly weren't in libraries. Fast forward to today's world . . . the library's still there, but there is the internet, which has wonderful resources, and the line between what's library and what's internet is not necessarily clear. We have a proxy server that does not make you authenticate each time you use a different database, so all this is just served up to you. So it's kind of transparent whether it's on the open internet or whether it's proprietary and it's restricted to TCU. It's not always clear what's fact-based and what's opinion-based. The user needs to be the one to interpret. So there's a need now for much more library instruction. This is where there's a growing role for libraries. One of the things that I've done in the last couple of years is strengthen the liaison model. We try to assign a librarian teaching the colleges, and if possible we have that librarian have two masters degrees, one in library science and one in the field of English, or in the field of science, so that there is comfortableness and knowledge of some of their research literature.

—**June Koelker**

ABOVE
Library renovations, spring 2014. Courtesy of TCU Marketing and Communication.

ABOVE
The main entrance for the Mary Couts Burnett Library in 2015, after major renovations were completed. Courtesy of *TCU Magazine*. Photograph by Amy Peterson.

RIGHT
Microfilm and microfiche readers at the Mary Couts Burnett Library, 1975. Courtesy of the Mark Couts Burnett Library.

There are a couple different areas that we targeted for focus in the 2015 renovation. One of them is more seating. Particularly during exams, students could not always find a place to sit down, so the seating had to be ramped up significantly. There will be a special area for graduate students that has a combination of a couple different features. One will be very small little rooms that are almost like monk cells. There'll be dissertation writing rooms. And then architecturally, Rees Jones Hall and the library will be joined by second floor bridges. So during twenty-four hour access, which is five nights a week, you'll be able to use the facilities and the seating in both buildings. So that you may choose a group study room in that building or a group study room in the library buildings.

Students are working more in groups. This change that I'm seeing is not library initiated; I think it's part of the campus culture. Libraries always had a history of quiet, and there is still a quiet space, but every bit as important is the conversation space, the place where you work in a group on your projects. [Before that], you read and you did your work alone and the seating tended to reflect that. Now we make sure that we have single and group seating.

There are a few things that we've discontinued because we've moved on. For example, we used to get thousands of print journals. If we can get electronic, it's available twenty-four hours a day, and it can be used by multiple people at the same time, whereas a print journal can be used when the building is open and by one person. I've run into some students that don't know what microfilm means. That's how you used to read old newspapers. Today you have full-text newspaper databases. The fact that a student has never used microfilm is fabulous, but if you need it we've got microfilm machines.

We needed to expand some of the tech support. Now for many projects, students may have a snippet that's audio or video, so we have some media editing suites and we have some high-powered computing that has, for example, GIS software. There are two special facilities that we're very excited about. The fablab is short for fabrication lab, which is primarily going to be 3D printing. One's called the vislab, and that's short for visualization lab. The vislab is a visualization feature where you're going to be able to see things much larger than on a computer monitor. We could have projection that would maybe be 270 degrees and show a large-scale image walking down the street in London in Shakespeare's time. It could be looking at molecular structures at two feet high and how the bonds hold those molecules together. It could be an Excel spreadsheet where you could see fifty columns, all at the same time. Years ago, video cassettes were a big deal. Now, there's so much more you can convey with the visual rendering of the information that's more mixed media. It's exciting.

It's fascinating. As the changes are occurring in the different disciplines, we need to be responsive. Most of what's in that library right now comes from North America or England, but we're getting much more international at our school, and the library needs to be reflecting our curriculum. We need to get research material that's from all over the world. That's one of the things I'm looking at right now—more international material.

—**June Koelker**

We had good support from the administration. When there was a budget cut here and there, the library was pretty much protected by the administration from making any drastic cuts, which was important. I guess the biggest obstacle was the funding to expand and remodel the library. That was something that we wanted to do for years, and I can't tell you how happy I am that it is happening right now. It is long overdue and students and faculty deserve a modern up-to-date library.

— **Robert Seal**

ABOVE
Chancellor Boschini on the steps inscribed with "Knowledge Is Power" inside the east entrance to the Mary Couts Burnett Library. Courtesy of TCU Marketing and Communication. Photograph by Amy Peterson.

This is a place that appreciates its library; they think the library's important. It has been aided by faculty support, administrative support; it has benefited by a lot of students using it. The library's not there to just be beautiful, it's there to be used and have people in the building twenty-four hours a day. If you're a librarian, that's just where you want to be. That's the part I like the best.

Nobody is an alum of the library. You're an alum of your college. Nobody graduates from the library. But really, if there were no library on campus, I think there may not be as many people graduating because there isn't a library to help them.

—**June Koelker**

ABOVE
Mary Couts Burnett Library, 2015. Courtesy of *TCU Magazine*. Photograph by Amy Peterson.

12.
Technology

ABOVE
Students with typewriters in a typing class, 1957. Published in Neeley School of Business yearbook. Courtesy of TCU Marketing and Communication.

BELOW
John V. Roach, former CEO of Tandy Corp, with an original 1971 Radio Shack TRS-80 Model 4P portable micro computer, 2019. Courtesy of *TCU Magazine*. Photograph by Rodger Mallison.

ABOVE
In 1961, TCU received its first computer, an IBM 1620 similar to the one pictured above, to support the work of the Institute for Behavioral Research. It was placed in Dan Rogers Hall. Courtesy of Erik Pitti via Wikimedia Commons.

RIGHT
Students from the Neeley School of Business work with computers, 1980s. Courtesy of TCU Marketing and Communication.

ABOVE
Students in a Neeley computer lab, 1990s. Courtesy of TCU Marketing and Communication.

LEFT
Professor Joe Lipscomb uses an overhead projector in the 1980s. Courtesy of TCU Marketing and Communication.

RIGHT
Opening of the Holme Geology Student Computer Lab, 1993. Courtesy of Mary Couts Burnett Library. Photograph by Linda Kaye.

LEFT
Computer lab, 1997. Courtesy of Mary Couts Burnett Library. Photograph by Linda Kaye.

LEFT
Library Information Commons, 2009. Courtesy of Texas Christian University. Photograph by Glen E. Ellman.

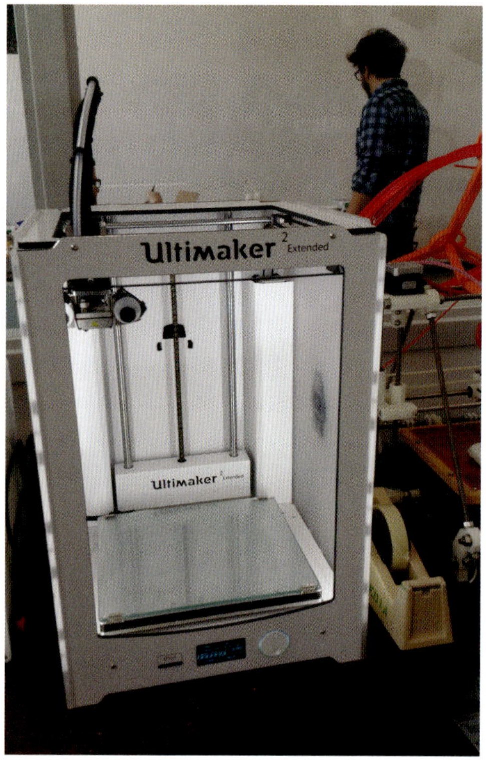

ABOVE
Students use computers in a strategic communication class, 2019. Courtesy of TCU Marketing and Communication. Photograph by Jeffrey McWhorter.

RIGHT
3D printer, 2016. Courtesy of *TCU Magazine*. Photograph by Rick Waters.

BELOW
Students work on computers in the newsroom in Moudy South, 2019. Courtesy of TCU Marketing and Communication. Photograph by Jeffrey McWhorter.

I think the biggest changes have been in technology. When I first got to TCU, we wrote on chalk boards. When we got really fancy we had these overhead transparencies that we would show on the screen. Now we've progressed to using PowerPoints and students bringing their laptops to class.

— Phil Hartman, Emeritus Professor of Biology and Dean, at TCU 1981-2022

My sophomore year, I took the first computer course that TCU offered, and I ended up going to work for IBM. Can you imagine a university without a major department that dealt with technology, and without computers? But it was such a different time. My father wanted me to get a degree in education, or to get my teaching certificate, because that was what was appropriate for a girl to do. I took one semester of an education course, and it was so awful. When I graduated, unlike many of my sorority sisters and female classmates, I didn't have a teaching certificate and I had to get a job. I had minored in math and majored in French, but because I had taken that one semester of a computer course, I interviewed with IBM, and they offered me a job. I was one of the first females hired by IBM as a systems engineer, not to be a secretary, and I loved the work. I would not have even known to apply to IBM had I not had that course.

— Deedie Rose, Trustee Emeritus, served 1988-2007

In 1984, we finally got a new computer system that integrated admission, financial aid, the business office, and the registrar's office. That allowed us to do better reporting and get more statistical analysis. At that time, we created what I call the "communication flow"; it changed our pattern of how we communicated with students over time. In 1985 or 1986, I saw an advertisement for a program at the Educational Testing Service in Princeton. It was called "Introduction to Personal Computers." Keep in mind we had no personal computers on campus at the time. We had magnetic card typewriters and eventually some memory typewriters. Admission letters could be stored, but the storage capability was small. So I went to Princeton for this program. It was a basic introduction to word processing, database, and spreadsheet capabilities, but I thought, gosh, this has so much power and potential. I got a Compaq PC when I came back, and I think it was one of the first ones on campus.

— Janet Herald, Associate Dean of Admissions, at TCU 1974-1989

I remember one night in 1985 walking to the library and looking at our first fax machine that was about the size of this table. The librarians called and said, "Oh, you must come, we've had our first copy come in." We had a print copy of a journal from UT Austin, and I stood there and looked at that and said, "This was transmitted over a telephone line!" It was amazing.

We've had a lifetime of changes in the way that the digital era has changed education, and what we do and how we learn and go about it. We worked with the O-IBM and IBM punch cards that you may have seen in history books. Then one day in an academic department, we got our first electronic calculator. Now the whole world is a classroom. At one time we had dual degrees classes with what was then our sister institution in Mexico. Their students were sitting in a classroom in Mexico; our students were sitting in a classroom at the Tucker building here on campus. The students would interact with each other and listen to lectures. You can see, then, what the internet did to education.

— Larry Adams, Emeritus Associate Provost and Associate Professor of Sociology, at TCU 1969-2011

Technology will continue to change. New gadgets, new techniques . . . Technology will always outrun other components of society.

— Larry Adams

In 1982 computers were still new. I wanted to use computers effectively in instruction. I had done some work at Carnegie Mellon University, and every one of their courses required that their students use technology. I sent some of our faculty members to Carnegie Mellon University, not because we wanted to be a carbon copy of them but to see what they were doing there that made sense for us at TCU. We had to tell people, "Just like Rome wasn't built in a day, we aren't going to make this change immediately. We're going to get the computers, we're going to offer professional development, and we're going to give you assistance while you're doing it."

— John Mangieri, Dean of the School of Education, at TCU 1982-1989

I grew up in Fort Worth, and when I was in high school I worked on campus in the student center. It was a lot slower paced than it is now, and the university was quite a bit smaller. The student body might have been six thousand. All our accounting work was done on pads, using pencils, and running tapes on calculators. There weren't any personal computers on people's desks; I bought the first personal computer in Sadler Hall. It was an IBM, when they first came out with personal computers. It was a huge thing, very heavy, about that thick [gesturing a gap of about eight inches], and it had an amber-colored screen. Until then, all our computer screens were green, so it was a big innovation. It had a ten-megabyte hard drive. Most files in Word or Excel now are bigger than ten megabytes. With technology, we're now able to do the accounting work much faster. It enables us to have time to do more analysis, and that's a good thing because it would be impossible to account complexities like the endowment all on scratch manually.

— Dick Hoban, Assistant Treasurer, at TCU 1981-2019

When they first came out with the typewriter that you could make some corrections electronically before you printed out, we were like . . . wow!

— Darron Turner, Chief Inclusion Officer and Title IX Coordinator, at TCU 1994-2021

I remember years ago when we didn't have any technology in the Alumni Office. Back in the day they had little cards. If you changed your address, you would call on the phone, and we would get our eraser out, erase it, put your new address, and stick it back in the card bank. Computers didn't exist. If you made a mistake on a typewriter, you'd have to rip it out and start over. It was much harder to communicate way back when. And so, I think technology has helped a lot. We can reach so many more people through technology than we ever could before.

— Kristi Hoban, Associate Vice Chancellor for Alumni Relations, at TCU 1980-2019

The changing world of computers at TCU may not be as visible as some of the big buildings that have been built, but there's been a huge shift in our emphasis on computer support systems. We're able to provide the technology to you as students that you're accustomed to and that our faculty need to use when they're teaching. The WiFi you enjoy or the software that you use to register for classes or the email systems that you have—there's been a huge investment by TCU over the last twenty years to bring all of our computer support systems up to speed. The infrastructure of the campus has really changed, far more than most people realize. It also reminds me about how dependent we are on technology, all the grading systems and class registrations and things that this institution is relying on.

— Roby Key, Associate Vice Chancellor for Advancement Operations, at TCU 1988-2016

One of the challenges to technology is communication. When you send an email, some of the language details that you pick up with conversation are easily lost. We have students who write exactly how they talk on their instant messaging on their cell phones, and we have to figure out how to correct that. The other part of that is how do you help students communicate when they're shy and technology becomes the crutch? I think we need to understand the limits of technology and how it may handicap our children. But, when used effectively, you can do a host of things. We can communicate with folks from across the planet and exchange ideas.

— Darron Turner

Technology changed everything. We used to give this speech at orientation of, "Say goodbye to your parents, and call them once a week or write to them." Now you talk to your parents once a day or every other day. We get frequent calls in the campus life office from frantic parents whose students have been out of touch for twenty-four hours and they assume the worst has happened because we are so connected [by] technology. The first computer I used belonged to Panhellenic; the university didn't supply computers to the student affairs office I was in, which was in the old student center. It's been a huge cost factor for universities, but it's been phenomenal.

Technology presents different challenges because you get the skills to text each other, but then you forget how to talk face-to-face, or you don't get the opportunity to do that. But you'll work it out because it's enhanced so many other things. Another thing it's done is make the world smaller. It used to be that Spain or Japan or Brazil or Columbia were so far away. Not any more, because you can Skype, and it makes you really want to go there and understand you're a global citizen, just like it says in our mission statement.

— Susan Adams, Associate Vice Chancellor for Student Affairs, at TCU 1975-2014

When I arrived in 2000, we had those pink and blue application folders. We did everything manually. We had the paper and pen applications. That has morphed into essentially everything online now. Not only applications, but all the supporting documents are transmitted to us electronically. We have become more sophisticated in how we manipulate data. The software system that we use is called PeopleSoft. It is a difficult software system to use, but if you have the right people who know how to manipulate it, it can provide us an awful lot of information.

— Ray Brown, Dean of Admissions, at TCU 2000-2016

At one time we were so far behind with technology. I think we were the only place besides the mom and pop grocery stores that did not have online job applications. We were still doing everything in the old paper-and-pencil way. We have really come out of the dark ages and advanced technologically.

— **Shari Barnes, Director of Employee Relations, at TCU 1983-2014**

We were a bit behind the times technologically when I got here. From about 1987 to 1994 I was pretty involved in PC computers, those old IBM computers, and I left my last job with everyone having their own computers. I came here, and nobody had computers. I got a big box computer that sat on my desk, and I had a little tiny terminal which acted as the information system.

The secretaries in the offices at the time were using carbon paper. In 1994, if they typed a letter to a faculty member, it had to be on a typewriter with carbon paper, and it was tough to do it well. You took a piece of paper, a piece of carbon, and another piece of paper on top and put them into the typewriter together so that the impact of the key hit through the carbon paper. Which is great, till you make a mistake. Then you have to back the thing back out again, correct the original and go with a razor blade to correct the carbon and scrape it off. People who ran the typewriters with carbon paper were gifted typists, and they could type flawless letters at a reasonable pace. One of my first moves was to say, we don't really need to use carbon paper anymore.

The information system that we kept on students was all homegrown. If they wanted to keep track of grades, somebody had to write a computer database program. And they had to keep that system running. Someone had to write the financial system. The people that worked in those places were either purebred computer scientists or self-taught [and] were mostly TCU people and TCU grads. Modifications or any new information we wanted to collect was difficult, because someone had to go into the original software and write a new subroutine and then collect all that. We have since moved to PeopleSoft, in 1996 or 1997. I lived through the transition of taking off the old system, translating the data into the new system, and starting to use PeopleSoft. The sophistication is much stronger, the security is a lot higher, the level of quality of the data is better. It is not as easy to use sometimes.

— **Michael Russel, Associate Vice Chancellor for Student Affairs**

We have wireless technology all over campus now. Ten years ago that was a pipe dream, and things like that changed the way that we can pursue all sorts of learning opportunities.

— **Patrick Miller, Registrar, 1981-2016**

We were one of the first universities to do a digital view book. It used to be that we, like most universities, would send it in the mail. We've had a lot of universities look at that and say, "Oh, we are interested in doing that." It's updateable because it's not in print. That's good and bad, because that means then you've got something that's very content hungry all the time.

The buildings that are coming online now, such as Rees-Jones Hall, are wonderful. It is what happens inside a facility that I think has been one of the fantastic hallmarks here at TCU: to use a building in interdisciplinary ways, to use a building that utilizes smart technology to help professors teach or engage their students better. Learning and teaching, just like marketing and communication, are undergoing tremendous change thanks to technology. Now a professor utilizes technology to assist the learning process and ensure that the students understand how to use technology in the right way.

We [the Marketing and Communications division] are making sure our structure is where it needs to be so that we are ready to assist the university as we evolve with the technology in the classroom or in the lobbies. The challenge is, with something digital, you have to have the content. We need to be ready to use our content to assist colleges who have websites now. That's huge for us, being in a position structurally where we can assist the university as it goes through evolutions with technology and a need for content or the need for marketing.

— **Tracy Syler-Jones, Vice Chancellor for Marketing And Communication**

When you're successful, you always have a danger of failing because you become complacent. In the case of engineering, if you don't change as the technology changes, you're going to fall behind. And it's hard to catch up. You always have to be on the alert to keep up with present technology.

— **Harold Nelson, Chair of the Department of Engineering, at TCU 1991-1998**

Every semester the people who teach business information systems have to redo their lectures because technology is changing so fast. We're doing several things to try to keep up. For example, in Marketing, we just put in a digital marketing course. We put in a social media course. We're having a course taught right now by Dr. Stacy Grau, who's team-teaching it with an advertising executive in New York. He's doing lectures from Skype. He's bringing real projects from New York into this class. We're trying some different things to keep up with the changing world.

— Bill Moncrief, Emeritus Professor of Marketing, at TCU 1982-2023

I think we should move toward not just applying technology to our workflow at the university, but integrating relevant technology and analytics into all curricula. If we could graduate students who understand how analytics affects their field, it would really put them ahead. A number of the deans have analytics with respect to their fields on their radars.

— Teresa Abi-Nader Dahlberg, Provost

There are areas where the technology changes rapidly. For example, in Radio/TV/Film, you've got to keep up with the technology, which means you have to change out your equipment. Same thing is true with respect to laboratory equipment in the sciences and computers on campus. I think we have done a relatively good job of that.

— Don Jackson, Emeritus Professor of Political Science, at TCU 1975-2010

When I became dean of Fine Arts and Communication, this building was untouched. It was built in the early 1980s, and frankly, very little had been done to the building or the furniture. When I came over here, we had analog technology and were behind the times by a long shot. I spent a tremendous amount of time and continue to spend a lot time making sure that our students have as much of the newest technology as we can afford at their fingertips. All of that comes from saying that we're never going to be behind again. We've been very successful at that. We've been able to raise the funds to keep equipment up to date. When the accreditation for journalism came, a lady from CBS San Francisco said that we had better equipment than they did. When ESPN came this last spring [for] the baseball playoffs, they left their truck at home because they felt what we had surpassed what they had. That says a lot. People say, "Well, it's just equipment," and you're right, it is just equipment, but it's also a tool. If our students don't know how to use the most current tools, they're not going to do well in the marketplace, and that's why we do it.

— David Whillock, Dean of the Schieffer College Of Communication, at TCU 1991-2019

In the most general sense, I am responsible for all technology at the university. That includes the networking, the servers, and the infrastructure piece, and not just the equipment. It is the conduit and fiber cables in the ground as well. We are involved in the construction of new buildings and managing the applications that sit on top of that infrastructure, whether that is the portal to check your grades, pay your bill, or select your dining plan. Then there is the security around all that: the accounts, the passwords, the firewall. There is the programming team that runs a customized version of those applications, and the customer service aspect, which takes support calls and helps people use the systems. There are about one hundred people across a variety of groups that handle everything technology at TCU. It is a lot to think about on a regular basis. But it helps that we have a lot of good people working for us.

I can remember when I lived in Milton Daniel, we had phone lines and dial-up phones. The year I graduated they put in network lines, which was revolutionary at the time. As a department, we've done some amazing things. You look at where the university's technology was seven to ten years ago, and it has really changed. There is a great perception from the budget office, the finance team, and the chancellor about the importance of technology. They make sure that it is well-planned and well-funded, and they treat it like a strategic asset. There have been many accomplishments, but getting the university to recognize the importance of technology has been huge for us.

Right now a challenge my team is going through is this period of decentralization. Before, all the data lived in a few systems, so if you wanted to know enrollment or financial trends or any other kind of data you could go to one or two systems and get that archived information. Now, with the adoption of the cloud, so many systems are being purchased quickly, and that data lives everywhere, and the data is difficult to bring all together and correlate. We are fixing that challenge now by looking at how to integrate the systems so that we can provide back meaningful data to people who need it.

We are also basically writing the systems for the School of Medicine from scratch. We are implementing and integrating their admission systems, their curriculum management system, and they need certain specialized things because it is a medical school.

— Bryan Lucas, Chief Technology Officer

13.
Title IX

ABOVE
Susan Bachelor Adams. Published in TCU 1998 yearbook. Courtesy of Mary Couts Burnett Library.

RIGHT
Vernell Armstrong tipping off the ball at a TCU women's basketball game vs. TWU, 1977-1978. Courtesy of Mary Couts Burnett Library. Photograph by Linda Kaye.

RIGHT
Laura Shrode Miller. Published in TCU 1979 yearbook. Courtesy of Mary Couts Burnett Library.

A change that has affected me is Title IX, and Title IX is not just about women's sports, which is what most people think. It's also sexual harassment policies and rules; it's equal opportunity in the classrooms. I've seen a huge change to the commitment to Title IX in all aspects of college sports. There are more women students in the School of Business than there were when I first came here. Everything is more open and equal. I think Title IX has been a huge change in university life.

I've seen big changes in the diversity in both gender and ethnic background of those in leadership positions and on the Board of Trustees. That's for the better.

2012 is the fortieth year of Title IX. I started working thirty-five years ago, so I've taken part in that because I've been the sexual harassment officer for nineteen years. We've done a lot of work helping people understand appropriate behaviors and professionalism and respect. What Title IX says is that for everyone there has to be equity and equal programs. That's not just so that you have a women's basketball team—that's so that women can learn what men learn: how to be competitive, teamwork, and how to lose and get back up and win the next time. Those are all real important life skills and professional skills. This is why it's important that women have equal access. Increasing access has probably been my biggest leadership impact on Title IX.

Women have more opportunities now. In the 1980s, when I was the student government adviser, Laura Miller asked, "Where are all the women leaders?" Before her, there had not been a woman student body president. Now nobody thinks anything of it when a woman runs for president. There are more national role models for women than there have ever been.

I think Student Affairs did absolutely everything it could to make sure that the same opportunities were available for every single student, so that everybody has a chance to succeed. That still happens today. Students who are uncomfortable in a classroom or with a faculty member, or are experiencing a problem, come to someone in Student Affairs.

This university made a good faith commitment not because it was a law but because it was the right thing to do.

We still carry the Disciples of Christ principle of inclusiveness. When the brothers founded TCU, it was the AddRan Male and Female College. We're committed to Title IX, that's not a change. We're just trying to move forward with what's happening in the greater society.

— Susan Adams, Associate Vice Chancellor for Student Affairs, at TCU 1975-2014

ABOVE
TCU Women's basketball vs. TWU, 1977-1978. Courtesy of Mary Couts Burnett Library. Photograph by Linda Kaye.

In 1974-1975, I coached the first TCU women's basketball team. We had no scholarships. We had no uniforms. We had no basketballs. We had no players. I went around and said, "Oh Jenn, You're tall . . . can you dribble? Can you shoot? Can you play defense?" When I'm walking across the campus, I still see a member of the volleyball team and I think, "Gee, I wish you could have been her in 1974. We could have used you." We won three games and came in second twelve times.

My spouse, my TCU roommate, sewed some of the uniforms, and we had to buy some of the jerseys. We had about twenty people come out. . . . We wound up with nine young women who could comb the court. It was five on five, but in high school most of these young women played three on three for defense and three on three for offense. The defense would play on one end of the court, get the ball to the middle of the court and have to pass it off and rest. Back then people thought that women shouldn't exert themselves. This was before Title IX and before people were better informed.

— Bob Frye, Emeritus Professor of English, at TCU 1966-2003

All of a sudden men's soccer vanished. Today there's a lot of people who don't even know we had it. That was a time when TCU said, "If we are going to have a sport, let's be very good at it or not have it. And a calculated decision was made to add women's soccer. Women's sports were growing. Coach Garmen in women's basketball had probably a fraction of the men's budget. I can remember when I first got into finance looking at the expenses and wondering "Why do the men have four beautiful outfits, and the women are still wearing what they wore last year?" I felt like it was almost a lawsuit waiting to happen.

—Jack Hesselbrock, Associate Athletics Director, at TCU 1988-2018

ABOVE
TCU Women's Soccer vs. SMU, 1986. Courtesy of Mary Couts Burnett Library. Photograph by Linda Kaye.

ABOVE
TCU Women's Tennis doubles, 1986. Courtesy of Mary Couts Burnett Library. Photograph by Linda Kaye.

LEFT
TCU rifle team (Sherryl Stine, Cheryl, Garrett, Linda Robinson, and Carolyn Faubion) and Coach George Beak, 1970. Courtesy of Mary Couts Burnett Library.

We have seen growth in Title IX and opportunities for women in sport. The university has embraced that growth. We've got a tennis facility and a collegiate soccer facility that are second to none. There has been great support for women's athletics. In the future, you'll see some more changes. TCU is about 60 percent female and 40 percent male, and we've got to grow our number of women's sports. We've are looking into the various options now to see what the next step is.

— Ross Bailey, Associate Athletics Director, at TCU 1977-2021

ABOVE
TCU Women's Soccer game against UT Austin, 2022. Courtesy of TCU Marketing and Communication. Photograph by James Anger.

ABOVE
A TCU track and field athlete during the TCU Invitational, 2015. Courtesy of TCU Marketing and Communication. Photograph by Michael Clements.

14. Inclusivity

To discriminate against another on the basis of skin color, sex, religion, and handicap is not merely stupid. It is absurd. And it is unacceptable on this campus.

— Chancellor Emeritus Bill Tucker

What is essential to this university is inclusiveness—inclusiveness in every meaning of that term.

— Chancellor Emeritus Bill Tucker

ABOVE
Image from a series of photos of a walk on the TCU Heritage Trail as part of TCU's Race and Reconciliation Initiative Week, 2022. Courtesy of TCU Marketing and Communication. Photograph by James Anger.

ABOVE
TCU's Holi celebration hosted by the Students for Asian-Indian Cultural Awareness (SAICA) and The Crew, 2022. Courtesy of TCU Marketing and Communication. Photograph by James Anger.

I think that inclusiveness—creating diversity—is one of the greatest changes since I started TCU.

— Eugene Brice, Trustee Emeritus, served 1992-1998

When I came here in 1958 there were no minorities. White as snow. I think the first Black student was in the nursing college, and then shortly after, Linzy Cole was a backfield runner who was Black. It would have been maybe a year or two after that that we were integrated.

In my field of geology, there might be one or two, maybe three girls, out of twenty-five, who would go into geology. because at that time a lot of big oil companies wouldn't even hire women. Of course, that's all by the boards now.

— Art Ehlmann, Chair and Professor of Geology, at TCU 1958-1993

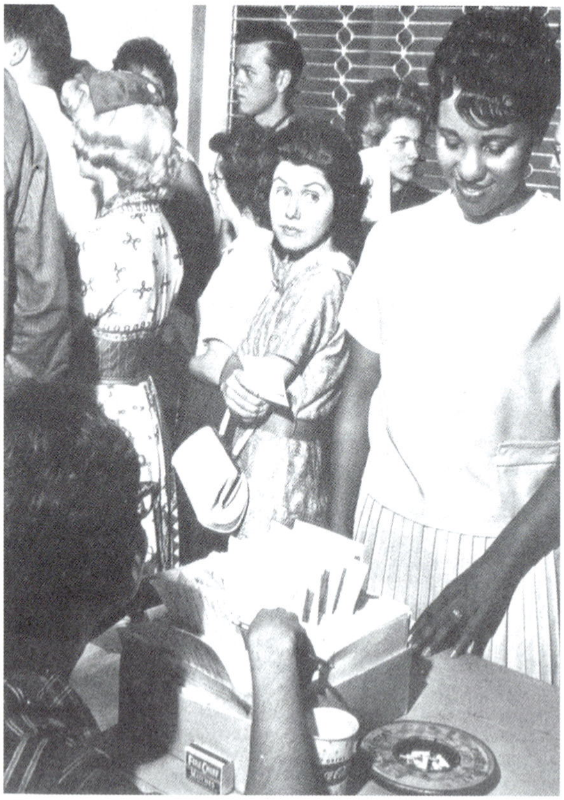

ABOVE
Allene Jones class of '63 registering for classes in 1962. Jones was one of TCU's first Black graduates, and in 1968 became the university's first Black professor, specializing in clinical psychiatric nursing. Courtesy of TCU Marketing and Communication.

Thirty-five years ago I think the white population was about 94 percent. The Black students on campus were almost exclusively athletes and as such, if you were Black on campus, the assumption was that you were an athlete, even if you weren't. That's even an issue today. I have a lot of Black students on this campus who aren't athletes, but every single one of them has been asked what sport they play.

— Linda Moore, Emeritus Professor of Social Work, at TCU 1977-2017

There were a lot of social organizations in the 1980s to get into, but Black students would really push to be a part of them and to be in leadership positions.

— Darron Turner, Chief Inclusion Officer and Title IX Coordinator, at TCU 1994-2021

The growth of Student Affairs has helped the campus progress for two reasons. It's helped diversify the campus and support students. When I came, this was a mostly white campus, but we now have international students and students of color from different ethnic backgrounds.

— Susan Adams, Associate Vice Chancellor for Student Affairs, at TCU 1975-2014

Anything we do to make it better for female faculty makes it better for all faculty, and if we make it better for faculty it's better for students. It's really in our best interest to pay attention to the places where we can improve, and we've been slowly working on that.

— Bonnie Melhart, Emeritus Dean of University Programs and Associate Provost, at TCU 1990-2019

I was one of the first people to bring openly gay people on campus. Never once at this university have I been questioned about any of the issues that I brought up related to ethnicity or sexual orientation. Those taboo subjects have been given nothing but carte blanche . . . They changed the internal anti-discrimination policy at TCU to include sexual orientation . . . There have been so many changes.

— Linda Moore

Chancellor Ferrari worked hard on benefits for faculty and staff. That's how the conversation started the first time about having benefits for same-sex couples. That process moved through but was not completed when Ferrari was here.

— Don Mills, Vice Chancellor Emeritus for Student Affairs, at TCU 1969-2022

ABOVE
TCU's Spectrum student group participated in the Tarrant County Pride Parade for the first time, 2019. Courtesy of TCU Marketing and Communication. Photograph by Kyle Cartwright.

ABOVE
Students at the Intercultural Center on campus demonstrating how to be an ally ahead of Pride month, 2022. Courtesy of TCU Marketing and Communication. Photograph by James Anger.

I am a member of the Shawnee tribe, and I've always had a strong belief in helping other Natives of the US attend college. I worked to bring other students in through participation with the tribes of the US Southwest and throughout the heartland of America. When tribes would award scholarships for Natives to attend a college or a particular university, I worked specifically with a financial aid director, Mike Scott, who said, "We will match every tribal scholarship at TCU to bring those students and help them."

What I attempted to do with the programs at TCU was provide a lot of support, including interpersonal support. Many of these students were first generation and away from cultural elements, and I knew what that meant. These students, even though we have strong support networks at TCU, still need special kinds of support.

— **Larry Adams, Emeritus Associate Provost and Associate Professor of Sociology, at TCU 1969-2011**

ABOVE
Haylee Chiariello, a TCU student and member of the Cherokee Nation, was one of the featured speakers at Reconciliation Day, April 21, 2021. Courtesy of TCU Marketing and Communication. Photograph by Amy Peterson.

When I looked at TCU back in '99, I thought, "Gosh, I like this university, but it doesn't have a lot of diversity." I was concerned about that. When you're talking about a university experience, you want to make sure it is as well-rounded as possible. We want to get students from different parts of the world, different genders, different socioeconomic backgrounds, and different ethnicities to come to TCU.

I think we've done a good job in terms of where the university wants to head with diversity amongst its student body and employees. I'm seeing a tremendous shift. It is part of our strategic goal to recruit a student body that is more diverse, not only ethnically, but gender-wise. To have a really nice university experience, you have to have a student body that can share with one another different life experiences. It's not only skin color, but also different socioeconomic levels, so students can bring a different kind of experience to the classroom. That is so important for a university that talks about educating students that are going to go out and change the world. You have to understand how the world operates, and you won't if you are with people who look like you, act like you, and think like you. You've got to bring in that diversity of thought in order to have an impact.

— **Tracy Syler-Jones, Vice Chancellor for Marketing and Communication**

ABOVE
Tracy Syler-Jones (left) interviews Fort Worth civil rights icon Opal Lee at the TCU vs. Baylor women's basketball game at Schollmaier Arena in Fort Worth, Texas, 2022. Courtesy of TCU Marketing and Communication. Photograph by Sharon Ellman.

I came to TCU really hoping to help move us forward in recognizing and celebrating diversity of all kinds. One of the things I did was help create the Chancellor's Council on Diversity with Cornell Thomas. In 1998, I was involved in starting Allies, the Women's Resource Center, and Community Scholars. These were all meant to help us become more reflective of society and more conscious and celebratory toward of all kinds of identities.

— Barbara Herman, Associate Vice Chancellor for Student Affairs, at TCU 1986-2021

I would say one of the really important things that, if we're talking about diversity and inclusiveness, is honoring and serving our first-generation students, because for them the journey is a little bit different, and for their parents also. That's been an emphasis.

— Barbara Herman

ABOVE
First Generation Day 2019, an annual event that honors students who are the first in their families to enroll in a higher educational institution. Courtesy of TCU Marketing and Communication. Photograph by Amy Peterson.

When I came to TCU, it was a predominantly white university, even more predominantly white than it is now. There are real efforts in terms of making structural changes through scholarship programs and recruitment strategies that came out of admissions and that came from the leadership of Ferrari. Michael Ferrari hired Cornell Thomas in the College of Education to provide him with some of the strategic leadership around DEI work before it was called DEI. We started the Community Scholars program.

— Karen Steele, Special Assistant to the Provost and Professor of English

DEI

The Diversity, Equity, and Inclusion Committee works to ensure equitable access and inclusion of opportunities, benefits, and resources for all members of the Horned Frog family. The committee's charge is to monitor all existing and future initiatives regarding diversity, equity, and inclusion on campus; and actively participate in developing a vision for diversity, equity, and inclusion that represents the entire campus community.

— DEI Mission Statement

ABOVE
Presentation of banner honoring TCU as a Special Olympics National Unified Champion School, 2022. Courtesy of TCU Marketing and Communication. Photograph by James Anger.

In June of 2016, one of two English Department faculty of color, who had just gotten tenure, resigned. He graciously wrote a detailed and measured letter of his experience working at TCU. It was a real wakeup call for the chancellor, who was shocked that anybody would have a miserable time working at TCU. There were things in the letter that I had a hard time imagining could have happened on our campus, but I've since learned are a daily occurrence for students, staff, and faculty of color.

In July of 2016 the Chancellor convened a group of his cabinet, and he invited me to come along to this meeting to think about how to make sense of this resignation and how to do better. The chancellor partnered Aisha Torrey-Sawyer and me together to lead the DEI effort. I wanted to be sure that I had someone who's lived experience could guide the effort, and it's been one of the most rewarding partnerships that I've had in my career. It's certainly one of the areas where I've grown the most in terms of understanding one of the top three challenges in higher education today.

We were formed by the Faculty Senate, but unlike most ad hoc faculty senate committees, it would report directly to the chancellor, so it would have more spine and more teeth.

ABOVE
Karen Steele. Courtesy of TCU Marketing and Communication. Photograph by Amy Peterson.

Prior to getting started, I did a little bit of traveling to different universities that have done some really striking work with DEI, getting input from their leadership and some of their faculty on their process. We also had a letter issued by Black students, and their demands about the experiences and the changes that they were requiring. It was also the same time that Comparative Race and Ethnic Studies was forming as a program. All of these things were all part of the experiences in starting us out.

The committee was comprised initially of people who were long-standing advocates for different aspects of diversity, equity, and inclusion. We assume that the broader range of the perspectives will give us more successful, nimble, creative solutions. When we set up the DEI Committee, we created a working group structure, and we asked every working group and the co-chairs of those working groups to recruit broadly. We wanted to make sure that there was diversity in terms of disciplinary backgrounds, colleges, and identities.

There are students who contribute to our committee work. The leader of the social justice group right now, Shelby Johnson, was a member of the DEI Committee last year . . . I couldn't believe what an incredibly analytical thinker she was and how forthright and powerful she was, among a bunch of faculty and staff. She was just so advanced in her thinking. She was often leading the work that we were doing.

We try to have DEI members and faculty who are listening, showing up, and providing support for students who are activists on our campus, because there's a toll to doing that work. Students want to see things happen so quickly. The timetable is utterly inadequate for many of our student activists. They are involved in lots of important changes, though they may not be beneficiaries of those changes during their four years at TCU.

The work that we've done over our first three years initially was trying to gather data to get a handle on what the realities were for our community. We did a lot of focus groups surveys to get a better sense of their experiences on our campus. We worked as a committee to identify what we thought were the high-level priorities, and we've ultimately distilled them in four pillars that are easily understandable. How do we attract faculty and staff to work here or students to study here? How do we teach them, and that can be about training for those who are employed here as well as for educating our students? How do we reach beyond campus to connect to our communities, especially our underserved communities? And then how do we address the campus culture? Campus culture is the biggest, baggiest, most complicated challenge because there are so many different dimensions.

Yesterday the Faculty Senate approved the second level of the implementation for the Diversity, Equity and Inclusion as an Essential Competency for our undergraduate core curriculum. We know that there will be specialists who teach the DEI courses for the undergraduate curriculum. But we want all faculty to build skills and inclusive teaching practices.

— Karen Steele

ABOVE
Aisha Torrey-Sawyer with students at the Faculty, Staff, and Students of Color Mixer hosted by the Office of Diversity and Inclusion, 2022. Courtesy of TCU Marketing and Communication. Photograph by James Anger.

In fall of 2016, Karen and I were tasked to lead the DEI Committee, and we officially began the committee in January 2017. I would say the first thing that we did with the committee was just to come together and consider what are the topics we want to talk about . . . We let the committee have discussions and figure out what the main topics were, and it came down to recruitment of students, faculty, and staff of color; training, education, and curriculum; reaching out to the Fort Worth community—and more specifically the community that does not always feel welcome at TCU; and finally campus culture.

Our charge was to come up with some of the ideas and strategies and put them forward to Chancellor Boschini. Karen and I meet with Chancellor Boschini probably every quarter to sit down and talk. I think what really helped us was that our first meeting was with Chancellor Boschini. He didn't tell us what we had to do. He wanted to really hear from us. He said, "I'm looking to you to tell me what it is that should happen, put forth those recommendations."

Chancellor Boschini has been an advocate for DEI. Chancellor Boschini always says, "If you have an idea, if you have something to share, come see me."

We have a lot of suggestions. How do we actually implement those? I would say in the past recommendations were made, and they were reviewed. What someone could do, they may have done it. Where it needs to change is to have a detailed strategy on moving recommendation forward. In the past, it has been very much reaching out and having one-on-one conversations with someone, and then that person thought about how they're going to do that. But that person may have ten other priorities that they have to get done. Now there is some shift where DEI is getting bumped up. . . . My vision is that we will lay out a plan that details step by step how we can get to all of the things that we want to happen, whether it's recruitment, inclusion, or campus climate. They are happening slowly—we have to take it to a different level.

My goal for DEI is really one where people feel like they're valued and part of the community. I think it is important that our students feel like this is a place for them no matter what marginalized group they come from. DEI's goal is to make sure that we are a world-class university that embraces, respects, and recognizes diversity, equity and inclusion for all. We're getting there.

I would say there's even been a shift at TCU, four years ago versus today. There have been huge differences in getting behind DEI. Although DEI is a challenge, we're moving in the right direction. There are individual faculty, staff, and students who are wholeheartedly invested in seeing TCU become a more inclusive university.

— Aisha Torrey-Sawyer, Director of the Office of Diversity and Inclusion

What's interesting to me is that in that first Faculty Assembly about the DEI Essential Competency proposal, there was a lot of push-back. Once it was all over and I had had some time to process the experience, I concluded that a lot of those negative statements came from a place of fear. Just fear of change, fear of the unknown. What has happened since then is that those fears are not as prominent because we are moving forward with our strategies for diversity, equity, and inclusion.

In the broadest sense, my goal is to embed DEI in everything we do, so that it really does become like fluoride in the water and such an organic part of what we do that we're not even aware we're doing it.

— Claire Sanders, Provost's Faculty Fellow for Diversity, Equity, and Inclusion

ABOVE
Students in the John V. Roach Honors College's Engaging Difference and Diversity class, taught by Lynn Hampton, 2018. Courtesy of TCU Marketing and Communication. Photograph by Jeffrey McWhorter.

I think especially in the last three to five years, TCU really started to focus on DEI and moving that effort forward. We now have the most diverse provost council or provost direct reports in the history of TCU. I can't say enough about how it changes the feelings inside of faculty, staff, and students from underrepresented groups. I got emails like, "Wow, I never thought my dean would be someone that looks like me." That, I think, is a real positive future thing.

We're going to go through a lot of pain in order to get to good. I don't think the civil rights movement in this country has ever taken a big step forward without a lot of angst.

— Teresa Abi-Nader Dahlberg, Provost

A monument recognizing Native American and Indigenous peoples will be dedicated Monday [October 22, 2018]. The plaque is dedicated to the Native American tribes who lived on the land that TCU now occupies and it's located between Reed Hall and Jarvis Hall. The following is in-scribed on it:

"We respectfully acknowledge all Native American peoples who have lived on this land since time immemorial. TCU especially acknowledges and pays respect to the Wichita and Affiliated Tribes upon whose historical homeland our university is located."

The plaque also features the quote "this ancient land, for all our relations," in both English and Wichita. The original plan was to have the entire quote in both languages, but when the last fluent speaker of Wichita died in 2016, that became impossible.

— ***TCU 360*, October 11, 2018**

ABOVE
Seminole Nation member Chebon Kernell speaks at the dedication ceremony for TCU's Native American monument, October 15, 2018. Courtesy of TCU Marketing and Communication. Photograph by Amy Peterson.

ABOVE
Between Jarvis Hall and Reed Hall stands a bronze plaque commemorating the Wichita and Affiliated Tribes. It states: "We respectfully acknowledge all Native American peoples who have lived on this land since time immemorial. TCU especially acknowledges and pays respect to the Wichita and Affiliated Tribes upon whose historical home land our university is located." Courtesy of TCU Marketing and Communication. Photograph by Eric Sasadeusz.

Race and Reconciliation Initiative

We are at pivotal point in America today. Racism has been present for far too long, and the many recent incidents, including the deaths of George Floyd and many others, have awakened a passion for true equity and justice. It is imperative that we, as stewards of TCU, do everything we can to instill, and live, very real change.

— **Email from Chancellor Victor Boschini and Mark Johnson, Chair of the TCU Board of Trustees, July 15, 2020**

Some of our race and equity response from students came before George Floyd. We had some local concerns. But George Floyd hit home to so many, and so I think that between Tracy Syler-Jones's office and the Chancellor's Office we crafted some messages that acknowledge the fact that we know that this is problematic and that as a campus we have our own issues. That's when the race and reconciliation stuff really got underway.

— **Kathy Cavins-Tull, Vice Chancellor of Student Affairs**

I can't make any promises to you or anyone as to what we will find and what we will do, but at the very least I can make the commitment to find and discover the history so that we can continue to have these conversations and honor the history as we look to making a new legacy for ourselves. . . . What I've been saying to those who will listen is that we should be prepared to embrace our past and not erase it. There is nothing to be afraid of; knowing our history and acknowledging it make us stronger in terms of our foundation for moving forward in the future.

— **Frederick Gooding, Honors Professor of African American Studies and Former Chair of the Race and Reconciliation Initiative**

You can't go somewhere if you don't know where you've been.

— **Chancellor Victor Boschini**

In the aftermath of the George Floyd murder, TCU had to reconcile with the idea of having to do something. We have to demonstrate and show our students that we're dynamic, that we're able to respond to the moment and step up. These factors helped culminate in the creation of the Race and Reconciliation Initiative.

It was daunting at the beginning, because we had no template. I think the best thing that we did was try to manage those expectations by stating what we were and what we were not. There's a lot going on in the world right now, and there's a lot going on at TCU, but we are here to study the history. We're not a magic wand, we're not here to cure everything. We're just here to help start a conversation that hopefully can grow in size, substance, and quality.

— **Frederick Gooding**

Reviewing, understanding, and transparently sharing information about our history will make us a stronger institution as we plan for the years ahead.

— **Chancellor Victor Boschini and Mark Johnson**

Through new understanding, we can—and must—take action that will lead to healing of any inequality here and more broadly in our world.

— **Chancellor Victor Boschini**

ABOVE
Frederick Gooding (left) and Marcellis Perkins (right) lead the Race and Reconciliation Initiative, 2021. Courtesy of TCU Marketing and Communication. Photograph by Amy Peterson.

Reconciliation Day

We accomplished the objective of creating something that was tangible, and we shared it publicly on April 21, 2021, on what now is known as Reconciliation Day. The event was just a beautiful sight to see. We wanted to make sure that we expressed that this was important, and one way to demonstrate that was by having the buy-in of the power brokers and the dignitaries. For Reconciliation Day, we had the Chancellor and the Provost speak . . . In addition, we had the Dean of Admissions, the Athletic Director, the Vice Chancellor of Student Affairs, and the Chair of the TCU Board of Trustees show up and speak.

We also created what was called RRI week. We ended with a block party out in the Campus Commons, where we had music and food to send a message that reconciliation doesn't have to be all doom and gloom. Whenever we talk about race, it doesn't have to be so heavy we're feeling a bit out of shape and depressed.

I think the idea that made this initiative different as opposed to others from the past is that it was backed with funding through the Provost's Office, so we had the means to bring in speakers and pay for the labor to do the research. These resources—and the Chancellor stating that Reconciliation Day should be annual event—were absolutely instrumental in demonstrating that this was a serious event. This idea of perpetuity suggests commitment, that there's going to be a space to reflect upon how TCU is doing and how it can improve. I think that's significant.

— **Frederick Gooding**

ABOVE
Performers from the dance group Ballet Folklorico de Fort Worth are featured at Reconciliation Day (April 20, 2022). Courtesy of TCU Marketing and Communication. Photograph by Leo Wesson.

In the last few years, we have certainly focused on Race and Reconciliation, our African American students, faculty, and staff, and I think that was an important place to start given the darkness and depth of our nation's history. I think that many people in Student Affairs who run the Inclusiveness and Intercultural Services did a great job. What I am hoping is that we continue to look at all identities and don't stop at bringing diversity to campus but continue to create community.

— **Barbara Herman**

I particularly want my white brothers and sisters to know that reconciliation is not just for Black, Indigenous, and people of color, but it's for all of us who dare to wear the purple. It's for an entire community.

— **Frederick Gooding**

Reconciliation means, to me, the opportunity to influence the future. This idea that we acknowledge the past, we tell the truth, and we tell the whole truth. By making a stronger connection with the past, we have the opportunity to influence the future. I can't change the past, but I can change my interpretation of it, my understanding of it, and what I want to do with it.

— **Frederick Gooding**

Aisha Torrey-Sawyer and I have been working with a lot of important input from the college diversity advocates. We've been working on a hiring guide that will be a checklist for all of Academic Affairs. It's going to call for and require departments to run their searches, not in a way that's fundamentally different, but in a way that they haven't been run in the past that is more attentive to details.

— **Claire Sanders**

LEFT
At Reconciliation Day (April 20, 2022), TCU extended a special welcome to several of Charley and Kate Thorps' living descendants (shown). Courtesy of TCU Marketing and Communication. Photograph by Leo Wesson.

ABOVE
Mural created as part of TCU's Race and Reconciliation Initiative, installed near the Clark Brothers statue on the Intellectual Commons, 2021. The artwork on the east side of the wall (shown) was created by Fine Arts students Lauren Fleniken, Quin Frazier, Faith Glass, Micah Matherne, and Katalina Watson. Courtesy of TCU Marketing and Communication. Photograph by Andrew Emery.

One thing that I would say is that if you just look at the hires we've made in the past two years, there's definitely a lot more diversity on the administrative staff, particularly when you look at deans, associate provosts, and others in Academic Affairs. We also have the initiatives to look at the history of TCU with Race and Reconciliation. We have different initiatives being led by the chancellor and the provost to look at how inclusive our curriculum is and what we are doing at the university to educate people for the future. We are being intentional about where we are in this environment going forward in the future.

— **Floyd Wormley, Associate Provost for Research and Dean of Graduate Studies**

If we're really going to celebrate and value and learn from the multiplicity of identities that we all represent, we're going to have to talk to each other more. So many of the things that Student Affairs has tried to do is have dialogues through programs such as the Family Table or the Crucial Conversations as well as in the classroom. Just saying, "Look at our percentages of various groups," is not enough, and certainly we have leaders who know that. I believe firmly that this chancellor and the previous two that I had the privilege of working with were and are deeply committed to doing the right thing and to have TCU be a leader in having a diverse, welcoming, inclusive, and respectful community, and that's so much of what Disciples of Christ is built on—making sure that individual identities and paths are recognized.

— **Barbara Herman**

15.

The Burnett School of Medicine

The medical school opening will be a huge accomplishment for TCU, especially since—if I am remembering this correctly—Fort Worth is the largest metropolitan area in the country without an allopathic medical school. This can be transformative not only for the TCU students who might ultimately go to that medical school, but also for the community, addressing more healthcare concerns. That's the huge thing that's on the horizon with TCU right now.

— **Cheryl Wilson, Associate Vice Chancellor and Controller, at TCU 2001-2019**

Our singular mission is to create the best future physicians. We want to ensure that our medical students are equipped to be skilled and empathetic physicians when they graduate.

— **Stuart Flynn, Dean of the Burnett School of Medicine**

We will maintain what they start medical school with, which is a very high level of empathy, which traditionally disappears in medical school. Our tagline is that we will train empathetic scholars.

— **Stuart Flynn**

ABOVE
Members of the inaugural class of TCU and UNTHSC School of Medicine, 2019. Courtesy of Texas Christian University. Photograph by Glen Ellman.

The program is trying to set itself apart from traditional medical schools with a communication-based curriculum meant to teach students empathy and to be active listeners.

— ***TCU 360* September 23, 2019**

The risk and the excitement and the charge to go forward with this medical school is a huge thing. I think we will look back and believe that it's been a really pivotal moment for TCU.

— **Brenda Cline, Member of the TCU Board of Trustees**

ABOVE
Stuart D. Flynn, the founding dean of the Burnett School of Medicine. Courtesy of TCU Marketing and Communication. Photograph by Amy Peterson.

Chancellor Boschini gives all of the deans a lot of leash, and he lets us lead . . . I've tremendously respected that. With a little bit of elbow grease, come next June, [we will be] a fully accredited medical school. I'm infinitely appreciative and respectful of what the chancellor has done vis-a-vis this medical school.

We invited the two leaders of the accreditation body for allopathic (MD-granting) medical schools, and we told them what our curriculum was going to be and, that if we really put our noses down, we could potentially submit everything a year later. They said something that was prescient and profound: "Your curriculum is something really special. Do not rush it. Take your time and submit in two years." That was amazing to hear and great advice.

At the end of their site visit the accrediting committee read a letter that basically said: "You don't have any issues of compliance." In other words, we got a 100 percent on the exam, which, I've been told, has never been done before by a new medical school. I was especially proud of that and proud for the university.

— **Stuart Flynn**

I think that Dean Flynn is visionary and is trying to create something that's new and innovative and that can impact medical education more broadly. He's trying to look at things like how do we make doctors better able to connect with their patients, how do we introduce new medical school technology, and how do we introduce augmented and virtual reality into medical education . . . I think the medical school is already impacting us greatly . . . It will create an enormous amount of attention in the community locally but also nationally.

— **Magnus Rittby, Professor of Physics**

The medical school offers a curriculum that focuses on the future of medicine, medical knowledge, communication skills, empathy, compassion, and lifelong learning.

— ***TCU 360*, March 2022**

To accommodate TCU's forward-thinking approach to medical education, the design includes flipped classrooms without lectures and spaces that enable students to partner with physicians from their first day in medical school.

— ***TCU 360*, March 2022**

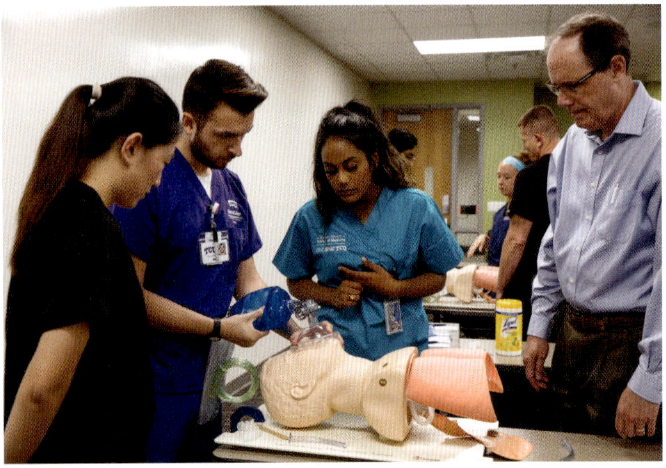

In a traditional curriculum, they do block clerkships. That's where they do eight weeks of internal medicine or eight weeks of pediatrics. They focus on one at one time. It's primarily hospital based, so they're seeing patients who are on one end of the spectrum, who have a condition that has advanced far enough to require urgent care. We do a longitudinal integrated clerkship (LIC), where they do all of their clerkships at one time, and we do the majority of the training in the clinical setting. One of the advantages is that it helps to expose our learners to where most of medicine is practiced, which is in clinics. Only really sick patients have to go to the hospital. If you orient our learners' gazes only on seeing the sickest of the sick, they can really never capture prevention, which is where medicine needs to move toward. That's one asset of utilizing an LIC.

The other part of it is that when they're in a block clerkship model, a lot of their interactions with patients are transactional. They're in the hospital for a week or two, and then they never see that patient again. What would it look like if you can help foster learning in an environment where they can have a longitudinal relationship with patients? For example, if I'm a preceptor and I'm an internist, and I accept one of our students, I am inviting them into a forty-week experience of learning in the clinic that I run, with the patients that I have the privilege of taking care of. I invite this learner to take on two or three of the patients that I care for. They see those patients on a regular cadence. Let's say a patient has to go into the hospital. Our learner will follow that patient into the hospital. When that patient gets discharged, they follow them right back again. They foster an actual relationship, and it helps to maintain empathy.

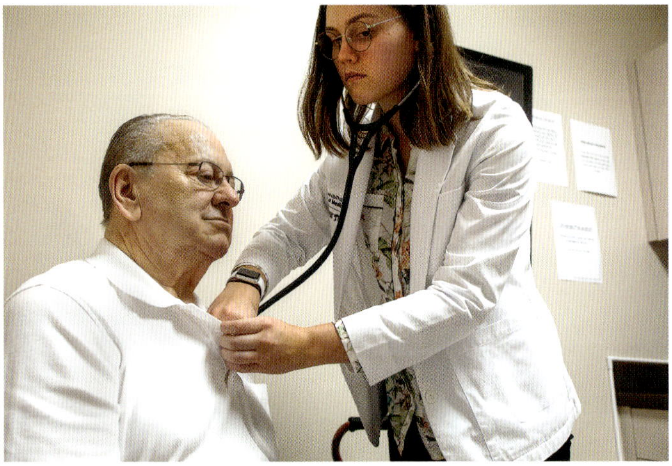

ABOVE
First year medical student Quinn Losefsky examines a patient at Mansfield Medical Associates as part of the Longitudinal Integrated Clerkship (LIC), 2020. Photograph by Mark Graham.

We know that medical students come in with a lot of empathy, but they don't leave with a lot of it. This has to do primarily with the learning environment. Longitudinal Integrated Clerkships is one way to shift that. It helps them foster actual relationships with patients. What's really nice about it is that the patients get invested in it too. When they get to have their own medical student, they're invested in helping to shape that student to being the doctor that they ultimately want. That's powerful. That's what I love about this model. Patients are just as responsible for helping our students learn. The founding dean, Stuart Flynn, along with Jacqueline Chadwick, the founding vice dean, brought these concepts to the table.

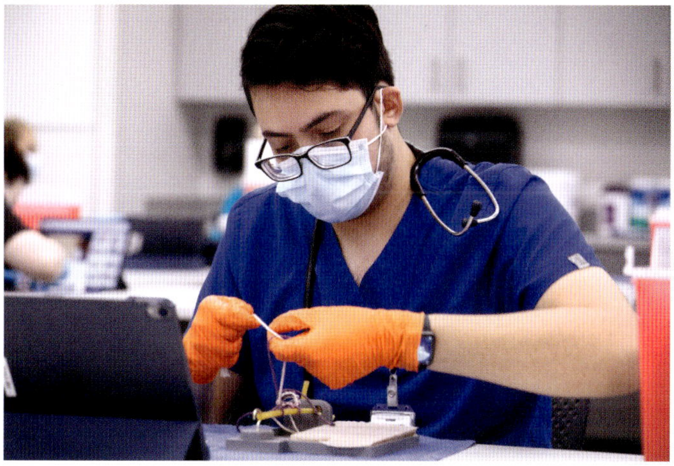

ABOVE
Edmundo Esparza practices suturing and knot tying, 2020. Courtesy of *TCU Magazine*. Photograph by Joyce Marshall

One of the big switches was actually going from a didactic or a lecture-based curriculum into the concept of the flipped classroom. In flipped classrooms, we all learn from one another. We have our students access information, and then we put them into classroom environments where they are typically doing case-based learning, problem-based learning, where they are coming together as a team and working out key concepts with an instructor, who is a content expert in the room, to help flesh out things that may not have been learned accurately. Working in teams is essential to being an excellent physician, because we do not work in silos. The more we encourage physicians to rely on the expertise of their teammates, the nurses, the techs, the respiratory technicians, and everyone who is there to do a job within an expertise, the better the outcome is for the patient.

— **Danika Franks, Assistant Dean of Student Affairs for Burnett School of Medicine, at TCU 2017-2022**

ABOVE
Jonas Kruse and Charna Kinard, members of the inaugural class of the TCU and UNTHSC School of Medicine, 2020. Courtesy of *TCU Magazine*. Photograph by Joyce Marshall.

We have a little bit of a national reputation, and the national reputation is two things. It's not how well we teach the basic sciences. It's the fact that we are training empathetic scholars. That word empathy resonates with people wanting to go to medical school. In fact, that's the reason I came to Fort Worth to start this medical school. The other is our nationally recognized communication curriculum. Communication and compassion. . . . Those two things give us a national cachet for some applicants that other schools aren't talking about. We had over 8,000 applicants in 2019 that came from all fifty states. I've been at big medical centers that never have seen that before.

— **Stuart Flynn**

Diversity, inclusion, belonging, equity, all of that is vital to us being able to accomplish what we do. If you don't have students that represent the patients who are being cared for, you are missing a whole gap of things. Representation matters. Your lived experiences are similar or are connected in such a way that there's an unspoken language. You can't train that. Our admissions focus on being able to have representation.

We strategically have admitted sixty students per class. We will stay that size because the amount of investment that we have to train them relies on a one-to-one pairing with their own preceptors in eight different disciplines. We have to keep our numbers strategic so that we don't over-shoot the community who has agreed to partner and train our students.

— **Danika Franks**

ABOVE
Paul Dorman at the Leadership Fort Worth breakfast event where the announcement of the H. Paul Dorman Charter Scholarship Program was made on April 18, 2017. Courtesy of Burnett School of Medicine. Photograph by Joyce Marshall.

ABOVE
Benefactor H. Paul Dorman (center left) received an honorary white coat and framed photo of the School of Medicine's inaugural class. On stage with Dorman are (L to R) Dean Stuart D. Flynn and first-year students Quinn Losefsky and Connor Rodriguez, 2019. Courtesy of *TCU Magazine*. Photograph by Mark Graham.

The Medical School has received a transformational gift that Chancellor Boschini was able to secure with Mr. Paul Dorman. Mr. Dorman will be paying for the first year of all the medical students and that will help reduce the debt of those medical school students. A lot of students will want to gravitate to us because we'll be able to help curb their debt with this transformational gift, and I attribute that to Chancellor Boschini.

—Jean Pickett, Chief of Staff

I'm working right now on what I refer to as a clinical trial research consortium. It will be housed in the School of Medicine. It will be with three of our big partners, John Peter Smith, Baylor, Texas Health Resources . . . We will be the biggest clinical trial site in the country times ten. Fort Worth is going to become the magnet for pharma and biotech to knock on our door first to ask us if we want to open and close studies for them, because to them time is money. If this even remotely plays out the way it should play out, it will be a game changer that I would've never predicted when I arrived. When I met a few months ago with Mr. Dorman, who does clinical trials, and gave him an update about the school, I told him this, and he leaned forward in his chair and said, "You just changed the national perception of your medical school and TCU." That may be something pretty profound that will attract companies to move here, and it will result in our Fort Worth clinical partners having national recognition for being cutting-edge discovery and delivery of healthcare.

— Stuart Flynn

Improving the academic profile of the university has been kickstarted with the addition of the medical school. That's a crucial step.

—Jack Hesselbrock, Associate Athletics Director, at TCU 1988-2018

The first class will begin in fall 2019. We want to see the medical school be successful, and I think it's going to be a game changer in ten years. People looking at TCU will be looking at TCU in a different way. I think the medical school will elevate us to a position of being one of the top fifty schools in the country, maybe even top thirty to forty.

— Mark Johnson, Member of the Board of Trustees and former Chair

The medical school I think is probably going to be the biggest change here from an academic perspective because it adds a piece to the institution that we'd been looking for—a professional graduate program to help us grow. It's really exciting for this university and for the Fort Worth community. It'll be even more exciting when that first class graduates. From a national perspective, we're going to get a lot of attention. Anytime we embark on something at TCU, it's done quite well. There is a need in this community and particularly in the state of Texas for more doctors.

— Andrea Nordmann, Chief University Compliance Officer

The TCU School of Medicine is having a truly exponential impact on our community.

— Chancellor Victor Boschini

16.
Global Community

ABOVE
Students in Harris College of Nursing and Health Sciences tour a university health care simulation facility during a study abroad course in Santiago, Chile. Courtesy of TCU Marketing and Communication. Photograph by Scott Murdock.

Students are going to live in a global community. The future in all dimensions is global. Universities must give students the best educational opportunities. Our world is continuing to change, evolve, and shrink. We have to live as our mission statement says—"To educate individuals to think and act as ethical leaders and responsible citizens in the global community."

A passion of mine for twenty-five years has been international education. We developed a collaborative, cooperative way to give each of our students an opportunity to go to another culture, become involved in that culture, and learn. My goal also was to bring the world to the university because I thought it was a two-way affair . . . When we bring international students to campus, that's a vitally important mix in a classroom. All of us learn about diversity from students from other countries rich in culture and tradition. Our students come back from studying abroad and one or two would say to me just about every year, "Now I know what international students feel like on campus, because I was that way on another campus."

— Larry Adams, Emeritus Associate Provost and Associate Professor of Sociology, at TCU 1969-2011

ABOVE
Students at the International Student Association banquet, a fundraiser for food donations to Latin American and Caribbean countries, 2012. Courtesy of TCU Marketing and Communication. Photograph by Carolyn Cruz.

ABOVE
Students on a trip to France in 1966. Courtesy of the Mary Couts Burnett Library. Photograph by Castleman.

We've been actively involved in international education for decades. Actually, the first study abroad program was back in the 1950s, when our Spanish department would take students to Mexico for intensive language programs. We moved into a period of inactivity for a while but gained momentum in the '80s. In the early 1990s we moved as an institution to internationalize our university when faculty started taking students abroad in the summer. Then we developed programs and liaisons with other universities, where our students could go abroad and have a period of study in another culture.

In the grand scheme of things, my vision was more than just sending students abroad, although that was a vital part of it. Attendant to that was the notion to bring international students from other universities and other cultures and other societies to TCU. Because in my mind, if you're going to have an international university, then we must make it truly international by having international faculty and students on this campus, participating in class discussions and to the life of our campus. True international education includes study abroad . . . and having visiting students and faculty from other universities here on our campus.

One specific challenge is always the finances. But we worked with that and found good cooperation and interest from faculty and staff. I give credit to all of those faculty and staff who've participated in international education in a variety of ways. They worked with our students going abroad and worked with non-US students coming here. We found good support from Chancellor Tucker and Chancellor Ferrari, and now from Chancellor Boschini. It was indeed a group effort.

— **Larry Adams**

ABOVE
Suzy Lockwood, from TCU Nursing, and Irmgard Payne, from the Davies School of Communication Sciences and Disorders, give the "Go Frogs" sign in the Andes during a study abroad course in Chile, 2017. Photograph by Scott Murdock.

I really think we're trying to become a great international university, a global university where you can train for most fields and go out and do the things you train for. We bring students in who have a host of information and ways of understanding life, who interact with each other, who can then go out and change the world in ways we don't know right now.

— **Darron Turner, Chief Inclusion Officer and Title IX Coordinator, at TCU 1994-2021**

I was quite concerned when the number of our international students went down briefly over COVID because, without them, our campus is not the same. Looking back to the past, when almost all international students were in one residence hall, TCU was not taking advantage of the richness that they bring. It's having those interactions and learning from them. Peggy Watson and I share a fairly strong belief that all of our students should be bilingual. I personally believe that a language other than English should be required in the core curriculum. All of our international students are at least bilingual, and many of them tri- and multi-lingual. I think that on the level of world experience, intelligence and drive are things that we all can learn from, and that's why I believe that, if students study abroad, doing it in a place where they can really immerse with the culture and the language is so important.

— **Barbara Herman, Associate Vice Chancellor for Student Affairs, at TCU 1986-2021**

ABOVE
An international student from South Africa displays her heritage during the TCU Commencement Reception for the Class of 2022. Courtesy of TCU Marketing and Communication. Photograph by James Anger.

The international admission process doesn't differ dramatically from traditional domestic student undergraduate admission. The big difference is the ability to pay. That's going to take on a greater role with international students than it does with traditional domestic undergraduate students. We don't give out nearly as much need-based financial aid to international students as we do to domestic students. Beyond that, the process is pretty much the same. I think most of us would like to see a few more percentage points of international students here. The spice that they add is extraordinary, and I wish more of our domestic students would take advantage of that in their undergraduate experience here at TCU.

We have an interesting practice here at TCU that predates me. Right now, we could pretty much fill our entire freshman class with Chinese students. Not too long ago, we could have done the same with Indian students. And thirty years ago we could have done that with Japanese students. We made the decision that we didn't want a majority of international students coming from one country to happen. We want to have as many countries in the freshman class represented as we possibly can. We have between sixty and seventy nations represented in the university as a whole. In every freshman class, we generally have seventy-five freshmen from international addresses. Those students generally come from about twenty-five different nations. The mix is pretty broad there, and that is intentional. We really would like to have as broad a mix of just about every background that we possibly can muster here. We don't want every student to come from one type of high school or one type of metropolitan area or one state, and the same holds true with international students.

— Ray Brown, Dean of Admissions, at TCU 2000-2016

ABOVE
The International Student Association participates in the Homecoming 2005 parade. Courtesy of Mary Couts Burnett Library. Photograph by Linda Kaye.

ABOVE
The main floor of Tandy Hall photographed from the mezzanine, 2019. Courtesy of TCU Marketing and Communication. Photograph by Jeffrey McWhorter.

Model UN

One thing I have tried to emphasize is an integrated education, a holistic education linking Student Affairs to Academic Affairs and making sure that students see connections between what they do out of class and what they do in class, and between what they do here and now and their future. I have been quite involved in global programs and helping to start the Model United Nations program. In 2002, our former Provost, Nowell Donovan, and I co-chaired a committee called the Collaboration Group, and it was all about creating a holistic, integrated student experience mirroring academic affairs and student affairs. We looked at lots of ideas, and one of them that I just got crazy about was Model United Nations. I hired Eric Cox, and we ran Model United Nations out of Student Affairs for a few years, and when he moved to Political Science we continued to do it together. That's a perfect example of students expanding their horizons and an important thing to do. With Model United Nations students not only get that international experience, but also learn to analyze their own ideas and those of others and learn to articulate ideas, whether you agree with them or not. I am proud of the global things I have done, particularly with the Model UN, because I think it has helped to make students more aware of their place in the world.

— Barbara Herman

Studying Abroad

Back in the late 1980s, there was one woman, Roberta Corder in the English Department, who would help students figure out how to study abroad. Larry Adams was particularly interested in international outreach, so he began to organize things in the international arena, making them more important. TCU had been sending some students for a summer program, TCU in Oxford. We stayed in the Florida State University building for ten years, and when we closed there, we opened the TCU London Center in 1998, hiring a director and renting an office. It was a time when people were beginning to understand that international wasn't any longer about, "it would be really cool to study somewhere else." It became clear to all of us at the university that, if students didn't have some international contact, they really weren't going to be educated.

The London Center was a direct enrollment into the University of Westminster instead of our having a little island program, where our students lived together and took classes together, which falls short of being integrative. Now our students live with people from all over the world and go to class with Brits. Around that same time, I think around 2005, we opened the Center in Florence and around 2006 we opened Seville.

ABOVE
Students pose by the Tower Bridge in London during the June 2012 study abroad program. Courtesy of TCU Marketing and Communication. Photograph by Amy Peterson.

ABOVE
TCU Nursing students explore the shoreline of Isla Negra during a study abroad course in Chile. Courtesy of TCU Marketing and Communication. Photograph by Scott Murdock.

I get pretty close to most of our study-abroad students, and when they come back I see that they've changed. Besides the international aspect of it, they look different, and they're more confident. They just grow up. They're away from their support system and their family, and they're having to figure out how to get where they're going, problem solve, be sick abroad, and so many other things. The students manage to live in another country, communicate with other people, and understand the differences in the world. The other thing I see is that many go a second time or pursue an international career. They come back with their eyes open to how much they love this country, to how much they have, to things that they've never questioned, to things they are comfortable with, and to things they want to re-examine for themselves. They're amazed that in Italy you can't turn the heat on until the government says you can turn the heat on. We really feel that students who study abroad gain depth.

I've helped students who didn't think they could study abroad figure out how to make that work. We've now harnessed our returned study-abroad students, and those students do peer advising. We've been given some grant money to help students get merit scholarships. Everyone at the university has said this is a priority.

I think we are providing the experiences, and we know they are safe by providing good locations. I think what we work on a lot in my office now is for it to be a meaningful experience. We're trying to help them pay attention and have a deeper breadth and depth of the experience by offering a one-hour cultural enhancement course. We've come so far with getting under-represented populations to be able to go. Now we would really like our students to stretch their boundaries about what locations they're choosing. We have a group going to India this summer, and we pushed so hard to try to make that work. We're trying to get to these under-represented places.

ABOVE
Students pose at the Great Wall of China during a study abroad program in 2007. Courtesy of TCU Marketing and Communication.

The Global Academy is kicking off now, and that's a new dimension to study abroad besides going a semester or summer. It's going to be multidisciplinary, so that students and teachers from different disciplines will pick a topic together, like sustainability, and they'll all be working on it, and then they'll go on location, and everybody in their own perspective will work on the location together. The pilot program went out to Panama, and it was highly successful.

Our study abroad program is in the heart of the TCU curriculum and the TCU experience.

— **Susan Layne, Study Abroad Adviser, 1987-2018**

The TCU Global Academy is an innovative study abroad program that brings together communities, organizations, TCU faculty, and students to explore global issues and solutions. This unique program gives students an opportunity to study a global issue in the classroom and then spend 1–2 weeks abroad working with organizations leading change. Students will explore multiple perspectives on the issue, see first-hand how other countries are solving problems, and engage in cooperative ways with community-driven projects.

— **TCU Global website**

I think the international program is one of our best changes. There was not an international program when I first came here. It's having a good support system for international students when they come here and also encouraging American students to go study in whatever country they want. We overcome the, "Oh, that's not going to fit in my major" barrier.

The increase in international students and students from different geographical regions of the US is now making us better stewards of our globe. We understand what we're doing to the environment and what happens in Japan matters in California, or Texas, or New York. The connectedness is the biggest piece, and the more we learn about different cultures, the more we learn we're the same.

— **Susan Adams, Associate Vice Chancellor for Student Affairs, at TCU 1975-2014**

ABOVE
A student from TCU's Neeley School of Business poses with local students in Addis Ababa, 2016. The trip focused on creating job opportunities for Ethiopian women, and was organized through the Neeley School's partnership with the Adera Foundation. Courtesy of TCU Marketing and Communication.

ABOVE
International students partake in the Homecoming 2015 parade in anticipation of the TCU vs. Texas football game. Courtesy of Ellman Photography. Photograph by Sharon Ellman.

The third Honors Abroad program was created by Theresa Gaul from the English Department and Dr. Betsy Flowers from Religion, a really creative idea called Cultural Pilgrimages. They go to London, Paris, and Rome, and each student decides what their personal pilgrimage is. We had some do a literary pilgrimage, where they would read certain authors and then go look into where they had lived and what they had done. We had people do architectural pilgrimages. We had one student do a fantastic sports pilgrimage. The World Cup was going on in Europe while he was there, and he did a study of sports fans in the three places. The single most interesting one was a student whose grandmother had visited at age eighteen the same three places and had kept a diary. She had her grandmother's diary with pictures, and she talked to her grandmother before they went. Her pilgrimage was to retrace her grandmother's steps, and she was shocked at how similar some of their experiences were and yet how different some of them were.

— Peggy Watson, Emeritus Professor in the John V. Roach Honors College and Dean, at TCU 1983-2012

I went through peaks and valleys at TCU, but still the most powerful learning for me was Spain, where I had the unique opportunity of reflecting on who I was and realizing what I was given. TCU and Honors gave me invaluable lessons. Honors taught me that we have to build a bridge to the next generation. Spain showed me just how much we need to reciprocate for what we receive.

— Austin Marple, class of 2014

I had read of Italy's history and had a vague idea of how much has happened since the birth of Rome and the flowering of Florence. We met a restaurant owner named Fabio in Florence, and after our meal he led us underneath his restaurant where we encountered ancient Florentine streets and architecture. There I gained a visual, tangible lesson about Italian history.

– Kasey Williamson, class of 2017

ABOVE
Students pose with the TCU flag during a study abroad course sponsored by the College of Education. Courtesy of TCU College of Education.

Our professor split us into teams and gave us a list of things to go and see all across Berlin before dinner. Along with that list, he gave us some cash, a map, a public transit pass, and a sly grin that said, "Good luck! You are on your own from here." We experienced total freedom in a totally foreign place.

– Daniel Floren, class of 2013

17.

Faculty Senate and Staff Assembly

Faculty Senate

The Faculty Senate was created by a small faculty committee in 1967 and approved by the entire faculty, Chancellor Moudy, and the board of trustees in 1968. The Faculty Senate is the representative body of the Faculty Assembly, designed primarily to express the views of the teaching and research members of the faculty. It is one branch of the shared governance of Texas Christian University. Views may be expressed upon any matter affecting the university, including educational policies, degree requirements, curricula, questions of academic freedom, student-faculty relations, faculty-administration relations, and practices of the university. Resolutions and recommendations voted by the Faculty Senate are passed on to the provost and chancellor and, when appropriate, the board of trustees.

— **Faculty Senate website**

I think it's fair to say that there were some faculty members who thought that we weren't raising salaries fast enough. When I was chair of the Faculty Senate in 1981 and we had the opening luncheon for faculty and staff in the Daniel-Meyer Coliseum, I said one of the things that we were going to work on in the Faculty Senate was faculty salaries. In the relationship between the executive committee of the Faculty Senate and the administration, especially the chancellor and vice chancellor for Academic Affairs, we would be talking about these issues.

Sometimes people talk about "the administration" as if it's an abstraction, I always try to caution my colleagues that those are people too. They have their ups and down, as we all do. When we try to negotiate through Faculty Senate, or through whatever department with administrators, deans, I think it's important to always remember that they are not some sort of abstraction—they are human beings. As we all try to be.

— **Bob Frye, Emeritus Professor of English, at TCU 1966-2003**

I thought during my years in the Faculty Senate, we all worked hard to get better communication with the administration. I think we achieved that. I wish more faculty would see the importance of contributing to leadership in the Faculty Senate at some point in their career.

— **David Grant, Emeritus Professor of Religion, at TCU 1981-2022**

If faculty are not involved in self-governance, they save a lot of time, and administration saves a lot of bother because, of course, if you have four hundred faculty, you have four hundred opinions. But even though it might not be as efficient to encourage a shared governance model, I think you do get a better product. When I was in practice, we didn't have any kind of notion of shared governance, and I think our decisions were the poorer for it. When faculty give up shared governance, they give up the opportunity to influence the direction of the institution. I believe with all my heart that administration needs a faculty that is aware of that tension and perfectly comfortable with it. We need for administration to be comfortable with it.

— **Rhonda Keen, Emeritus Professor of Nursing and Dean, at TCU 1982-2020**

The relationship between the staff, faculty, and administration has been positive. Since we have a Faculty Senate and Staff Assembly, we have a university that works together. When you get everyone on the same page and pulling together, good things happen. It's not the easiest way, but we've been fortunate to have people with open minds and who accept input. It's kept students, faculty, and staff exceptionally cohesive.

— **Ken Morgan, Director of the TCU Energy Institute, at TCU 1978-2018**

Colleagues, thank you for this moment of personal privilege . . . . My comments will be brief but not extemporaneous. Someone [Coach John Wooden] once said, "The most important things I know are those that I learned after I knew everything." This is probably where I am in my life. I have worked with you directly for over two decades. You have never betrayed a confidence and more importantly, you have taught me to trust you, the faculty. I am convinced that if you are given sufficient information, you collectively will make rational decisions that are in the best interest of TCU. And the Senate is in a position to do just that. I once read, "The most common way people give up their power is by thinking they don't have any." [Alice Walker, *The Color Purple*.]

As I depart, I challenge the Senate to create opportunities and affirm the responsibility of leadership. Specifically:

Continue to shoulder the responsibility of seeing that our students achieve,
Assume the responsibility for the professional welfare of our colleagues, and
Accept the responsibility for the ethical conduct of our profession.

With regard to student achievement, do not reject assessment; rather use the results of assessment to improve the educational experience of future students. Do not become fixated on the assessment of every student in every instructional setting. Find ways to examine the learning of your class, your majors collectively, and find ways to know if the new core is producing the results you want for the majority of students. At times you will be advantaged by seeing the forest as a panorama rather than a collection of trees. As to the welfare of our colleagues, try to move beyond the almost meaningless exercise in which we participate under the guise of post-tenure review. We need to do post-tenure review for the sake of our colleagues, not for the Southern Association of Colleges and Schools (SACS). Take time to reflect on your own professional interests. Do they not change with time? Throw away the cookie cutter of teaching, research, and service and find ways to weave the current interests and enthusiasm of a colleague into the tapestry of departmental and university activities. Help one another understand that each of us contributes in different ways at different times in our careers, and that's okay. Use these differences constructively; do not penalize colleagues for it.

We adopted the American Association of University Professors (AAUP) Statement on Professional Ethics. Have we implemented it? I challenge you to deal with breeches of professional ethics in ways similar to those used by the medical and legal professions. Would it not be more appropriate for peers to review and sanction colleagues as appropriate, than to leave such professional judgments to administrators? Why do we not have a faculty ethics committee? I know, without doubt, you, individually and collectively, can achieve meaningful goals; accomplish great things that will significantly change this university for the better forever. Just do it! Thanks for the memories!

— **Provost Emeritus Bill Koehler's final remarks to the Faculty Senate, May 6, 2004**

The Faculty Senate consists of the faculty members who represent the faculty and their needs. There really wasn't a group that represented staff and their needs and came up with ideas of things we could do until the Staff Assembly started during Ferrari's time. It's made up of staff from all areas of the campus.

— **Kristi Hoban, Associate Vice Chancellor for Alumni Relations, at TCU 1980-2019**

Everybody talks about shared governance . . . and you wonder at some institutions if they really have shared governance or if it's actually a top-down model. The Core is a really interesting example of shared governance at TCU. Faculty were given the responsibility to create it.

— **Peggy Watson, Emeritus Professor in the John V. Roach Honors College and Dean, at TCU 1983-2012**

With Chancellor Boschini I have had an opportunity to work with him much more closely. One of the things that gave me confidence to accept this new administrative role is that I have great confidence in his leadership. I also see him quite collaborative and willing to honor the traditions of shared governance that TCU has. When decisions are made, he's careful to include Faculty Senate, the Staff Assembly, and the Student Government Association. And I think that's important to maintain the climate and the culture that we have at TCU.

— **Susan Weeks, Vice Provost**

The governance of the university has changed fairly dramatically over the last thirty years. Governance has become much more open, much more transparent. The board has become more involved, and I think more people have access to decision making and more students, faculty, and staff are heard in decision making.

— **Laura Miller, former President of the National TCU Alumni Board and ex officio Board of Trustees member, served 2000-2006**

Faculty Senate Resolution on Diversity, Equity, and Inclusiveness, 2016

The Faculty Senate of Texas Christian University, representing the faculty, reaffirms its commitment to the university's core values of academic achievement, personal freedom and integrity, the dignity and respect of the individual, and a heritage of inclusiveness, tolerance, and service. The faculty supports the TCU community's ongoing efforts to fully realize those values and their expression in diversity in all its forms: equity, inclusiveness, freedom of expression, and academic freedom.

Faculty Senate Resolution on Community Dialogue, 2019

Mirroring the broader world around us, the TCU community strives to accommodate a diversity of opinions, perspectives, and experiences on many issues of importance. Given these differing views, authentic and respectful dialogue must guide faculty discussions on current and future issues of concern to the university. Especially now, as we begin work toward crafting a structure for teaching our students how to speak, relate, and work productively across differences, it is imperative that faculty model this skill set. A willingness to address differences respectfully and frankly, with an attitude of curiosity, humility, and a desire to understand, should be our ground rule in all matters involving discourse and debate. We therefore call upon all TCU faculty, regardless of rank, discipline, or perspective, to listen carefully to one another, to seek understanding over divisiveness, and to engage in respectful dialogue in their discussions with one another.

Faculty Senate Statement in Support of All TCU Students

As the elected representatives of the TCU faculty, we believe that every individual deserves respect, inclusion, and support. We find it unacceptable for anyone to discriminate against or degrade students. To all of our students, please know that you are not alone, and your identity is valid and valuable. We stand with you, and we are committed to creating a safe and inclusive environment for you to learn and grow. We encourage all members of our campus community to celebrate diversity and promote equality, and we condemn any form of hate speech or discrimination. We believe that everyone has the right to be themselves, and we will continue to advocate for the rights and well-being of all students.

Staff Assembly

One of the things that is a fairly new occurrence is the Staff Assembly, which is a comparable body to the Faculty Senate. I love it when those two bodies speak with one voice about benefits for employees, or about an honor code for students, or about something in the community.

— Barbara Herman, Associate Vice Chancellor for Student Affairs, at TCU 1986-2021

Dr. Ferrari helped start the Staff Assembly, which partners with the Faculty Senate in governing the university.

— Mary Nell Kirk, Executive Assistant to the Chancellor, at TCU 1989-2021

I felt the staff needed a voice. These people knew a lot more about the university. They were a wealth of information. They loved the university and would do anything for the university. They needed to have a voice. The Staff Assembly ensured that they had a seat at the table.

— Chancellor Emeritus Mick Ferrari

The Staff Assembly began under Ferrari's term, and that was pretty controversial, but he said, "No, you have to let people have a place to talk."

— Don Mills, Vice Chancellor for Student Affairs Emeritus, at TCU 1969-2022

Ferrari propelled the feelings of the faculty and staff of the university to be more positive. He did things like change some of the benefits system, especially for our general staff employees, and created the Staff Assembly.

— Leo Munson, Associate Provost for Academic Support, at TCU 1983-2018

From my position as a faculty member, TCU is a better place than when I started thirty years ago. It is a more horizontal kind of structure than a vertical structure. Inevitably, in administration, someone has to make decisions; the chancellor and the provost have to play their roles. But in terms of consultation, both formal and informal with faculty and staff, this place is much more consultative—that's what I mean by horizontal.

When Ferrari came, there was a shift toward empowering the faculty and the staff. I was quite impressed with the inclusion of the staff as full partners with the university . . . As a faculty member, I only know it from a distance, but the Staff Assembly is an equal and equally respected partner . . . Ferrari was really committed to that, and Boschini is, too.

— Andrew Fort, Emeritus Professor of Religion, at TCU 1982-2017

18.

Texas Construction University

The Tucker Years

Tucker was adamant about focusing on one project at a time, so we would finish one and then do the next one. He insisted on being systematic about it, and we ended up meeting all of our goals.

— **Bronson Davis, Vice Chancellor for University Advancement, at TCU 1990-2006**

At this time, a facility was not built unless all the money was in hand, and not just for the building but there was an endowment for the maintenance.

— **Robert Garwell, Dean of the College of Fine Arts and Communication, at TCU 1989-2012**

ABOVE
Moncrief Hall, built in 1988. Courtesy of TCU Marketing and Communication.

We were bulging at the seams and were having triples in residence halls. We made the case to the governing board that we needed more space, and Mr. Moncrief came forward with the money to build Moncrief Hall. The first time we went out for bids on that building, we were way over budget, and I can remember going to talk to Tex Moncrief with Chancellor Tucker about the fact that we were over budget, and he said, "TCU is too important. Go ahead and build what you think we should have to serve the students." I've always been impressed with that. You have a board there that really cares about the welfare of the students and puts a lot of effort into student scholarships and supporting student events and activities. Many of the things we did we could not have done without board support.

— **Peggy Barr, Vice Chancellor for Student Affairs, at TCU 1985-1992**

Buildings completed 1980-1998

1980, Moody North and South

1980, Indoor Tennis Courts

1988, Moncrief Hall

1989, Tandy Hall

1992, Winthrop Rockefeller Building for Ranch Management

1997, Dee J. Kelly Alumni and Visitors Center

1997, TCU Police Department

1998, Tom Brown/Pete Wright Apartments

1998, Walsh Performing Arts

ABOVE
Tandy Hall with statue of Charles Tandy, built in 1989. Courtesy of TCU Marketing and Communication. Photograph by James Anger.

The school was stable and had a lot of the personality of today throughout that period [1990s]. We built several buildings. One was the Dee J. Kelly Center. It let people of the community and alumni have a place where they can come on campus and do things often to TCU's benefit. Before the only way they could participate in a meeting was go to the old student center, and there was no place to park. The Kelly Center and moving the bookstore out of the old student center really opened up TCU more to the community. Prior to that it was hard to visit TCU. The Kelly Center has been a big benefit to the university.

— **John V. Roach, Trustee Emeritus and former Chair, served 1981-2005**

ABOVE
Newly remodeled Dee J. Kelly Alumni Center, 2018. Originally built in 1997. Courtesy of Linbeck Group, LLC. Photograph by Leo Wesson.

At one point we had a couple of offices on the third floor of Sadler. And then the Alumni Office moved from there to a house on Princeton, where the new addition to Brite is. We had two bedrooms upstairs and then a bedroom downstairs that were our offices. We had a table that would seat eight people, and if we had a meeting that was bigger than eight we had to reserve a room in the old Brown Lupton Student Center. The difference between this little house that has since been torn down and the Kelley Center where we are today is totally different. To have room in a facility like this helps to program and to grow.

— **Kristi Hoban, Associate Vice Chancellor for Alumni Relations, at TCU 1980-2019**

ABOVE
Walsh Center for Performing Arts, built in 1998. Courtesy of TCU Marketing and Communication. Photograph by Amy Peterson.

ABOVE
PepsiCo Recital Hall. Courtesy of Dixie Dixon.

There were two key things that we were looking at in the Walsh Center: the PepsiCo Recital Hall and the Hays Theater. We wanted to have a performance facility for music that was unique, and that's what we built with the PepsiCo Recital Hall. The trick in it was for the architect, Malcom Holzman, to give the spaciousness and the sound of a large, cathedral-like setting within the space of only 350 people. He came up with the concept of a house within a house. The result was an excellent acoustic situation.

The PepsiCo is unique, and that we wondered what could we do in the Hays that would be unique. the Hays Theater was done after some theaters that were done back in the 1920s.

When we started looking at the Walsh Center, the size of the Music Department had doubled from one hundred to two hundred majors, and now it's up to three hundred majors. The theater department tripled in size. There were already expansive needs that we needed in terms of space. We solved some of those with the Walsh Center, but there were still many more that needed to be taken care of. We didn't quite get everything. But we made a dent in accommodating the dramatic growth that was taking place our programs.

— **Robert Garwell**

Buildings completed 1998-2003

1999, Garvey-Rosenthal Soccer Stadium

1999, Lowdon Track and Field Center

2000, Justin Center

2000, Leibrock Village

2002, Tucker Technology Center

2003, Smith Hall

2003, University Recreation Center

2003, Varsity Tennis Building

2003, Lupton Baseball Stadium

The Ferrari Years

One of Dr. Tucker's initiatives was preserving the money we had in the endowment. When Chancellor Ferrari came, he said we needed to spend some of that. We need to update the campus, we need to get our facilities in line with what our clients, the students, wanted and expected. Of the buildings that came online when Dr. Ferrari was here, one of the significant ones was the student rec center. Another was the Tucker Technology Center. There were also a lot of the additions to the athletic facilities because we were still viewed as a school with not a very competitive athletic program. Additions to our weight facility and some serious improvements to the basketball arena and other athletic facilities took place during the Ferrari years.

— **Ann Louden, Chancellor's Associate for Strategic Partnerships, at TCU 1978-2017**

ABOVE
University Recreation Center, built in 2003. Courtesy of TCU Marketing and Communication. Photograph by Jeffrey McWhorter.

The old recreation center was built in 1972, and it was obsolete when it opened. We had students who were joining fitness clubs elsewhere, and we knew that it was important for students to have a place to do recreation. We put together a team and got Chancellor Ferrari to see where we ought to go, and we ended up with what is truly a world-class building.

— **Don Mills, Vice Chancellor for Student Affairs Emeritus, at TCU 1969-2022**

ABOVE
Tom Brown / Pete Wright apartments, built in 1998. Courtesy of TCU Marketing and Communication.

The facilities back then were acceptable, but they weren't wow. Ferrari wanted you to walk in the rec and see that purple arch glass and indoor track and think, "This is a remarkable place."

— **Ann Louden**

We were barely able to house all the freshmen and maybe half of the sophomores. At the end of Chancellor Tucker's era we started a housing master plan, and then we got a go-ahead to build Tom Brown and Pete Wright. That showed with the right housing, students would want to live on campus. But there was still nothing for them to do on campus, so Chancellor Ferrari made certain that we looked at what it would take to build a new student center and a new recreation center, which were the two primary spaces for non-academic student activity on campus. The decision was made to go with the rec center primarily because we had a much better sense of what would be in it, what it would do.

— **Don Mills**

Chancellor Ferrari opened up the purse strings a little more; we started remodeling some of the classrooms and laboratories. And we had the Tucker Technology Center in recognition of Bill Tucker's contribution to the university. The Smith building also came along during that time frame, and the fitness center, which was a big hit with the students from day one.

— **John V. Roach**

Mick Ferrari started us on a building program that really changed the face of the university. We started putting all the technology into the classrooms and improving the classrooms' look and feel. Mick Ferrari started the building push, but Victor Boschini went through the entire campus. It's had a complete makeover as part of his tenure.

— **Dick Hoban, Assistant Treasurer, at TCU 1981-2019**

Reshoring Program

There were some basic infrastructure things that needed to be done before we could build more. For example, our classrooms needed badly to be updated, which essentially meant more technology. Our laboratories needed to be upgraded. In some cases, it was a matter of basic things like replacing roofs and making sure that the sprinkler systems were installed over the whole campus. I would say that Ferrari got most of that accomplished before he retired and that Boschini was able to think on top of that and say, "Okay, now what more do we need?" What we needed was more buildings. Some of it was also rethinking how the campus was going to look over a long period of time. Chancellor Boschini decided we were going to build a campus that looks unified, and it has made a big difference because the place just looks gorgeous. It looks distinct, and then it becomes part of the visual identity of the place, because no other place looks like it.

When you've lived through it all as I have . . . it's just been exciting to be a part of it, to be able to live through it, and watch it happen. I don't know any other university in America that has transformed their campus in such a short period of time as this one.

— **Larry Lauer, Emeritus Vice Chancellor for Government Affairs**

ABOVE
Classroom in Scharbauer Hall. Courtesy of TCU Marketing and Communication. Photograph by Jeffrey McWhorter.

ABOVE
Aerial of TCU Campus Commons, 2022. Courtesy of TCU Marketing and Communication. Photograph by James Anger.

When Mick Ferrari took over, we started to see a few new buildings rise, and along with that this magical thing called the Reshoring Program. And it's because a student, Sarah Donaldson, didn't think much of some of the facilities, particularly in Winton Scott. The labs were out of date, the roof leaked, and the microscopes were old. She got some photographs of the bad conditions and got some photographs of what it was like in local high schools, which was much better, and went to the trustees. The trustees instituted the reshoring program. Every year they gave us several million dollars to improve labs and classrooms. That was a major thing in my life to suddenly realize finally I was getting labs that actually met my needs.

When I came here and wanted a desk for my office, I had to go across to a metal gym which was situated about where the Tom Brown housing complex is. When the administration got new stuff, they would put that old stuff in the gym to be recycled. We had a colossal recycling mechanism for sub-standard furniture. There was an atmosphere that we weren't affluent enough to be able to pay for a good desk, a chair, a computer for a new faculty member. Now it's all changed, of course, because we're doing much better.

— **Nowell Donovan, Provost Emeritus**

The Boschini Years

Huge changes and all for the better have taken place during my time here. Obviously, the buildings have dramatically changed. Alumni in their sixties come back and say this isn't the same university, and in many respects it's not. The chapel is still there, Sadler Hall is still here, and some of the dorms are still there, but they've all been renovated. The chancellor has always thought that first appearances count. When you come on this campus with your parents, he wants you to say, "This is a neat place."

—**Nowell Donovan**

There hasn't been a year since I've arrived when we haven't been embarking on some significant building project. Chancellor Boschini likes to joke about Texas Construction University, but it has made a remarkable change. My neighbors who have lived in Fort Worth since the seventies said TCU used to be a campus that grounds matched the buff colors of the brick, but today it's a beautiful campus.

— **Karen Steele, Special Assistant to the Provost**

Buildings Completed 2004-2022

2004, Schollmaier Basketball Complex

2007, Carter Hall

2007, King Hall

2007, Samuelson Hall

2007, Wright Hall

2007, Palko Hall

2007, Sam Baugh Indoor Practice Facility and Cox Field

2008, Brown Lupton University Union

2008, TCU Campus Store

2009, Scharbauer Hall

2010, Wright Admission Center

2011, Erma Lowe Hall

2012, Amon G. Carter Stadium (major renovation)

2013, P. E. Clark Hall (Worth Hills)

2013, Marion Hall

2014, Rees-Jones Hall

2014, Hays Hall

2015, Frog Alley Parking Garage

2015, King Family Commons

2015, Mary Couts Burnett Library
(renovation and expansion)

2016, Worth Hills Parking Garage

2017-2018, Greek Village (eleven buildings)

2019, Arnold Hall

2019, Fine Arts Building

2019, Richards Hall

2020, The Harrison

2020, Spencer and Marlene Hays Business Commons
(Sumner Hall, Hays Hall)

2022, Van Cliburn Concert Hall

ABOVE
Sadler Hall, built in 1960. Courtesy of TCU Marketing and Communication. Photograph by James Anger.

ABOVE
SuperFrog with Don Mills during the construction of the BLUU. Courtesy of Mary Couts Burnett Library. Photograph by Linda Kaye.

Mick Ferrari began to picture just a bit more of what TCU could be, and then Victor Boschini arrived here like a bolt of lightning. He has more vision and creativity and imagination than anybody I've ever run into . . . The entire commons area, everything from what is now Scharbauer Hall down to the stadium, was nothing but asphalt and parking, and it was awful looking. Victor is the one who really conceived the idea of what the center of the campus could be with the new commons area and the Brown-Lupton University Union. We are a physically attractive university and getting more so as time goes on.

— **Eugene Brice, Trustee Emeritus, served 1992-1998**

ABOVE
Campus Commons, 2021. Courtesy of TCU Marketing and Communication. Photograph by James Anger.

BELOW
Building the Campus Commons, 2007. Courtesy of Texas Christian University. Photograph by Gary Logan.

ABOVE
Demolition of the Brown Lupton Student Center, 2008. Courtesy of Texas Christian University.

ABOVE
Hays and Sumner Halls, 2019. Courtesy of TCU Neeley School of Business. Photograph by Leo Wesson.

ABOVE
Fine Arts Building, built in 2019. Courtesy of TCU Marketing and Communication. Photograph by James Anger.

When I arrived in 2012, the board had recently come from their strategic planning efforts at Rough Creek. It was a thorough roadmap that laid out what they envisioned for the campus. I hit the ground running here with the team, and it was full bore. In the ten years we've been here, we've done over $1.2 billion of construction. We've increased the square footage of campus by more than 60 percent. It's been tremendous growth.

— **Todd Waldvogel, Associate Vice Chancellor for Facilities and Campus Planning**

We are in the final stages of completing the east side of the library [2015]. The library and Rees-Jones will be joined by two bridges and opened in August. The School of Business is currently in the process of a $90 million fundraising effort that will completely change the school. Smith Hall will be rearranged on the inside. Dan Rogers Hall will be torn down and a new and larger building will be put up. That building will not only parallel the street east of Dan Rogers but also swing around the building toward where Bass is. Tandy will also be completely refigured.

The Reshoring Program will continue this summer. We'll be primarily redoing the second and third floors of Winton Scott. Next summer, 2016, we will be in the Sid Richardson in the Environmental Science and Geology areas and in Tucker. A third senior design lab will be created in the basement of Tucker. The hope is that we will build a new performance building for Music in the not-too-distant future, and the goal is to build an additional facility that will bring in some of the Fine Arts departments like Design and Merchandising, and the theater costume shop into main campus.

— **Leo Munson, Associate Provost for Academic Support, at TCU 1983-2018**

Rees-Jones Hall is a great facility, and all the people love to be in it and teach in those classrooms. There's been a marked change to the facilities here. When I have the opportunity to meet with alumni who haven't been coming back regularly, the one thing they always say is, "It is so different and so much improved." It's hard to believe that all of this has taken place in the eleven years from when I got here. It's a great testament to the senior leadership of the university, in particular Chancellor Boschini, and it certainly speaks well for our board of trustees and their confidence, trust, and support for basically redoing this campus. The changes are going to continue. It's not like anybody's taking their foot off the accelerator pedal in terms of campus improvement.

— **Andrew Schoolmaster, Emeritus Professor of Geography and Dean, at TCU 2007-2021**

I think the last ten years under Chancellor Boschini you've seen the most change in the facilities. Chancellor Ferrari started the building process, but most of it has happened in the last ten years under Chancellor Boschini.

— **Jim Atwood, Professor of Religion and Assistant to the Dean of Admissions, at TCU 1979-2020**

At present there is an expansion of residence halls, and more are on the drawing board. That's simply because if we wish to become a residential campus, then there's a need for spaces for students to live on campus.

— **Larry Adams, Emeritus Associate Provost and Associate Professor of Sociology, at TCU 1969-2011**

ABOVE
Rees-Jones Hall, built in 2014. Third floor study area. Courtesy of TCU Marketing and Communication. Photograph by Jeffrey McWhorter.

ABOVE
Arnold Hall (left) and Richards Hall (right), built in 2019. Courtesy of TCU Physical Plant.

ABOVE
TCU's Greek Village, built in 2017-2018. Courtesy of TCU Marketing and Communication. Photograph by Amy Peterson.

Chancellor Boschini had a vision of residentiality that we've been working toward since he came. Every place is a nice place to live, a place where you want to be on campus and be involved in things that are going on. Campus is a 24/7 living and learning space now. . . . We've never ignored academics, but it's not as visible as a new stadium, new dormitories, reshoring all of the science labs, and a new business building. Now it's time to figure out a way to really show where TCU shines.

— Bonnie Melhart, Emeritus Dean of University Programs and Associate Provost, at TCU 1990-2019

The ability to house half the student body is a big deal. We'd like to keep moving forward and house even more. We built the stadium, we redid the Daniel Meyer and the Schollmaier Arena, and now we are redoing the business school. We've got a music performance hall on the horizon, which is really exciting. The music program, which has been outstanding for a long time, is now going to have facilities that are going to help that program tremendously.

— Mark Johnson, Member of the Board of Trustees and former Chair

ABOVE
Atrium of the Van Cliburn Concert Hall, completed in 2022. Courtesy of Bora Architecture + Interiors. Photograph by Peter Molick.

Chancellor Boschini has so much vision on how to make this campus look and feel like the quality institution he found it to be when he got here . . . you've seen how the buildings have changed in four years, and it's not just the buildings. It's the continued quality everywhere.

— **Susan Adams, Associate Vice Chancellor for Student Affairs, at TCU 1975-2019**

ABOVE
Campus flowers, 2018. Courtesy of TCU Marketing and Communication.

The TCU Landscape

Making the campus more inviting and attractive was an absolute priority to me, and that meant flowers and shrubbery, things of that sort. When I became chancellor there was no nursery in the Physical Plant—nothing like that. But if we were going to have more success in admissions, we needed to have an attractive campus. Not everyone agreed when they started seeing flowers sprouting here and there, but it did happen, and of course today TCU's campus is absolutely gorgeous.

— **Chancellor Emeritus Bill Tucker, at TCU 1979-1998**

I arrived in Fort Worth in the first week of August, walked onto campus, and thought this was the ugliest place I had ever been in my whole entire life. The grass was brown, the ground was brown, the trees were brown, the buildings were brown.

— **Kay Higgins, Associate Dean of Student Development, at TCU 1977-2021**

Dr. Tucker started the beatification around campus. It is probably hard to believe, but when I was in school they didn't even water the grass . . . over in Worth Hills, and a lot of people called it "goat hills" because there so many big stickers called a "goat head" growing over there. Victor Boschini has further promoted beautification of the campus. The whole transformation of the campus over the last five years is just phenomenal.

—**John V. Roach, Trustee Emeritus and former Chair, served 1981-2005**

ABOVE
Worth Hills, 1973. Courtesy of Mary Couts Burnett Library.

When I moved to Fort Worth in 1977, campus had practically gone back to prairie. It was stark, dry, woebegone . . . but during the years that I worked here the transformation has been phenomenal. It began to change because one of the early donors that Chancellor Tucker was able to interest in the university was Mary Beasley. She had an interest in landscapes and gardens, and she gave a substantial gift that was designated just for campus beautification. It used to amuse Mary Nell Kirk and me because students would write letters to the editor in the *Skiff* to complain about their tuition being spent on replacing the pansies with the begonias every year.

— **Nowell Donovan, Provost Emeritus, at TCU 1986-2019**

One of the things that Chancellor Tucker did under his watch was campus beautification. This beautiful campus and all the landscaping now didn't look anything like this when I came. The yellow-brick buildings certainly look nicer with a lot of green and color around than they did when it was just kind of bare earth.

— **Janet Herald, Associate Dean of Admissions, at TCU 1974-1989**

It was funny because at that time, people were saying: you're not really taking time to fix up any of these old buildings, but the landscaping is beautiful. What people didn't realize is there was a foundation that had been set up to make sure that the grounds had been set up and the flowers were being changed out, and that everything really looked nice. The tulips were blooming in the spring and the pansies in the winter, and different flowers in the fall and spring. I mean if someone hadn't created that endowment, or have the foresight to endow a fund to keep the landscaping up for the future, we wouldn't have what we have today, and it makes a huge difference.

— **Steve McGee, Chief of TCU Police, at TCU 1995-2020**

ABOVE
Tulips bloom each spring on TCU's campus, 2016. Courtesy of TCU Marketing and Communication. Photograph by Amy Peterson.

In the 1980s Chancellor Tucker said we would love to have some trees on the campus. We at the city said, you know I think we can get you the trees. We had a forestry department that grew and gave trees to nonprofits that could take care of trees. Dr. Tucker said, "Well Bob, that's fine that you're going to get me fifty trees, but we cannot do that because we have to put in a water sprinkler system, and that's $100,000." But the next year a lady gave TCU a tank truck, and TCU committed to hand water those trees long enough to give them a chance to survive—that's three years. So we started with a few trees and over the years we added another fifty and another fifty and another fifty. So now if you look around the entire campus you have trees all down the medians, and that came from the city knowing where to get the trees. We did several joint projects like that, and it has contributed to the look of the school and the neighborhood around it.

— **Bob Bolen, former Fort Worth Mayor and Senior Advisor to the Chancellor, at TCU 1991-2014**

ABOVE
Creative writing class at Froghenge, 2018. Courtesy of TCU Marketing and Communication. Photograph by Jeffrey McWhorter.

It's a prettier campus than it was when I was here as a student—and I thought it was really pretty back then. I just love, especially during the springtime, when you see all the beautiful flowers outside. I think TCU works really hard to make it a pleasant environment for students, faculty, and staff to live, work, and be in every day. The transformation of the campus with the Campus Commons has probably been one of the most physically transformative developments on campus. All that beautiful green space was a big, ugly parking lot until about ten years ago. During all the construction on the east side of campus, I think everyone was afraid we would lose all the green space. And I think TCU has done a really good job being intentional about keeping green space even in the midst of all the construction that goes on.

— Cheryl Wilson, Associate Vice Chancellor and Controller, at TCU 2001-2019

TCU, when I first got here, had a beautiful infrastructure, but it wasn't a beautiful campus. Bill Tucker made it become a beautiful campus. It wasn't just paint on walls, it was bushes planted and sidewalks put it in; he really made it a beautiful campus.

— John Mangieri, Dean of the School of Education, at TCU 1982-1989

You've probably heard many other people say that if you went down there ten years ago, it was a parking lot surrounded by buildings. And it was. You could look from where Milton Daniel now is to where Colby is and see only space and cars. For Vision in Action, we got some landscape architects up here, and they said, "You're completely wasting space here. You could put at least two lines of halls of residence in here and still have good views, and still keep a lot of trees and make it look pleasant." So that's what we decided to do. Every single tree on this campus has been planted. It was prairie.

—Nowell Donovan

ABOVE
TCU campus, 1914. Courtesy of Mary Couts Burnett Library. Photograph by Bryant Studio.

There was serious consternation about changing the rhythm and the traffic pattern of the university in moving the BLUU and building a commons. The old student center sat basically where Scharbauer is now, and everything from the stadium to into it was parking lot. It was really not very attractive, and it was just a big loop of traffic. You know most great universities have these lawns, these commons, that signature look. I think some of us were very worried it would feel claustrophobic. Because the space was really from Colby and Foster on one side toTom Brown Pete Wright and Milton Daniel, and what would that look like all filled in? It's so funny to me to think about that. About a month ago I was walking with some friends who were looking at TCU for their daughter, and they were like, "Oh my gosh this is so wide open and wonderful in here," and I just laughed, because I thought how nervous we were and how humorous that is retrospectively. I think about what space was like when ESPN Game Day came, what it's like when there's a concert, what it's like at graduation, and how that looks and feels. It's just remarkable.

— Laura Miller, former President of the National TCU Alumni Board and ex officio Board of Trustees member, served 2000-2006

ABOVE
Campus Commons, 2020. Courtesy of TCU Marketing and Communication. Photograph by Andrew Emery.

There were so many things going on at TCU, at the same time. When the history is totally written, this will be one of the "Golden Ages" of TCU. The campus looked tired, and all of a sudden it looked vibrant. When you come to visit a place, one of the things you are affected by is what it looks like. Dr. Tucker had made it certain that the grounds always looked beautiful. It was Dr. Tucker who said we would have flowers all year long. When you work someplace like that, it helps morale, it helps you feel better about it, students liked it better, so the idea of wonderful grounds then got married with a vibrancy in the buildings. There was a time when you literally could not walk from north to south at TCU without either going on Stadium Drive or University Drive. There was no pathway through like there is now between Reed and Scharbauer and between the new buildings on the Commons. The walkways, the arches, all of that was designed to make people feel connected to other parts of the campus.

— **Don Mills**

19. Pandemic Response

It started in January of 2020. Jane Torgerson, the director of our health center, heard through her networks that there was this virus in other parts of the world. By February we were seeing it move through Asia and get to Europe. We had students in Italy at that time, and we had a couple students studying in China. That was our greatest concern. I remember early in March we were trying to make decisions about whether or not we should bring those students back.

On campus, we had some students who couldn't go home, international students, mostly students whose borders were closed . . . It was really quiet around campus that spring.

— Kathy Cavins-Tull, Vice Chancellor of Student Affairs

ABOVE
The fall 2020 semester began amidst the coronavirus pandemic: a sign urges students to stay home if they feel sick, August 2020. Courtesy of TCU Marketing and Communication. Photograph by Amy Peterson.

ABOVE
Campus Commons looking east toward Scharbauer Hall, viewed through the BLUU arch, March 2020. Courtesy of TCU Marketing and Communication. Photograph by Amy Peterson.

We thought extending spring break by a week was going to fix all our problems, and surely this thing will be gone by the summer. It's like the flu. The warm weather will come and zap it.

—Jeremiah Donati, Athletics Director

I think we saw it coming, but we weren't sure what the light at the end of the tunnel was, and it was a train.

Like most colleges and universities, we have a disaster and continuity plan. But I don't think anyone had a disaster or continuity plan that they had developed and expected it would last for eighteen months.

— Yohna Chambers, Vice Chancellor for Human Resources

The Chancellor hired the epidemiologist Dr. [Elie F.] Berbari from Mayo Clinic. When this was first starting, he was meeting with him every Monday morning to get the lay of the land. Then he and I would talk about what he was hearing from them.

— Kathy Cavins-Tull

One of the things I would've done differently is I would have hired the Mayo Clinic immediately after hearing the word pandemic, because not only did it help the Campus Readiness Committee get advice, it also helped me personally. They gave me a lot of reassurance. I also would have been more decisive from the beginning, but I was afraid—all of us were.

— Chancellor Victor Boschini

I think that our Mayo people affirmed what we were doing and encouraged us . . . they've been pretty supportive all the way through.

— Kathy Cavins-Tull

We had all the right people in the right places, and we all trusted one another. I think that folks were so committed to making sure that the show went on, that our students didn't suffer, and that we continued forward with our mission. Nobody wanted to drop the ball. Nobody wanted to punt. We just kept going.

— Yohna Chambers

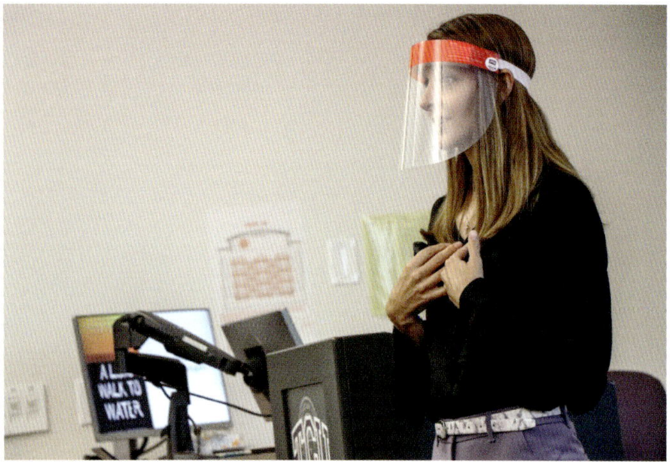

ABOVE
Professor Jennifer Smith teaches Critical Literacy and Children's Literature while wearing a face shield, August 2020. Courtesy of TCU Marketing and Communication. Photograph by Jenny Moore.

ABOVE
The fall 2020 semester begins amidst the coronavirus pandemic: students sit in a class that is being taught both in person and online, August 2020. Courtesy of TCU Marketing and Communication. Photograph by Amy Peterson.

When COVID first hit, there were three groups of people. There was one group of people that ran away from me on campus. There was one group of people that tried to run over me. And then the third group was a small but mighty group that ran with me and said, "We can do this. We're going to make this happen." Dr. Kathy Cavins-Tull chaired our COVID-19 preparedness task force. She was just one of many people on that group that just seized it and said, "We can do this." They were calm and rational at a time when a lot of people, including me, were not calm and rational.

— **Chancellor Victor Boschini**

Honestly, it shocks me that we got all of the courses flipped online in a week in March and that we got all of the faculty teaching fall courses to take the Koehler Center training and to redesign their courses in the summer.

— **Teresa Abi-Nader Dahlberg, Provost**

ABOVE
Theatre Department adjunct faculty member Kelsey Milbourn instructs a group of theatre majors in a Musical Theatre Dance class. Face coverings and personal spaces outlined with white tape on the stage help ensure a safe environment; cameras and a video screen facilitate distance learning, October 2020. Courtesy of TCU Marketing and Communication. Photograph by Andrew Emery.

We promised our students to prepare them to be ethical leaders. If we're going to help prepare them to be ethical leaders, then we have to be, too. Part of that was clearly understanding the expectations of what delivering the academic experience in this pandemic environment would look like.

— **Yohna Chambers**

We established a readiness team that was co-chaired by Kathy Cavins-Tull and Sean Taylor, our emergency manager, and myself as chief facilities officer. Sean and I worked hand in hand supporting Kathy as she developed certain committees. There were no competing interests. Everybody was trying to succeed for our students, for our staff, for our faculty.

— **Todd Waldvogel, Associate Vice Chancellor for Facilities and Campus Planning**

ABOVE
Provost Dahlberg and Chancellor Boschini celebrate new graduates of the class of 2020 in a video after the spring commencement ceremonies were postponed, May 2020. Courtesy of TCU Marketing and Communication. Photograph by Amy Peterson.

ABOVE
Faculty member Clark Jones in the College of Science and Engineering leads a class via the videoconferencing platform Zoom, April 2020. Courtesy of TCU Marketing and Communication. Photograph by Andy Emery.

It's so bizarre to reflect back now. We acknowledge that everything we did was difficult. We had an employee in HR who lost three family members to COVID. We had some tough times. I can't say enough about the HR team. They did what they had to do.

— **Yohna Chambers**

Everybody gave everybody a little more grace than we're used to. We've all been through a collective trauma, and we don't think about that enough.

— **Chancellor Victor Boschini**

All of our lives have been shaken by the COVID-19 pandemic. I think what we learned through that pandemic is how we can chart our way through a pandemic and hold onto our mission, our values, and our priorities. . . . We took intentional steps to train everybody on how to be in a virtual atmosphere, because we wanted to be sure that we provided quality experience even in the online environment.

— **Floyd Wormley, Associate Provost for Research and Dean of Graduate Studies**

Something that we adopted is that we always tried to come at things assuming positive intent, recognizing that when people were a little jacked up, it was because they were worried about something. Everyone had a different set of concerns going into this.

— **Yohna Chambers**

COVID was like a dream, to be honest. It was exactly two years ago when I was sitting in this office by myself and literally I'd look out and wouldn't see any cars. It was a pretty lonely existence . . . I'm really proud of the way we managed it.

I think the thing that I worried more about than kids getting sick from COVID was the mental health aspect of it. The mental health aspect of the pandemic was probably much more damaging to the younger age group.

— **Jeremiah Donati**

In 2019 there were 298 telehealth calls of employees or their covered family members; in 2020 there were 5,465 telehealth calls. That is a 1,734% increase in the use of telehealth. In 2020 40% of the calls were mental health related compared to 10% in 2019. This demonstrates a 300% increase in mental health-related calls from 2019 to 2020.

— **Yohna Chambers**

Zoom forever changed the ways in which we show up to work, and had it not been for technology, I don't know if we would've been successful getting through that. We had to pivot quickly. My calendar was just filled with Zoom calls all day.

There was obviously a tremendous amount of stress and uncertainty, but I really did see people stepping up for each other. You saw people wearing multiple hats, and I think that's always been a hallmark of this school. And they do it proudly. They do it willingly.

—Jeremiah Donati

We did a lot of relocating people. People have been willing to step out of their roles and step into other roles on a temporary basis throughout this whole thing.

— Teresa Abi-Nader Dahlberg

We quickly pivoted in March of 2020 to an online medical school. We did telemedicine, and our students learned a lot of skills they wouldn't have learned without COVID.

TCU went into a hiring freeze, and we were this tiny little medical school. We did not have the sustainability to go over the next hurdle unless—and this is what happened—a bunch of amazing people at this medical school started taking on two jobs, three jobs, four jobs.

— Stuart Flynn, Dean of the Burnett School of Medicine

ABOVE
Landing zones in TCU buildings provide spaces for students to "attend" online classes, January 2021. Courtesy of TCU Marketing and Communication. Photograph by Eric Sasadeusz.

You just forget how important human interaction is. It was Kathy Cavins-Tull and I in this whole building... and it was lonely. I never realized how much people feed on each other. It really made me realize how much that connection means, how you not only are dependent on it but thrive on it.

— Chancellor Victor Boschini

It wasn't great at the time, but we just didn't know what else we could do. We take orders from the state. We take orders from the county. We take orders from the federal government. Trying to make sense of all of that and provide students the experience they wanted was interesting.

It felt like we were running an infirmary.

As things started getting better for us, we brought a lot of furniture in that we rented and allowed people to gather outside, which seemed to be well received by the students. It gave them an opportunity to gather. We needed to give students opportunities to gather because, if we didn't do it, they were doing it at off-campus parties.

— Kathy Cavins-Tull

ABOVE
Students gather safely in the Campus Commons during the COVID-19 pandemic, November 2020. Courtesy of TCU Marketing and Communication. Photograph by Eric Sasadeusz.

I don't live student experience, but I observe it a lot, and I think the student experience has changed a lot in the past year. The one thing most students and parents say is, "It's so much better than if I was at home."

— Chancellor Victor Boschini

Because of COVID and because of our inability to do much on campus, I was worried about us losing what is our key ethos of our connected campus culture. I'm glad we can do stuff online, but our goal is not to be the best online campus. I don't think we want to change what we are at our heart, at our core, and that is this personalized, connected culture.

— Teresa Abi-Nader Dahlberg

ABOVE
A TCU Facilities employee uses an electrostatic sprayer to disinfect a conference room, June 2020. Courtesy of TCU Marketing and Communication. Photograph by Andy Emery.

ABOVE
Professor Amy Roehl and students in Interior Design II, October 2020. Courtesy of TCU Marketing and Communication. Photograph by Andrew Emery.

I think we learn in community, and that's the best way to learn. Not only are students learning the knowledge and the content for what they're going to go on and do or what their vocation will look like, they do that in a community of diversity. Taking the community aspect out of learning only gives you one hand to clap. If students are sitting in their bedroom at home, tuning into their class, they're sitting in the same place where all of their values have been shaped. Part of going to college is to broaden your perspective and challenge your values. I strongly believe in education through community.

— **Yohna Chambers**

My biggest lesson from the whole pandemic is that the hardest challenge is communication. Communication is the key, and then the central communications team just was overwhelmed. In the middle of the summer I went and asked the deans to loan their communications people to me. And they did.

— **Teresa Abi-Nader Dahlberg**

In Neeley we started looking at it from the eyes of the students. We were seeing so many graduating seniors lose their job offers because of the global pandemic. We knew the marketplace was looking for more business analytics, and we had a lot of students in need. We created an all-new Master of Science in Business Analytics program that would be a fifth-year option for our graduating seniors who were otherwise displaced from a continuity of professional development and a lack of jobs upon graduation. What would take typically two to three years to devise and pass through all the committees and then operationalize an all-new curriculum, we turned into three weeks. We went from concept to approved program in three weeks. Ultimately, we yielded a first-year class of over fifty students for this graduate program. It was almost like our version of the ventilator to provide oxygen to our graduating seniors.

— **President Daniel Pullin**

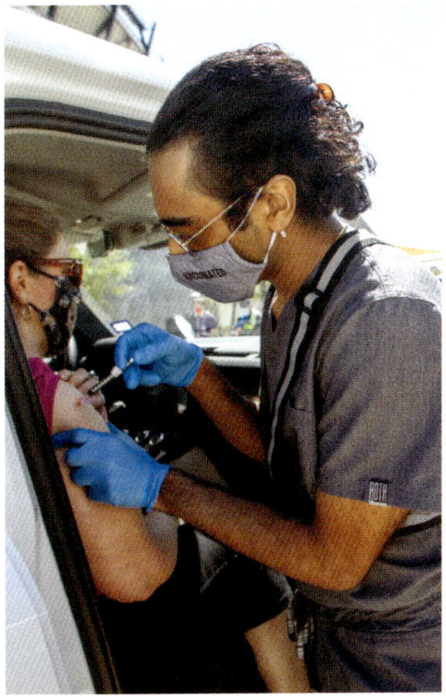

ABOVE
Medical student Dilan Shah administers a vaccine during a drive-through COVID-19 vaccine clinic held at TCU, March 2021. Courtesy of TCU Magazine. Photograph by Mark Graham.

We did something worth noting in the spring of last year [2021]. Nobody was letting student staff into their spaces at that time, but we had students in the nursing program who needed clinical experiences. We also wanted to be as aggressive as we could be to get the vaccine on our campus, and small clinics like ours were not being given the vaccine at that time. . . . Last February [2021], starting right after the ice storm, every Saturday we set up a drive-through clinic all the way through lots one, two, three, and four behind the stadium, so that the community could come and get the shots. Our nursing students got to do it and got clinical experience from it. We provided all the staff for all the traffic control. Any vaccine that was left over from no-shows we gave to our own students, faculty, and staff. It was a great partnership. . . . We were working from 4:45 in the morning until 7:00 at night.

— **Kathy Cavins-Tull**

ABOVE
An employee in one of the food service areas wears a face covering to ensure food safety, July 2020. Courtesy of TCU Marketing and Communication. Photograph by Andy Emery.

There are challenges here like there are anywhere, but I continue to say this is still the healthiest university I've ever been at or been associated with. Since we went into this healthier, we're going to come out of it healthier.

— **Teresa Abi-Nader Dahlberg**

ABOVE
TCU students wear face coverings to prevent the spread of the coronavirus, June 2020. Courtesy of TCU Marketing and Communication. Photograph by Andrew Emery.

One thing that the past eighteen months made us all realize is that we shouldn't be so sure about what tomorrow holds, in a good way. . . . It helped me realize that I've got to start thinking three steps ahead rather than one step ahead as a leader.

— **Chancellor Victor Boschini**

We protected our staff too . . . we made it through as a university and we didn't furlough anybody. The community of TCU is more than just the students and the alumni. The faculty and staff are family. We're all working hard together. We're all equally dedicated to this success . . . success was our only option.

— **Todd Waldvogel**

TCU was really hurt by the pandemic financially, but I think we will come out of it stronger. TCU is almost 150 years old now. We're older than countries, standing armies. When people in town complained to me, I would say, "How old is your company?" And they'll say, "Oh, 32 years old." Mine's 150 years old, and it's still here. We must be doing something right.

— **Chancellor Victor Boschini**

What we saw in the COVID-19 pandemic that many other institutions had to do—furloughing faculty, shutting down majors—we didn't have to do at TCU because of good financial planning. I think a lot of people take that for granted.
The fact that we are financially stable and that we are making plans to remain financially stable going forward is something important in our strategic plan to make sure that we see another 147 years.

— **Floyd Wormley**

I think your secret weapon on navigating COVID or any unexpected event for which there is no roadmap is your culture—the work ethic, the civility with which we treat ourselves and each other, and the deep love for the importance of an institution and the recognition that it must endure, not just for us, but for the next generation. How lucky are we to have been situated at Texas Christian University when this happened! How fortunate we are to know that we have colleagues that we can lean on and who can lean on us, and that we're going to do whatever it takes to unleash a spirit of innovation to lead and continue to navigate, not just to survive this but to position the institution to flourish as we emerge from this.

— **President Daniel Pullin**

ABOVE
TCU honored its graduates from the classes of 2020 and 2021 with commencement ceremonies in May 2021. Courtesy of TCU Marketing and Communication. Photograph by Glen E. Ellman.

20. TCU Culture

ABOVE
TCU welcomes students to campus, 2021. Courtesy of TCU Marketing and Communication. Photograph by Andrew Emery.

I think the values have stayed the same. I think the culture is still the same. Kids change, environment changes, but I think TCU has stayed pretty close to the values it was established on.

— **Ron Clinkscale, Trustee Emeritus, served 1985-2016**

TCU was quite a bit smaller in the 1990s . . . and of course a lot of the structures that are here now were not here at that time, so it was a much different environment in terms of the campus geography. But I think the basic culture is the same. It was a very open, warm, and receptive group of people. I really enjoyed being there and I miss being there.

— **Harold Nelson, Chair of the Department of Engineering, at TCU 1991-1998**

I actually first came to TCU as a student when I was eighteen . . . [during] my senior year in high school. I just fell in love with it.

When I think about then and now, it's amazing, even after all these years. The first word that comes to my mind is still friendliness. That's probably the most consistent thing that I've seen. When you come to campus, people say "hi" to you, are welcoming whether you're a student or faculty or staff. It's still a friendly place, and it's never lost that culture through all these years.

As TCU continues to grow and become a larger university, I hope that we don't ever lose that small college culture, friendliness, and inclusiveness. As we grow, we must be mindful of the challenge of keeping this culture that everyone loves so much.

— **Cheryl Wilson, Associate Vice Chancellor and Controller, at TCU 2001-2019**

Compared to ten years ago the university is bigger, it's more complicated, there are more students, more activities, and more national attention. But at the core the values of the university have remained just as strong— the appreciation for the culture and the friendliness of the culture—those continue to remain intact. I think that with all the change, the one thing that hasn't changed is probably the most important thing. That is the university's heart seems to be just as strong as it was when I got here—the friendly relationships that we maintained with one another. With all the change, that continues to be woven into the fabric.

— Brian Gutierrez, Vice Chancellor for Finance and Administration, at TCU 2006-2022

ABOVE
Students study together in a Women's Studies class, 2009. Courtesy of TCU Marketing and Communication. Photograph by Amy Peterson.

Through it all, the thing I have been most impressed with is our culture at TCU, the idea of a connection culture where we make sure our employees and our students are aware of what our vision is and are engaged in it, and we make sure each one knows that we are available to you, that we make an impact on their lives by the way that we connect with them. That's still very much a part of who we are, and that's what has kept me here all these years.

— Ann Louden, Chancellor's Associate for Strategic Partnerships, at TCU 1978-2017

We like to trumpet all of our successes, the wonderful things, and the progress that we've made over time, but I think it's important for us to be mindful of what got us here. I think it's important that we be mindful that there are some things about TCU that have not changed, that we hope will not change, and that is the essence of this place. We still take pride that we are nice people, that we are friendly, that we are collaborative not competitive, and that we respect those who've come before us.

— Ray Brown, Dean of Admissions, at TCU 2000-2016

ABOVE
The TCU community gathers together to celebrate Christmas with the 42nd annual Carols by Candlelight held at Robert Carr Chapel, 2019. Courtesy of TCU Marketing and Communication. Photograph by Amy Peterson.

There's an ethos here that I believe has remained the same. Recently I've had a lot of contact with Honors alumni from the 1960s, when the Honors Program had just barely started, and they all talk about community. They remember an interest in doing what's right, in trying to figure out what is right. That has remained constant. I've always felt that TCU has a culture of respect. We had a culture of respect in the 1960s; we had a culture of respect in the 1980s when I started, and I think we have a culture of respect today. We respect students, and students respect faculty. It's not just being polite. I think respecting each other is on a much deeper level. I believe that has remained the same. The difference has been in the academic excellence.

— **Peggy Watson, Emeritus Professor in the John V. Roach Honors College and Dean, at TCU 1983-2012**

I think that's one of the distinguishing characteristics, that we have a caring community.

— **Barbara Herman, Associate Vice Chancellor for Student Affairs, at TCU 1986-2021**

ABOVE
Students congregate between classes, 2021. Courtesy of TCU Marketing and Communication. Photograph by James Anger.

I think we have a very value-centered or value-based culture on this campus, but that's not by accident; and I think you lose that if you aren't purposeful about it. I want to be purposeful about saying it; like here's one of my best values: that if you're in this class and two years from now, you see a kid from this class on the corner crying, you go up to them. That's what TCU is.

If you look back at the things Addison and Randolph Clark did when they founded TCU, part of the culture of the Disciples of Christ is that they're very inclusive. I think that started 140-something years ago on this campus. People here feel like they have a stake in what's going on at every level, and I think that's good.

— **Chancellor Victor Boschini**

We had a new person in the athletic department recently. I asked him, "What do you think about TCU?"

He said, "I have to tell you it's the most 'puppies-and-ice-cream' place I've ever worked at. Everyone here is just so kind and gentle." He had never worked at a school like that. I've been at eleven schools and I've never been at one this friendly either.

The whole TCU culture is kind of family oriented. I think it gets reflected a lot. Like you see a lot of professors' kids on this campus at events, and it's fun. I've worked at places where that wouldn't be encouraged. People would think that's unprofessional.

— **Chancellor Victor Boschini**

ABOVE
Associate Chaplain Britt Luby with her son at TCU's Blessing of the Animals, 2018. Courtesy of TCU Marketing and Communication. Photograph by Amy Peterson.

The culture has never changed. It's permeating in our ethos. It's how we react to success, the culture of how we treat people; it's the culture of the type of kids that we get to come here.

— Chris Del Conte, Athletics Director, at TCU 2009-2017

Many people did not understand about the affiliation with the Disciple of Christ Christian Church. TCU has always been inclusive and recognized as leaders in coed education from the very beginning at Thorp Spring. It was a whole history that you had to explain in order for people to understand that kind of culture and acceptance that people everywhere would find at TCU.

— Sandra Ware, Dean of Admissions, at TCU 1986-2000

TCU had been small and even though it has grown, they retained that closeness. They retained that family feel of student to faculty to administrator. I hope we never outgrow that. I hope we never get so big that we become strained or lose that connectivity that we have have with each other.

— Scott Sullivan, Emeritus Professor of Art History and Dean, at TCU 2000-2016

Some things haven't changed. There is still a feeling of family and community and definitely a student-centeredness.

— Barbara Herman

We used to have single sex halls, and there was an older woman who worked in the front office of one of the residence halls. I discovered that every year on Valentine's Day, when the flowers came in for the girls in residence halls, she would use money out of her own pocket to go over to the local grocery store and buy flowers and little vases for the girls who didn't get flowers, so everyone in the building got a flower. That's what TCU is all about. That kind of a dedication to students.

— Peggy Barr, Vice Chancellor for Student Affairs, at TCU 1985-1992

ABOVE
Staff, faculty, and students at the Welcome Back Mixer hosted by the Office of Diversity and Inclusion, 2022. Courtesy of TCU Marketing and Communication. Photograph by James Anger.

We've maintained that student-centric, human-centric feel about the place, even though we've grown. And that's very hard to do, to maintain and not lose your character or your culture. It is a strength of ours.

— President Daniel Pullin

If you put students first at your university, good things will happen. When you put students first, you're probably going to make good decisions. That's the growth of the university, that's why we're here.

— Ken Morgan, Director of the TCU Energy Institute, at TCU 1978-2018

ABOVE
TCU faculty and staff host incoming students for dinner to welcome them to TCU, 2021. Courtesy of TCU Marketing and Communication. Photograph by Andrew Emery.

At TCU, one of the things that's unique is the overall commitment to the student. My perception of our leadership is that if something is about the students and enriching their experience, we find a way to say yes. Everything supports the excellence of their education. We support their sense of community, because community doesn't end when they throw their mortar boards and they head out the door. TCU has an emotional connection for so many people, and it's part of our city. It's a part of our culture.

— Todd Waldvogel, Associate Vice Chancellor for Facilities and Campus Planning

The people that are here love working here; you can tell. I see people working after five o'clock here, always helping students, to the "nth" degree.

— Chancellor Victor Boschini

I've always appreciated, from the day I started, the level of care that faculty and staff had for students.

— Michael Russel, Associate Vice Chancellor for Student Affairs

At every university I have been at, I would tell the people that we have great faculty and that they take a personal interest in their students. TCU is a cut above that. TCU raised the bar for me when I came here and saw the devotion of faculty to students. They loved the students, and they were here because they wanted to teach. They wanted to share their passion for what they do with students: help them become successful in their chosen fields. You know what's amazing to me, students who graduate keep in touch with their faculty. I tell the faculty that when you're hired here, your relationship with the students doesn't stop after four years. It continues, and that's great because then you know that you've really made a difference in their lives.

— Scott Sullivan

ABOVE
Honors academic advisor Donna Schonerstedt meets with a student, 2019. Courtesy of TCU Marketing and Communication. Photograph by Jeffrey McWhorter.

The faculty I know don't care just about their job or discipline, but about their students, and helping them find careers and jobs. I see the hours that they spend going above and beyond for students. That has been a neat thing about being involved with the Wassenich Award, because I read what students write about their faculty and about their staff advisers and how they have made a difference in their lives, and the things that they have done that nobody knows about, the extra hours that they put in, and that's pretty special. To read these nominations is just fantastic. I don't think the students realize how special and meaningful it is to the faculty and staff who read those nominations to know they made a difference in a student's life

— Barbara Herman

There's a commitment to care for students. It shows from the time you arrive on campus and meet the first representative of the university—everybody here cares. In the military, we would've said one team, one fight. That sounds a little overdramatic for an academic environment. But everybody's singular commitment to the totality of our community is special, and it makes a difference. It's a great place to be.

— Todd Waldvogel

It really is a group effort of everybody pulling together. That has been the great thing about here that you don't see elsewhere. I think it's part of our culture at TCU.

— Bill Moncrief, Emeritus Professor of Marketing, at TCU 1982-2023

ABOVE
Mary Nell Kirk. Courtesy of Texas Christian University.

The commitment to community makes this a great place to work. The students are what we are here for every day and are the reason we exist, so we want to be there to help and do whatever we can for them. I think TCU has such a warm and fuzzy feeling that generations of horned frogs stay with TCU once they have been here. For the most part everybody wants to help everybody out. We want to be there for each other. I don't take for granted the amazing work environment with others who share my passion for TCU and want to make it a good school for the students.

— **Mary Nell Kirk, Executive Assistant to the Chancellor, at TCU 1989-2021**

People really dedicate themselves above and beyond what they get paid for . . . and it shows.

— **Bonnie Melhart**

It doesn't surprise me, but the quality of people that TCU attracts in faculty, staff, students, and families thrills me. When ninety-eight to ninety-nine percent of the entire community are really amazing people, it makes going to work every day a really wonderful opportunity.

— **Kay Higgins, Associate Dean of Student Development, at TCU 1977-2021**

The thing I've learned over the last thirty years is that there is a lot of passion here to make things happen. We deliver.

— **Clarence Scharbauer III, Trustee Emeritus and former Chair, served 1990-2017**

I was very well established with great friendships and opportunities in Georgia, and the only way I got the courage to leave was to say I'm just going for three years. But it didn't take long before I knew that I wasn't going anywhere. TCU wasn't a particularly attractive place. It still was brown in the winter, brown in the summer, and a few other colors in the fall and spring. But great, great people. The faculty and staff that continue to be here and the students are equally remarkable. After all these years it still does not change. Graduation is such a bittersweet moment for me because the relationships that have developed over four years have been so wonderful.

— **Kay Higgins**

ABOVE
Nowell Donovan and Kathy Cavins-Tull, 2018. Courtesy of TCU Marketing and Communication. Photograph by Amy Peterson.

When I was first here I couldn't believe the atmosphere. It's very family-like, it's very friendly . . . just warm in some ways. I had to pinch myself. "Is this really for real?" This place is not only beautiful, but people seem to enjoy their jobs and enjoy working for the institution.

— Jean Pickett, Chief of Staff

TCU always felt like a family to me. Not that everyone always got along or felt the same way all the time, which you have probably experienced with your sister occasionally.

— Sandra Ware, Dean of Admissions, at TCU 1986-2000

Most people do not stay in one institution for as long as I've been here. But I had a chance to grow up with TCU. I wanted to be a part of the institution. It was just a good place . . . it was a family atmosphere in a way. What I loved about TCU was that people who were here were serious about their work but very open and non-elitist. We work hard, but we are also a community, and we respect each other. It was an easy place to figure out who I was and what I wanted to do and how to go about it. It was a culture that to me was unique. Not every academic institution had that kind of culture.

— Larry Lauer, Emeritus Vice Chancellor for Government Affairs, at TCU 1966-2014

Growing the endowment was really a huge feeling of security, but more than just security. The thing that I really felt was the quiet optimism that we can do what we want to do because we have the resources to do it. It was also careful planning, deliberate steps forward. This was a place with a strong and quiet trajectory. It was going to be very good for a very long time, and it was good to be a part of that. I think that is what attracted faculty and administrators and kept them there so long. The turnover at TCU is low. People came, people stayed.

I treasure my time at TCU. Those years were formative in my life. I love looking at it now and what is has become—a nationally recognized university, and every student should be proud to have that degree. I consider myself fortunate to have been there and to have been there in the years of Bill Tucker, because I learned so much from him about core values and how higher education should be.

— Fred Heath, University Librarian, at TCU 1987-1993

TCU is open to ideas. That is one thing we ought to be proud of. We often don't say very much about it. Some universities are pretty rigid about how you get new things started. Here they like to invest in new ideas. When you can take good ideas forward and see the realities come to you, then you're at the right place. All of the things I've ever wanted or dreamed of have come true because of the kinds of people we have here.

— Ken Morgan

It never occurred to me that individuals had the power to effect change. It seemed like there were people in authority, and they were the ones that made the decisions, and we just followed along. I was surprised when I came to TCU that individuals, faculty members and students, really have the power to effect change. That's one of the reasons I stayed. I felt like, if I worked hard enough and had some good ideas and could bring other people on board, that we actually could effect change, and I was right about that. I think that makes TCU unique.

— Peggy Watson, Emeritus Professor in John V. Roach Honors College and Dean, at TCU 1985-2021

I could name people that have been here for twenty years, and that tells you something about an institution where people want to stay. There's something about the institution that keeps people. I think people stay at TCU because it's a community. I think they stay there because there's opportunity for growth within that community. You can experience change there and make a difference.

— Peggy Barr, Vice Chancellor for Student Affairs, at TCU 1985-1992

Thirty years ago TCU was nothing like it is today. TCU seemed fairly rural and small townish . . . lots of parking and lots of yellow brick buildings. But people were very nice, and everyone I met was so welcoming. The changes that we've undergone at TCU have made it a place where people want to stay. Not just because of the physical infrastructure that wasn't here fifteen years ago, but also because of how leadership has really tried to make TCU a unique place.

— Manfred Reinecke, Professor of Chemistry, at TCU 1964-2006

ABOVE
Manfred Reinecke. Courtesy of *TCU Magazine*.
Photograph by Carolyn Cruz.

I came to TCU five years ago, July 2016, and really fell in love with the mission and the growth and trajectory of TCU.

— **Yohna Chambers, Vice Chancellor For Human Resources**

I think it says a lot about the kind of leadership we have had over the last thirty-five years that people want to stay. People really like it here.

— **Linda Moore, Emeritus Professor of Social Work, at TCU 1977-2017**

There is obviously a lot of excitement as TCU receives recognition as one of the top colleges to work at.

— **Chancellor Emeritus Mick Ferrari, at TCU 1998-2003**

TCU is very fortunate. We don't really need recruiters because TCU has such an incredible reputation in the community that everyone wants to work here.

— **Shari Barnes, Director of Employee Relations, at TCU 1983-2014**

The staff in the chancellor's office was one in a million. It was a great privilege to work with them on a daily basis.

— **Karen Baker, Chief of Staff and Vice Chancellor for Human Resources, at TCU 1992-2016**

We have a very good staff here. Turnover is virtually zero. People like working at TCU. They come and stay. That's how we got from there to where we are now.

— **Will Stallworth, Associate Vice Chancellor for Physical Plant, at TCU 1989-2012**

TCU has been a great place to work. I've been here all these years because of the city of Fort Worth, the university, the quality of the students and the faculty, and the support I get from the administration.

— **Sharon Fairchild, Emeritus Professor of Modern Language Studies, at TCU 1978-2017**

One of the nicest things about TCU is the accessibility of the upper administration. The transparency and the accessibility of the administration are things that make TCU a great institution.

— **Phil Hartman, Emeritus Professor of Biology and Dean, at TCU 1981-2022**

ABOVE
Shark Tank judges (L to R) Phil Hartman, Mohanakrishnan Sathyamoorthy, and Sathishkumar Gopalaswamy, 2020. Courtesy of Mark Graham and *TCU Magazine*.

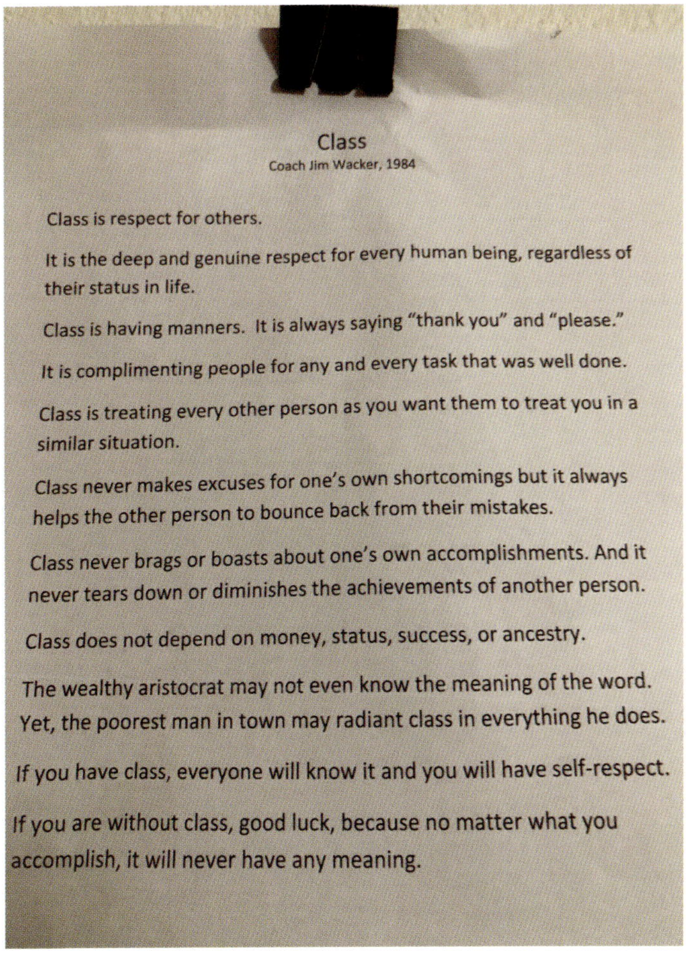

Class
Coach Jim Wacker, 1984

Class is respect for others.

It is the deep and genuine respect for every human being, regardless of their status in life.

Class is having manners. It is always saying "thank you" and "please."

It is complimenting people for any and every task that was well done.

Class is treating every other person as you want them to treat you in a similar situation.

Class never makes excuses for one's own shortcomings but it always helps the other person to bounce back from their mistakes.

Class never brags or boasts about one's own accomplishments. And it never tears down or diminishes the achievements of another person.

Class does not depend on money, status, success, or ancestry.

The wealthy aristocrat may not even know the meaning of the word. Yet, the poorest man in town may radiant class in everything he does.

If you have class, everyone will know it and you will have self-respect.

If you are without class, good luck, because no matter what you accomplish, it will never have any meaning.

ABOVE
"Class" by Jim Wacker, 1984.

I think being a community in terms of our faculty and staff is important for how we deal with problems on a day-to-day basis. If I have a problem, I know from experience which office and which person I need to contact to resolve something. I am always sure that I can get good service. It's a personal relationship.

— **Magnus Rittby, Professor of Physics**

We've got the best staff of any institution or place I've ever been involved with.

— **Malcolm Louden, Trustee Emeritus, served 1978-2020**

This is my third university, and this is the most congenial place I have been. This is a place that people like to come to work. They enjoy each other. There is no animosity between the administration and the faculty, or the faculty and the staff, or the staff and the administration.

— **Scott Sullivan**

TCU is such a unique place. . . . What we have here is special. It's an exceptional higher ed experience, and I do believe that this is one of the best places to be.

— **Jean Pickett, Chief of Staff**

I would say the academic profile is unbelievably different from before. But the similarities perhaps are more important—the friendly atmosphere, the feeling of family, the ability to go talk to any professor at any time. As trustees, one of our goals is maintaining the community and sense of culture at TCU and examining what that is and making sure we retain that.

— **Brenda Cline, member of the TCU Board of Trustees**

When Moncrief was built to house the student athletes, my office was inside the residence hall. If anybody wanted to know about those young men or women, whether they missed a class, had an injury, they'd call. It was a time of my life here that I've never had again. I'd be at my house at night, and my wife would say that there's someone at the door. There would be one of our players. It was really tight knit. If you ever talked to any athlete from 1986 or 1987 to 1992 or 1993, they would share that. There's a bond that's unbelievable between myself and those groups, both men and women.

—**Jack Hesselbrock, Associate Athletic Director, at TCU 1988-2018**

This campus was such a great place to be and nothing has changed. I love this place, and there are a lot of reasons. When my husband died twelve years ago, John Butler, who was the University minister, was in the ICU sitting with me and two faculty from Social Work, the chair of the Sociology Department, the Harris College Dean; and when my husband died, within thirty minutes the Provost, Larry Adams, and the Assistant Provost were all at the hospital. The Director of Research and Sponsored Projects drove my car home so my neighbor could take me home. When I got there, there was already pizza for the kids, courtesy of Rhonda King, and sandwiches from the Provost. And then Kay Higgins and John Butler were at the house helping me plan the funeral. They did it all. I did nothing. That kind of family is incredible.

— **Linda Moore, Emeritus Professor of Social Work and Chair of the Faculty Senate, at TCU 1977-2017**

I've come to appreciate it more in my later career, but this is an unusually friendly, supportive place. It's got the trials and tribulations of anywhere, but on balance this is really a generally kinder and friendlier place than average, and it's supportive. That's not a trivial thing, and if it goes, it'll be missed, and then the people who didn't have it won't realize what's missing.

— **Andrew Fort, Emeritus Professor of Religion, at TCU 1982-2017**

I think we would all do well to realize that the experience that you have here at TCU is unique. Whether it is that personal experience, where so many folks know each other by name, or whether it's the physical environment or cultural environment. Those things just don't exist in a lot of places, and I think it's important to realize how special this place is. I think about when I leave this university, I want the people who will come behind me to be able to enjoy all that makes TCU so special, just as I did. Somebody thought about it before I got here, and, if they hadn't done the great work that they did, I wouldn't have been able to do the work that I'm doing, and we as students or faculty wouldn't be experiencing this great, amazing place today. We've all got to remember that responsibility.

— **Brian Gutierrez, Vice Chancellor for Finance, at TCU 2006-2022**

Chancellor Boschini wants to treat people like he would like to be treated. That culture has pervaded this university. I can't think of a better culture or a better kind of foundation for having a positive and successful environment. There's not a lot of turnover in key people here at TCU. I think that speaks volumes about the university and people wanting to be here. It's been voted one of the best places to work several years in a row now. I want to maintain the culture of this school. I think that's something that will preserve this institution well into the future.

— **Mark Johnson, Member of the Board of Trustees and former Chair**

TCU is a great university. I'm really excited to see it continue to grow and move forward, and it is because of the people who are here—it really is. It is the people who make this university work every day, from the people in the physical plant on up through the administration. There's such a sense of family here and such a sense of camaraderie and wanting to see this university succeed.

— **Tracy Syler-Jones, Vice Chancellor for Marketing and Communication**

ABOVE
The billboard on University and Park Hill Drives when classes were remote during the pandemic, April 2020. Courtesy of TCU Marketing and Communication. Photo by Amy Peterson.

I feel optimistic about TCU's future. I have witnessed the changes that have taken place at TCU, and all of them have been positive. We have managed to keep those great qualities that make us unique, especially our values and culture of respect. We've managed to do so many things and yet keep what was good about what's original. I feel privileged to have been a part of all of that. It makes me optimistic. I love working with students who come in with so much optimism that they think they can change the world. I think they can too. It's a privilege to work with them.

— **Peggy Watson**

21.
Then and Now

Aerial Photos

LEFT
Aerial photo of TCU campus, 1970s. Courtesy of Fort Worth Police Historical Association and Fort Worth Fire Department.

BELOW
Aerial view of TCU campus, 2022. Courtesy of TCU Marketing and Communication. Photograph by James Anger.

Student Union

RIGHT
Brown-Lupton Student Center, 1968. Courtesy of Mary Couts Burnett Library. Photograph by Linda Kaye.

BELOW
Brown-Lupton University Union (BLUU), 2018. Courtesy of TCU Marketing and Communication. Photograph by Jeffery McWhorter.

Cafeteria

LEFT
Student Center cafeteria, 1974. Courtesy of Mary Couts Burnett Library. Photograph by Linda Kaye.

BELOW
Market Square dining area on the second floor of the Brown-Lupton University Union, 2010. Courtesy of TCU Marketing and Communication. Photo by Carolyn Cruz.

Registration

RIGHT
Students register for classes at the Daniel-Meyer Coliseum, 1975. Courtesy of Mary Couts Burnett Library. Photograph by Linda Kaye.

BELOW
Orientation leaders and academic advisors help incoming students register for classes at computer labs around campus during First-Year Orientation, 2022. Courtesy of TCU Marketing and Communication. Photograph by James Anger.

Move In

LEFT
Students move out of Colby Hall, ca. 1980. Courtesy of TCU Marketing and Communication.

BELOW
Students move into Colby Hall, 2017. Courtesy of TCU Marketing and Communication. Photograph by Amy Peterson.

Dorm Room

RIGHT
Students in a Jarvis dorm room, 1971. Courtesy of Mary Couts Burnett Library. Photograph by Linda Kaye.

BELOW
Residence hall room in Colby Hall, 2017. Courtesy of TCU Marketing and Communication. Photograph by Amy Peterson.

University Drive

LEFT
University Drive, 1972. Courtesy of Mary Couts Burnett Library Special Collections

BELOW
University Drive, 2023. Courtesy of Kareyn Hellmann.

Campus Concert

RIGHT
The Jefferson Airplane performs at Daniel-Meyer Coliseum, 1970. Photo published in the 1971 TCU yearbook. Courtesy of Mary Couts Burnett Library.

BELOW
SGA concert featuring Keesha in the Campus Commons, 2022. Courtesy of TCU Yearbook. Photograph by Jillian Miller.

Fort Worth

LEFT
TCU / Fort Worth Week banner in downtown Fort Worth, 1973. Courtesy of Mary Couts Burnett Library. Photograph by Linda Kaye.

BELOW
The TCU Marching Band participates in the Fort Worth Stock Show and Rodeo parade, 2023. Courtesy of TCU Marketing and Communication. Photograph by Glen E. Ellman.

Student Fans

RIGHT
Students in the stands, 1975. Courtesy of Mary Couts Burnett Library. Photograph by Linda Kaye.

BELOW
Fans cheer for the Horned Frogs during TCU's game against Oklahoma University at Amon G. Carter Stadium, 2022. Courtesy of TCU Marketing & Communication. Photograph by Marina Magnant.

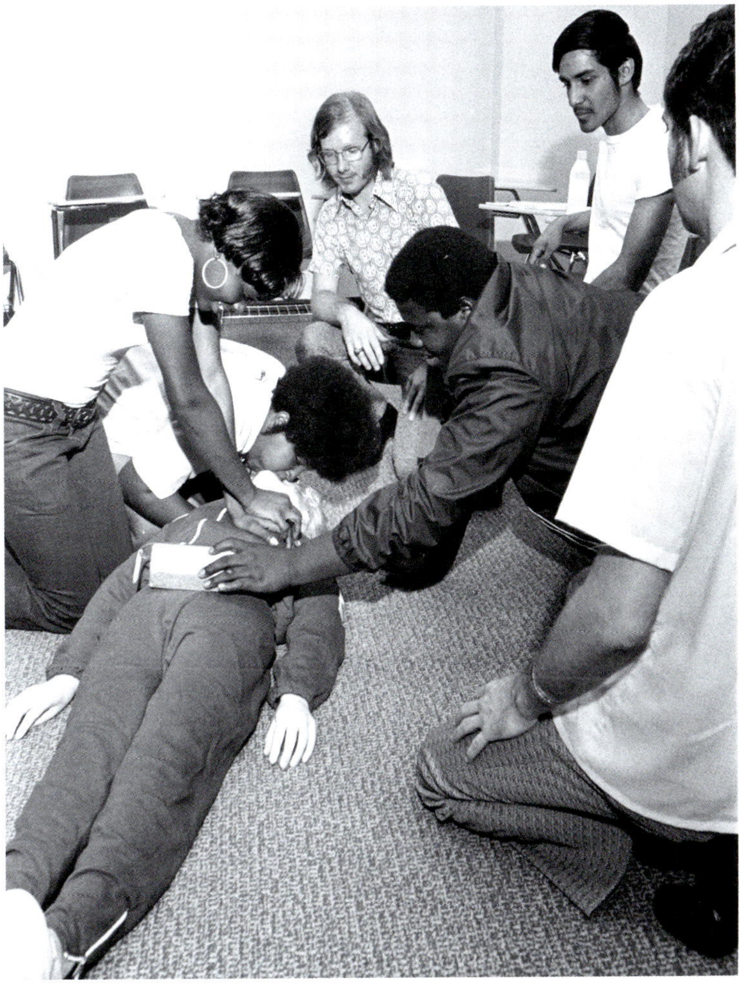

Students in the Harris College of Nursing and Health Sciences

LEFT
Nursing students learning CPR, 1972.
Courtesy of Mary Couts Burnett Library.
Photograph by Linda Kaye.

BELOW
Nursing students learning CPR, 2018.
Courtesy of Texas Christian University.
Photograph by Scott Murdock.

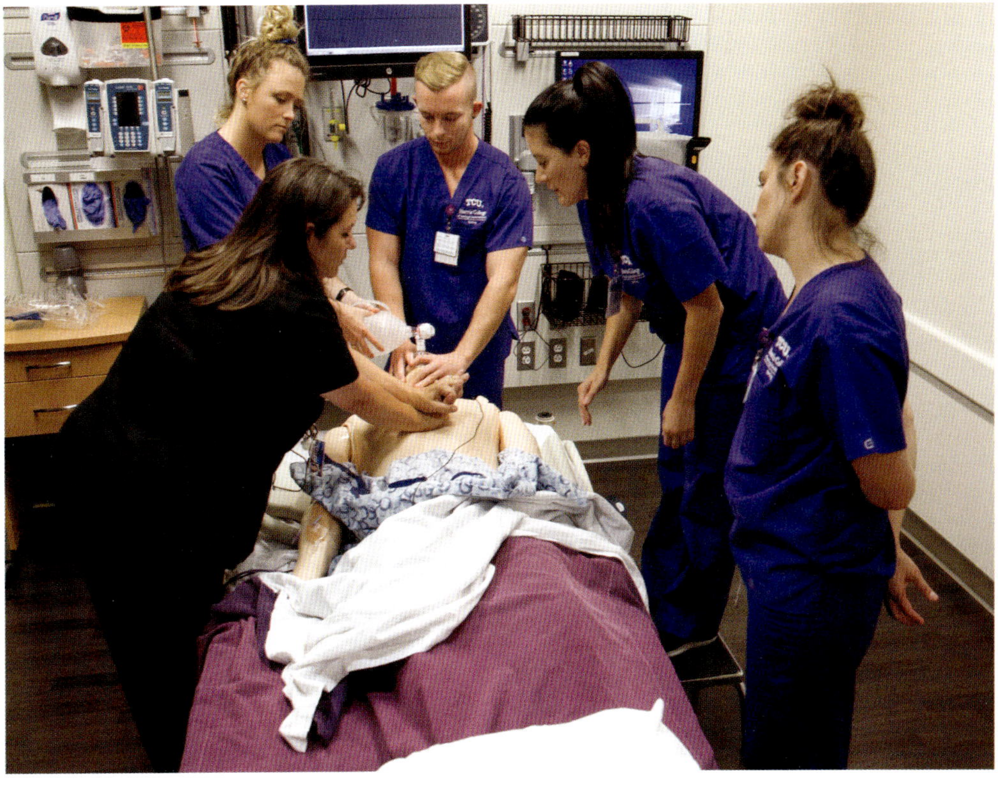

Showgirls

RIGHT
TCU Showgirl at Amon G. Carter Stadium, 1978. Courtesy of Mary Couts Burnett Library.

BELOW
The TCU Showgirls perform at the College Football Playoff's Fiesta Bowl, 2022. Courtesy of TCU Marketing and Communication. Photo by Amy Peterson.

Centennial and Sesquicentennial

LEFT
Mary Couts Burnett Library at the TCU Centennial, pictured with the centennial flag and memorial urn, 1973. Courtesy of Mary Couts Burnett Library.

BELOW
Mary Couts Burnett Library at the TCU Sesquicentennial, 2023. Courtesy of TCU Marketing and Communication. Photograph by James Anger.

IV.

Thoughts on the Future: A Personal Reflection

Chancellor Victor J. Boschini Jr.

As TCU was celebrating its centennial fifty years ago, Chancellor James M. Moudy was asked to anticipate its future, and he did so by imagining a great future based several conditional ifs: if TCU remained committed to its high values, if it remained an independent school, if it remained rooted in the real world, and if it remained aware of its past and of its responsibilities for the future. If the institution embraced these conditional ifs, he concluded that TCU would "probably survive many centuries, and the world would be better for its having survived."

LEFT
Chancellor Moudy at the Centennial Convocation in 1973. Courtesy of Mary Couts Burnett Library.

Moudy had been asked to anticipate TCU's future as the conclusion to Jerome Moore's centennial history, and I have been asked to do something similar at the end of this sesquicentennial publication. But people have been attempting to predict the future ever since there were people. Throughout the ages, a lot of really smart people have spent a lot of time making that attempt, and none of them have been particularly successful. I am certainly not going to be any more successful. With our world constantly changing, I don't think anyone can accurately predict what will happen tomorrow, next year, or years from now. There's too much change and too much uncertainty.

Yet I will state I am one-hundred-percent certain that TCU's future will be joined with its past and present by its strong sense of community. Everyone—students, faculty, staff, and alumni—feels this strong sense of connection with each other and with the campus. We are a campus community threaded by strong attachments and supportive collaborations. I have never worked for a school that engendered such loyalty from its community, and I am certain this will continue well into the next 150 of Texas Christian University. Chancellor Moudy acknowledged that TCU's future would inevitably be influenced by its past. What TCU had achieved in its first 150 years was, he stated, "an amazing and marvelous thing." I have no doubt whatsoever that TCU will achieve even greater amazing and marvelous things. Our connections and our community will remain strong.

The future is not something to predict—it is rather something to build. Growth is inevitable. TCU will continue to grow in the future, and it's our responsibility to help manage this growth by building on our foundational strengths. Student enrollments will increase, but TCU will remain student-centered. We will always have a great faculty to student ratio, and by maintaining our teacher-scholar model for faculty we will ensure our culture of connection and community, regardless of our student numbers. Growth will bring greater diversity. While we are growing, the world is shrinking, and our global connections will deepen, and we will have more international students and more collaborations with colleagues across oceans and continents. In terms of our mission and vision, I think that we will always be committed to helping students become responsible citizens and ethical leaders in the global community. This commitment has lasted 150 years, and it will last another 150 years or more.

As TCU grows, so will our physical footprint grow. As we evolve and adapt to the needs of future students, our campus will be bigger. I believe this will be a necessity to meet the changing demands of future learners and teachers. We will have even more residence halls, and a majority of students will be living in on-campus housing. As current trends indicate, our buildings will be much more flexible spaces than they are today. At one time in the past there was a general belief that TCU needed a giant parking lot in the middle of campus because students, faculty, and staff wanted to park close to everything. We replaced that with the Campus Commons. This shift will continue. It's possible that our current parking garages will be retrofitted into instructional, multi-use buildings as fewer students, faculty, and staff will be driving their own personal vehicles to campus every day. Given the constant desire for more green spaces, it's also possible to imagine an almost park-like campus with new outdoor areas that will serve our community in a variety of ways.

Learning will be different in the future. This is probably the most difficult area to

And what shall be TCU's future. God knows. And so do we in part. The reason we do not say that *only* God knows the future is that man is able to make some experience-based estimates of what the future will be, for the laws of cause and effect are sufficiently well known that man can predict the future, at least conditionally.

Chancellor James M. Moudy

I think the future's bright, I really do. I think it's going to be great. I think people still love this place like no place else I've ever worked, and that'll get us through any problems.

Chancellor Victor J. Boschini Jr.

The best way to predict your future is to create it.

Abraham Lincoln

Never make predictions, especially about the future.

Casey Stengel

Without continual growth and progress, such words as improvement, achievement, and success have no meaning.

— Benjamin Franklin

OPPOSITE
Frog Fountain, summer 2021. Courtesy of TCU Marketing and Communication. Photograph by Jeffrey McWhorter.

project, but one thing I know for certain is that we will probably not offer classes on the traditional schedules we currently have. I foresee a time when students will be able to access any and all of their academic content whenever and wherever they want them. Access will become key, and access will be almost universal throughout the twenty-four hours in each day. Clearly this access will be deliverable online, but it is my hope that TCU will never lose its personal touch, that no matter when or how students, faculty, and staff will always be able to communicate directly with each other, that whenever students have an issue or question they can speak to someone quickly and without a computer-generated intermediary. Artificial intelligence will surely become a part of everyone's life in ways yet unimagined, but while we speak to computers we should always be able to speak to each other. TCU's great strength is that it has always been a caring community committed to student success. This will never change.

Growth always carries a hefty price tag, and future campus leaders and trustees will have to be mindful of maintaining a budget that balances yet still allows for innovation and expansion. As the past indicates, TCU's financial affairs will grow more complicated and require greater and more skillful management to make sure the tuition increases are matched with increases in financial aid. We have dedicated great amounts of time and effort to grow our endowment, and these efforts will continue so that we can remain stable during times of economic instability. Our capacities to connect and communicate with each other will also continue to expand, and this expansion will increase greater transparency and cooperation. There will be problems, sudden crises that demand attention and intervention, and there will be times when some are unhappy with policies and decisions because there is never enough money to do everything that everyone wants. But I repeat: our connections and community will remain strong.

Chancellor Moudy based his thoughts on the future on four conditional ifs. My thoughts are not conditional. Texas Christian University will continue to advance, achieve, and progress. As a caring community dedicated to teaching and learning, we will continue to help all of our students lead responsible lives of tolerance, empathy, and service. TCU's origins trace back to Thorp Spring, but European universities began in places like Bologna, Paris, Oxford, and Cambridge as centers of learning where professors and students came together to extend knowledge; where free inquiry was promoted, and narrow-minded, short-sighted thinking was rejected; and where differences were embraced as strengths. TCU will continue to bring people together, to promote creative thinking, and to embrace our differences.

ABOVE
Frog Fountain, fall 2020. Courtesy of TCU Marketing and Communication. Photograph by Amy Peterson.

OPPOSITE
Frog Fountain, winter 2021. Courtesy of TCU Marketing and Communication. Photograph by Eric Sasadeusz.

PAGES 310-311
Frog Fountain, spring 2021. Courtesy of TCU Marketing and Communication. Photograph by Amy Peterson.

APPENDIX

Visualizing Growth by Numbers

Maggie Williams and Cathan Coghlan

Undergraduate & Graduate Enrollment 1973 - 2022

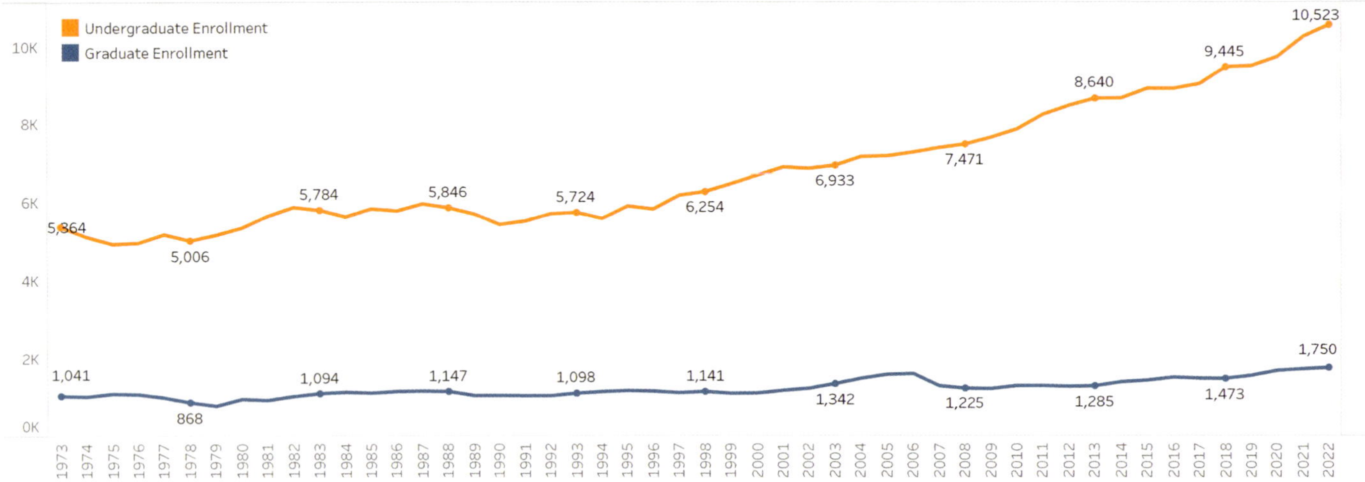

Source: 1973 - 2022 Fact Book

Geographic Origin of Students 1973 - 2022

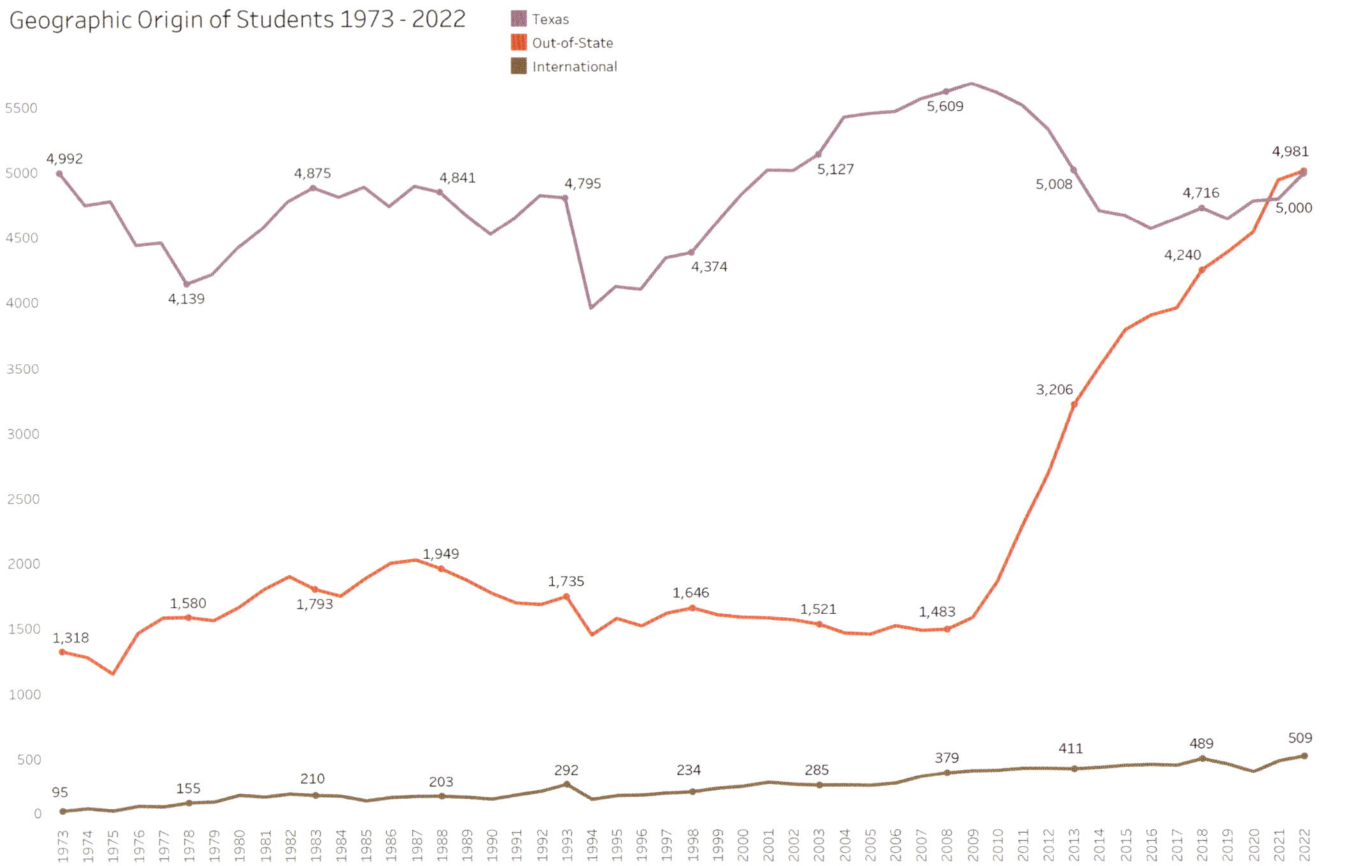

Source: 1973 - 2022 Fact Book

Percent of Total Ethnicities - Undergraduates 1980-2021

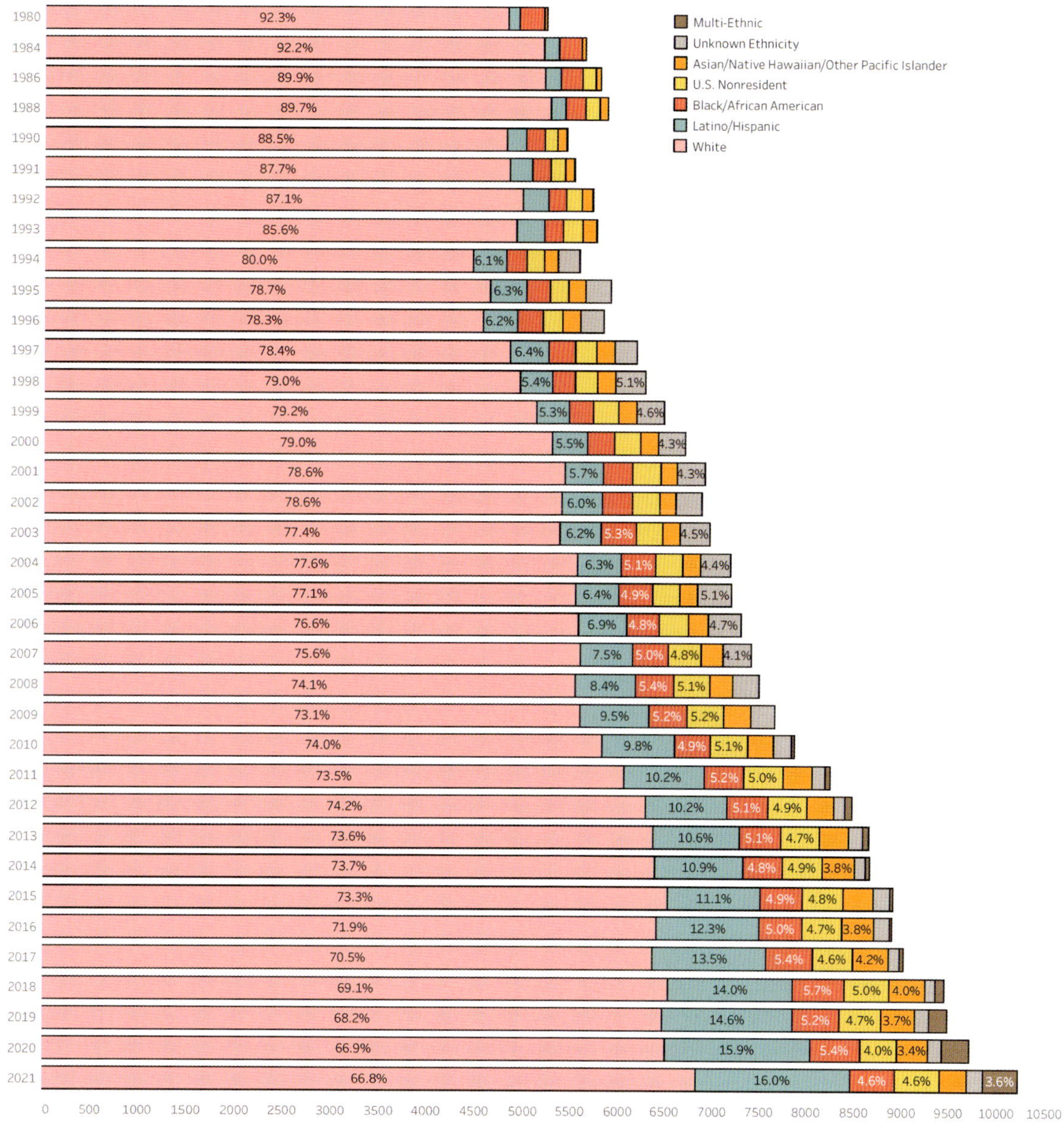

Source: 1980 - 2021 U.S. Department of Education, Institute of Education Sciences, National Center for Education Statistics

Notes: First professional applicable 1980-2008. Brite Divinity School enrollment included until split in 2007.

Data Missing: 1981, 1982, 1983, 1985, 1987, 1989

Percent of Total Ethnicities - Graduates 1980-2021

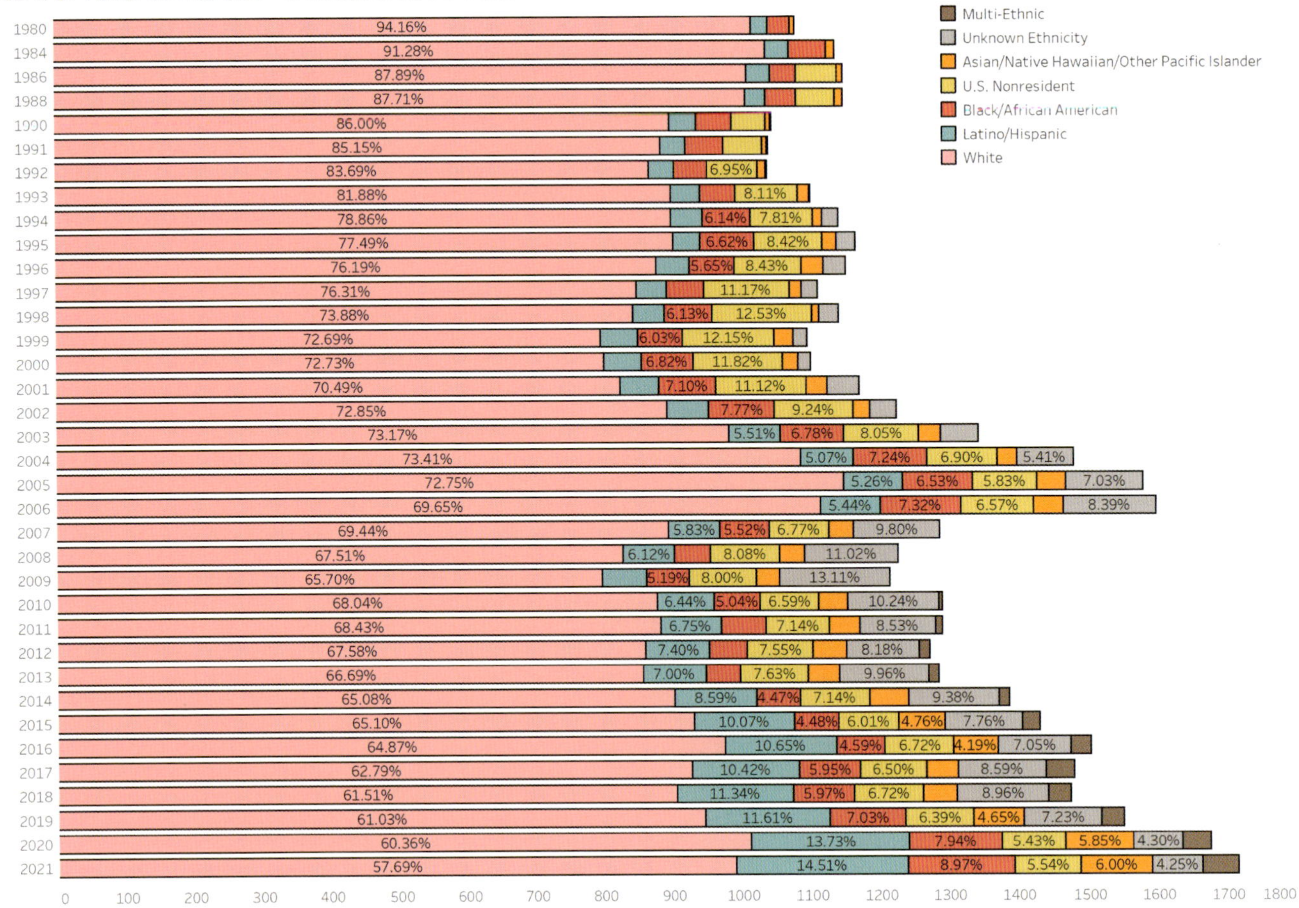

TCU Gender Distribution 1973 - 2022

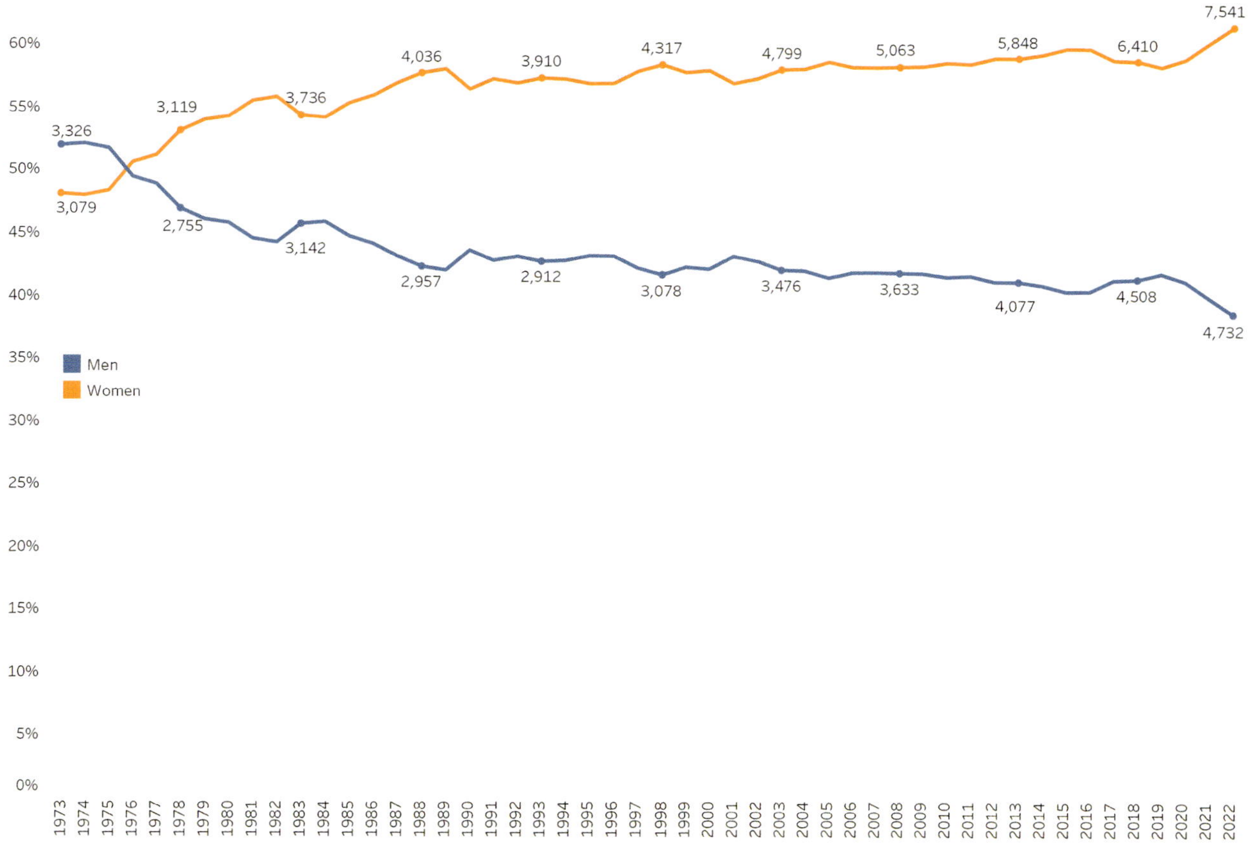

Sources: 1980 - 2021 U.S. Department of Education, Institute of Education Sciences, National Center for Education Statistics, 1980-1983, 2022 Fact Book

Notes: First professional applicable 1980-2008. Brite Divinity School enrollment included until split in 2007.

Student-to-Faculty Ratio 1973 - 2022

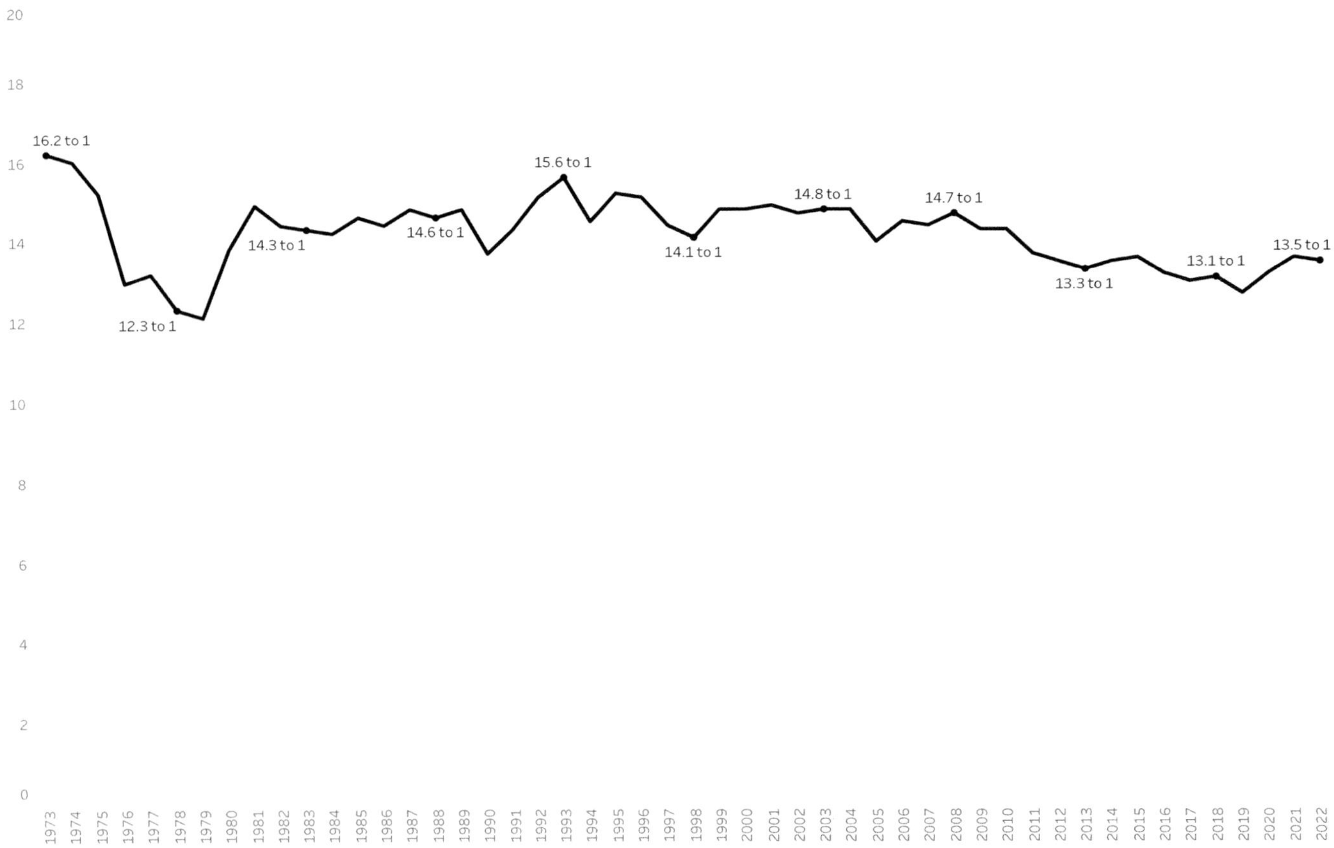

Source: 1973 - 1976 IR Scanned Archive Files, 1978 - 2022 Fact Book

TCU Full-Time Faculty 2002 - 2022

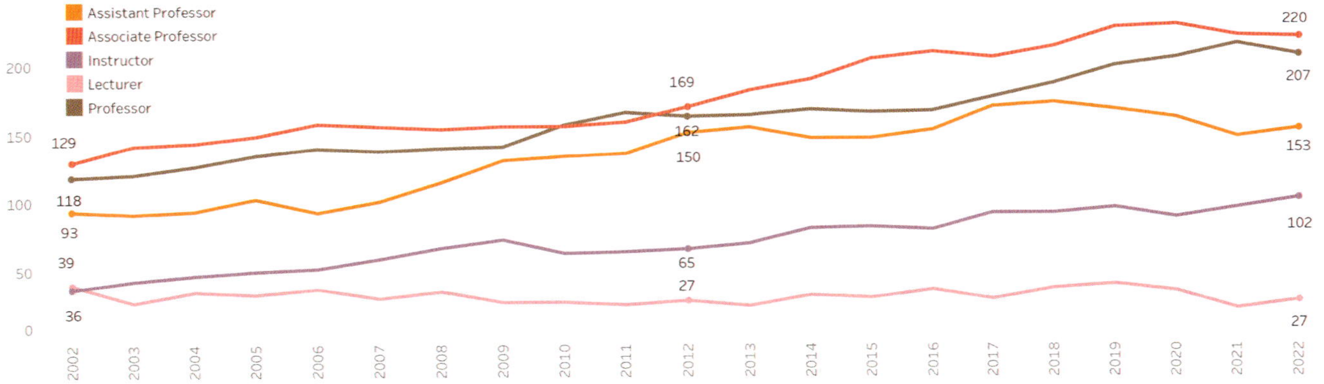

TCU Part-Time Faculty 2002 - 2022

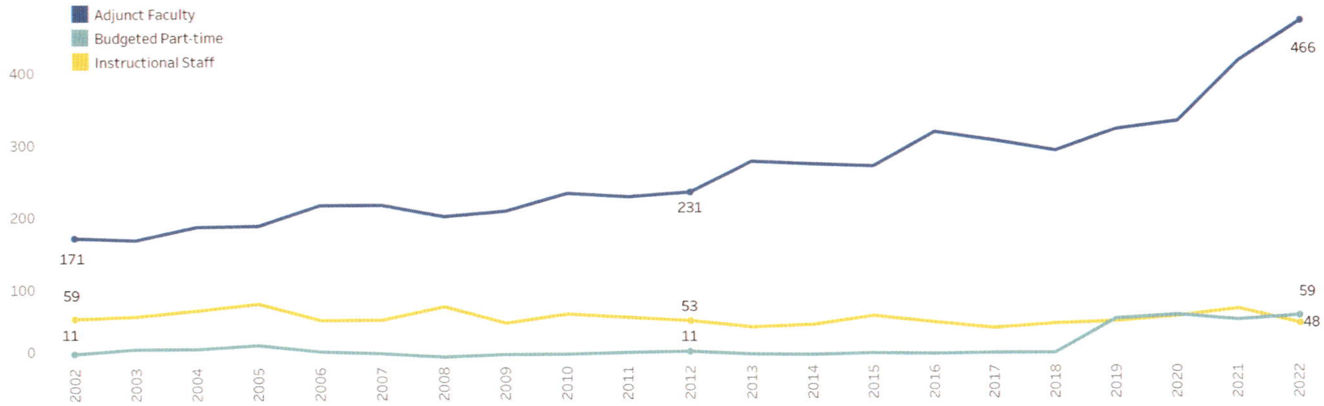

Source: 20002 - 2022 Office of Instituional Research

TCU Full-Time Faculty - Female and Minority Percentage 1985 - 2022

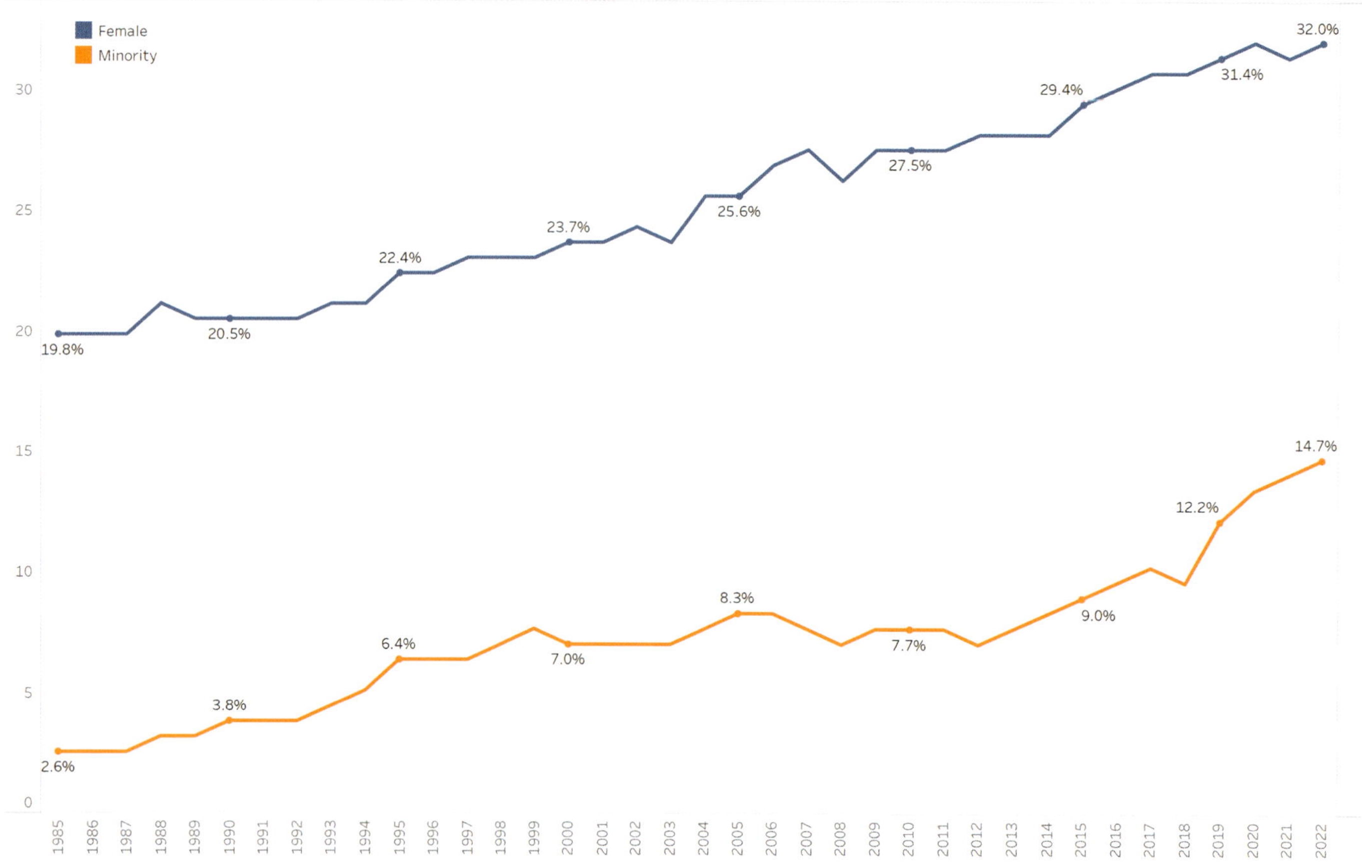

Source: 1985 - 2022 Fact Book

Data Missing: 1973 - 1984

Total Credit Hours for Fall Semesters 1973 - 2022

Sources: 1973 - 1979 Institutional Research, Special Collections, Mary Couts Burnett Library, Texas Christian University, 1980 - 2022 Fact Book

Notes: 1976 imputed using average of 1974, 1975, 1977, and 1978. Brite Divinity School enrollment included until split in 2007.

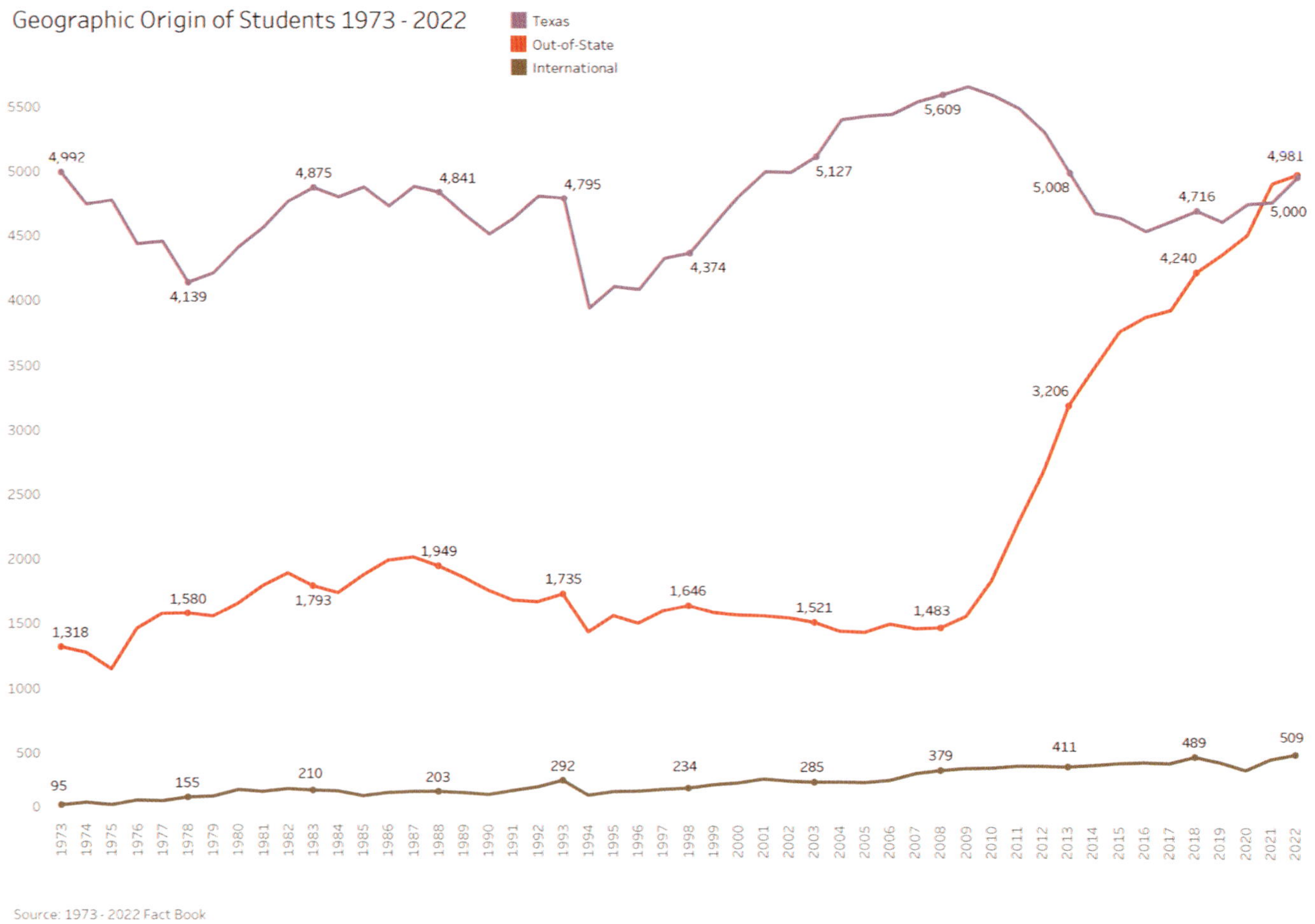
Geographic Origin of Students 1973 - 2022
Texas
Out-of-State
International
5500
5000
4500
4000
3500
3000
2500
2000
1500
1000
500
0
4,992
4,139
4,875
4,841
4,795
4,374
5,127
5,609
5,008
4,716
4,981
5,000
4,240
3,206
1,318
1,580
1,793
1,949
1,735
1,646
1,521
1,483
95
155
210
203
292
234
285
379
411
489
509
1973 1974 1975 1976 1977 1978 1979 1980 1981 1982 1983 1984 1985 1986 1987 1988 1989 1990 1991 1992 1993 1994 1995 1996 1997 1998 1999 2000 2001 2002 2003 2004 2005 2006 2007 2008 2009 2010 2011 2012 2013 2014 2015 2016 2017 2018 2019 2020 2021 2022
Source: 1973 - 2022 Fact Book

TCU Total Programs Offered 1973 - 2022

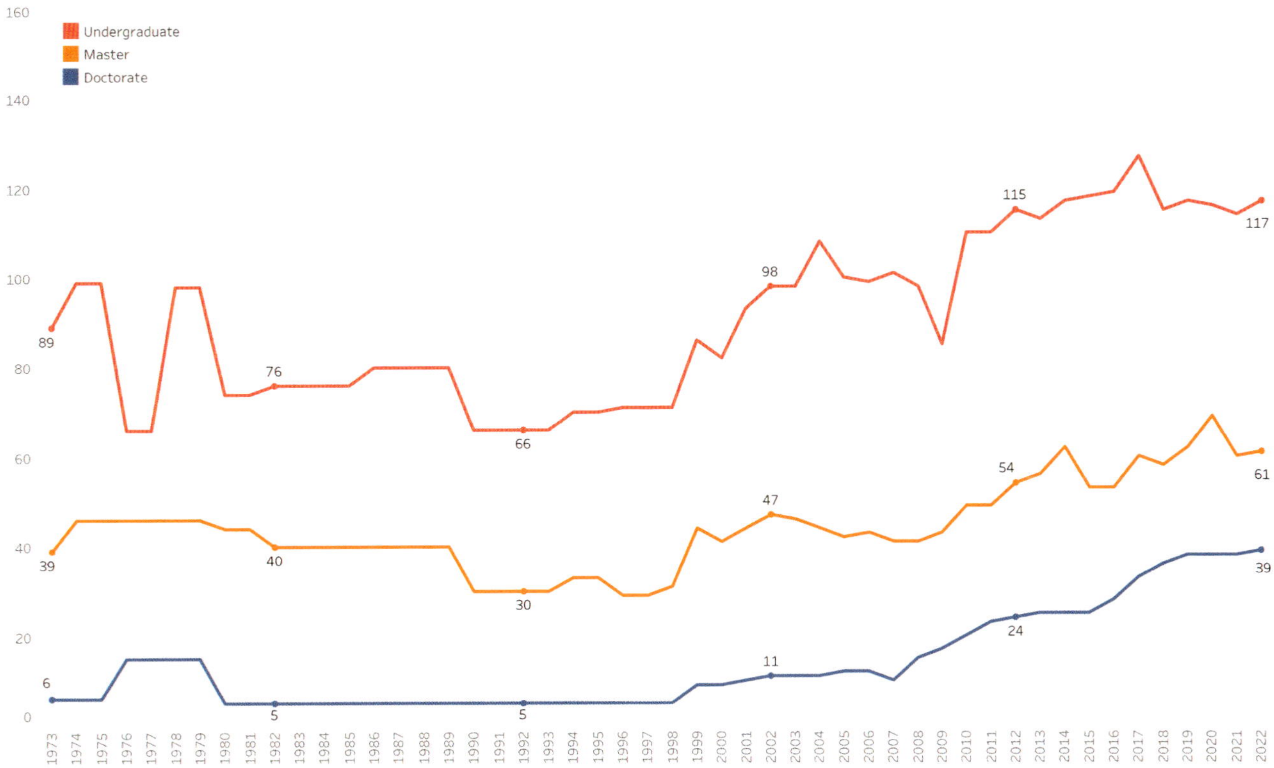

Source: 1999 - 2022 Fact Book, 1973 - 1998 TCU Course Catalog Special Collections, Mary Couts Burnett Library, Texas Christian University

Notes: Brite Divinity School enrollment included until split in 2007. Please note that changes in numbers of programs offered during a year could be due to how the programs were classified in that given year.

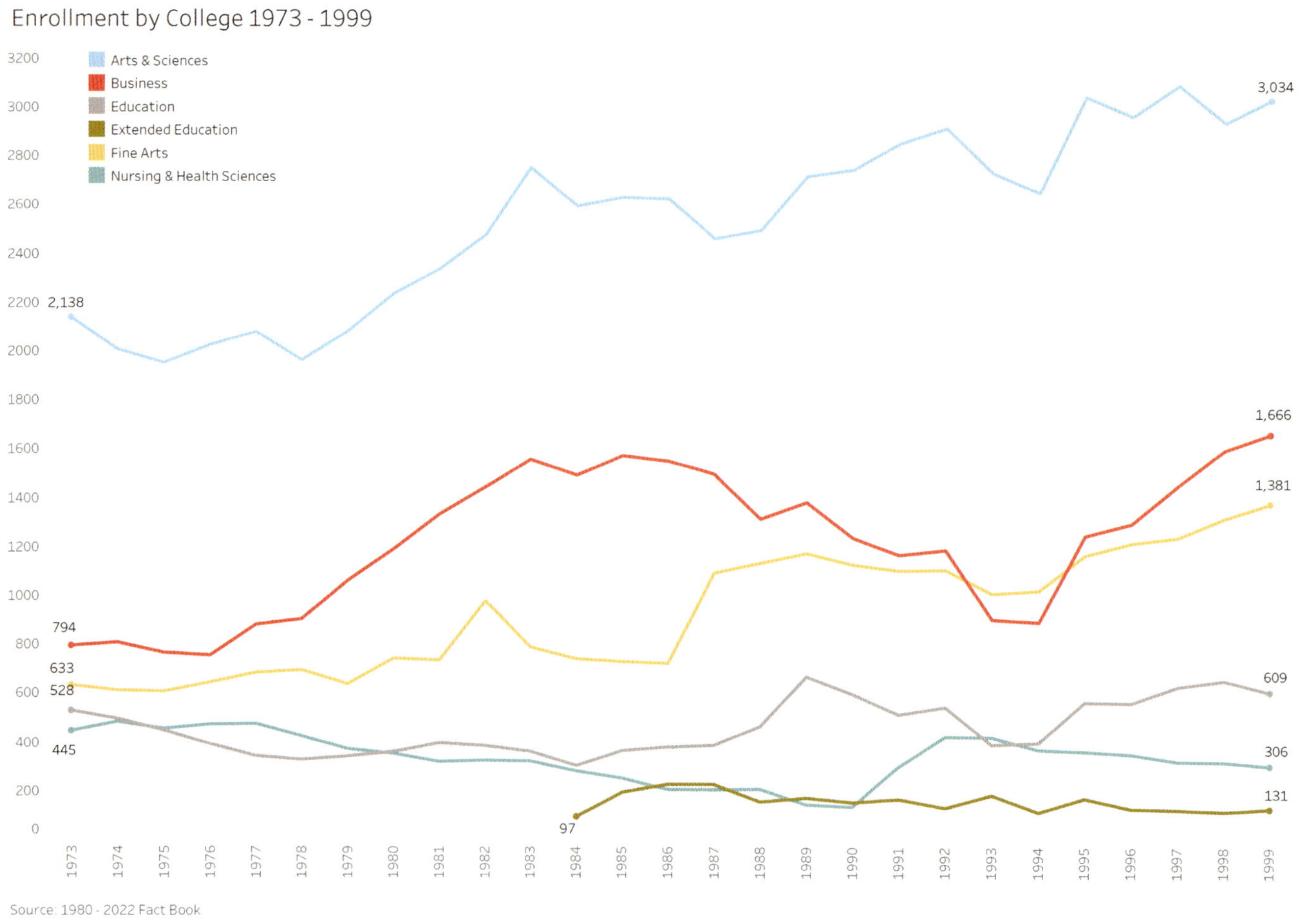
Enrollment by College 1973 - 1999
Arts & Sciences
Business
Education
Extended Education
Fine Arts
Nursing & Health Sciences
3200
3000
2800
2600
2400
2200
2000
1800
1600
1400
1200
1000
800
600
400
200
0
2,138
3,034
1,666
1,381
794
633
528
445
609
306
131
97
1973
1974
1975
1976
1977
1978
1979
1980
1981
1982
1983
1984
1985
1986
1987
1988
1989
1990
1991
1992
1993
1994
1995
1996
1997
1998
1999
Source: 1980 - 2022 Fact Book

Enrollment by College 2000 - 2022

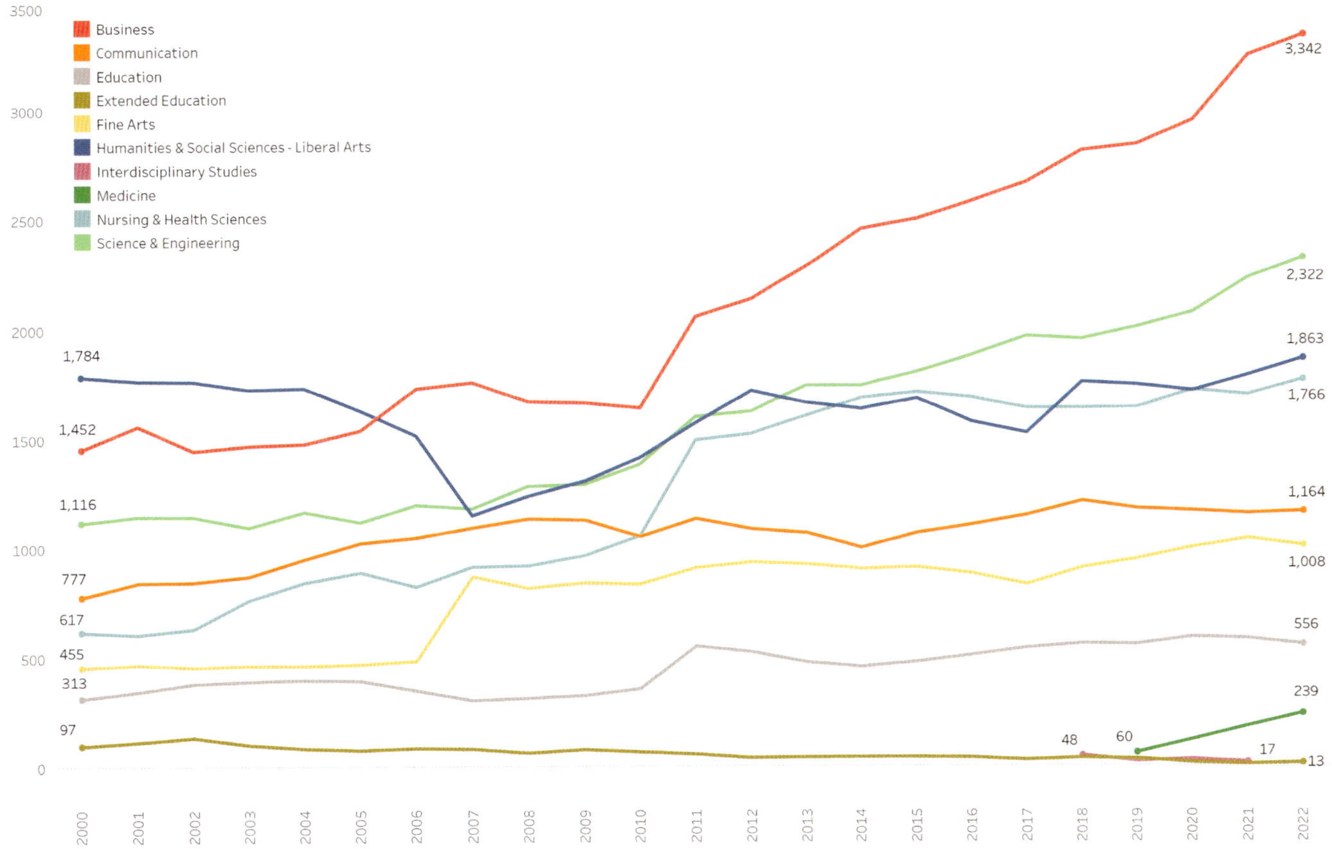

Source: 1980 - 2022 Fact Book

Degrees Awarded 1972-73 through 2021-22

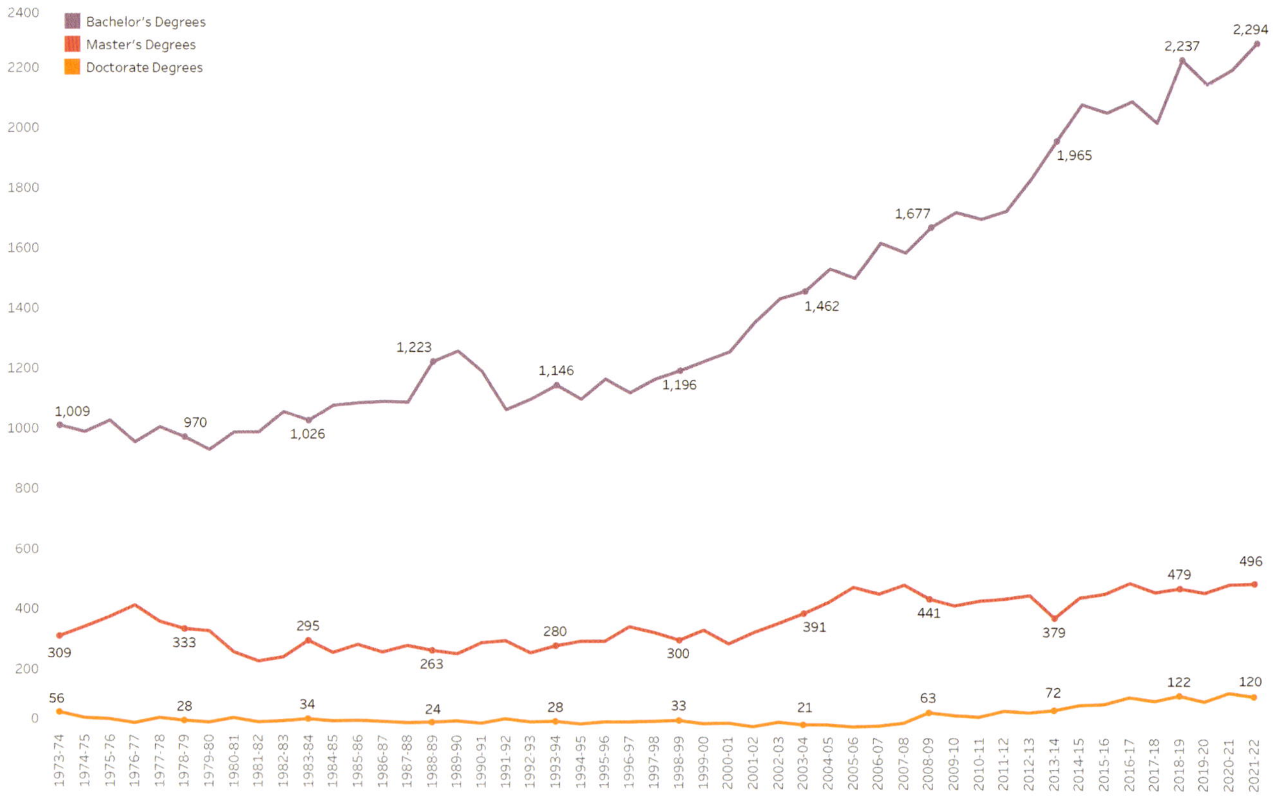

Source: 1972 - 2022 Fact Book

Notes: Brite Divinity School enrollment included until split in 2007.

Percent of Students Retained after 1 Year & Graduated within 6 Years 1984 - 2021

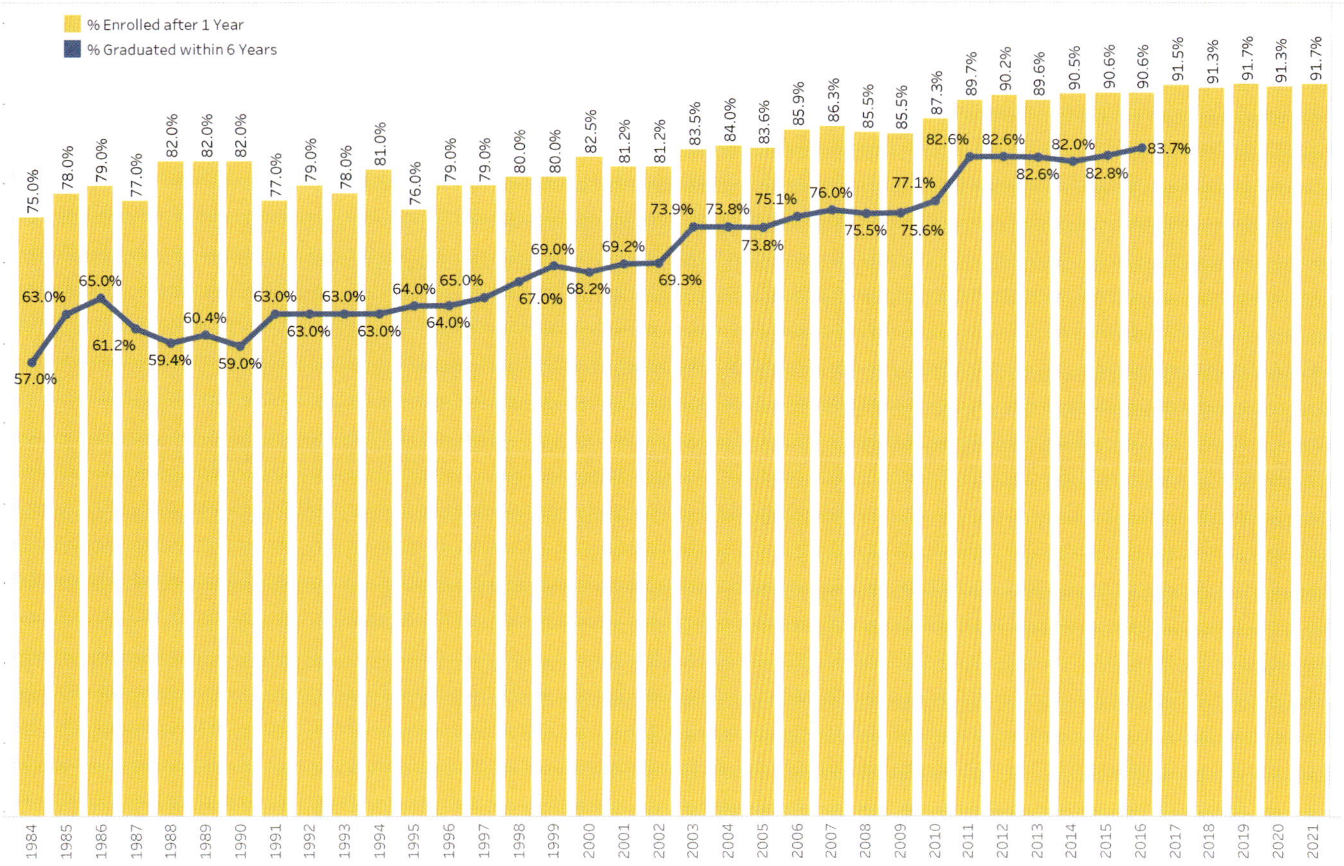

Source: 1985 - 2021 Fact Book

Notes: Brite Divinity School enrollment included until split in 2007.

TCU Campus Square Footage 1973 - 2020

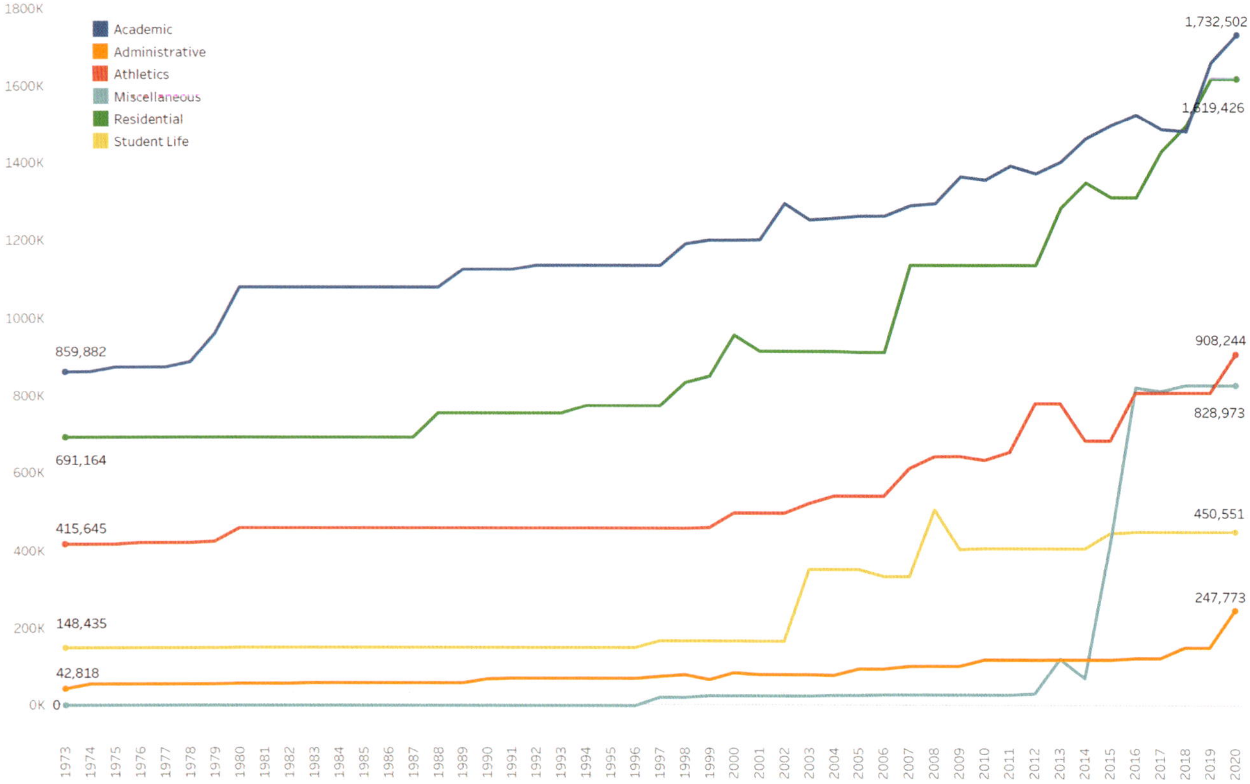

Source: 1973 - 2020 TCU Facilities

Tuition & Fees 1973 - 2022

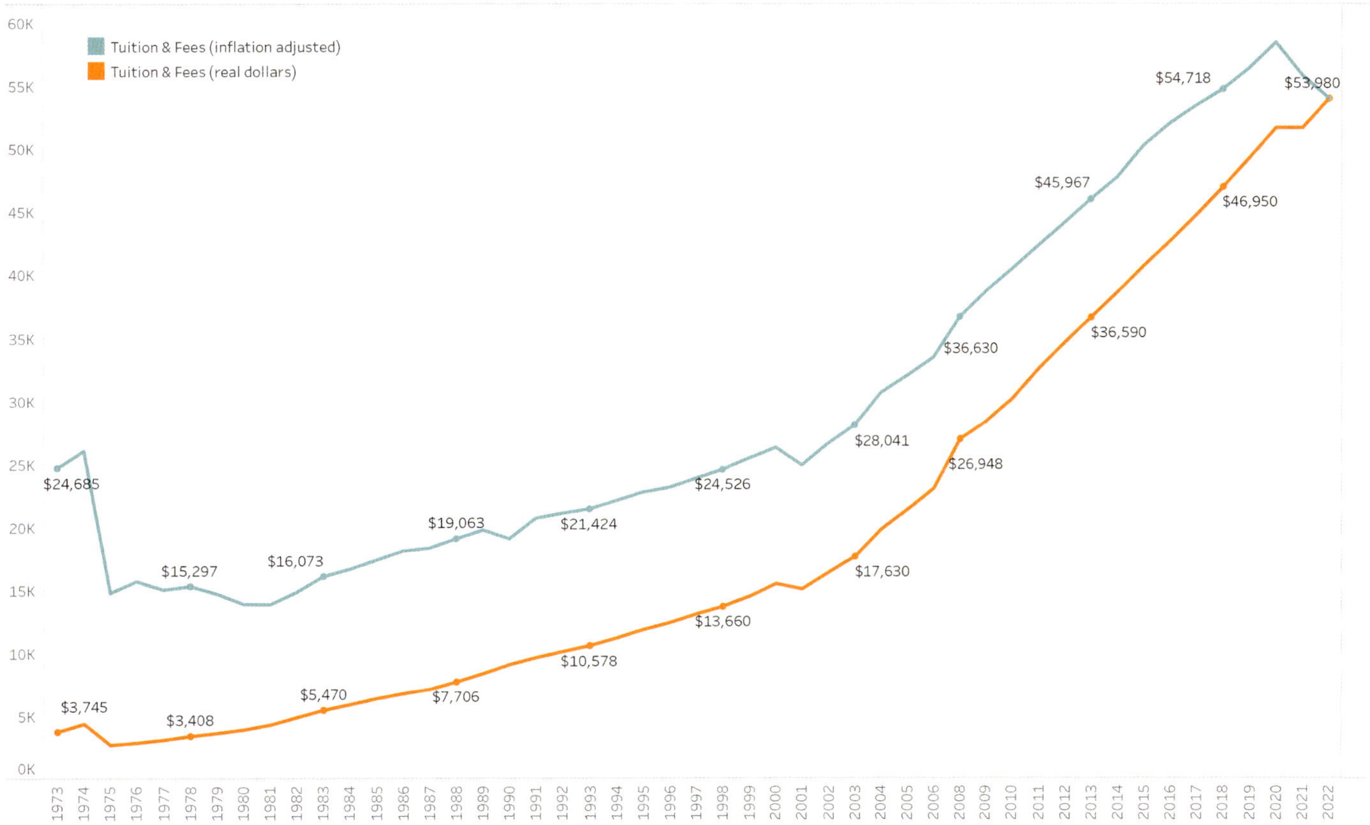

Sources: 1973 - 1979 Institutional Research, Special Collections, Mary Couts Burnett Library, Texas Christian University, 1980 - 2022 Fact Book

Data Missing: 2007

Notes: Inflation calculated using www.usinflationcalculator.com.

Male Housing - General & Greek 1975 - 2022

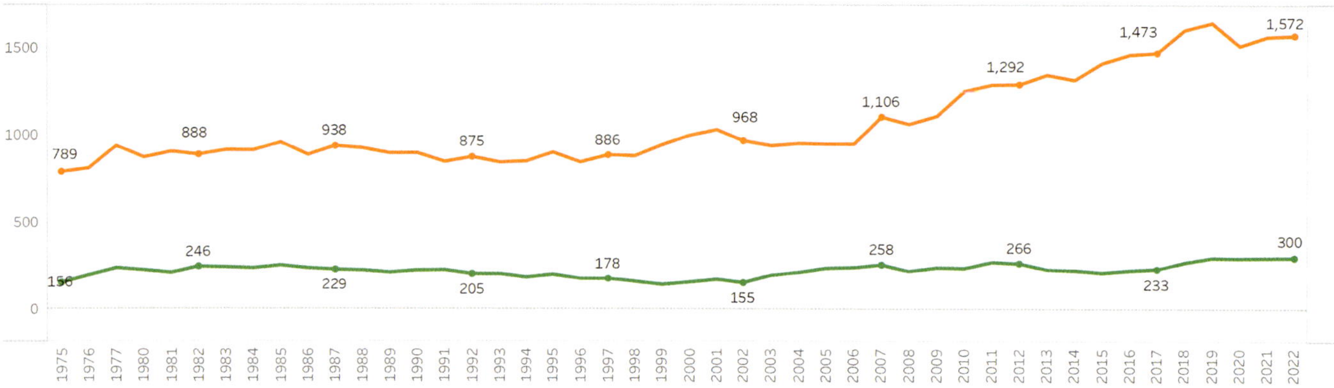

Female Housing - General & Greek 1975 - 2022

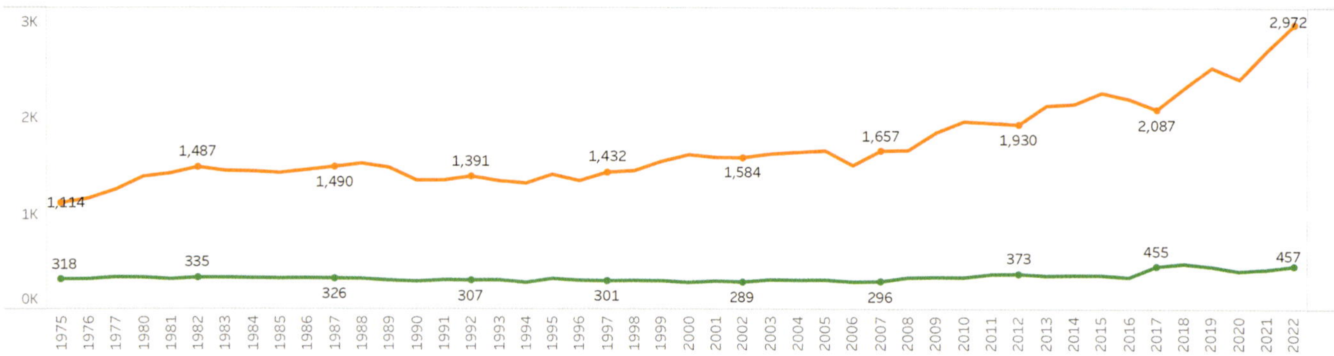

Greek Housing
General Housing

Sources: 1975, 1976, 1977 Residental Services Special Collections, Mary Couts Burnett Library, Texas Christian University, 1980 - 2022 Fact Book

Data Missing: 1973, 1974, 1978, 1979 missing and not imputed

TCU Endowment and Gross Annual Payout 1992 - 2023

Source: Endowment and Gift Accounting

U.S. News TCU Ranking 1991 - 2023

1991-1994

Rank	1991	1992	1993	1994
Quartile 2				●
Quartile 3	●	●	●	

1995-2002

Rank	1995	1996	1997	1998	1999	2000	2001	2002
2nd tier			●	●	●	●	●	●
3rd tier	●	●						

2003-2023

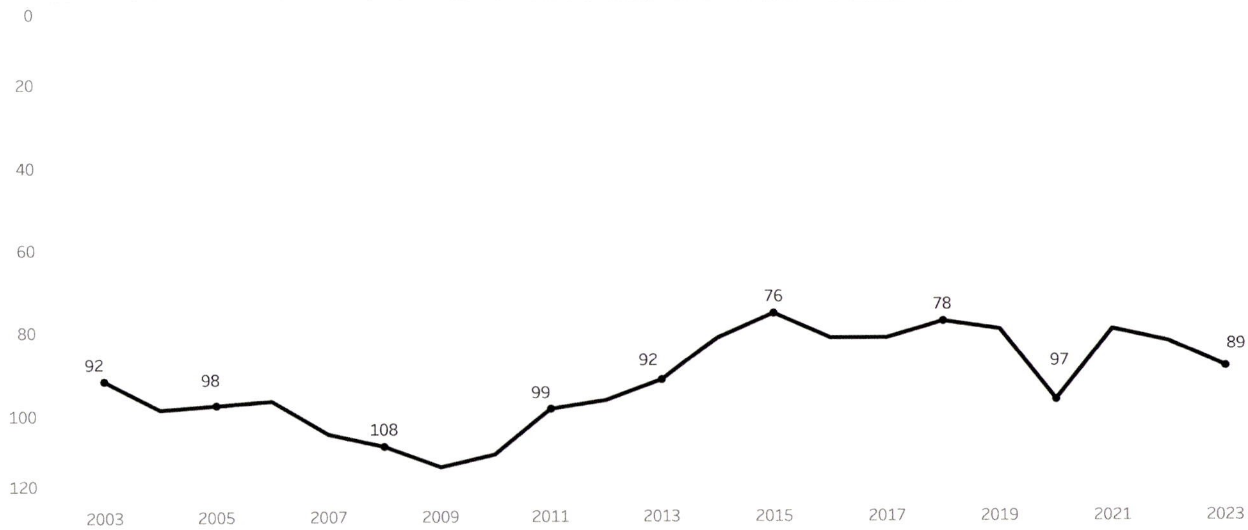

Source: 1991 - 2023 Annual Report, U.S. News & World Report